D1336761

Rise Up My Love

Rise Up My Love

*The drama of Salvation History
and the Song of Songs*

C. E. Hocking

PRECIOUS SEED PUBLICATIONS

© Copyright Precious Seed Publications 1988

ISBN 1-871642-00-0 (hardback)
ISBN 1-871642-01-9 (paperback)

This book and other Precious Seed publications

Church Doctrine and Practice (336 pages)
Day by Day through the New Testament (408 pages)
Day by Day through the Old Testament (416 pages)
Treasury of Bible Doctrine (468 pages)

are obtainable from

Precious Seed Publications
PO Box 8
Neath
West Glamorgan SA11 1QB
UK

Printed by Hillman Printers (Frome) Ltd

Preface

A VISIT TO ISRAEL in 1983/4 prompted the writing of this book. I had always
been persuaded, Biblically, that the confusing of Israel and the Church
robbed both of their peculiar God-given heritage. During that particular
stay in Israel I was urged to develop some of the hints given in this direction which I had opened up there previously in the Song of Songs. The
course of ten lectures which resulted from this request provided the basis
for this book, and is given here a more permanent and much more complete form.

That the Song of Songs is Biblically unique in its extended unfolding of
the loving intimacies of a man/woman relationship is patent. As Encyclopedia Judaica expresses it 'the Song of Songs is unique in the Bible,
for nowhere else within it can be found such a sustained paean to the
warmth of love between man and woman'. The justifying of its inclusion
in the Canon of Scripture, consequently, has resulted in a spate of differing interpretations ranging from the naturalistic to the solely spiritual. In
pursuing a spiritualized view of the Song's contents, the concensus
among believers seems to fall into two interpretive categories. For the one,
it is best construed as pursuing the varying moods and phases of an individual's relationship with his Lord, while for the other, it unfolds the
larger or more corporate relationship between the Lord and His Church.
Fatal to these proposals as tools of true interpretation is the inescapable
fact that the Song is an Old Testament book. Of course, we have been, and
shall continue to be refreshed, challenged, and drawn closer to the great
Lover of our souls as we meditate in this book which is concerned with
the deep emotions of the human heart. Our contention is, however, that
the book can be interpreted consistently and completely only when it is
seen as an actual developing human love relationship which mirrors that
which is being worked out between the Lord and Israel. Israel is the loved
and elevated partner of the One who is described as both her Maker and
her Husband, Isa.54.5. The changing fortunes of the love relationship between Israel and her God is given considerable space elsewhere in Old
Testament Scripture, figuratively, allegorically and typologically. This encourages us to use the Bible as its own interpreter in approaching the contents of the Song of Songs. We have sought to do this in these pages, paying attention to the Biblical use of the Hebrew terms once the immediate
contextual use is understood. For us, it becomes clear that the Song of
Songs traces the love relationship between the Lord and Israel from the

beginning of its history to the end, from the patriarch Abraham through to the grand messianic millennial reign. Throughout these passing millennia, Israel's Lord, her Beloved, remains the unchanging and faithful One. The woman of the Song however, whom her Beloved describes as 'my love, my fair one', represents those who are true to the Lord among the nation in every generation. The failures here are those of one whose love for her God ebbs and flows. No place is given in the Song of Songs to that 'dust' seed of Abraham, those who are his children according to the flesh alone. It is not only for its air of springtime that the Song features liturgically on the intermediate Sabbath of the Passover Festival to this day. The spiritual climate of the poems radiates the increasing experience and warmth of divine redeeming love which is the great Passover theme.

To appreciate the basis for understanding the Song in this way, I have dealt first with the Biblical approach to man/woman relationships, marriage and love in some detail, which are so different from those in the West. Then it has been necessary to review the informing background material drawn upon by the inspired poet from the Fauna, Flora and Seasons with which he was so familiar. Our own many extended visits to Israel have enhanced greatly our appreciation of these too. These things provide the writer with some of the great motifs of the Song. In considering them we have sought to provide the Biblical means to interpret consistently the Song as being the presentation of the heart of Israel's God revealed in the history of the faithful among the nation.

As my task was nearing completion, I was given a copy of the late O. L. Barnes privately produced book on the Song. He was a highly qualified engineer with an avid interest in the Word of God, and with considerable ability in Semitic languages also. I found his own English translation refreshing, and sought, and was kindly given permission to incorporate it into my book with a few small modifications. This will give to it a much wider reading public which it deserves, and will enhance my book with his sweet translation. I have set it in separate parts before each of my chapters on the six Poems of the Song, so as to provide them with a lively and fresh introduction. I would like to record my thanks to Mr. Roy Miller of Long Horsley for permission to do this.

May the Lord bless this book to many, and through it may many more be drawn to run after Him. In particular, our prayer to God is that not a few out of the nation today may search for and find that One Who is deservedly described by the Israel of God as her Beloved and Friend, the glorified Messiah, Who is the chiefest among ten thousand and the altogether lovely One.

C. E. Hocking

Contents

9

Contents

Appendices

Indices

Abbreviations

*	indicates that all the OT or NT references to a word are listed
‡	indicates that all the references to a word in the Song are listed
†	indicates a word occurs here only (a hapax legomenon)
//or =	indicates parallel Biblical passages follow
[ ]	enclose transliterated Hebrew or Greek words, or chapter/verse numbers in Hebrew
cf.	compare
ct.	contrast
1.1f	chapter 1 verses 1 and 2
1.1ff	chapter 1 verses 1 to 3
1.1–8	chapter 1 verses 1 to 8

Abbreviated references to sources are listed in the Bibliography

Quotations are from the Revised Version unless stated otherwise.

Illustrations

The photographs for the colour illustrations throughout the book were all taken by the author.

The painting of the male & female gazelles used on the front cover is the work of the Israeli artist Walter Ferguson, whose kind permission to include it is acknowledged. The beloved in the Song is described 'as a roe', and is heard to appeal to his loved one, 'Rise up, my love', Song 2.10. See pp. 60–63.

The photograph on the back cover is of the beautiful 'Madonna Lily' in one of Carmel's Mountain Valleys, May-time. It is used as a simile by the beloved to describe his loved one 'As a lily among thorns, so is my love among the daughters', Song 2.2. See pp.83–88.

Part 1

BY
WAY OF
INTRODUCTION

Contents – Part 1

1

THE SETTING, SIGNIFICANCE AND STYLE OF THE SONG

ALL WHO READ THE SONG OF SONGS through at a sitting are impressed with the vividness of its expression drawn from the beauty of its surroundings. The nature lover is immediately at home in it though walking through unfamiliar terrain. The sophisticated might be more impressed with the sense of splendour and wealth that filters through its poetry. We shall collect some of the elements designed to make us at home in the history and topography of the Song's setting, learning not only the identity but something of the literary genius of its author at the same time.

The Setting and the Author

The very first sentence of the Song provides us with its title, and directs us to Solomon, 1.1. His name appears also in six other places in the book.[1] We are left in no doubt that it is the famous King Solomon who is in view.[2] Even where the word king appears without his name added, Solomon is still before us.[3] For many, this is little more than a literary device. For us, it slots the Song into its proper historical setting.[4] It belongs to Solomon's era, which spanned a forty year period of the tenth century, between 970 and 930 BC. As we shall see, it is to the happier and

---

[1] 1.1,5; 3.7,9,11; 8.11,12‡.   [2] 3.9,11‡.   [3] 1.4,12; 7.5[6]‡.
[4] Familiarity with 1 Kings 1–11//2 Chron. 1–9 is essential.

13

earlier part of his reign that the Song relates.[5] We refer to the more typologically viewed period recorded in the first nine and a half chapters of 1 Kings and in 2 Chronicles 1–9. The mention of but sixty queens and eighty concubines in the Song points to this.[6] The latter years of Solomon's reign were thoroughly corrupted through his love of many women, reference then being made to some seven hundred wives and three hundred concubines.[7]

The external splendour radiating through parts of the Song match what we expect of Solomon's reign of glory. His box-like carriage, in which he was borne on men's shoulders, was resplendent with silver, gold and purple. And when he travelled, his train was redolent with 'all powders of the merchant'.[8] Precious stones, marble, ivory, were all familiar items in this king's fabulous reign.[9] We are pointed to the king's chambers, his banqueting house, the queens, concubines and virgins without number who enhance his palaces.[10] The reference to Pharaoh, chariots, horses, all drive us back to the historical background of Solomon's times.[11] His reign externally was one of superlatives; its 'prosperity exceeded the fame' which it generated. Of his throne we read that 'there was not the like made in any kingdom'. Silver 'was nothing accounted of in the days of Solomon', and he made it 'to be in Jerusalem as stones, and cedars made he to be as the sycomore trees that are in the lowland, for abundance'.[12] For both history and the Song, Solomon is the king of glory. It would seem ludicrous, therefore, to place the Song in the comparatively run down period after the exile as some seek to do.

The places to which our attention is directed in this story in song belong to the greater Israel and its environs in the Solomon era. Solomon's kingdom stretched far and wide. He and his

---

[5] Critical scholarship produces datings ranging from the third millennium BC through to the third century BC with evidence to establish each proposal. More recently Carr, having faced the differing arguments, has concluded that 'there is enough evidence of archaic grammatical and linguistic forms in the Song ... to sustain the argument for a date around the time of Solomon', Tyn. p. 18, esp. n.1.   [6] 6.8.   [7] 1 Kings 11.1–8.   [8] See 3.6–11; 1.11.   [9] 1.10; 5.11, 14, 15; 7.1, 5[2,5].   [10] 1.4; 2.4; 6.8f.   [11] 1 Kings 3.1; 4.26[5.6]; 9.16, 19, 22; 10.26, 28f.   [12] 1 Kings 10.8, 20f, 27.

people basked in the sunshine of David's military successes. The Song reflects this period of territorial enlargement and more 'international' influence.[13] Solomon's capital city was Jerusalem, eight references to which appear in the Song.[14] There David's impregnable tower, made the more impressive through the exploits of his mighty men, was to be seen.[15] Places mentioned, and obviously very familiar to the writer, include those we should expect, like En-gedi on the western shore of the Dead Sea, Tirzah on the central mountain range of Samaria,[16] Baal-hamon near to the south-eastern entrance to the Jezreel Valley from Samaria at modern Jenin, the Sharon Plain bordering the Mediterranean on the west, and the beautifully impressive Carmel Range which terminates it on the north.[17] We are conducted still further afield, however, to Keder in the northern part of Arabia, Heshbon, Bether, Mahanaim,[18] and the great mountain range of Gilead, all of which are to the east of the Jordan River, and from there to the north where the towering Hermon, Amana, or Senir in the Anti-Lebanon Range provide us with the look-out toward Damascus in Syria,[19] while Lebanon itself is referred to seven times.[20]

We return again to the opening verse which claims that it is 'The Song of Songs, which is Solomon's'.[21] His reign alone, one of

---

[13] 1 Kings 4.21, 24f[5.1, 4f].　　[14] 1.5; 2.7; 3.5, 10; 5.8, 16; 6.4; 8.4‡; cf. Zion in 3.11‡.　　[15] 4.4. This is not the so-called David's Tower featured in the Citadel at the Jaffa Gate today. David's and Solomon's Jerusalem did not extend to the Western Hill as it did in later kingdom times.　　[16] Later to become the capital of the Northern Kingdom, Israel until Omri's sixth year, 1 Kings 16.24f. [17] 1.14; 6.4; 8.11; 2.1; 7.5[6].　　[18] Specially relevant for the Song is the incident in Jacob's life as he was returning from Haran to the promised land, climaxed at Gen. 32.2.　　[19] Notice the topographical detail in some of these references: 1.5, 'the vineyards of En-gedi'; 7.4[5], the location of the pools 'in Heshbon, by the gate of Bath-rabbim'; 2.17, 'the mountains of Bether'; 4.2; 6.5, 'mount Gilead'; 4.8, 'from the top of Amana . . . Senir . . . Hermon, from the lions' dens, from the mountains of the leopards'.　　[20] Lebanon's forests, 3.9, fragrance, 4.11, flowing streams, 4.15, and majestic elevation, 5.15, feature along with other more general references to the country, 4.8(2); 7.4[5].　　[21] Two psalms bear the same Hebrew construction [Heb.lishlomoh] in their titles, 72.[1] and 127[1]. The letter l

undisturbed peace, when political, marital, social, economic, educational and art links with Egypt were closely forged, provides the perfect as well as the obvious setting.[22]

The Significance

What is the Song of Songs about? Primarily, it is a love story the course of which is traced in a series of poems which were set to music. It relates the fortunes of a special love relationship between Solomon and a particular maiden. Each found the other to be altogether unique. The king was prompted to write, as none other could have done, this poetic masterpiece concerning their developing love. For King Solomon had unrivalled creative talents as history informs us, for 'he spake three thousand proverbs: and his songs were one thousand and five'.[23] Yet not one of his many compositions equals the Song as a poetic unfolding of human love. The progress of their natural relationship we shall consider in various parts of this book.[24] Enough to say here that the thrills and chills affecting their love, betrothal and marriage, the happinesses and the hindrances, the delights and the dangers, all pursue intertwined paths to their grand and inevitable goal, for 'love never faileth'.

---

[21] *cont*. [Heb.lamedh] affixed to Solomon's name indicates his authorship rather than that the Song was 'for him', or even simply 'concerned with him' as its subject. It is certainly no 'literary fiction'. The classical particle translated *which* [Heb. ʾasher] in the title appears here only in the Song. An abbreviated form [Heb.she] occurs over 30 times, and is equally dominant in Ecclesiastes (68 times), another of Solomon's literary productions. There are about 40 other references only in the whole OT.   [22] 1 Kings 3.1 and chaps. 9–10. See E. W. Heaton for the Egyptian connection. The Egyptian love poetry genre is considered to be the closest literary parallel to that used in the Song, using much of the same vocabulary, stock phrases, and detailed physical descriptions of the love partner. See e.g. Carr, JETS, 25, '82, 489–98. Goulder, Song 73, has pointed out recently however that 'There are no Egyptian pieces which approach the Song in length or complexity', questioning the relevance of the Egyptian parallels adduced.   [23] 1 Kings 4.30[5.10].
[24] See esp. pp.146ff. Goulder, 2f, discerns a semi-continuous sequence of 14 scenes, moving in a progression from the arrival of the princess at Solomon's court to her acknowledgement by the king as his favourite queen(?).

But this is not what the Song is *all* about. As is the case with all great literature, there is another dimension to be found here.[25] Solomon himself had some awareness of divine calling and sovereign choice in his own elevation to the throne. He sensed that he had something of a messianic place in history as a 'fulfiller' of God's covenant with his father David.[26]

Solomon's two other extant song compositions suggest something of this deeper significance. *Psalm 72* concludes Book 2 of the Psalms, and predicts the happy conditions which shall obtain on earth when the kingdom of God is established at last under a greater king than Solomon. It is here truly that the 'prayers of David the son of Jesse are ended'.[27] Rashi interpreted this psalm as David's, 'for' or on behalf of his son, being his last and composed on the occasion when he endorsed the nomination of Solomon as his successor.[28] Clarke's comment on the specially fitting character of this psalm as it closes Book 2 is more to the point. 'David's prayers have reached their highest peak. With prophetic insight he looks beyond the peaceful reign of Solomon to the more glorious reign of the Messiah, who is both his greater Son and sovereign Lord'.[29] However, we would prefer to see it as a true psalm of Solomon in which the conditions described realize all of David's prayers.[30] The climax of the Song of Songs, we believe, conducts us to this wonderful period when 'the whole earth (will) be filled with his glory'.[31] Though this psalm provides a grand supplement to the Song, the Song itself clearly excels it, for it sweeps within its embrace, not only the climax, but the whole range of salvation history. *Psalm 127*, the other of Solomon's

---

[25] See pp.144–48.   [26] 2 Sam. 7; 1 Kings 1; 3.4–13; 5.2–5[16–19]; 8.15–21 and 2 Chron.//.   [27] Ps. 72.20.   [28] Referred to in Cohen, Pss 230. [29] Clarke, Pss 185.   [30] The word 'ended' [Heb.kallu, pual of kalah found elsewhere only in 3 mpl at Gen. 2.1] would be better rendered here 'accomplished', perfected by being fulfilled, completed, finished in that the goal has been achieved. The elder Kimchi wrote concerning this 'When all shall have been fulfilled, so that Israel, brought back from exile, shall have been restored to their land, and the Messiah, the son of David, rules over them, then will they need no more atonement, and deliverance, and blessing, for they will possess all, and then will be ended the prayers of David the son of Jesse', quoted in Perowne, Pss 323. [31] Ps. 72.19; cf. Hab. 2.14.

song compositions, is central in the series of the Psalms of Ascents. The grand finale of this group is that bright millennial day when the prayer 'The Lord bless thee out of Zion; even he that made heaven and earth' will be fulfilled.[32]

Further, the man who resolved all the enigmas presented for his unravelling, has provided us in the Song with the most heart-warming enigma of all. This is suggested by the fact that, though the song is composed by Solomon, in it he presents more often the words, even the soliloquys, thoughts and reveries of the maiden. He writes as one who knows what is in her heart and mind, as is specifically stated of Jesus who 'needed not that any one should bear witness concerning man; for he himself knew what was in man'.[33] Here then is highlighted that extremely penetrating discernment of the one to whom was given 'wisdom and understanding exceeding much, and largeness of heart, even as the sand that is on the seashore. And Solomon's wisdom excelled the wisdom of all the children of the east, and all the wisdom of Egypt. For he was wiser than all men; than Ethan the Ezrahite, and Heman, and Chalcol, and Darda, the sons of Mahol: and his fame was in all the nations round about'.[34] However much he might have had in common with others, Scripture is clear that Solomon excelled, so that we should not be surprised to find significant evidence for this in the Song, as in other products of his wisdom.

The Style

By way of genre the Song is to be classified among the wisdom literature, and in particular as love poetry within this. As Hebrew poetry generally, it makes capital of *sound patterns*, e.g. shemen and shemekha (ointment and your name) in 1.3, *unusual words* of which it has many, e.g. charuzim (strings of jewels) in 1.10, *word and phrase repetitions* (see specially chap. 12 where their function structurally is considered), and *parallelism*, e.g. 'they made me keeper of the vineyards; (but) mine own vineyard have I not kept' in 1.6d,e, and *chiasm*, e.g. 2.10c–13e. And yet,

---

[32] Ps.134.3.　　[33] 1 Kings 10.1–3; John 2.25.　　[34] 1 Kings 4.29ff[5.9ff].

there is no real parallel elsewhere in the whole of Biblical poetry. There is nothing to equal its rich, luxurious language, as it taps the realms of magnificence in architecture and artifact to describe the beauties of the beloved and of the loved one. Gold alone befits them both, 5.11,14,15: 1.11. Precious stones fitly set express their preciousness, 5.14: 1.10; 4.9; 7.1[2]. The splendour and wealth of Solomon's court and capital city, never to be surpassed in the nation's history, are plundered by the poet otherwise beggared for suited description. For the beloved is a king, and his loved one is described eventually as princess, 1.4,12; 3.9,11; 7.5[6]: 7.1[2]. The impenetrable walls, and the great projecting towers adorned with warriors' shields supply further similes and metaphors, 4.4; 7.4; 8.10. All of this wealth, this weight of glory, betokens unprecedented divine blessing granted to the king, 1 Kings 3.15, and now something of it is seen upon her. This motif, like the others which the poet exploits to enrich our appreciation of that which the lovers are to one another, has no evil connotations whatsoever.

To all of this our poet adds, even intermingles, the descriptive range of nature, with its birds and beasts, the beauties of field and forest, mountain and valley. We shall devote several chapters to nature imagery. Stylistically, this must be the love poem of all love poems.

Using a human love relationship therefore, Solomon was led by the Spirit to create a most charming means of unfolding the love relationship between the Lord and Israel. He was familiar with this grand theme through the Scriptures already in his hands.[35] His detailed development of it by means of the man/woman relationship provided an informing motif for the later prophets of the Old Testament. The Song, then, provides a kind of literary bridge between the earlier covenant love concept of the Pentateuch, and the marriage motif later exploited so tellingly by the prophets. We shall consider this love/marriage theme, so vital for the appreciation of the Song, as it is developed in the Old Testament. The two chapters immediately following this one are devoted to this.

---

[35] Deut.17.14–20, esp. v.18f.

2

IT IS NOT GOOD THAT THE MAN SHOULD BE ALONE

AS THE SONG OF SONGS CONCENTRATES in an unparalleled way upon the more intimate and personal love relationship, the betrothal and marriage of a man and a woman, there is need to bring into focus those elements of the Old Testament revelation which touch upon the mind and purpose of God relating to these matters.

That the fruitful union of man and woman was a crowning purpose of God in creation is evident from the very beginning of Genesis. Of them alone do we read 'God created man in his own image, in the image of God created he him; male and female created he them'.[1] Genesis 2 has the phases of God's creatorial handiwork regarding the man and the woman particularly in view. Here we learn that the man, like the beasts and the birds, was formed out of 'the dust of the ground'. He was created first,[2] and in the process of naming every creature 'there was not found an help meet for him'. Among the beasts and the birds the man remained 'alone'. The Lord God had already said 'It is not good that the man should be alone', and had determined to 'make him an help meet for him'[3] once the man's awareness of loneliness had dawned upon him. His future partner's creation however was quite different from his own. The Lord God built her out of one of Adam's ribs, which He removed from him while he was in a

---

[1] Gen.1.27.   [2] Gen.2.7,19; I Tim.2.13; 1 Cor.11.8.   [3] Gen.2.18,20;
1 Cor.11.9.

21

deep sleep. This 'woman', different from the man, yet belonging to him and essential for him, was brought now to the man.[4] His jubilation could not be contained: 'This is now', he says, at long last, 'the one for whom I have felt such a deep longing'. Thinking of her origination provided yet another thrill for him, for she was a definite part of him! Because he knew that she was 'bone of my bones, and flesh of my flesh', they belonged together. What she is to him essentially prompts this 'formula of possession'. It remained only for the man to indicate their union and yet their distinction by calling his perfect partner 'Woman [Heb. ˊishshah], because she was taken out of Man [Heb. ˊish]'. If in nature they were one, in sex they were different and distinct.[5] In this creation cameo, the embryo for the future of the race was enveloped. The man, we are told, would 'leave his father and mother' in order to 'cleave [Heb.dabhaq] unto his wife: and they shall be one flesh'.[6] In the marriage union of our first parents, divine purpose was realized in their togetherness and their fruitfulness. From then on, the sons born would yearn for partners who were altogether suited to them, and on finding them they would leave the provisions of parental love in order to cleave to their wives, that they, in turn, might not be 'alone'. Remarkably, in this leaving of father and mother, the sons would build up the father's house [Heb.beth ˊabh], ensuring the continuation and multiplication of family and tribe.

From the beginning then there existed a socially healthy and accepted institution of monogamous marriage.[7] This involved minimally a desire for union which was entered upon with the permission and blessing of the parents, tribe and society. Physical union consummated and finally ratified the marriage. The bond between the couple was irrevocable, and they were to cleave to one another. What do we know of those formalities leading into marriage, and those privileges and responsibilities entered upon in

---

[4] Gen.2.21f.   [5] Gen.2.23.   [6] Gen.24; Matt.19.5; Mark 10.8; 1 Cor.6.16; Eph.5.31. To 'become one flesh' refers to a change of state, not to a process, BDB 226,IIe. It emphasizes also the irrevocable character of the marriage bond. Marriage involves and yet does not consist in physical union alone, cf.Gen.34.2ff.

[7] The legislation places the emphasis upon this as the norm. The very first bigamist belonged to the godless line of Cain, Gen.4.19.

marriage? What safeguards against abuses and breakdown were written into the Biblical legislation?

The Formalities Leading into Marriage

Mating by mutual consent, or promiscuous living with those of the opposite sex are practices unacceptable to God. They may provide for more abandoned and carefree physical gratification outside of formal constraints in the short term, but they cannot develop nor sustain a stable society, neither can they extend the whole being and the best interests of the parties concerned. Worse still, loose living only leads to irreparable physical and emotional damage. Uncontrolled lust, born out of unhealthy concentration upon the physical attractiveness of the opposite sex, has always led to the corruption of the pure, and the dissatisfaction, if not the revulsion, of the offender.[8] What has the projection and exploitation of sex, as such, to do with true love, and the pure joy of the union of man and woman according to the mind of God? As in many other spheres of life, the divine purpose and provision for man and woman, pure and without cause for shame as given by Him, has been transformed into the impure and shameful by the devil.[9]

Marriage is presented as the norm for men and women in the Scriptures.[10] True marriage provides for so much more than a physical union. It creates a perfect completeness as two people realize that they are truly one whole, and provides for a unique companionship which their individual distinctivenesses only serve to enrich and extend. It promotes mutual care and concern, and opens up fields of practical co-operation. It is God's provision

---

[8] See esp.2 Sam.13.1–22; also Rom.1.26f.   [9] Gen.3.1–7; 1 Cor.6.13c–20.

[10] Gen.2.24; Heb.13.4. Those who forbid to marry are teaching 'doctrines of demons', 1 Tim.4.1–3a. Some equipped to accept it may make themselves 'eunuchs for the kingdom of heaven's sake', Matt.19.12; cf.1 Cor.7.2,7ff,17,32f. Where a climate of imminent judgment or 'present distress' obtains, God's servants are encouraged to keep themselves 'free from care' necessarily involved in marriage. However, these are accomodations to the abnormal. Legislation regarding forbidden marriage unions is to be found in Lev.18.6–18; 20.11f,14,17,19ff; Deut.22.30; 27.20,22f. The restrictive regulation of Deut.24.1–4 is not intended to define grounds for divorce, but rather to legislate where, through sin, it has taken place.

for the building up of the family through procreation/generation, and is the stable and secure cradle in which children are reared and trained for their future acceptance in, and contribution to God's congregation and society at large. The home, which provides the external framework for the marriage, is intended to be a sanctuary, a school, and a centre of blessing to all.

Initiation. In the wisdom and purpose of God, society was organized patriarchally, that is, the family was seen as 'the father's house' [Heb.beth ´ abh]. It was the father's family name and inheritance that was to be perpetuated. Marriage, therefore, effected legally the transfer of a woman from 'her father's house' to the 'house' of her husband's father. Consequently, the initiative in establishing a marriage contract belonged with the head of the house of the man involved, and he is found acting on behalf of his son in the negotiations with the father of the maiden involved. Thus Abraham commissioned his servant to 'take a wife for my son Isaac'. The woman was consulted only at the end of all the other procedure.[11] In Samson's case, he found the woman of his choice and insisted that his parents 'get her for me to wife'.[12] In the Song, it was in the very sphere where his mother had brought him forth that the maiden had first aroused in her beloved yearnings after her.[13] His initial yearnings after her, brought him from his home to her home.[14] Later still, he brought her from her home to his home 'in the day of the gladness of his heart'.[15] Unmarried women might be met in public while engaged in daily tasks,[16] but unmarried members of opposite sexes did not mingle freely, nor share in the love and courtship phases of modern western society prior to their formal betrothal. The woman did not seek the man; the initiative, springing out of an inner yearning for a suited life partner, was always on the man's side.

Compensation. As a marriage would deplete the one family of a daughter, while enlarging another family by the addition of another daughter, and by the envisaged children who would be

---

[11] Gen.24.4.　　　　[12] Jud.14.1f. This marriage was unlawful in terms of the developed Mosaic legislation, Lev.18.6–18; Deut.7.1–4.　　　　[13] Song 8.5c–e.
[14] 3.4.　　　[15] 3.11.　　　[16] e.g. when visiting a well to obtain water, as with Rebecca, and Rachel, Gen.24.15–20; 29.9,11.

added to that house, the bride's father would expect some return for the loss sustained by him and the gain accruing to the bridegroom's family. The 'marriage fee' or 'bride-price' [Heb.mohar][17] was paid to the bride's father, and was subject to negotiation. The amount seems to be specified only in that case where an unbetrothed daughter had been the victim of rape and the guilty party was forced to marry her.[18] Clearly then, sexual relations are not equated with marriage. Further, where the suitor was unable to pay in cash, payment in kind might be acceptable, as in Jacob's case who *served*, or in Othniel's case who *stormed* and *secured* a city, or in David's case who *slaughtered* the enemy, for their respective fathers-in-law.[19]

Betrothal. With the compensation issue settled satisfactorily, the betrothal[20] of the pair was formally sealed. The bride-to-be's father was committed to 'give to wife' his daughter.[21] For the 'bride', an unfaithful act during the betrothal period was punishable as adultery.[22] Should she be the victim of rape while betrothed, the offender was guilty of adultery and was punished.[23] For the man the 'bride' was his already, although living together was not yet permitted. His liability to military call-up and service was also waived.[24] Should he have second thoughts, and wish to dissolve his betrothal, nothing short of the issue of a writ

---

[17] The word [Heb.mohar] is translated wrongly 'dowry' in Gen.34.12. It is distinguished also from the word 'gift' [Heb.mattan], 34.12, which refers to the presents that might be passed to the bride-to-be, and/or to her family when final agreement had been reached, cf.24.28,30,47,53. A dowry, in the form of a gift from the bride's father to her is mentioned only in the cases of Rebecca, Leah and Rachel, each of whom were given their attendant nurse, or slave girl, 24.59; 29.24, 29, Achsah who was given springs of water, Josh.15.19, and Pharaoh's daughter who was given the city of Gezer when she married Solomon, 1 Kings 9.6.
[18] Deut.22.28f; Exod.22.16f[15f]; cf.Gen.34.2,12. [19] Gen.29.20,28; Josh.15.16ff; 1 Sam.18.23ff; 2 Sam.3.14. [20] The word 'betroth' [Heb.pi̅ el of ῾rs, ῾eras] means 'to win legally for one's own', for which see especially 2 Sam.3.14; Hos.2.19f,21f. In the NT the word [Grk.mnesteuo] means to woo or win, betroth, Matt.1.18; Luke 1.27; 2.5. [21] For the phrase [Heb.nathan ... le̅ ishshah] see Gen.29.28; 34.8,12; Josh.15.16f//Jud.1.12f. [22] Deut.22.23f. [23] Deut.22.25ff. [24] Deut.20.7.

of divorce would annul the bond.[25]

The Marriage Itself

So far the prospective bridegroom has visited *his loved one's house.* This did not bring about their union. The marriage of a couple was effected when the bridegroom brought the bride to *his house.*[26] Of Samson we read in connection with the one his parents had obtained 'for him to wife', that 'after a while he returned to take her'.[27]

Celebration. With the passage of time, the actual wedding event, which originally was a very simple affair,[28] became more public, formal and elaborate. Special wedding garments became the order of the day for the guests, and also 'a bridegroom decketh himself with a garland', and 'a bride adorneth herself with her jewels' though remaining veiled.[29] The formal procedure, on the day and at the appointed time, was for the bridegroom to make his way to the bride's parental home. He was accompanied by his close friends and the master of ceremonies, the best man, the 'friend of the bridegroom'.[30] The bride too had her own entourage of female companions as she came out to meet her husband.[31] The colourful procession now made its way to the bridegroom's home, to the joyous accompaniment of singing and dancing.[32] Well-wishers lined the route and shared in the joy. As the group approached their destination, other guests would come out to meet them, lighting their lamps and greeting the coming bridegroom and his bride.[33] The invited guests that were ready and fitly attired entered the home, and surrounded the loaded tables at the

---

[25] For quite different reasons see Matt.1.18f. Humanly, Joseph may have taken the tolerant view that Mary had been forced in the countryside, which would permit the sparing of her life whilst freeing him from his obligation to marry her, Deut.22.28f.   [26] Song 3.4,10f.   [27] Jud.14.8.   [28] Gen.24.66f.

[29] Matt.22.11f; Isa.61.10; Ezek.16.9–13; Gen.24.65; Ps.45.8f,12–15[9f,13–16].

[30] Jud.14.11; Matt.9.15 = Mark 2.17 = Luke 5.34; John 3.27; Jud.14.20.

[31] Ps.45.14[15]; 1 Macc.9.39.   [32] ct.Ps.78.63; Jer.7.34, where as an evidence of God's judgment upon His people, He would 'cause to cease from the cities of Judah, and from the streets of Jerusalem, the voice of mirth and the voice of gladness, the voice of the bridegroom and the voice of the bride: for the land shall become desolate'; cf.16.9; 25.10.   [33] Song 3.11; Matt.25.1–9.

marriage feast.[34] The festivities might continue through a week.[35] By these means the marriage was witnessed and ratified publicly.

Consummation. The climax of the wedding festivities was the bridegroom's physically 'taking to wife' the one whom, in the betrothal, had been 'given him to wife'.[36] The couple entered a special tent or bridal chamber where the marriage was consummated immediately.[37] Those yearnings stimulated in his heart toward her in his house initially, which had led him with his parents to her house, were at last satisfied on bringing her home to his house. The parents of the bride were given the sheets of the wedding night bed as the corroboratory tokens of their daughter's virginity, so as to safeguard her against possible false accusations later.[38]

Continuation. Throughout the course of marriage, a developing and satisfying love relationship in all its aspects was to be enjoyed as God's gift. 'Live joyfully with the wife whom thou lovest all the days of the life of thy vanity, which he hath given thee under the sun ... for that is thy portion in life'.[39] True love would never take the partner of one's youth for granted. In terms of their

---

[34] Matt.22.2–10; 25.10; cf.Gen.29.22; Jud.14.10.   [35] cf.Jud.14.12–18. Some since Wetzstein's paper on the subject in 1873, have proposed that the 19th century AD Syrian marriage customs, extending throughout one week, during which the couple are crowned as 'king and queen', provide the nearest parallel to the Song. Highly descriptive love songs (known as wasfs, with which Song 7.1–5[2–6] has been compared, and even a sword dance, cf.6.13d[7.1d]) are featured. See Delitzsch SoS 162–176 for a review in English. It is to be observed that, while the 'king' and Solomon are referred to often, the bride of the Song is never addressed as queen. See also our p.141f.   [36] 'take to wife' [Heb.laqach leˉishah], Gen.4.19; 6.2; 11.29; 12.19; Exod.21.10; Lev.21.7; Deut.20.7; 22.13; 1 Sam.25.43a; Hos.1.2. Taking a wife = marrying her, Deut.24.1. Compare the words 'to know' [Heb.yadhaˉ], Gen.4.1,17,25, 'to lie with, to ravish'[Heb.shakhabh], Gen.30.15,16; 39.7,10,12,14; 2 Sam.11.11,13.   [37] cf. Isaac who 'brought her into his mother's tent, and took [Heb.wayyaqqech] Rebecca, and she became his wife; and he loved her', Gen.24.67. See also the phrases 'go in unto her' or 'went in unto her' [Heb.ˉabhoˉah ˉeleha and yabhoˉah ˉeleha], 29.21,23. Note in Deut.21.13d–f, 'thou shalt go in unto her, and be her husband, and she shall be thy wife'. [38] Deut.22.13–21.   [39] Eccles.9.9.

physical relationships, the couple were to find increasing pleasure in one another, and rejoice in those children given them as an heritage of the Lord.[40] Freely, and with no sense of shame, the husband was to 'rejoice in the wife of thy youth. As a loving hind [Heb. ̄ayyeleth ̄ahabhim] and as a pleasant doe [Heb.ya' alath chen], let her breasts satisfy thee at all times; and be thou ravished always with her love [Heb.be ̄ahabhathah]'.[41] This is to be compared with the language of the Song. In this connection, it is important to observe that the use of more detailed and intimate physical descriptions on the lips of both bridegroom and bride is reserved for the wedding day and during their ensuing marriage relationship, that is, from chapter 3.6 onward in the Song.[42] In the marriage each was to consider the other in all that had to do with the intimacies of their shared life.[43]

Marriage provides measureless fields for love to sow and reap its peculiar rewards. The ideal wife lives energetically for the enriching of her husband and household. As the proverb has it 'A virtuous woman is a crown to her husband'.[44] The benefits of her selfless and tireless love become known far and wide. Her children will 'rise up, and call her blessed; her husband also, and he praiseth her, saying: Many daughters have done virtuously, but thou excelleth them all'.[45] The husband provides, funds, and maintains the home, and by his diligence enriches his wife and family. Through his kindly understanding, he encourages and supports his wife. In the family, he supplements the mother's gentleness and succour with a father's authority and stimulation in the children's upbringing.[46] Together they inculcate the fear of the Lord in those lives committed to their charge. The man's ideal wife so extends him and his capacities that, above and beyond the delights of their love, and the demands of daily work and family responsibility, his administrative influence and wise judgment is known by the people of the land generally.[47] The sense of the incomparable qualities of each other not only engages the thoughts of each, but it finds expression in word and action. So in the Song, if the husband was to her 'the chiefest

---

[40] Ps.127.3.   [41] Prov.5.18f.   [42] Song 4.5; 7.3[4].   [43] 1 Cor.7.3–6.
[44] Prov.12.4.   [45] 31.1–31; cf. Song 6.9d,e.   [46] cf.1 Thess.2.7,11f.
[47] Prov.31.23.

among ten thousand', then she was to him 'but one; the only one of her mother; she is the choice one of her that bare her'.[48] Fittingly, such a wife could say 'I am my beloved's, and his desire is toward me'.[49]

Covenant Character. Malachi clearly describes marriage as a covenant. The wife of one's youth is both 'thy companion [Heb.chabhertekha], and the wife of thy covenant [Heb.we esheth berithekha]'.[50] The promises and vows made on their wedding day were serious and sacred, committing them to mutual obligations for all time, 'as long as they both shall live'. Compare the solemn vows uttered by both parties to marriage even today. Divorce was nauseous to the God that said 'I hate putting away, saith the Lord, the God of Israel'.[51] The man who left father and mother did so in order to 'cleave [Heb.dabhaq] unto his wife'.[52] They both become 'one flesh', which includes more than the sexual union of the pair. Rather it unfolds the formation of a new family relationship, demonstrating in tangible terms the irrevocable covenant which the Lord has with His people.

The Lord Jesus pointed out that, while Moses had 'written you this commandment' *permitting* divorce but never *commanding* it, it had been an accommodation to the hardness of their hearts. The intention of God had been made clear 'from the beginning of the creation'. 'Male and female made he them. For this cause shall a man leave his father and mother, and shall cleave to his wife; and the twain shall become one flesh: so that they are no more twain, but one flesh. What therefore God hath joined together, let not man put asunder'.[53] Note the absolute character of this impera-

---

[48] Song 5.10b; 6.9a–c.   [49] 7.10.   [50] Mal.2.14. For 'the wife of one's youth' [Heb. esheth ne urekha] see also Prov.5.18; cf. 'the husband of her youth' [Heb.ba al ne urekha], Joel 1.8. Yet another description of a man's wife is 'friend' [Heb. alluph, AV = guide], Prov.2.17.   [51] Mal.2.16.
[52] 'cleave'[Heb.dabhaq] = cling to, stick to another. It is a prominent technical term in the field of covenant making, e.g. Deut. 10.20; 11.22; 13.4; 30.20; Josh.22.5; 23.8, expressing both the affection and loyalty of Israel who fear, serve, love and obey their Lord, TWOT I. 178. Its use in Gen.2 suggests the ratification of a marriage covenant.   [53] Mark 10.5–9//. Reference to 'bone' and 'flesh' in a variety of contexts denotes kinship or blood relations, Gen.29.12–14; 37.27; Jud.9.2; 2 Sam.19.13.

tive. In the light of this, the Lord went on to explain to His disciples that 'Whosoever shall put away his wife, and marry another, committeth adultery against her: and if she herself shall put away her husband, and marry another, she committeth adultery'.[54] The irrevocable character of the marriage relationship, and the faithfulness of both the husband and wife to one another, is aptly represented in covenant terms.

Authority. The authority in the marriage partnership was vested in the man, who is referred to as 'the woman's husband' [Heb.ba`al ha`ishshah].[55] The word stresses possession, ownership,[56] which takes us back to the initiative of the man, and that act of purchase which had sealed the relationship at the beginning. Sarah illustrates the acceptance of this by calling Abraham her husband 'my lord' [Heb. `adhoni].[57] It was Abraham who named Isaac,[58] as Adam had done for all over which he had been given authority by God. It is the man's name and 'house' that was continued in the marriage. The Bible genealogies are an object lesson in the patriarchal authority which they represent. The wives enjoyed tremendous freedom and influence in the family circle, but all was tempered with the spirit of subjection to their husbands. The extension of this into the teaching of the New Testament indicates its ongoing relevance for our own times.[59]

Breakdown. In the course of time the sanctity of marriage and of family life was hedged about with legislative safeguards. For our purpose, the most important of these has to do with the sin of adultery. In instances where the case is proven, and a man's wife has been party to illicit intercourse with another man, the judgment was to be as severe as it was swift. 'If a man be found lying with a woman married to an husband, then they shall both of them die, the man that lay with the woman, and the woman: so shalt thou put away the evil from Israel'.[60] Such summary judgment also falls upon the offenders where the woman is as yet only

---

[54] Mark 10.11f. [55] Exod.21.22; cf.2 Sam.11.26. [56] Gen.20.3.
[57] Gen.18.12; 1 Pet.3.6. [58] Gen.21.3; cf.2.20. [59] 1 Cor.11.3; 14.34f;
Eph.5.22; Col.3.18; 1 Tim.2.12ff; Tit.2.3ff; 1 Pet.3.1-6. [60] Deut.22.22; ct. John
8.2.

betrothed to a husband.[61] In the case of rape, the man only was condemned to die.[62]

A man's wife, in entering upon marriage, was committed to absolute faithfulness to her husband. Should she become guilty of adultery, she violated her marriage covenant, which was even more strongly condemned as a forgetting of 'the covenant of her God' because of the divine legislation regarding it.[63] This confronts us again with the sacredness and the seriousness of the marriage bond in the sight of God, and that sanctity in it upon which He insists. 'Thou shalt not commit adultery'.[64] That law has never been rescinded nor modified. Hence the writer of Hebrews insists 'Let marriage be had in honour among all, and let the bed be undefiled: for fornicators and adulterers God will judge'.[65] There was provision even against the nagging uncertainty in the mind of a husband regarding his wife's faithfulness, catered for by the 'law of jealousy'.[66] In such cases, the man's wife was to be brought, along with 'a meal offering of jealousy', to the priest, and he in turn, was to bring her before the Lord. The woman was to 'swear with the oath of cursing', and drink the 'water of bitterness', which would test her inward parts with all their secrets. Should she be guilty, or as the paragraph repeatedly has it 'defiled' [Heb.nitma‾ ah],[67] the Lord would bring the deserved curses upon her. Should she be 'clean; then she shall be free, and shall conceive seed'.[68]

The breaking of known divine laws with respect to the marriage relationship is to 'trespass' [Heb.ma‾ al] against one's partner.[69] This, in turn, is because of the twisted, sinful nature, and its fruit is described as 'iniquity' [Heb.‾ awon].[70] The one guilty of such sin is said 'to deal treacherously' [Heb.baghadh] toward their marriage partner.[71]

---

[61] Deut.22.23f.   [62] 22.25ff.   [63] Prov.2.17.   [64] Exod.20.14. [65] Heb.13.4.   [66] Num.5.11–31.   [67] Seven references in all, Num.5.13,14(2),20,27,28,29; cf. 'uncleanness' [Heb.tum‾ ah], v.19.   [68] v.28. [69] vv.12,27.   [70] vv.15,31(2).   [71] The word is used of human marriage faithlessness, e.g. Exod.21.8; Jer.3.20, and of treachery against God, e.g. Jer.3.20; 9.2[1]; Hos.6.7; Mal.2.10ff. In the latter case, the covenant relationship with God is viewed metaphorically as a marriage union in which the nation has been faithless, see TDOT 1.470–73, Erlandsson.

The breakdown in human relationships reflects the sadder and more disastrous breakdown in the relationship between man and God through sin. As Wolff expresses it 'It is always a disturbance in the relationship to God which shows itself – in different ways – in the disturbances within the common life of men and women'.[72]

This review of man/woman relationships Biblically has laid the foundation for a consideration of the use of this as a motif to express the intimacies of God's relationship with men. We shall develop this in the next chapter.

---

[72] Wolff, AOT 176.

3

THE MARRIAGE RELATIONSHIP BETWEEN THE LORD
AND ISRAEL

GOD'S PURPOSE IN CREATION was to glorify Himself, and latent in all
His works and ways, therefore, there is a revelation of Himself.
This is particularly so in the creation of man and woman. Paul
writes concerning their union 'This mystery is great: but I speak
in regard of Christ and the church'.[1] It should come as no surprise, therefore, that the marriage relationship is used theologically
to describe the oneness, the intimacy and the indissoluble
character of that relationship which exists between the Lord and
Israel.

Already we have touched upon many of those facets of human
marital affairs dealt with in the Old Testament. Each of these finds
a place as God's love for the nation of Israel is unfolded in the
Scriptures. Everything started with His yearnings, His love for
her;[2] she was the one He chose. The Lord redeemed her, and
betrothed her,[3] and how well He recalled 'the love of thine
espousals'. He went on to marry the nation, being bound to her
by covenant ties.[4] He provided and cared for her, and was all that
a loving husband should be, and so much more, to the Israel that
He loved.[5] The nation can never fault her God in His matchless
love and unchanging faithfulness to her.

Tragically, there was a breakdown in the marriage relationship

---

[1] Eph.5.32. [2] Deut.7.7f; Ezek.16.16f. [3] Deut.7.8; Jer.2.2.
[4] Ezek.16.8 [5] 16.9–14; Hos.2.8

33

and the joy which attended it. The cause of this is placed at the nation's door. Israel was unfaithful to her God. She went after other gods, worshipped the Baals and the Ashtoroth as 'lovers' [Heb.me ahabhim].[6] Religiously, spiritually, the nation became an adulteress to the dishonour and displeasure of her God.[7] The Lord, whose name is Jealous,[8] would not share her with another. She was put out of her land, and lost all the joys and blessings of her marriage, but she was never divorced by the God who was her Husband: 'For I hate putting away, saith the Lord, the God of Israel'.[9]

Among the many salvation motifs by which the nation is encouraged,[10] is that of the love [Heb. ahabh], and of the steadfast, faithful, covenant love [Heb.chesedh] of her divine Husband. It is upon God and His love for her that her hope rests. We must consider a little more specifically the contribution of Israel's prophets to this theme.

The Marriage Motif of the Prophets

It was given to **Hosea** to develop most fully and suggestively this aspect of the relationship between God and the nation. His own tragic experience of a broken marriage, fitted him to enter into the heartbreak of the God of Israel.[11] In brief, the prophet had married, his wife bore three children, only the first being clearly his own. Gomer was unfaithful to him, and said 'I will go after my lovers'.[12] She neither appreciated the matchless love of her husband, nor realized that the munificent benefits she enjoyed were all tangible proofs of his commitment to her.[13] The marriage ended in disaster, and she was put away from the house and stripped of those gifts which love had bestowed upon her. This tale of woe is too familiar in our day, when adultery stalks unchecked, and there are so many wrecked marriages, and broken homes.

---

[6] cf.Hos.2.5,7,10,12,13[7,9,12,14,15]; 3.1. [7] Note the constant use of the word 'to commit adultery' [Heb.na aph] of Israel figuratively, Isa.57.3; Jer.3.8,9; 13.27; Ezek.23.27; Hos.2.4. [8] Exod.34.14. [9] Mal.2.16. [10] See 'Love', Baur EBT,2.519f. [11] see chs.1–3 where the prophet's own domestic experience is interwoven with its application to the history of God's relationship with the nation. [12] Hos.2.5,7,13[7,9,15]. [13] Hos.2.5,8,9,12[7,10,11,14].

The relating of the human tragedy involved would hardly have warranted a place in Scripture were it not that Hosea's experience mirrored something more defiling and disastrous. Despite God's love for Israel from the beginning and the wealthy inheritance which He gave her, the nation did not appreciate all that He was to her, or all that He had done for her. In wrongly attributing her bounty to the Baals, she gave herself to their worship, committing spiritual adultery which, in turn, led to all kinds of physical promiscuity also. This inevitable life-corrupting effect of departure from God has been before us earlier; the 'gods many, and lords many', together with all that the devil supplies on 'the table of demons', have always proved to be the ruination of those whose love for God has waned.[14] The outraged holiness of God demanded that the defiled nation be put aside, whilst His inflexible righteousness decreed judgment upon their wickedness. In all of this, the prophet's experience was a clear parable and an exact parallel of God's. There was one amazing distinction however, which the Lord revealed to Hosea in order that even in this feature of divine love, he might follow the pattern of God's determined ways with the nation. Hosea's wife, now abandoned by her lovers after she had become degraded and defiled, was to be redeemed and restored to home and husband 'even as the Lord loveth the children of Israel, though they turn unto other gods, and love cakes of raisins'.[15] This the prophet did, and became a living embodiment of the message of the Lord to the nation He loved.

As Hosea adopted the metaphor of the marriage relationship to warn and woo the Northern Kingdom, Israel, before the judgment of God resulted in their exile, so Jeremiah and Ezekiel used that same relationship to expose and denounce the Southern Kingdom, Judah, before God's purging judgment resulted in its carrying away also.

For **Jeremiah** the beginnings of Israel's relationship with her God were holy and utterly absorbing and thrilling like a true first love.

---

[14] See pp.31f. Also 1 Cor.8.5; 10.20–22. Even during the wilderness wanderings, Israel was defiled through sexual relations with Moabitesses, promoted through the vile influences of Baal-peor, Num.25.1–9; 1 Cor.10.8. Pagan cult and human corruption went hand in hand.   [15] Hos.3.1.

With what joyous satisfaction the Lord recalled 'the love of thine espousals; how thou wentest after me in the wilderness'.[16] As the years passed, however, the house of Jacob rejected their God saying 'I will not serve; for upon every high hill and under every green tree thou didst bow thyself, playing the harlot'.[17] They became totally insensible to sin, and far from fleeing from its advances, they freely paired up with the Baals and the corrupting sexual promiscuousness associated with this worship. The prophet's boldly condemning parallel to the nation's abandonment of all restraint is the behaviour in the love-life of the 'wild ass'. In her pairing season, observes the prophet, 'all they that seek her will not weary themselves; in her month they shall find her'. So, in the nation's apostasy, she says 'for I have loved strangers, and after them will I go'. She says 'to a stock (wooden Asherah), Thou art my father; and to a stone (pillar), Thou hast brought me forth: for they have turned their back unto me, and not their face'.[18] Even 'the sun, and the moon, and all the host of heaven ... they have loved'. The judgment of God was inevitable, and 'all thy lovers are destroyed', 'thy lovers shall go into captivity', and 'All thy lovers have forgotten thee'.[19]

For **Ezekiel**, the behaviour of the nation in the light of the pitying and elevating love of God, only exposes the more luridly the incredible perversion shown in their shameless abominations. When the Lord saw her initially in her blood He said 'live'. And 'when I passed by thee, and looked upon thee, behold, thy time was the time of love; and I spread my skirt over thee, and covered thy nakedness: yea, I sware unto thee, and entered into a covenant with thee, saith the Lord God, and thou becamest mine'. He washed her, anointed her, clothed her, placed ornaments on her, crowned her, fed her, and then confessed 'thou wast exceeding beautiful'. Her beauty was perfect 'through my majesty which I had put upon thee'.[20] The opening word of Ezekiel 16.15, 'But', introduces the inexplicably ungrateful and indescribably perverted response of the sinful nation. Unparalleled promiscuity betrayed their total heart-alienation from a God of unsullied holiness, as

---

[16] Jer.2.2.   [17] 2.20.   [18] 2.24,25,27; cf.v.33; 3.1f.   [19] 8.2; 22.20,22; 30.14.   [20] Ezek.16.6,8,9–14.

she poured out her whoredoms 'on every one that passed by; his it was'. All that God had given her, she prostituted in the unbridled pursuit of the forbidden, never considering the grace that met her in the days of her youth. Religiously, politically, and morally she unashamedly committed whoredom. She was 'A wife that committeth adultery! that taketh strangers instead of her husband!'[21] The divine judgment of the nation was inevitable, therefore, for 'behold, I will gather all thy lovers, with whom thou hast taken pleasure, and all them that thou hast loved ... and will discover thy nakedness unto them'. 'Because thou hast not remembered the days of thy youth, but hast fretted me in all these things; therefore, behold, I will bring thy way upon thine head'.[22]

Praise God! His ways are not irrevocably governmental. Judgment is His strange work. He crowns His ways, rather, with grace. This is evident in both of the major prophets we have been considering. For Jeremiah, the last word to a faithless and an adulterous nation which is to pass under the judgment of God vibrates with sovereign grace. He recalls that 'The Lord appeared of old unto me, saying, Yea, I have loved thee with an everlasting love: therefore with lovingkindness have I drawn thee'. The word which breathes with hope in Ezekiel 16 is 'Nevertheless'. Had not the Lord sovereignly determined to 'remember my covenant with thee in the days of thy youth, and I will establish unto thee an everlasting covenant'?[23]

In both of these major prophets, therefore, marital love, the intimate relationships of husband and wife, and that adultery which betrays and defiles it, become figures of the union of the Lord and Israel and the course through which it ran. By means of this figure, as well as many others, the Lord's people are shown not merely to fail in reciprocating His love, but to be guilty of shamefully degrading themselves and of dishonouring Him.

The prophet **Isaiah** however utilizes the marriage bond in

---

[21] Ezek.16.15; see also vv.16–34.   [22] 16.37,43; read vv.35–43. The whole of Ezek.23 pursues, in a similar vein, the adulteries of the nation and the offence these were to God.   [23] Jer.31.3; Ezek.16.60,62.

comforting the nation which would feel their case irretrievably lost. Totally dispirited, they would consider that their God had divorced them once and for all. How quickly the Lord commissioned Isaiah to ask on His behalf, 'Where is the bill of your mother's divorcement, wherewith I have put her away?' Of course, there was no such document in existence. Has He not said elsewhere 'For I hate putting away, saith the Lord, the God of Israel'?[24] He aims for the nation's heart when He says 'Thou shalt be no longer termed Forsaken; neither shall thy land any more be termed Desolate: but thou shalt be called Hephzi-bah, and thy land Beulah: for (explaining the significance of the names) the Lord delighteth in thee, and thy land shall be married'. The happy prospect of Israel's reuniting with her God causes the outburst 'Sing, O barren, ... for more are the children of the desolate than the children of the married wife'. The secret is 'thy Maker is thine husband; the Lord of hosts is his name: and the Holy One of Israel is thy redeemer; the God of the whole earth shall he be called. For the Lord hath called thee as a wife forsaken and grieved in spirit, even a wife of youth, when she is cast off, saith thy God'.[25] Israel's Maker, who is her Husband, will not rest until He has her at His side, enjoying His love once again.

---

[24] Isa.50.1; Mal.2.16.   [25] Isa.62.4; 54.1,5f.

4

LOVE IS THE GREATEST

LOVE is a predominant Biblical theme and is wrought into the poetic tapestry of the Song. It demands our attention before we venture into the Song particularly. First, then, we shall consider:

Love in the Old Testament

The most important word for love in the Old Testament [Heb. root ´hb] is used in reference to 1). God's love to men, to Israel in particular, to Jerusalem etc. 2). man's love to God and 3). man's love to man and to those of the opposite sex. The use of one word to embrace such a wide spectrum of meanings has resulted in differences of view as to the origin of the term itself. The order in which this analysis of its use has been expressed here is fundamentally opposed to much that is written today on the subject of love in the Bible. It is stated authoritatively by some that the original use of the concept of love [Heb. ´ahabh] 'belongs to the realm of sexual love, of physical desire, of lust, and even of sensual pleasure'.[1] Such a conclusion can be maintained only where the Bible is conceived solely as a prodigy of its Near Eastern environment rather than having been inspired by God, and where man is held to be naturally progressing from partial to more perfect light in the course of his religious development. We reject all such pro-

---

[1] TDOT 1.107, Wallis; TDNT 1.22, Quell.

39

positions and the shaky foundations on which they are built. The hymn writer saw and expressed the point more clearly in the words,

> And yet I want to love Thee, Lord:
> Oh, light the flame within my heart,
> And I will love Thee more and more
> Until I see Thee as thou art.

We must start from the great premise, succinctly stated in the New Testament, that 'God is love'.[2] Further to this, we are to own that 'love is of God; and every one that loveth is begotten of God, and knoweth God'.[3] In this also God must be owned as the great originator, as surely as He is the creator and sustainer of the universe. The believer is quick to say 'Herein is love, not that we loved God, but that he loved us, and sent his Son to be the propitiation for our sins. Beloved, if God so loved us, we also ought to love one another ... We love, because he first loved us'.[4] Of course, we acknowledge that we are using New Testament words to refute what we see as erroneous statements regarding an Old Testament word. We do so because of the very pithiness of the quotations, rather than because evidence of God's love as the great first cause is not forthcoming from the Old Testament canon. Another has arrived at the same conclusion from the theocentric character of the Biblical revelation as a whole. 'Biblical thought is, from the outset, orientated theocentrically – one might almost say theocratically – and therefore has as its central point the idea of God as Creator and Lord of all, as well as deliverer and judge of mankind. For this reason it is of the love which is predicated of God Himself that we must first speak'.[5]

The first Biblical reference to love [Heb. ˋahabh] refers to human love, expressing Abraham's affection for his 'only son Isaac'.[6] It is

---

[2] 1 John 4.8,16.   [3] 4.7.   [4] 4.10f,19.   [5] See 'Love', Baur EBT 2.519. For another conservative and detailed approach to the subject of God's love in the OT see CIBPI 277–88 in which Walker insists that 'God is love' as an abstract theological statement 'is alien to the character of the OT and is not found there', p.277. However, it is one of those *eternal facts* brought to light by the coming of the Son of God's love.   [6] Gen.22.2; cf. Isaac's love for Esau, 25.28, and Israel's love for Joseph, 37.3f, and Benjamin, 44.20.

clearly used of love for one of the opposite sex too, and in a sexual sense as when Rebecca[7] became Isaac's wife 'and he loved her'. However, at the back of all this, stands the great fact of God's prior love for these very fathers. Deuteronomy records of Israel's God that 'because he loved thy fathers, therefore he chose their seed after them, and brought thee out with his presence, with his great power, out of Egypt; to drive out nations from before thee greater and mightier than thou, to bring thee in, to give thee their land for an inheritance, as at this day'.[8] Israel's unique place among the nations found its originating cause in God's love. 'The Lord did not set his love [Heb.chashaq] upon you, nor choose [Heb.bachar] you, because ye were more in number than any people ... but because the Lord loveth [Heb. ahabhah] you, and because he would keep the oath which he sware unto your fathers, hath the Lord brought you out with a mighty hand, and redeemed you out of the house of bondage, from the hand of Pharaoh king of Egypt'. The close association of divine love and the nation's election here emphasizes the divine initiative. It was when Israel was but a child that the Lord 'loved him, and called my son out of Egypt'.[9] In a variety of ways Israel experienced the Lord's ongoing love.[10] They were precious in His sight, and He loved them.[11] 'Yea, I have loved thee with an everlasting love: therefore with lovingkindness have I drawn thee'.[12] Although the nation in a backslidden state may question the fact, their God truthfully states 'I have loved you'.[13] Is not the very future of the nation guaranteed in the love of their God? He cannot rest until, at last, the day will dawn when 'The Lord thy God is in the midst of thee, a mighty one who will save: he will rejoice over thee with joy, he will rest in his love, he will joy over thee with singing'. He says 'I will love them freely'.[14] In the previous chapter we considered the revelation of God as developed in the *prophets'* writings. The selections here from the *Pentateuch through to the Prophets* are sufficient to establish that the love of God initiated salvation history, and is revealed throughout its course.

---

[7] Gen.24.67; cf. Jacob's love for Rachel, 29.18,30, Leah's hope of regaining Jacob's love, 29.32, and Shechem's sexual abuse of Dinah, 34.3.   [8] Deut.4.37f; cf. 10.15.
[9] Deut.7.8; Isa.63.9; Hos.11.1.   [10] Deut.23.5[6]; Ps.47.4[5]; 1 Kings 10.9;
2 Chron.9.8.   [11] Isa.43.4; 48.14.   [12] Jer.31.3.   [13] Mal.1.2(3).
[14] Zeph.3.17; Hos.14.4[5].

41

Individuals, too, enjoyed the causeless love of their God, whether it be Abraham, the father of the nation, or Solomon.[15] Hiram, king of Tyre, and the queen of Sheba acknowledged that it was because the Lord loved [Heb. ʾahabhah] His people Israel that He had made Solomon king over them.[16] There is a kind of messianic anticipation in this.

It is clear that the love initiative is with God, and that He actively pursues the object of His love with a view to her blessing, and at tremendous cost to Himself. His love brings the nation into a covenant relationship with Himself and sustains her in it. This is unfolded in other forms of the divine love expressed by the terms 'steadfast love or loyalty' [Heb.chesedh], 'compassion or pity' [Heb.racham], and 'favour or grace' [Heb.chen]. Also, the nation He has chosen in sovereign love, He 'knows' [Heb.yadhaʾ], a term which is used of the intimate physical union of man and woman, and also of that personal and national intimate relationship which God's people realized.[17] Here is the true prototype. As a result of this, He now calls upon the one upon whom He has bestowed His love to reciprocate it in an undivided and pure devotion to Him, and in obedience to His commands. Is there any department of life outside the claims of divine redeeming love?

Humanism may propose that man himself must apply his energies properly, and determine to live out a concern for others on purely humanitarian principles. This takes no account of man's fall and bondage to sin. It preaches a gospel of 'man can'. Rather, the Bible insists that 'man cannot', and that he urgently needs a divine rescue and a motivation to love. Israel experienced this when her God brought her out of Egypt, 'the house of bondage', and set her at liberty to serve him out of love for Him, and for all that He had done for her. Israel's behaviour should now reflect her blessing.

The first claim was upward, as the words of the Shemʿa show: 'Hear, O Israel: the Lord our God is one Lord: and thou shalt love the Lord thy God with all thine heart, and with all thy soul, and with all thy might'.[18] Their God would continue with them as

---

[15] 2 Chron.20.7; Isa.41.8, in each case translated 'friend'; 2 Sam.12.24; Neh.13.26.
[16] 1 Kings 10.9; 2 Chron.2.11[10]; 9.8.   [17] Gen.4.1,2,5; Exod.33.12; Hos.13.5; Amos 3.2.   [18] Deut.6.4.

the one 'which keepeth covenant and mercy with them that love him and keep his commandments'. In fact, what did the Lord require of them but 'to walk in all his ways, and to love him, and to serve the Lord thy God with all thy heart and with all thy soul, to keep the commandments of the Lord, and his statutes . . . for thy good'. They were 'to love the Lord thy God, to obey his voice, and to cleave unto him'. The associating, almost merging, of the ideas of love and obedience finds its NT corollary in the words of our Lord: 'If ye love me, ye will keep my commandments', and 'If ye shall keep my commandments, ye shall abide in my love, as I have kept my Father's commandments and abide in his love'.[19] God's people should love 'his name', 'the habitation of his house', 'thy salvation'.[20] This would become apparent to all as they loved 'the stranger', 'his law', 'pureness of heart', 'the good', 'mercy', 'truth and peace'.[21] Shall we not respond to the psalmist's appeal, 'O love the Lord, all ye his saints: the Lord preserveth the faithful'?[22]

In saying this, does this not place love far beyond the sphere of the emotions, as it also denies emphatically that the true origins of love are in the sensual and the erotic? Surely, it is because man has given up the God of pure love that he has turned to the false gods of his own devising. Herein lies the explanation of the perversion of love into something synonymous with lust, with all the consequent wrecking of the human body and mind.[23] In man's sin and departure from God under the subtle and successful influence of the devil, lies the explanation of the crude and corrupting mythological creations of the Canaanite pantheon. And man, deifying his own passions, became enslaved, travelling the broad road downward to destruction. It must be erroneous to propose eroticism and pagan mythology as the informing background of the Song.

---

[19] John 14.14; 15.10.   [20] Deut.7.9; 10.12; 30.20; cf. 11.1,13,22; 13.3f[4f]; 19.19; 30.6,16; Josh.22.5; 23.11; Neh.1.5; Ps.31.23; 145.20; Exod.20.6; Deut.5.10; Dan.9.4. See also Ps.69.36[37]; Isa.56.6: Ps.119.97,113,165; cf. 119.47,119,127,140,159,167: Ps.40.16[17]; 70.4[5].

[21] Deut.10.19: Ps.119.165: Prov.22.11: Amos 5.15: Mic.6.8: Zech.8.19.

[22] Ps.31.23[24].   [23] Rom.1.21ff,24–27.

Love in the Song

It has been remarked that, Biblically, it is in the Song that we meet for the first time the poetic praise of love. The Solomon who had been divinely equipped to compose both proverb and song, excelled himself in leading the way into one thing too wonderful for us, 'the way of a man with a maid', which mystery reaches up to the very heart of God.

In the Song, the love relationship is presented positively as a motif, and establishes by this token its right to the foundational place. The utter breakdown, the prostitution of that which is truly pure, is left for others to portray, namely the prophets. As with New Testament teaching, a classic treatment of a truth is developed in one book whilst the perversion of this at the theoretical and practical levels necessarily follows elsewhere. So it is with the Song and the prophets as we have noticed. It is the love theme with all its rapturous mysteries, its dreams and disappointments, and yet its guaranteed final triumph, for 'love never faileth', that sets the Song of songs far above all others. Of course, in the maiden failure is evident, and her appreciation of both love and her lover clearly advances, yet there is a total absence of infidelity and unchastity throughout. We are convinced that this spiritually creative masterpiece has influenced all the prophetic writings which post-date it. It was only subsequent to the emergence of this love song that the prophets boldly use the love affair and the marriage union, to such telling effect, in reviewing the divine programme with the nation, past, present and future. With them, however, it is the appalling breakdown of the relationship, through the impurity of the nation, which is then met through divine grace.

Let us consider this dominant love theme in the Song. The word love occurs often[24] though we cannot anticipate the whole range of its use in the Song here. We respond instinctively to the words falling from the lips of the fairest of women 'his banner over me was love', 2.4. For her, he was 'thou whom my soul loveth', 1.7; 3.1,2,3,4.

---

[24] Verb [ˊahabh‡] 7 times at 1.3,4,7; 3.1,2,3,4: noun (fem) [ˊahabhah‡] 11 times at 2.7; 3.5; 8.4,7(2) with the article, and at 2.4,5; 3.10; 5.8; 7.6[7]; 8.6 without the article; for the subject generally see Appendix 2.

The two chief characters in the book speak endearingly of one another. In doing so they adopt words translated 'my love' (him of her) or 'my beloved' (her of him). In considering these we shall be encountering the recurring love theme.

Her beloved regularly described her as **'my love'** [Heb.ra˘yathi].[25] The general meaning of the word family from which this is drawn is 'comrade, friend, companion'. In some contexts the closeness and intimacy suggested by the relationship is obvious. Notice, for example, its correlation with family terms: 'thy brother, the son of thy mother, or thy son, or thy daughter, or the wife of thy bosom, or thy friend, which is as thine own soul', Deut.13.6[7]. Further, there is a certain binding character to such a relationship, and Leviticus even adds the *command* to love for 'thou shalt love thy neighbour [Heb.rea˘] as thyself', 19.18. Another form of the root [Heb.re˘ah] interestingly links us with Psalm 45 where the female companions of the queen are so designated.[26] At Qumran the word was used of any member of the community, or even of the community corporately. In one instance in the Song the word is used, in the masculine form, of her beloved: 'This is my beloved [Heb.dodhi], and this is my friend [Heb.re˘i,masc]', 5.16. The two terms are in obvious parallelism. The former is her more usual way of addressing her beloved, whilst the latter, in the feminine form, is the equivalent term by which he refers to her.

Her frequent description of him as **'my beloved'** [Heb.dodhi], is also bound up with the theme of love [Heb.dodh]. Outside of the Song it is used mostly to designate one's uncle,[27] and only rarely is it used of love.[28] In the Song it is found in the plural six

---

[25] The word with its possessive suffix is found only at 1.9,15; 2.2,10,13; 4.1,7; 5.2; 6.4 and in the plural at Jud.11.37*. [26] Ps.45.14[15]; see also Jud.11.38. Yet another form of the word is referred to the 'king's friend', a technical term for a high court official, an intimate counsellor, or even of 'the best man' at Samson's wedding, Jud.14.20. [27] Some 18 times. [28] In the plural abstract of sexual love in Prov.7.18; Ezek.16.8; 23.17: in the singular it is used once to designate the Lord as the wellbeloved in Isa.5.1. The latter reference provides the only parallel to the Song's extensive use of the singular as the designation for the Beloved. Notice particularly its bold application to the Lord Himself.

times,[29] and in the singular as a designation for the beloved one, thirty three times.[30] Let the fairest of women be heard as she speaks of the one dear to her: 'My beloved is mine, and I am his', 2.16, 'I am my beloved's, and my beloved is mine', 6.3, 'I am my beloved's, and his desire is toward me', 7.10[11]. This emphatic use of an Old Testament love term[31] prevents our missing its fundamental importance in the Song.

The Song and Psalm 45

Perhaps the closest parallel to this unique book is that found in Psalm 45, the title [v.1] to which reads 'A song of loves' [Heb.yedhidhoth derived from the root dodh]. This word usually refers to the Lord's love for Israel.[32] The psalm is understood as an actual royal marriage song. 'The question how a secular poem of this kind was included in the Psalter is answered by the analogy of the Song of Songs' according to Cohen. The psalm was taken to refer to 'King Messiah, and the marriage as an allusion to his redemption of Israel'. Similarly, the Song was seen to be 'descriptive of the covenant relationship between God and Israel'.[33] Of course, differences are to be expected. The God that ensured a place in the Scriptures for both of them drew on more than one aspect of the love theme to help us to appreciate His purpose. The psalm is concerned more with the grand climax, the Song with the developing course of salvation history. The warrior king must remove his enemies and take over his kingdom before his queen is seen in gold of Ophir, according to the psalm. Just how the king has such a partner in that day is the concern of the Song. The king's right hand may be a terror to the foe, and yet his loved one may thrill in its warm embrace. The country scene may initiate, enrich, and even sustain first love, but a royal wedding requires the city, yea the city of the great king, and the palace where the union displays all the glorious ramifications of their love. The country maiden is the

---

[29] Song 1.2,4; 4.10(2); 5.1; 7.12[13].   [30] 1.13,14,16; 2.3,8,9,10,16,17; 4.16; 5.2,4,5,6(2),8,9(4),10,16; 6.1(2),2,3(2); 7.9,10,11,13[10,11,12,14]; 8.5,14.   [31] 39 out of 43 such uses excluding the 18 cases where it signifies uncle*.   [32] See Deut.33.12; Ps.60.5[7]; 108.6[7]; cf.127.2; Jer.11.17.   [33] Cohen Pss 140.

prince's daughter after all![34] The distinctions are there. The psalm is more theological and obviously eschatological (true to form), whilst the Song is more personal and devotional. However, the points of contact are numerous, supplying us with ample Biblical material which adopts the poetry of pure love, a love which finds its zenith in the intimate relationship between God and His people.

We recall one further connection with our love theme regarding Solomon. The second child born to David and Bathsheba was named by David 'Solomon', and 'the Lord loved him'. The prophet Nathan was sent to name the child Jedidiah [Heb.Yedhidhyah, from the same root dodh], which means 'loved of the Lord', 2 Sam.12.25†. Causeless and changeless love is in evidence throughout the Song, and this love triumphs at last despite all the failures in its object. Truly 'Many waters cannot quench love', 8.7.

The Claim Inherent in the Title of the Song

The title of this book, 'The Song of songs', 1.1, describes its character. What does it convey to us?

Song [Heb.shir] occurs often in the Old Testament.[35] Apart from the two references in verse 1 it does not reappear in our book. It is the usual term for the glad as distinct from the sad song, cf. Amos 8.10. It is the medium in which to express both joy, Isa.30.29, and triumph, Jud.5.12. By its means the heart overflowed to God also, whether in prayer, Ps.42.8[9], in praise, 69.30[31], or in psalm, 48 title [1]. In realizing what God was to them, the Spirit creatively touched His people's hearts and lips producing yet more songs.[36] Further, the Levitical ministry of music and song swelled the chorus

---

[34] Ps.45.3–7,9[4–8,10]; ct. Song 2.4 'his banner over me was love', 8.5 she is leaning on his arm: Ps.45.4c[5c]; ct. Song 2.6; 8.3: Ps.45.8b,13[9b,14]; cf. Song 3.6–11: Ps.45.9b[10b] 'queen'; cf. Song 7.1[2] 'prince's daughter'.　　[35] The masc. noun 77 times, the fem. noun [Heb.shirah*] only 13 times at Exod.15.1; Num.21.17; Deut.31.19(2),21,22,30; 32.44; 2 Sam.22.1 = Ps.18 title [1]; Isa.5.1; 23.15; Amos 8.3*, and the verb 86 times.　　[36] Ps.33.3; 40.3[4]; 96.1; 98.1; 144.9; 149.1; Isa.42.10.

of praise rising to God from His house, 1 Chron.6.31,32 [16,17]; 13.8; 25.6,7. Both in the popular *lyrics* of the people, and in the more priestly and *liturgical responses* of people and Levites alike, Israel resounded with songs.

The Song of songs [Heb.shir hashshirim], as a phrase, has attracted a number of different interpretations, of which only two claim attention. *The first*, proposed by a Jewish commentary,[37] construes it as suggesting a minimum of three songs.[38] Proverbs, Ecclesiastes, and the Song of songs were the three outstanding poetic products of Solomon. Their obvious differences in spirit and content indicate the several phases of Solomon's life and experience. His promising youth is mirrored in the Song, the penetrating and prodigious output of his mature wisdom is represented in Proverbs, whilst old age reflects on the net results of trying everything under the sun and warns of the vanity of all things in Ecclesiastes. Given that these are the three excelling literary works of Solomon, the Song of songs, like Abishai, 'was chief of the three', 1 Chron.11.20f. This is spiritually suggestive, though the proposition lacks convincing grammatical support.

Secondly, grammatical consideration of the phrase establishes its true meaning. Hebrew construes the singular followed by the plural form of the same noun in phrases descriptive of the pre-eminence, the superlative character of a thing.[39] Perhaps the phrase 'the holy of holies' provides us with the most familiar Biblical parallel. The whole of God's sanctuary was holy. Within it an area open to priests alone was described as 'the holy place', but that innermost room where God's presence was evident, and into which the high priest alone could enter on one day in the year, was called 'the holy of holies' [Heb.qodhesh haqqodhashim]. This place peculiarly could be described as 'the most holy place', Exod.26.33,34. The

---

[37] Midrash Rabbah 1.1.10.   [38] cf. the phrase 'time and times and half a time', Dan.7.25; 12.7; Rev.12.14, meaning three and a half times.

[39] cf. Heb.qodhesh qodhashim, meaning 'most holy' of   1) the brazen altar, Exod.29.37; 30.10; 40.10,   2) the incense altar, 30.36,   3) the meal offering, Lev.2.3, 4) the sin offering, 6.25; 10.17,   5) the trespass offering, 7.1; 14.13,   6) the shewbread, 24.9,   7) the heave offering, Num.18.7, and   8) the Temple, Dan. 9.24.

phrase 'Song of songs' hence introduces the song par excellence, the most outstanding song of all the songs.[40] Rabbi Aqibha's assessment is specially appropriate here: 'For in all the world there is nothing to equal the day on which the Song of Songs was given to Israel, for all the Writings are holy, but the Song of Songs is the Holy of Holies'.[41]

What Makes The Song The Most Excellent Of All Songs?

The Old Testament contains many outstanding songs. The Targum selects ten uttered in this world, hailing the Song of songs as the best of them all.[42] For the Church Father Origen there were just seven songs of peculiar worth, carefully selected so as to present the Song of songs as the climax of them all.[43] In both of these enumerations there is unanimity in according the Song of songs the chiefest place. There must be unequivocal support for this, independent of the claim inherent in the title of the Song itself. The fundamental note of the Song, its essential subject-matter, together with its many moving stylistic and thematic harmonics, would have won for it the pre-eminent place in the field of song-writing. But surely, it is *love*, the undisputed keynote of the Song, which accords it its very special place amongst the Bible songs.

---

[40] cf. the phrases servant of servants, Gen.9.25, prince of the princes Num.3.32, God of gods, and Lord of lords, Deut.10.17; cf. Rev.17.14; 19.16, the heaven of heavens, 1 Kings 8.27, king of kings, Dan.2.37; Ezra 7.12, vanity of vanities, Eccles.1.2, excellent (RV marg. ornament of) ornaments, Ezek.16.7.

[41] Mishnah Yadayim, 3.5.   [42] The ten were: 1) Adam's song for the sabbath, Ps.92,   2) Moses' song at the Reed Sea, Exod.15.1,   3) Israel's song when water was given, Num.21.17,   4) Moses' song when his departure was at hand, Deut.32,   5) Joshua's song as he pursued his foes, 10.12,   6) Deborah and Barak's song after their God-given victory, Jud.5.1,   7) Hannah's song when granted a son, 1 Sam.2.1,   8) David's song when delivered from all his foes, 2 Sam.22 = Ps.18,   9) Solomon's song, and   10) Israel's song when the Lord finally heals the very wounds He had inflicted, Isa.30.29.   [43] The first six songs for him were: 1) the Song of the Sea, Exod.15.1,   2) the Song of the Well, Num.21.17,   3) the Song of Moses, Deut.32,   4) the Song of Deborah, Jud.5,   5) the Song of David's deliverance, 2 Sam.22 = Ps.18, and   6) the Song of Asaph, 1 Chron.16.8ff. Note that the first 5 of his selections feature among the Targum's choices.

By Way of Introduction

The Song, then, is introduced most appropriately as 'The Song of songs'. Love forms its very warp and woof. It is this that causes it to surpass all other songs. For whilst among the galaxy of spiritual graces urged upon us in the Scriptures, there is the supreme triad of 'faith, hope, love' which abide, yet, among these three 'the greatest . . . is love'. Follow after love.[44]

---

[44] 1 Cor.13.13; 14.1.

Part 2

SOME
MAJOR MOTIFS

Contents – Part 2

5

FAUNA

PERHAPS IT WAS WISDOM, peculiarly God-given, in which Solomon most excelled.[1] As king he sought that divine endowment necessary to properly administer justice among God's people. However, his wisdom was more wide ranging than this, as the penetrating depth and breadth of his proverbs indicate. To help us in our appreciation of the Song we shall concentrate on its demonstration of his wisdom in the fields of flora and fauna. Already in 1 Kings this useful analysis had been proposed, for we read that 'he spake of trees, from the cedar that is in Lebanon even unto the hyssop that springeth out of the wall: he spake also of beasts, and of fowl, and of creeping things, and of fishes', 4.33[5.13]. Drawing upon a delightful acquaintance with the countryside, 'all things bright and beautiful, all creatures great and small' not only enhance the Song's scenic appeal, but also enrich its many apt and attractive similes.

We shall consider first the faunal motif. The number of creatures referred to in the Song has been noticed by many.

Concerning Birds

Among the birds of the air the **dove** [Heb.yonah] is specially emphasized in the Song. The word may refer to any of the smaller species of pigeon, numbers of the characteristics of which

[1] 1 Kings 3.12; 4.29ff.

53

are pointed out in the Scriptures. Here it signifies the rock pigeon.[2] The dove hides away from danger among the stony crevices of the rock-face.[3] Among the birds, it is the pigeon and the turtledove alone that are acceptable as a burnt offering.[4] Can anything less than perfect devotion be acceptable to Israel's God? The beloved's endearing description 'my dove' [Heb.yonathi] is tellingly paralleled by a notice of that absence of all defilement in her which appeals to him so much.[5] The dove's gentleness and guilelessness are suggested in the New Testament, Matt.10.16. Similes not only add great poetic beauty to Biblical expression but enrich it as they are pondered. It should not escape our attention that the dove in simile is not infrequently associated either with the fugitive state of one saddened by the *loss of divine favour*,[6] or with the favoured state of those returning from exile into *the blessing of divine favour*.[7] In the light of this, the appropriateness of the use of the dove for his loved one in the Song will become more apparent when we have considered the interpretation of the book as a whole.

Both of the lovers describe the other's eyes as 'doves'.[8] Her eyes are a true mirror image of his. Usually doves are seen together in pairs, as are eyes. Beauty and constancy are suggested, for the dove has its mate alone before its eyes, and mourns when its mate is absent.[9]

---

[2] The Columba livia, 1.15; 2.14; 4.1; 5.2,12; 6.9‡: Lev. alone has more references(9) all translated pigeon (as also Num.6.10).   [3] Song 2.14; cf. Jer.48.28; its wings carry it to safety, Ps.55.6[7]; cf. also the enjoyed peace and prosperity suggested by Ps.68.13[14]; ct. the silly dove which becomes ensnared, Hos.7.11.
[4] Lev.1.14 + 8 times, and Num.6.10. Always offered in pairs. The 'turtledove' is mentioned in Song 2.12b‡.   [5] Song 5.2; 6.9; cf. the dove released from the ark which found no suited place to rest, Gen.8.8–12.   [6] Esp. Ps.55.6[7] with first part of the title of Ps.56[1a]. Here David desires to fly away from the troubles he is experiencing during the period of Absalom's rebellion.   [7] Ps.68.13[14]; Hos.11.11.   [8] Song 1.15; 4.1; 5.12. The reference may be to their largeness, to their glistening colour, their quick movements, or even to their shape as Egyptian art and sculpture stylized human eyes in the form of the bodies of birds. However, for Delitzsch in 5.12 the doves are the dark pupils. Goulder p.5 proposes doves (tails) are eyelids (which flutter), milk is the iris, pools are the pupils, 7.4[5], brooks of water are the tear ducts.   [9] The dove is a figure of beauty only in the Song in the OT, 1.15; 4.1; 5.12.

The book also introduces the '**singing birds**' [Heb.zamirt].[10] This word is a general term for those birds happily breaking forth into chorus when the spring follows the hard winter months.

The **turtledove's** [Heb.tor‡] voice heard in the land is another pointer to the arrival of the spring season. Through Jeremiah the Lord complained that 'the turtle (dove) and the swallow and the crane observe the time of their coming; but my people know not the ordinance of the Lord'.[11] This bird is another of the small pigeon family and is associated with the pigeon (or dove) in the appointed sacrifices of the Lord in 11 of its 14 Old Testament references. The Targum on Song 2.12 associates the voice of the turtledove with 'the voice of the Holy Spirit of redemption'.[12] It is used as a metaphor for Israel in Psalm 74.19.

One other bird is used in a simile concerning the beloved's hair; it is the **raven** [Heb. ˉorebh].[13] The point in the simile is the blackness of his hair, suggesting youthfulness and vigour, unlike the nation of Israel of whom it was said in Hosea's day: 'Strangers have devoured his strength, and he knoweth it not: yea, gray hairs are here and there upon him, and he knoweth it not', 7.9.

Concerning Mammals

Among the animals introduced in the Song, **the mare's** role is rarely appreciated. Translations of the word [Heb.susaht],

---

[10] Song 2.12†. The sweet psalmist of Israel is, in Hebrew the sweet zemor (same root). Another word from the same root [Heb.mizmor] is found as a technical designation in the titles of many psalms. We join with the hymn writer: 'Let all creation join in one to bless the sacred name'.

[11] Jer.8.7.   [12] According to the Targum that was the voice heard by Abraham in Gen.15.14; see also bT.Ber.3a.   [13] This is a member of the Corridae family which include rooks, crows etc. It is conspicuous by its black plumage. Though numbered among the unclean, Lev.11.15 = Deut.14.14, and an obvious scavenger, Job.38.41; Prov.30.17; cf. Gen.8.7, it acts as waiter for God's servant in time of famine, 1 Kings 17.4,6, and survives the Lord's judgment of the earth, Isa.34.11. The Lord who gathers together the outcasts of Israel, gives also 'to the ravens which cry' as further evidence of His providential care throughout creation, Ps.147.2,7*.

e.g. 'a steed' (RV), 'a company of horses' (AV), have obscured the fact that the word is feminine, and the AV has also further confused the issue by introducing the term in the plural. Firstly her beloved is not thinking of horses but a horse, and that a mare.[14] Further, in putting 'chariots' in the plural, neither can he be thinking of 'a mare in Pharoah's chariots'. Pharoah's chariotry was drawn by pairs of beautiful stallions. He is comparing her to 'a mare', a solitary female among the countless male steeds belonging to Pharoah's chariotry. Hence, she is altogether unique among this matchless force. Seemingly weaker, yet one mare among these many stallions would cause complete chaos. Is not this the terrifying uniqueness through weakness intended in the simile?[15] As at the Exodus at the beginning of the nation's history, so shall it be at the end. When Israel returns to the Lord it will confess: 'Asshur shall not save us; we will not ride upon horses (for which Egypt was famed): neither will we say any more to the work of our hands, Ye are our gods: for in thee the fatherless findeth mercy', Hos.14.3[4].

Next, we are reminded that it is **'the foxes** [Heb.shu ̄alim], the little foxes, that spoil the vineyards', Song 2.15‡. It is jackals that are referred to. They move about in packs, leaving a trail of destruction behind them. Special care is needed in blossom time, if the harvest is not to be impaired. The appeal has overtones regarding all that might nip in the bud the longed for fruitfulness. However, the call to duty interfered with the developing romance of the lovers.

The lion [Heb. ̄aryeh] and **the leopard** [Heb.namer] which have their lairs in the Hermon, 4.8‡, are an obvious menace to life. Not only fruit but even life itself is at risk in such dangerous situ-

---

[14] Song 1.9. The singular was construed as collective by Rashi and Rambam, prompting the AV's 'company of horses'. Ibn Ezra saw in the singular the contrast of a humble mare amid the others.   [15] Pharoah's chariotry was doomed at the Reed Sea. He, like many others had put his 'trust in chariots, and some in horses' [Heb.sus, masculine, and often in the OT]. For the Exodus event and Pharoah's chariotry see specially Exod.14.9,28; 15.1,21,19. We see this behind the reference to Pharoah's chariots in Song 1.9, as the proposed interpretation will demonstrate. For the theme of misplaced trust pointedly developed around the stallion, or male horse see Ps.20.7; cf. 33.17; 147.10; Prov.21.31; Isa.31.1,3; 36.9.

ations. In connection with interpreting the Song it is important to notice even this heightening of the danger to which his loved one is exposed suggested by the change of faunal simile. It is clear that those peaceful and secure conditions obtaining in Eden, and yet to be restored when 'the wolf shall dwell with the lamb, and the leopard shall lie down with the kid; and the calf and the young lion and the fatling together; and a little child shall lead them. And the cow and the bear shall feed; their young ones shall lie down together: and the lion shall eat straw like the ox', neither obtained at that point in salvation history anticipated in chapter 4 of the Song, nor have they been arrived at yet.[16] When the kingdom of God is established on earth, such Edenic conditions will obtain again.

We look now at more domesticated animals. The Song, by means of a number of words, focuses on the flock whether of **sheep or goats**. Among other things claiming their attention, both the beloved, and his loved one care for flocks. She knows what he will be doing; he will be feeding [Heb.ra`ah],[17] and making to rest [Heb. rabhats][18] at noon those committed to his charge. At first she does not know where he will be so engaged, 1.7, though others would quickly rectify this, 1.8. Later, 6.2,3, she knows exactly where he will be, as well as what he will be doing without any assistance from others. This, strangely at first sight, only dawns on her after asking others to help her in her search for him. It was by describing to others in considerable detail *who* he was and *what* he meant to her, that she was brought to know *where* he would be.[19] Again, notice the development associated with this, a completely different theme. Perhaps we should take time to point out that this shepherd has been considered by some[20] to be a different person

---

[16] Isa.11.6f.   [17] At 1.7,8; 2.16/ /6.2,3; 4.5‡. Only once is it used of her in an obvious simile, 4.5.   [18] 1.7‡.   [19] For detail see 5.8–6.3.   [20] The view has gained considerable ground since Ewald developed (in 1826) an earlier proposal claiming that there were three chief characters in the drama, King Solomon, a shepherd lover, and the Shulammite. This 'shepherd hypothesis', treated in detail by Driver, ILOT 413–420, and briefly assessed by Harrison, IOT 1053f, was adopted by Scroggie KYB I.117–121, and surprisingly, and more recently, by Clarke in his commentary on the Song. Rejected categorically by Falk LL 63. See our chap. 12 under Drama.

from the king, Solomon. We shall have to treat this question in greater detail when we consider the interpretation of the book later. Enough here to say that the king and shepherd roles are often interwoven in the Word of God, and this is the case in the Song also. The shepherd of Psalm 23 who makes his own lie down in green pastures, is also the sovereign of Psalm 24, the King of glory. Though this anticipates the question of interpretation, it is well to do so in order to alert ourselves to the spiritual overtones to be weighed in the references to animals and occupations in the Song.[21]

The shepherd was to be found by following the footprint trail of the flock [Heb.tso´n]. This is the most common Old Testament word for flock. It is often adopted in simile and metaphor of the multitude of Israel, and specially as under the Lord's care.[22] There is no simile here, though a spiritual, typological truth is suggested. Similarly, she refers to the flocks [Heb. ´edher],[23] of his companions. The root suggests the meaning of those who follow behind. The sheep hear the shepherd's voice, and they follow him, a fact still seen to be true in the Near East.

The beloved describes his loved one's teeth by comparing them to '**a flock (of ewes)** that are (newly) shorn, which are come up from the washing; whereof every one hath twins, and none is bereaved among them'.[24] Their whiteness and purity, symmetry, completeness, and perfection, not only attract him, but provide him with further cause to speak well of her. One may have been blessed with a fine set of teeth which, through neglect, become depleted, their appearance becoming spoiled by many a gap. Jacob, in reviewing his unswerving attention to Laban's flocks beyond the claims of mere duty, could say 'thy ewes and thy she-

---

[21] To pasture [Heb.ra´ah] to tend, graze from which the participle [Heb.ro´im] translated 'shepherds', 'feeders' of sheep in Gen.46.32, is derived. Compare the NT verb [Grk.poimaino] to act as shepherd, tend flocks, used of the Messiah in Matt.2.6; Rev.7.17; 12.5; 19.15, and of the elders in the churches in John 21.16; Acts 20.28; 1 Pet.5.2. The verb in the Song has no object when used of his activity, see 1.7; 2.16; 6.2,3. She is said to be engaged specifically with kids (young goats NIV), 1.8.   [22] Flock [Heb.tso´n] 1.8‡; metaphorically Ps.74.1; 79.13; 100.3; Ezek.34.31.   [23] Song 1.7; 4.1,2; 6.5,6‡.   [24] 4.2.

goats have not cast their young', Gen.31.38. Endowment is to be matched by industry if we are to be all that we can be! It is this with which she is credited. Chapter 6.6, while identifying the animals concerned as ewes [Heb.rachel*, cf. the name Rachel, Laban's daughter and Jacob's wife],[25] omits reference to the shearing, otherwise it repeats the simile of 4.2. We can hardly doubt that the change is meaningful. Concerning the Servant of the Lord we read 'as a lamb [Heb.seh] that is led to the slaughter, and as a sheep [Heb.rachel = our word for ewe] that before her shearers is dumb' he opened not his mouth, Isa.53.7. He knew the personal cost of such non-retaliatory response. Costliness is essential to that cleanliness reflected in the one in whom the king finds delight also: it is in the measure in which she follows the steps of the Servant that such descriptions become true of her.[26] While present with His own disciples, Jesus the Messiah spoke not only of His own sufferings at the hands of men, but also of those experienced by all who would take up their cross and follow Him.

When her beloved wishes to describe the hair of the one he loves, he turns to the flock[27] of **goats** [Heb. ˘ez][28] for his simile. If the whiteness of the sheep fitly portrays her teeth, it is the blackness of the goats' coats that provides him with the most apt simile for his loved one's hair. The tents of Kedar were made of goats' hair, as are the Bedouin tents today, and were black, as the parallel in 1.5 establishes. It should be noted that this simile is used concerning his loved one before that which exults in her whiteness. The order is spiritually significant. The beloved sees his loved one's hair,[29] as a flock of goats might appear to be a

---

[25] Gen.29.6 and often. Figuratively in Jer.31.15, and in a happy simile: 'The Lord make the woman (Ruth) that is come into thine house like Rachel and like Leah, which two did build the house of Israel', Ruth 4.11. [26] Only one other reference to ewe [Heb.rachel] in the OT, Gen.32.14[15]*. [27] This word for flock [Heb. ˘edher] is used figuratively for the nation of Israel in numbers of contexts, e.g. Isa.40.11; Jer.13.17,20; Zech.10.3. [28] Song 4.1; 6.5. The goat in the God-appointed sacrificial system is the predominant sin offering victim. The Tabernacle was covered with black goats' hair curtains, so that Balaam could say of the Lord 'He hath not beheld iniquity in Jacob, neither hath he seen perverseness in Israel', Num.23.21. [29] Given her for a covering, and her glory, 1 Cor.11.15.

black covering sweeping over the bare slopes of Mount Gilead as it falls away into the Jordan Valley. She was covered with the black goat's hair of the sin offering before the purity and submissive character of her devotion was developed.

Deserving of more careful consideration are the loveliest representatives of wild life in Israel, **the roes** (literally **does**) **and the hinds** which are used in the adjuration refrains of the Song.[30] The male gazelle (roe) [Heb.tsebhi*][31] and its female mate (doe) [Heb. tesbhiyyah*],[32] distinguished by their curved and hollow horns,[33] must be numbered among the most graceful of creatures. Two species are particularly common in Israel even now,[34] and one seen in the land in the past was known to have borne twin fawns.[35] A different animal, the male of which is translated 'hart' [Heb. ´ayyal][36] and the female 'hind' [Heb. ´ayyalah][37] in the Song, is one with which most of us are more familiar. It is the yellowish-brown deer, distinguished by its solid, forked horns, and is of larger proportions than the gazelle species. The animal was once fairly common in Israel, a fact supported by the places named Aijalon or 'Deer Field'.[38]

---

[30] Song 2.7; 3.5.　　　　　　　[31] 2.9,17; 8.14‡, a generic term embracing the many forms. It is found once spelled with an aleph in the plural form [Heb.tsebha ´yimt], 1 Chron.12.9. It should be noted that a word translated beauty, pleasant etc. [Heb.tsebhi] is usually taken to be derived from another root, though it may be that the gazelle was so named because of its beauty, in which case the root would be identical.　　　　　　[32] Found in the plural [Heb.tsebha ´oth*] at 2.7; 3.5, and without the aleph [Heb.tsebhiyyah*] at 4.5; 7.3[4].　　　　　　[33] 'Its antlers are not split', bT. Hullin 59b, and they are hollow similar to the shophar, jT. Erubin 1.19b.　　　　　　[34] The gazella arabica (or gazella) is dark fawn in colour, and two feet or a little more in height, the gazella dorcas is light fawn and stands 2 or 3 inches shorter than the former, cf. [Grk.dorkas] and Acts 9.36. [35] Gazella subgutterosa, cf. 4.5; 7.3[4].　　　　　　[36] The male fallow-deer Cervus Capreolus, or Carmel hart, Holladay CHAL 12; Feliks NMB 271, pace identification with the Red Deer, Cervus Elaphus, IDB 2.526 McCullough. In the Song at 2.9,17; 8.14‡.　　　　　　[37] It is the hind of the fallow-deer, found in the plural at 2.7; 3.5‡.　　　　　　[38] A Levitical city in Dan, Josh.19.42; 21.24, though later, after Dan's migration north, adopted by Benjamin, 1 Chron.8.13. The valley below the town was named 'the valley of Aijalon', Josh.10.12. There was also an Aijalon in the tribe of Zebulun, Jud.12.12.

It should be noted that in the adjuration refrains, 2.7; 3.5, it is the females of the two species that are brought together in the phrase 'by the roes (literally does), and by the hinds of the field'. In 2.9,17; 8.14 where her beloved is addressed, it is the two males that are linked together in the phrase 'a roe or a young hart'. The phrase 'two fawns (masc) that are twins of a roe (should be doe, fem)' refers to the young male and female of the one species, 4.5; 7.3[4]. Due to inconsistent translation, the pairs of each animal have become confused. We have consistently translated the male and female *gazelle* as 'roe' and 'doe' respectively, the *deer* as 'hart' and 'hind' respectively.

The hart panting after the water brooks, as during a severe drought, provides a vivid figure of the psalmist's soul thirst for God, who is the fountain of living waters.[39] Both gazelles and deer had a parted hoof and chewed the cud; they were clean animals and could be eaten.[40] Their meat was among the delicacies that loaded Solomon's lavish table.[41] As wild game they were hunted, and because of their swiftness,[42] surefootedness,[43] and agility, they were a great challenge to the hunter's skill and stamina. Among the tragic effects at the time of Jerusalem's overthrow, it was prophesied that 'Her princes are become like harts that find no pasture, and they are gone without strength before the pursuer'.[44] Particularly in the Song, beauty, grace, elegant form, and gentleness,[45] together with strength and agility,[46] prompt the use of roes/does (gazelles) and harts/hinds (deer) in similes of the beloved and his loved one respectively.

Observation of the habits of the gazelle and deer have served to emphasize the appropriateness of selecting them to mirror the rela-

---

[39] Ps.42.1[2].   [40] Lev.11.3; Deut.12.15,22; 14.5; 15.22.   [41] 1 Kings 4.23[5.3].   [42] This was proverbial, 2 Sam.2.18; 1 Chron.12.8[9].
[43] Becoming a fine simile in the phrase 'He maketh my feet like hinds' feet: and setteth me upon my high places', 2 Sam.22.34; cf. Hab.3.19. In that glorious day, 'the times of restoration of all things' when Israel's God will have come and saved them, 'Then the lame man shall leap as the hart' as just one of the spectacular changes effected, Isa.35.6.   [44] Lam.1.6 points to the hart deterred, by the fear of its pursuers, from the pasture it so sorely needs.   [45] 4.5; 7.3[4].
[46] 2.9,17; 8.14.

tionship of the couple in the Song. This must be the reason why they are introduced more frequently than other animals here.

We shall consider their living and mating habits, which obviously puzzled men in Job's time.[47] It has been established that the herd of harts normally live apart from the hinds. The young male fawns live under their mothers' care until they mature, when they make their way to the herd of harts also: 'they go forth, and return not again'. This mutual indifference of the sexes is characteristic until the spring time, the mating season, arrives. Then the harts begin to woo the hinds, first chasing them and then fleeing from them, movements which are reciprocated by the hind. The often timid hart throws caution to the wind as it seeks its mate. So her beloved, who is as a roe or a young hart, 'standeth behind our wall, he looketh in at the windows, he showeth himself through the lattice', Song 2.9. Following the approach there is the appeal, 'Rise up, my love', v.10, and although there is some response, love is not perfected yet. It is through absence that the heart is made fonder, and consequently the hart flees away, until a more auspicious time, 2.17. Finally, as sure as day follows night, both hart and hind search for and find each other, and their union is realized. In fact, in each stage of approach, attraction, appeal, and absence, there is definite progress made toward the goal. There is a pattern about their love cycle; its course is set, and its end is assured. At the beginning the end is seen in embryo; at the end the mysteries that are enshrined at the beginning burst forth into full view. So these graceful creatures, freed from all others to be solely for one another, make their way to the place of their birth to breed their young. How appropriate are the words then 'Under the apple tree I awakened thee: there thy mother was in travail with thee, there was she in travail that brought thee forth', 8.5. Solomon had been observant enough to see and unravel the mystery of this love cycle, and through it discerned an even more general truth. In later life he expressed it in these words: 'To everything there is a season, and a time to every purpose under heaven: a ... time to love, and a time to hate'.[48]

---

[47] Job 39.1–4; see Feliks NMB 270–4 and his Song Intro.10–16. [48] Eccles.3.1,8.
The hatred in question is that of sexual revulsion in 2 Sam.13.15(2); Deut.22.13,16; 24.3; Ezek.16.37. Compare the behaviour of the wild ass, which seeks her partner eagerly in the appropriate time, Jer.2.24.

Patently, the love cycle of the hart and hind finds its counterpart in the love affair of the king and the country girl. In the Song there are the several cycles initiated by the king's approach, in which he speaks to her heart and awaits her response, absenting himself meanwhile. What point this gives to the refrain, 'I adjure you, O daughters of Jerusalem, by the roes (does), and by the hinds of the field, that ye stir not up, nor awaken love, until it please'.[49] Some have found a difficulty in this oath, and have averred that, as human love alone was in view, to have included the name of God in its wording would have been inappropriate. Once the key place that the hart and hind cycle have in the drama is grasped, together with the indivisible link that exists for the author between the chief actors and these graceful and loving creatures, there can be no problem. As we consider the interpretation of the Song later, we shall see that the 'purpose under heaven' which the Lord has for Israel also has its several phases and its own time. This truth is unfolded in the Song in the eventual joyous union of the Messiah and the nation of Israel.

---

[49] Song 2.7; 3.5; cf. 8.4.

6

FOREST AND FRUIT TREES

WE RETURN TO that review of Solomon's accomplishments in
1 Kings. It is recorded that 'he spake of trees, from the cedar that
is in Lebanon even unto the hyssop that springeth out of the
wall'.[1] Solomon may have spoken at length, in fact discoursed on
a range of natural phenomena. A classified list covering this field
predating his reign by a century or more has been discovered in
Egypt.[2] The Old Testament displays a general interest in nature as
such.[3] More specifically, it adopts the field of nature in parable,
poetry and proverb to press home moral and spiritual lessons.
Figures of speech, including the more explicit and extended simile,
and the more concise and covert metaphor, sustain interest, and
draw out the emotions. Also they supply great motifs, for example
that of the shepherd and his sheep, or man/woman relationships
whether chaste or corrupt, and generally enrich the teaching of the
Bible. Attention needs to be given to the imagery used, and the
particular function it has. We should take note of imagery which
reappears in the course of salvation history with a certain
theological weighting, in judgment or blessing contexts, in
kingdom and glory settings. Imagery has a large place also in
typological anticipations of the eschatological goal.

In the Song great use is made of the botanical motif in un-

---

[1] 1 Kings 4.33[5.13].　　[2] Gardiner, AEO, ´48 in J. Gray on Kings OTL 145.
[3] Job 38–41; Prov.30.15–20,24–28.

folding the development of the love theme. The beauties and varieties of nature provide not only a breathtakingly attractive setting for lovers, but nature itself is seemingly in harmony with their changing moods.

The Forest Trees

Of these there are many in the Scriptures, and they are set in contrast to fruit trees such as the apple, with which they are compared less favourably sometimes.[4] Nonetheless, they are the source of wood for the carpenter, cabinet-maker, and builder alike.[5] Two such trees are singled out for mention in the Song.

The Fir [Heb.berosh; here a uniquely spelled plural, berothim†][6] is a collective name embracing three species.[7] It is numbered among the noble trees, often found in parallel with the cedar, as it is in the Song.[8] These two trees provided the Near East with its highest quality timber for building. The 'choice fir' was a tall tree with a straight trunk, and an appealing fragrance. Its wood was used in the construction of the Temple ceilings, floors, and doors.[9] The fir is used also in a variety of similes where strength, stateliness, and productiveness are signified.[10] It is to be used to glorify the Lord's future sanctuary. The thorn, a constant reminder of the curse brought in through the fall, is to be replaced by the fir in the kingdom age.[11] The glory of that period will be unquestionably the creatorial work of the Lord, for the wilderness will be stocked with seven trees, among which will be the fir.[12] Their homeward march to 'gloryland' will be refreshed

---

[4] Song 2.3; cf. Ps.148.9 'fruitful trees and all cedars'.   [5] Song 3.9; cf. 1.17.
[6] 1.17†; berosh occurs over 30 times.   [7] See Zohary, PB 106f. He suggests that whenever the fir is linked with the cedar of Lebanon that the tree signified is probably the Cilician Fir, Abies cilicica. The two trees grew in mixed forests. Feliks, NMB 110f, identifies it with the high juniper tree, Juniperus excelsa, which grows well in Lebanon. Further, it is called brotha by the Lebanese, which may explain the unique spelling, berothim, in Song 1.17. In modern Hebrew berosh designates the cypress, certainly not the tree signified by the term Biblically.   [8] Isa.14.8; 37.24 = 2 Kings 19.23; Isa.41.19; Ezek.31.8; Zech.11.2.   [9] 2 Chron.3.5; 1 Kings 6.15,34.   [10] Ezek.31.8; Hos.14.8[9]; Nah.2.3[4].   [11] Isa.60.13; 55.13.   [12] Isa.41.19.

by rivers, and sheltered by oases of trees as harbingers of the final salvation to which Israel is being brought. Then the nation will exclaim 'I am like a green fir tree'.[13] That will be a greater day for Jerusalem than that when David ascended to it with the ark of the covenant, accompanied by musicians with instruments of fir.[14] These contexts throb with hope.

The Cedar [Heb. ´erez] is referred to over 70 times in the Old Testament.[15] It occurs three times in the Song.[16] It was the loftiest and the loveliest of Lebanon's trees. The timber was of superior quality, durability, straightness, appearance, and fragrance. We read of goodly and choice cedars. Zohary aptly expresses it: 'what the lion was to the animal world, the cedar was to the plant world'.[17] David's royal palace was built of its wood; 'I dwell in an house of cedar'. We may compare that impressive part of Solomon's palace complex referred to as 'the house of the forest of Lebanon'.[18] It was the dominant wood used in the cladding of the Temple.[19]

The cedars of Lebanon are described as being planted by the Lord. Israel planted in her land had boughs 'like cedars of God'. They were living monuments to the Lord's creative omnipotence. The righteous, too, grow like the cedar for they are planted in the house of the Lord.[20] It must be realized that this tree flourishes in Lebanon. Scripture speaks of Lebanon as a synonym for the cedar, so closely bound up are the tree and its natural habitat. When Ezekiel speaks of an eagle transplanting a cedar to the plains and the heat of Babylon, he thereby indicates that there is no hope for it.[21] Conversely, when Hosea sees the amazing features of Israel's restoration including his casting 'forth his roots as Lebanon (i.e. like the cedar)', and that 'his smell (shall be) as Lebanon (i.e. like

---

[13] Hos.14.8[9].   [14] 2 Sam.6.5.   [15] When associated with Lebanon it signifies the Cedrus libani Loud. It is a coniferous tree attaining massive proportions; up to 100 feet high [30m] and over 6 feet [2m] in diameter. The height of the cedar is Biblically documented, 2 Kings 19.23; Isa.37.24; Amos 2.9. See excellent chaps. in Hareuveni, TSBH 93–116.   [16] Song 1.17; 5.15; 8.9‡.
[17] Zohary, PB 104.   [18] 2 Sam.7.2 = 1 Chron. 17.1; 1 Kings 7.2; 10.17,21.
[19] 1 Kings 6.9,10,15,16,18(2),20,36.   [20] Ps.80.10[11]; 104.16; 92.12[13].
[21] Ezek.17.3; see Feliks, NMB 135–138.

the fragrance of the cedar)' he is anticipating nothing short of a miracle performed by the Lord to effect such changes. To prove this point, cedars of Lebanon actually planted on Mount Scopus in Jerusalem, well before the State of Israel was re-established, have made little progress in their new location.

For the bride her beloved's 'aspect is like Lebanon, excellent as the cedars'.[22] The cedar is only one element in this composite portrait of her glorious lover. We must look beyond Solomon in all his glory, to One more glorious than he. Ezekiel looked beyond the more immediate fortunes of the house of David, to that day, excelling all others, when the nation would be blessed under the shadow of the branches of the Messiah, the promised son of David. The Lord said 'I will also take of the lofty top of the cedar, and will set it; I will crop off from the topmost of his young twigs a tender one, and I will plant it upon an high mountain and eminent (Zion) in the mountain of the height of Israel will I plant it: and it shall bring forth boughs, and bear fruit, and be a goodly cedar: and under it shall dwell all fowl of every wing; in the shadow of the branches thereof shall they dwell. And all the trees of the field shall know that I the Lord have brought down the high tree, have exalted the low tree, have dried up the green tree, and have made the dry tree to flourish'.[23] There can be only One of whom it can be truthfully said that 'he is altogether lovely'.[24] It points to the glorious Messiah whom the Israel of God already adores, and who is to be appreciated in all his beauty and splendour by the nation in the future.

The Fruit Trees

There are something like a dozen fruit bearing trees referred to

---

[22] Song 5.15. The word translated 'aspect' [Heb.mar ̃eh] has several nuances. Once it is used of an arresting spectacle, Exod.3.3; then it refers to the visible form, the outward appearance as opposed to the inner man. Of the Servant of the Lord, for example, we are told 'his visage was so marred more than any man', 1 Sam.16.7; Isa.52.14; see also 53.2 where it is translated 'beauty', ct. 'thy countenance (comprehending her whole form) is comely', Song 2.14(2)‡. Then, particularly in Ezekiel and Daniel, it signifies a supernatural vision. The word is derived from the verb 'to see' [Heb.ra ̃ah], used in the Song at 1.6; 2.12,14; cf. ro ̃eh, a seer, 1 Sam.9.9, and mar ̃ah, vision, 1 Sam.3.15.　 [23] Ezek.17.22–24.　 [24] Song 5.16. The unique phrase 'Israel of God' belongs to Israel's election of grace today, pp.241,244.

in the Old Testament. Six of these feature in the Song. Obedience was demanded of Israel if she was to enjoy the yield of fruit. 'If ye walk in my statutes, and keep my commandments, and do them; then I will give your rains in their season . . . and the trees of the field shall yield their fruit.'[25] It is so important to observe the sensitive association that exists between man and creation around him in the Scriptures. Sin disturbs the whole of nature,[26] and Israel's reconciliation to God brings in its train the responsive harmony of nature.[27] Something of this is reflected in the course of the Song, and is fully experienced at its climax. We shall consider the references to those trees and fruit introduced in the Song. They provide us with a fruitful thematic approach.[28]

The Apple Tree [Heb.tappuach]. The word for the tree and its fruit occurs only six times in the Old Testament. Tappuah is also found as a place name and as a person's name. A variety of trees have been proposed as signified by the Hebrew term. Recently, Zohary has challenged the basis for departing from the natural translation 'apple', the main case against it being the absence of archaeological evidence so far for that tree's existence in Israel at such an early date. Apple is certainly the meaning of the word in modern Hebrew, and we shall accept it as such.[29] The tree is attractive, growing up to 12 metres high. The colour of the fruit varies with the variety, and is both delicious and odiferous.[30]

For the maiden, her beloved was 'As the apple tree among the trees of the wood'.[31] This type of excelling description of one's partner she has learned from him.[32] It is important to see that the

---

[25] Lev.26.3f.   [26] cf. e.g. Gen.3.17ff; Lev.26.14f,19f.
[27] cf. e.g. Hos.2.19–23. Creation's groans will only cease when it enters into 'the liberty of the glory of the children of God', at the second advent of the Messiah in glory, cf. Rom.8.18–25.   [28] The word fruit [Heb.peri] occurs at Song 2.3; 4.13,16; 8.11,12‡. A word emphasizing the excellence of the fruit [Heb. meghedh*] is linked with it in 4.13,16, and stands alone in 7.13[14]. Elsewhere it is used only of Moses' blessing of Joseph, Deut.33.13,14(2),15,16, which see.
[29] See Zohary, PB 70 pace himself IDB 2.286,2b and Trever IDB 1.175f. The word used of tree or fruit is found in the Song at 2.3,5; 7.8[9]; 8.5‡. Also at Prov.25.11; Joel 1.12*.   [30] Song 2.3; 7.8[9].   [31] 2.3.   [32] 2.2.

initiative in this, as more generally in the Song, rests with him. A remarkable exception to this is found in chapter 8. There his bride claims to have awakened first her beloved. In the very place where his mother both conceived and bore him, under the apple tree, there their relationship began for her. It was there that his desire not to be alone, which drew him to her, became tangible for her.[33] Conversely, she sees her beloved himself 'as the Apple tree among the trees of the wood' in chapter 2. They may be grand, but he is grander still. She finds shade and shelter from the scorching sun under his shadow, and in doing so she finds rapture too. He himself thrills her. As though that were not enough, she finds that he bears fruit for her sustenance which is sweet to her palate.[34] In expressing his love for her, he creates an overwhelming love for him, and in turn he would sustain her in that experience. If he is born here, her love is developed and consummated here too. The use of the apple tree metaphor in the Song then, relates to a place where her beloved is born, and to a place where she awakens him and is satisfied by him. When the apple as a fruit is used metaphorically, she relates it to her beloved's person and on his part he finds her breath fragrant like the apple. She had been feeding upon him obviously. This may appear very complicated initially. However, we may compare the Old Testament's use of 'Israel' of the patriarch, then of the nation which sprang from his loins. Then we read of the land of Israel, the place given to the nation for an inheritance by God. After the division of the nation into two kingdoms, it is used of the people of the Northern Kingdom, and then typologically for a person, the nation's Messiah who is both the hope and the embodiment of the inheritance and the nation.

The Fig Tree. The word [Heb.te ̄enah] is used for the tree and its fruit. It is found 39 times in the Old Testament.[35] It is the first of the fruit trees mentioned in the Bible, where its leaves rather than its fruit are mentioned. These were used by Adam and Eve to produce aprons to cover their nakedness.[36] The men sent to spy out the

---

[33] Song 8.5. For connection with the habits of gazelles see pp.60–63.
[34] 2.5.   [35] The Ficus caricus L., Hareuveni, TSBH 60ff. In the NT [Grk.syke, sykon], e.g. Matt.21.19–21; Mark 11.13.
[36] Gen.3.7.

land of Canaan brought back figs, along with grapes and pomegranates, as firm evidence that it was truly the fruitful land which God had promised.[37] On the instruction of Isaiah, Hezekiah's attendants applied a plaster of figs, medicinally, to draw the inflamed and mortal ulcer, and the king recovered.[38] Only the cultivated female fig tree produces fruit which is edible. This is richly rewarding to the one who looks after it.[39] It is sweet and nutritious. The high sugar content facilitates its preservation; it is dried in order to store.

The fig is mentioned only once in the Song. Its blossoming or ripening of 'her green figs' [Heb.pag†], is one of a number of delightful characteristics of the spring-time, which the beloved uses to woo his loved one to himself. This occurs in mid to late March, and the early fig begins to form immediately on the branches of the previous season. This is the precursor of the true fig, which is produced on the new growth and matures in August and September. Her beloved urges her to come out of her house to enjoy the beauties of the countryside with him at this most pleasant of seasons. The tree is simply a part of the scenery, and is spoken of in a literal sense. However, its mention in that part of the Song suggestive of the post-exilic period up to the incarnation of the Messiah, the Son of God, is most appropriate. Even up to the time of Messiah's first advent, the nation was expected to produce early fruit, that is before the grand harvest when the kingdom of God would be set up.[40] In chapter 11 we shall give attention to time settings in the developing theme of the Song.

The fig is used Biblically mostly in figurative contexts. It is often associated with the vine in symbolizing that peace and plenty for which men long. What more idyllic conditions can be found than those which are described during Solomon's reign when 'Judah and Israel dwelt safely, every man under his vine and under his fig tree'.[41] The leaves of the tree thus provided a fine shelter from the

---

[37] Num.13.23,27; ct.20.5.   [38] 2 Kings 20.7 = Isa.38.21. The treatment is known extra-Biblically, Pliny, NH 22.7, etc.   [39] Prov.27.18.   [40] This is simply illustrated by Nathanael in John 1.48,50, himself a fine example of early fruit for God in the nation.   [41] 1 Kings 4.25[5.5]; cf. 2 Kings 18.31 = Isa.36.16. A similar hope is before Israel in the future, Mic.4.4; Zech.3.10; cf. Joel 2.22; Hag.2.19.

blazing sun. In Jotham's fable it is famed for its sweetness and good fruit, which it is not willing to leave to take up office as king of the trees.[42] The teaching which our Lord associated with the fig, clearly relates it to His ministry in Israel and its ramifications for the nation, whether considered in the past, the present or the future.[43]

The Pomegranate Tree. The word pomegranate [Heb.rimmon‡] is used of the tree itself and also for its fruit 32 times in the Old Testament.[44] It is a small tree reaching up to 4 metres in height. Its fruit, along with that of the vine and fig, was displayed by the returning spies to demonstrate the fruitfulness of the land of Canaan.[45] In ancient times it was much more predominant than it is today, as a number of places and people so named in the Bible would indicate.[46] Its scented and beautiful crimson flowers enhance the many glories of the late springtime in Israel.[47]

Its fruit is uniquely shaped, attractively coloured, and inside its rind it is packed full with refreshing, juicy seeds. In this latter feature it is unsurpassed as a symbol of multiplied fertility. It may be eaten fresh, or be included in a variety of table dishes, and wine may be made from the juice squeezed from its fruit.[48] The bark of the tree and the rind of the fruit once were used in the manufacture of ink, and the rind is still used in the tanning of leather.

It is to be noted that most of the Biblical references to the fruit are bound up with the God-appointed ritual in His house. The skirt

---

[42] Jud.9.10f.   [43] See in order Luke 13.6f; Matt.21.19(2),20,21//Mark 11.13,20,21; Matt.24.32//Mark 13.28//Luke 21.29.   [44] For the tree see Deut.8.8 where it is one of the land's seven varieties indicative of the large-handed blessing of God; cf. I Sam. 14.2; Song 4.13; and ct. with this its use of one of the gods of Syria, 2 Kings 5.18(3); and as devastated by the locust plague along with the other fruit trees mentioned in the Song, Joel 1.12f; Hag.2.19 where its returning fruitfulness, with that of the vine, fig and olive, is an evidence of the restoration of the favour of God to the nation. For the fruit see Num.13.23; Song 4.3; 6.7.
[45] Num.13.23.   [46] See e.g. the Rimmon in southern Judah, Josh.15.32 = Zech.14.10; Gath-rimmon, a Levitical city at the junction of the Aijalon and Yarkon rivers in modern Tel Aviv, Josh.19.45; 21.24, and another Rimmon in Zebulun, Josh.19.13. As a person's name see 2 Sam.4.2.   [47] Song 6.11; 7.12[13].   [48] 8.2.

of the high priest's blue 'robe of the ephod' was to have suspended from it emblems of pomegranates made in the dominating blue, purple, and scarlet threads specified for the Tabernacle.[49] Pomegranates wrought in bronze were festooned around the massive ornamented capitals on top of the Jachin and Boaz pillars at the entrance to Solomon's Temple, four hundred per capital. These two contexts alone cater for twenty of the Old Testament references.[50]

Outside of these contexts, it is only the Song which refers to the tree or its fruit more than twice. Here the beloved exhausts the fields of fauna and flora to describe his loved one's beauty, and the pomegranate has its own contribution to offer when he thinks about her temples or cheeks.[51] These are attractive in shape and rosy in colour, the very picture of youthfulness and health 'like a piece of a pomegranate'. Her charms, which were altogether shut up for him, he conceives as a veritable paradise of pomegranates, with all the unspoiled potential for reproducing itself that the simile suggests. We have noticed earlier that the setting of the developing love affair is largely among the beauties and freshness of the spring season. Two proposals, one on his part and one on hers,[52] to ascertain whether the time of the flowering of the pomegranate had arrived, bring us to the threshold of the final realized union of the pair in the story. There remains only one further reference to the fruit in the Song.[53] In this the loved one desires her beloved to drink 'of the juice of my pomegranate'. The juice concerned [Heb. ʿasis*] had been pressed out of the fruit, to produce a sweet, red wine.[54]

---

[49] Exod.28.33,34(2); 39.24,25(2),26(2).   [50] 1 Kings 7.18,20,42(2); 2 Kings 25.17; 2 Chron.3.16; 4.13(2); Jer.52.22(2),23(2).   [51] Song 4.3; 6.7. The word for 'temple' [Heb.raqqah*] appears outside the Song only at Judges 4.21,22; 5.26 where it clearly refers to the temple, the part of the skull to the side of the eye-sockets. Her veil may be seen as the rind framing the exposed brow and temples which are as an opened pomegranate, or as pith around the red fruit, so her net-like veil upon her rosy cheeks.   [52] Song 6.11; 7.12[13].   [53] 8.2.   [54] The noun's use is instructive regarding Israel's blessed future. Amos, speaking of the day when the Lord will raise up the tabernacle of David once again, says that, among other evidences of His bounty, 'the mountains shall drop sweet wine (= what is pressed out)', 9.13. Joel, referring to the time when the presence of the Lord in His holy mountain Zion, will be evidence of its holiness, adds to this 'that the mountains shall drop down

Anticipating a little, we see in this that joyous day which is still awaited by our Lord, when He will indeed not only accept the cup but will 'drink it new with you in my Father's kingdom'.[55]

The Walnut Tree. Most translations of Song 6.11 render one of its phrases 'the garden of nuts'. The NIV has 'the grove of nut trees'. The word for 'nuts' [Heb. ´egozt] appears only here in the Old Testament, and has been taken as a general term. However, Josephus uses the word specifically of the walnut trees of the Gennesaret plain in Galilee.[56] In post-Biblical Hebrew literature also, the word is used, not only of nuts generally, but of walnuts in particular. This tree grows up to 8 metres high. In the spring it is bedecked with flowers, after which the leaves appear. At the end of summer, the fruit ripens, the outer skin breaking open releasing the nut, which falls to the ground. Inside the wooden shell, is a peculiarly folded nut, which is very nutritious, containing in the order of 60% fat. Even the wood of the tree is in demand for furniture manufacture, the costliness of which is more than matched by its attractiveness.

In the Song the garden of nuts was visited by the beloved in yet another spring-time/early summer intrusion,[57] out of which developed the final unbroken union of the pair.

The Palm Tree. This tree [Heb.tamar*] is stately and erect in appearance, one associated by most with oases of the desert.[58] It can reach 20 metres in height, made the more impressive by its un-

---

[54] *cont.* sweet wine, and the hills shall flow with milk', 3.18[4.18]; ct.1.5. These conditions will be established after Israel's oppressors have been made drunken with their own blood 'as with sweet wine', Isa.49.26. The verb [Heb. ´asas*] is used only once, and in a similar vein, and the basic meaning of the word is apparent when Malachi says 'and ye shall tread down (i.e. to press or crush by treading) the wicked', 4.3[3.21]†.

[55] Matt.26.26//Mark 14.25//Luke 22.16.   [56] Wars 3.10.8.   [57] Song 6.11; see chap. 19.   [58] cf. the well-stocked oasis named Elim, where there were 70 palms, Exod.15.27. Jericho, the city of palms, continues to be that even to this day, a luscious oasis town in an utterly wilderness-like situation in the Jordan valley, Deut.34.3; Jud.1.16; 3.13; 2 Chron.28.15. The tree's leaves are among the four items to feature during the feast of the tabernacles, Lev.23.40; Neh.8.15. It features along

cluttered trunk crowned with a curved canopy of arching leaves between 2 and 3 metres long. In the spring-time the tree has great clusters of flowers, the harbingers of the more massive and heavy clusters of fruit, ripened by the end of the summer period. Each date in the cluster is up to 4 centimetres long, having a large stone or seed as the core, the fleshy fruit around this being very sweet and nutritious. A quality date honey may be produced from it. This is the more surprising as they grow often in areas having brackish water supplies. In modern Israel, there is an extensive programme of date-palm cultivation in the saline soil areas of the Jordan Valley, the Dead Sea, and the Arava. The place-name Tamar, belonging to a town near the south end of the Dead Sea, is an ancient witness to the profusion of these trees in that area. Its leaves, too, were woven into a variety of domestic items such as baskets or mats. Even its wood was put to good use for roofs and rafts.

Tamar, is a name borne by three women in the Bible, one particularly renowned for her beauty.[59]

---

[58] *cont*. with other fruit trees which suffer devastation in a locust plague, Joel 1.12. It is clearly used as a simile of spiritual prosperity, Ps.92.12[13]. A cognate [Heb. tomer*] associates the palm with the place where justice is dispensed, so as to link it with the symbolism of righteousness, Jud.4.5; cf. Jer.10.5. The palm figures as a dominant ornament upon the carved wood panelling of Solomon's Temple in the past, 1 Kings 6.29,32(2),35; 7.36; 2 Chron.3.5, and in Ezekiel's Temple in the future, Ezek.40.16,22,26,31,34,37; 41.18(2),19(2),20,25,26. These are all the uses of another cognate [Heb.timorah*]. The carved reliefs of this tree in these settings suggest the stateliness, fruitfulness and holiness that belong to that still future era of peace after the victory of God in establishing righteousness in the midst of the earth. See, for an anticipation of this, the palm strewn way by which the Messianic Lord entered the city of the great king in the last week of His life, John 12.13; cf. Matt.21.8; Mark 11.8.

[59] Tamar [Heb.Tamar*] is the name of 1) Judah's daughter-in-law, Gen.38.6,11(2),13,24; 1 Chron.2.4; Ruth 4.12. What sovereign grace is evident in this story, where despite sin, and illicit sexual relations, the messianic purpose pursued its pathway through to Immanuel, Matt.1.23. Then 2) David's daughter, and Absalom's sister also, 2 Sam.13.1,2,4,5,6,7,8,10(2),19,20,22,32; 1 Chron.3.9. This is another sad case of abuse and sin. Finally 3) Absalom's daughter, 2 Sam.14.27.

In the Song the word is used twice,[60] in similes regarding the bride-to-be. It is her upright and slim stature which draws from her beloved the comparison with the graceful palm. The hanging clusters of fruit provide him with another simile for her breasts.[61] She is to him a daughter of delights, and he would make her altogether his own. He thought [Heb. ´amar, to say, but in this context as elsewhere, to think, purpose], yea determined, to harvest all her precious fruits for himself. If, in 3.4, she would hold him, and not let him go, then here he will take hold of her for his own possession.[62]

The Grape Vine. In the Song, as in the Old Testament generally, the vine has a pre-eminent place. What the cedar is to the 'trees of the wood', the vine is to the fruitbearing varieties. Of the wide range of terms associated with viticulture in the Scriptures, the Song uses four. The vineyard [Heb.kerem] features nine times, the vine itself [Heb.gephen] occurs four times, wine [Heb.yayin] is mentioned six times, and raisins [Heb. ´ashishah] once.[63] As far back as Noah's time, Biblically, man was cultivating and caring for vines, climaxing the ingathering of the vintage with a season of joy.[64]

Vineyards are to be seen clothing the hill country in Israel, where it would not be possible to grow crops such as cereals. Their presence is a monument to the initial diligence, and ongoing maintenance work of the hill-farmer.[65] The vine is a woody, climbing shrub, sending out branches from its thick bases. If these

---

[60] Song 7.7,8[8,9]‡.   [61] 7.7[8]. Note the italicized words 'of grapes' for which there is no Hebrew equivalent, though the Targum has added them here. Where grape clusters are in the writer's mind he says so, see v.8[9]. The word 'cluster' [Heb. ´eshkol] is not confined to grapes for in the Song we have clusters of henna flowers, 1.14, of dates, 7.7[8], and of grapes, 7.8[9]‡.
[62] [Heb. ´achaz, = with some force, see 2.15; 3.4,8; 7.8[9]‡]. We might compare the cognate word 'possession' [Heb. ´achuzzah], used of the land of Canaan given to Abraham's seed, Gen.17.8, and the ends of the earth given to God's Son, Ps.2.8, for a possession.   [63] Vine [Heb.gephen‡] at 2.13; 6.11; 7.8[9],12[13]: vineyard [Heb.kerem‡] at 1.6(2),14; 2.15(2); 7.12[13]; 8.11(2),12: wine [Heb.yayin‡] at 1.2,4; 4.10; 5.1; 7.9[10]; 8.2: also house of wine, lit.2.4: raisins [´Heb.ashishah*] at 2.5, and 2 Sam.6.19; 1 Chron. 16.3; Hos.3.1.   [64] Gen.9.20; Deut.16.13ff.   [65] For a detailed description of the tasks involved in preparation and cultivation, Isa.5.1–6.

are not artificially supported, they will simply trail along the ground, without the full benefits of air and light for the fruit. Lifted, and strongly supported, however, they will entwine themselves with their support as they push out further from their root, sometimes as much as four metres in a season. They would climb any object in their path, even another tree. This may be envisaged in Song 7.8, where clusters of the vine are associated with the palm tree.[66] The leaves open out in early spring but finally fall in late summer. They are quite large, and sufficiently tightly spaced to provide an excellent shade from the sun's heat during the day if supported above head height. Not infrequently, a householder will train the branches of a vine over a high trellis adjoining his house, producing thereby a most attractive and efficient shaded patio.[67] Vine leaves are used in various tasty culinary dishes too. The flowers take the form of green clusters, which, through pollination, develop into delicious and refreshing grapes, the colour of which depends on the variety. Some of the grapes are soaked in oil and water, and after drying in the sun, are thus preserved. The dried fruit was pressed into nutritious blocks, known as raisin cakes [Heb. ´ashishah,[63]]. A great proportion of the vintage is set apart for wine production.

The vine is among the selected, sevenfold bounty which Israel's God-given inheritance boasts.[68] Its prominent use in Biblical imagery was to be expected therefore. In the Song, the vineyard, vine, and wine are used now in a literal sense, now equally clearly in simile, in metaphor, and still we have to question whether there is not also some typological/eschatological projection to be grasped.

At the beginning, and at the end of the Song, reference is made to vineyards [Heb.kerem, 1.6; 8.12(2)]. In the first case her mother's sons, she complains, were incensed against her, and 'they made me keeper of the vineyards'. She is describing her undesirable lot with its multiplicity of rigorous demands. The latter passage states,

---

[66] cf. Ezek.19.10f.   [67] cf. 1 Kings 4.25[5.5].

[68] Deut.8.8. The tale of the experiences of an Egyptian officer, Sinuhe, who fled from his own land and spent part of his time in the Yarmuk Valley area, includes a description of that region which lists six of the items above, omitting only the pomegranate, ANET 18ff.

quite dispassionately, that Solomon was the owner of a particular vineyard which he rented to a number of 'keepers' for a certain fixed fee from each one of them. Both of these passages are followed by a statement from his loved one about herself. In the former case, she insists that the responsibility thrust upon her by her 'mother's sons' prevented her from adequately looking after her own vineyard. Whilst the words might be taken literally, it is clear from the context that she has the vineyard of her own appearance, beauty or charms, in view. The phrase 'my vineyard' is being used metaphorically for herself. She was, indeed, black 'because the sun hath scorched me', and this in the course of enforced duty. We may compare the call to duty in the plurality of vineyards which is introduced in the setting of an appeal from her beloved for her sole attention in chapter 2.[69] A happier situation altogether is in view later as she calls to her beloved 'Let us get up early to the vineyards; let us see whether the vine hath budded, and its blossom be open, and the pomegranates be in flower: there will I give thee my love'.[70] The climax is reached when Solomon's single vineyard is in the hands of keepers; none are distracted by much serving there! Yet, each was responsible to provide the king with a handsome return from the profits made. They were to bring for the fruit assured 'a thousand pieces of silver'. The Shulammite has her own vineyard however. It, too, has its keepers, and they are to be enriched through their labours to the extent of a double tithe. Solomon, however shall have the thousand, that is, she is happy that all its profit should be his.[71] There is no neglect of her vineyard, nor is she pre-occupied with it to the point of being distracted from him, nor is she concerned about it for her own enrichment but rather for his. This points on to that fruitful and joyous period when Israel and her Lord Messiah are united throughout the millennial reign. Lastly, the plural 'vineyards' is used as part of a simile describing her beloved. He is to her 'as a cluster of henna-flowers[72] in the vineyards of En-gedi'.[73]

---

[69] Song 2.15(2).   [70] 7.12[13].   [71] 8.11(2),12.   [72] 1.14. For henna see pp.102f, n.3–11.   [73] En-gedi is on the western shore of the Dead Sea, a luscious and refreshingly beautiful oasis in an utterly barren and unbearably hot area. A powerful, perennial spring of fresh water, combined with the heat, encourages

The vine [Heb.gephen] in the Song generally features as one of the spring-time indicators. It is found blossoming as the fig ripens her green figs, and buds having its flowers open when the pomegranate is in flower.[74] At that time it beautifies the landscape and diffuses its fragrance far and wide. The clusters of the vine's mature fruit become similes for the Shulammite's breasts.[75]

As for wine [Heb.yayin], she uses it metaphorically of his love which 'is better than wine', and of which 'we will make mention . . . more than wine'.[76] Her beloved excels her in expressing what her love was to him, for, said he, 'How much better is thy love than wine', and 'thy mouth (is) like the best wine'.[77] Virtually at the centre of the Song, her beloved having responded to her poetic invitation to come into his garden, that is, to possess her completely, says 'I am come into my garden . . . I have gathered . . . I have eaten . . . I have drunk my wine with my milk'.[78] All that she was for him, he now enjoyed to the full. At last, she confesses that she has laid up 'all manner of precious fruits' for him. She expresses her intention to cause him 'to drink of spiced wine, of the juice of my pomegranate'.[79]

To grasp the typical, the more eschatological undertones of

---

[73] *cont.* a prolific fruitfulness. The henna flowers add to this the element of beauty and fragrance. Their whitish flowers grow in clusters very much like grapes. Toward the end of the kingdom period, En-gedi housed a thriving perfume industry, henna contributing a part toward this. In Ezekiel's vision of the future kingdom age, the changes to take place in this very area are quite staggering. Fishermen will be netting fish from the healed waters of what is at present a lifeless sea. 'And by the river upon the bank thereof, on this side and on that side, shall grow every tree for meat, whose leaf shall not wither, neither shall the fruit thereof fall: it shall bring forth new fruit every month, because the waters thereof issue out of the sanctuary: and the fruit thereof shall be for meat, and the leaf thereof for healing', 47.12, and see vv.9ff. En-gedi* was one of six cities in the area at the time of the conquest, Josh.15.62, an asylum for the hunted and rejected David, 1 Sam.23.29[24.1]; 24.1[2], and the place from which the daring Moabite thrust against Jerusalem and Jehoshaphat was launched, 2 Chron.20.2.

[74] Song 2.13; 6.11; 7.12[13].   [75] 7.8[9].   [76] 1.2,4.   [77] 4.10; 7.9[10].
[78] 5.1.   [79] 8.2.

all this, we need to consider the use of vine and wine in the Scriptures more generally. The vine/vineyard motif is richly developed in connection with Israel. The nation is sometimes likened to a vine, sometimes identified as a vine metaphorically.[80] The Song is uniquely linked with the idea of God and His vineyard in Isaiah 5, where the prophet sings 'a song of my beloved' [Heb.dodhi], a form of address dominating the whole of the Song, and not found elsewhere.[81] We have already suggested a link between the Shulammite's desire that her beloved should drink of her spiced wine, and the Messiah's forecast of that day when He would drink again the fruit of the vine when kingdom time had dawned.[82] This must be the grand and joyous climax toward which the Song moves. To express that hope in Amos' words 'Behold, the days come, saith the Lord, that the plowman shall overtake the reaper, and the treader of grapes him that soweth seed; and the mountains shall drop sweet wine, and all the hills shall melt. And I will bring again the captivity of my people Israel, and they shall build the waste cities, and inhabit them; and they shall plant vineyards, and drink the wine thereof; and they shall also make gardens, and eat the fruit of them. And I will plant them upon their land, and they shall no more be plucked up out of their land which I have given them, saith the Lord thy God', 9.13–15.

With this we come to the end of the Song's use of forest and fruit trees. We have observed that both groups provide pleasant and fragrant settings for the developing love story and the imagery by which to describe the beauties of the partners. Everything around them blends in with the overwhelming joy of their love, as this in turn projects typologically the delights of that time when the Lord 'will rest in his love'.[83]

---

[80] cf. Jer.6.9; Ezek.17.6; 19.10 and Jer.2.10; Hos.10.1. [81] pp.45f, n.27–31. [82] Song 8.2; Matt.26.29. [83] Biblical imagery concerning the vine, the fig, and the olive (suggested in the references to 'ointment, oil' in the Song), indicates their range typologically. Each presents a distinct aspect of the nation before God in the past, present and future: vine, *spiritual joy*, Ps.80.8–11,12–16; Isa.5.1–7; Matt.21.33–46: fig, *national sweetness*, see n.41–43: the olive, *spiritual witness*, Rom.11.17–20,21–25; Jer.11.17f; Zech.4.3,11f; cf. Rev.11.3–12; Hos.14.6.

7

FLOWERS AND GRASSES OF THE FIELD

HAVING CONSIDERED the Song's contribution to the subject of forest
and fruit trees, we shall make our way into field and garden with
Solomon as our inspired guide. Whilst each item needs to be noted
and identified, it is important to observe if the plant is being used
as a simile and to what purpose. Also, other Biblical usage may shed
further light on any metaphorical or typological/eschatological
significance in connection with the nation.

Israel is a particularly beautiful land in the spring season. The
winter rains have soaked the soil, and now the occasional showers,
the latter rains, interplaying with the lengthening periods of sunshine, provide ideal conditions for stimulating growth. The carpets
of colourful wild flowers put on a spectacular show. The cultivated
grasses develop apace, providing now a green and then a golden
landscape. The countryside is not as yet scorched brown. The
weather is delightful, the days being free from that intense heat
which, later, can be so enervating. Soon all of this changes, for
within two months the barley and the wheat are harvested, and the
flowers of the field shrivel under the glaring sun. The landscape appears quite different when summer has fully come. The prophet
Isaiah puts this dramatic landscape change to good use
eschatologically, vividly presenting the transitory nature of all
earthly might and splendour. The voice is heard saying 'All flesh is
grass, and all the goodliness thereof is as the flower of the field: the

grass withereth, the flower fadeth . . . but the word of our God shall stand forever'.[1] In the Song, a number of excursions into the fields acquaint us with a few of Israel's beauties and bounties in their season.

The Springtime Flowers. A general word [Heb.nitstsan], embracing numbers of the splendid wild flowers carpeting the countryside in the spring season, is used in chapter 2.[2] These are predominantly red in colour, and include anemones, tulips, and poppies. Although each variety tends to be comparatively short-lived when considered alone, their sequential appearance maintains the colourful display for a considerable period through to May-time. Fallow land is then flower-strewn land, an attractive divinely embroidered landscape. It is this that the beloved would have his loved one to enjoy in his company. He desires that their relationship might truly reflect the beauties and hopes of spring-time.

The rose [Heb.chabhatstseleth*] of Sharon is certainly not the English rose. The root from which the word is derived indicates that a flower which shoots from a bulb is intended.[3] Beyond this there is little agreement as to the identification of the flower concerned. Some equate it with 'a lily of the valleys' assuming the two descriptions to be in poetic parallelism.[4] Others see it as a reference to the autumn crocus, a view supported by the RV margin of Isaiah 35.1 which also directs our attention to Song 2.1, the only other Biblical reference to the word. The translation there runs 'the desert shall rejoice, and blossom as the autumn crocus'. Its association here with the Sharon, which also appears in the context of its only other use, has encouraged others to find a suitable flower whose natural habitat is the coastal plain south of Mount Carmel. The narcissus is one such, growing in the damp soil of

---

[1] Isa.40.6ff; cf. 1 Pet.1.24f where the contrast is with the incorruptible seed of the Word by which men are begotten again.   [2] Song 2.12†; cf. verb 'to bloom, blossom' [Heb.natsats*], 6.11; 7.12[13]; Eccles.12.5: in Qal Ezek.1.7 = to sparkle, related to brightness here. Note also n.fem. 'blossom' [Heb.nitstsah*], Job 15.33; Isa.18.5.   [3] cf. 'onion' [Heb.batsal†], Num.11.5.   [4] e.g. Zohary PB 176. He finds further support for this by proposing a parallel between Isa.35.1, 'blossom as the rose (lily)' and Hos.14.5, 'blossom as the lily' where the word is the one translated lily in Song 2.1b.

the plain and elsewhere in the land. It is winter flowering, becoming dormant in February. Another and better proposal is the beautiful and intensely fragrant sea daffodil, which the Arabs describe as 'the lily of the sea-shore'. It is at home in the sand dunes of the Sharon, and flowers quite late in the summer.[5] All of these proposals involve dominantly white flowers, and indicate a definite advance in the maiden's self-understanding. Had she not earlier confessed herself 'black' and therefore 'as the tents of Kedar'?

The lily [Heb.shoshanah] **of the valleys.** This, by definition is a flower characteristic of the mountain valleys [Heb. ˇemeq‡, derived from a verb meaning 'to be deep'], rather than of the wide open, unsurrounded plains. It is best identified as the white 'Madonna lily', once prolific in the good soil of the alluvial valleys and hollows in the Galilee and on Mount Carmel. Today it is much rarer.[6]

The lily is the dominant wild flower of the Song, and is one of the largest, loveliest and most fragrant in the land. It grows up to 1.5 metres high. Its stem is very leafy, and is crowned with a cluster of outstandingly beautiful flowers. Once these have bloomed in the early summer, they remain open day and night, being even more fragrant during the night. Obviously, it is a symbol of beauty and fragrance, and was adopted in Christendom as a symbol of purity, and resurrection. Hence the name 'Madonna lily', and its place in many churchyards.

---

[5] Feliks SoS 28, opts for the sea daffodil, the pancratium maritimum L. This and the narcissus tazetta L., belong to the Amaryllis family, Hareuveni NBH 119. Zohary PB 178f, rejects the identification of either of these with 'the rose of Sharon'. His detailed descriptions and pictures are excellent. JND opts for 'a narcissus of Sharon', others the red tulipa sharensis. [6] Lilium candidum L. The word in the masculine form occurs in Song 2.16; 4.5; 5.13; 6.2,3; 7.2[3], and also at 1 Kings 7.22,26 (note/ /in 2 Chron.4.5 is shoshanah, fem.form), and in titles of three psalms, 45[1]; 69[1]; 80.[1]*. A slightly different pointing of the masculine [Heb.shushan*] occurs at 1 Kings 7.19, and in the title of Psalm 60[1]. The feminine form [Heb. shoshanah*] occurs in Song 2.1,2, and also 2 Chron.4.5; Hos.14.5[6]. The name [Heb.shoshan] is suggestively derived from the numeral six [Heb.shesh], the flower having six-petal lobes, and stamens. Delitzsch, however, links it to the word for linen [Heb. also shesh] because of the white colour.

The maiden, in comparing herself to these two wild flowers, is more aware of her attractiveness and appealing fragrance since her beloved's advances, but she does not appreciate the excelling uniqueness which he finds in her. This he develops by accepting one of her similes, that of the lily, but enhancing its beauty by framing it 'among **thorns**' [Heb.choach]. This is a masterly touch indeed. Thorns and thistles are signs of the original curse of the ground through man's sin, and the ongoing fruit of sinning against the soil by neglecting it. Long before modern ecological research had established it, Job knew the association that existed between the type of soil and those things which would grow in it. 'Let thistles [our word choach] grow instead of wheat, and cockle instead of barley'.[7] Wheat requires good soil, but if that soil is not farmed it will produce thorns. Barley on the other hand grows in poorer soil. When the ground has been neglected, the very weeds which grow in it indicate those crops most suited to it. The beloved's setting the lily among thorns is a clear proof of the excellent quality of the soil, and the neglect of it by those responsible for it. It further helps in identifying the 'lily among thorns', for the soil must be excellent as we have seen. Such is the case in the mountain valleys of the Galilee, which also provide good pasturage for the flocks as the other references to lilies in the Song require. In a scene suffering the ill-effects of Adam's fall, and those caused by the sin and neglect of each succeeding generation, the beloved had eyes for none except his 'lily among thorns'.

It is important to notice the contexts outside the Song where reference is made to lilies. *Observation one* is that they form an important decorative element in Solomon's Temple. The top of the two massive bronze pillars in the porch, named Jachin and Boaz, which flanked the approach to the house, were decorated with 'lily

---

[7] See Gen.3.17ff; Job 31.39f. A penetrating observation on the Job verse was given by Rabbi Hoshaya: 'The Torah here taught you a law of nature: a field that produces chochim is suitable for the growing of wheat; a field that brings forth baashah points to soil suitable for the sowing of barley', Mid.Ran.Reʹeh 15, quoted in Feliks NMB 258; also Hareuveni TSBH 70, 114f. The 'thorn' of our verse is the so-called Golden Thistle, Scolymus maculatus L. Thorns and the fields sown with grain feature together in our Lord's parable, Matt.13.7,22; Mark 4.7,18; Luke 8.7,14.

work'. Also the brim of the great bronze sea in the court before the house was made 'like the brim of a cup, like the flower of a lily'. The four references in Kings/Chronicles added to the eight in the Song, incidentally lock the Song into its historical setting. In together accounting for 2/3 of the Old Testament usage of 'lilies', it suggests that in considering Solomon's period, and what it represents typically, we are likely to derive the most help in understanding the Song. That Solomon's reign is a messianic anticipation cannot be doubted. He built God's house, and bore the glory, as Messiah is yet to do.[8]

Observation two is that the other five references are all of interest with the typological/eschatological and the messianic aspects in mind. Psalm 45 is indisputably Messianic, and is the first of four psalms bearing Shoshannim in their titles. It is also, in its content, the closest parallel to the tone of the Song as a 'song of loves'. Psalm 69 is Messianic also, but totally different in tone. Here the Messiah's sufferings following upon his evident zeal for God's house, and climaxing at Golgotha, are plain from the New Testament quotations. So are the troubles through which the nation passes consequently, when 'their table before them becomes a snare'. The meek of the nation are glad however, and the nation's history is to be consummated when 'the heaven and earth praise him, the seas, and everything that moveth therein. For God will save Zion'. In the light of this, Psalm 80, where the title has 'Shoshannim Eduth', the threefold plea 'Turn us again ... cause thy face to shine, and we shall be saved' indicates the intense desire for God to create those conditions within His own which will bring them out of their troubles. Even more dramatically they address Him: 'Turn again, we beseech thee, O God of hosts: look down from heaven, and behold, and visit this vine'. Similarly, Psalm 60, bearing the 'Shushan Eduth' title, pleads with a God who has cast off His people, that He might intervene on their behalf. 'Through God we shall do valiantly'. Hosea 14 rounds off this review of Old Testament usage of the words for lily found so frequently in the Song. Again the context is one prefaced by

---

[8] 1 Kings 7.19,22,26; 2 Chron.4.5; cf. Zech.6.12f.

Israel's repentance and return to the Lord in the last days, when nationally they will be blessed and made a blessing. Among other similes used of the nation then, the prophet says 'he shall grow as the lily', v.4. Two distinct threads weave their way through the ministry of these prophecies. There is both that proclamation of the acceptable year of the Lord, and of the day of vengeance of our God. There is a ministry of comfort, and one of challenge. Beyond the present uncertainty and distress there is to be the exchange of beauty for ashes.

In this connection it is of interest to note the LXX rendering of these psalm titles, which runs 'Concerning those who are to be changed, or transformed'.[9] This is spiritually suggestive. For Israel, it anticipates the desire expressed in the words 'let the beauty of the Lord our God be upon us'.[10] One New Testament manuscript actually uses the word adopted in these titles in connection with our Lord's transfiguration.[11] What an outward change took place on that occasion!

In the Song the lily is used only once in a simile by the maiden, and then for her beloved's lips which are said to be 'as lilies, dropping liquid myrrh', 5.13. For some, this has required the word to be descriptive of a red flower rather than a white one. However, the second clause in the simile is the definitive one in interpreting it. It is their fragrance that is emphasized, not their colour, though the lily's form also adds the dimension of beauty and gracefulness. Lilies must have a place in the description of one who is altogether lovely! It points us to the One anointed of the Spirit of whom it was said 'Thou art fairer than the children of men; grace is poured into thy lips'.[12] This is referring to One 'greater than Solomon', which our Lord Jesus claimed to be when referring to the wisdom of His ministry.[13] It is to His gracious ministry, as now glorified in

---

[9] LXX titles of Pss.44, 59, 68, and 79 [Heb. and EVV = 45[1]; 60[1]; 69[1]; 80[1]]. It should be added that if 'the Chief Musician' element of psalm titles be taken as the subscript of the preceding psalm, as in Habakkuk 3.19, rather than as the superscript of the psalm which it opens, as in our text, then the 'Shoshannim' psalms would be 44, 59, 68, and 79. See Thirtle, Titles. In this case their ministry is clearly bound up prophetically with the remnant of Israel which passes through trouble to triumph.   [10] Ps.90.17.   [11] see AGD re 'to be changed' [passive of Grk. ´alloioo].   [12] Ps.45.2[3]; Song 5.13.   [13] Matt.12.42.

heaven, that chapter 5 refers.

The graceful roe or young hart and the fawns love to be among the beauties, fragrance, and serenity of nature. So it is that three times in the Song lilies decorate the scene where her beloved, who is likened to a roe or young hart, is found. We are informed that 'he feedeth among the lilies' (twice), for it is here, where something of his own beauty and fragrance is revealed along with serenity, that he finds satisfaction. His loved one's affections, too, find their satisfaction where he finds his – 'among the lilies'. It is also the beloved's purpose and occupation 'to gather lilies', each precious to him. This latter role, as we shall see, suggests the Lord's worldwide ministry in the present. He is now gathering a people for Himself out of all the peoples of the earth.[14]

'Consider the lilies of the field, how they grow; they toil not (as men do out of doors), neither do they spin (as women do in the home): yet I say unto you, that even Solomon (note this reference to this king in the context of 'lilies' once again) in all his glory was not arrayed like one of these. But if God doth so clothe the grass of the field (as also He feeds the birds of the heaven), which today is, and tomorrow is cast into the oven, shall he not much more clothe you, O ye of little faith'.[15] These familiar words of our beloved Lord insist that the beauty with which the 'lily' is adorned is God-provided. It is equally clear that God gives attention to such perfection though the flower's life is transitory in the extreme. What place is there for anxiety regarding our own clothing therefore? Will not faith be granted those things which the Father knows we need? Nature's harmonies and beauties unfold then, not only the handiwork of the Creator, but also the heart, the good pleasure of the Father. The 'lilies' in the Song are indeed to the praise of the glory of God's grace, and it is where this grace is prolific that the beloved one, and the one he loves find their satisfaction.[16]

We have already noted the occasions when the maiden sees

---

[14] See Song 2.16; 4.5; 6.2,3; cf. James in Acts 15.13f.   [15] Matt.6.28f.
[16] cf. Song 6.2 and 4.5.

herself as a 'lily of the valleys', and her beloved surpasses this by describing her as a 'lily among thorns'. These similes regarding the maiden suggest her lowly purity, and her beauty and fragrance the more captivating to her beloved when found in such inhospitable surroundings. Yet if she is, at one time, seen as a lily surrounded by thorns, on another occasion she hears appreciative onlookers say 'Thy belly is like a heap of **wheat** [Heb.chittah] set about with lilies'.[17] The 'belly' refers to the lower abdomen, which externally may be fat through excess, as in Eglon's case,[18] or be attractively rounded and surrounded as in the Shulammite's case. Excluding the use of the 'belly' [Heb.beten] as representing the inward parts of the body, the term has two chief associations.[19] On the one hand, our word stomach fits well those contexts where eating and the like is in view. On the other hand, our word womb would be a very suitable translation in many cases where procreation and related thoughts are intended. The description of the bride's gird-ed waist and stomach, supplementing the parallel reference to her navel in the earlier part of the same verse, takes us beyond the ex-ternal colour and form to the tremendous potential that is seen in her. It is not 'a grain of wheat', a simile specially suited to em-phasize the need for it to fall into the ground and die if it is not to abide 'by itself alone'.[20] The simile of the 'heap of wheat' demands rather that the corn of wheat has indeed been sown and has died, producing its glorious crop. The Suffering Servant is

---

[17] Wheat [Heb.chittah], Triticum durum, one of the grass family, a main crop of the land, one of the seven varieties betokening God's blessing, Deut.8.8, and highly nutritious, 32.14, the food of His people, Ps.81.16[17]. How this establishes, as we have seen earlier, that the natural habitat of the lily is that good ground where the thorn will grow if neglected, but where wheat grows if cared for. In chap. 2 of the Song Israel's beauties are seen amid the evidence of the curse. In chap. 7 her beauty and fruitfulness are seen apart from any evidence of the curse. The two distinct stages in the salvation history of the nation are matched by this and other changes in nature. [18] Jud.3.21f. [19] The word [Heb.beten] figuratively as the inner being and its faculties, Prov.18.3; 26.22; Ps.40.8[9]; Hab.3.16, as the stomach to be satisfied, Prov.13.25; Ezek.3.3,14; cf. Rev.10.8ff, as the womb or man's body as the instrument of procreation or genera-tion, Gen.25.23f; Hos.12.4; Ps.127.3; 132.11; 139.13; Mic.6.7. [20] John 12.24.

yet to 'see of the travail of his soul, and (he) shall be satisfied'. Also, it assumes that the crop of wheat has been harvested successfully, the threshing operation is over.[21] Eschatologically, this projects the history of the nation of Israel beyond the period of cataclysmic judgments during which the Messiah will have used His winnowing fork, and will have thoroughly cleansed His threshing-floor.[22] The threshing-floor is surrounded, not by a wall of thorns to safeguard the grain against intruders, but with an attractive girdle or bed of lilies. She had nothing to fear now as her reunion with her beloved was so near.[23]

The Mandrakes. This is a perennial herb of the fields, without stem, but featuring large crinkled leaves. Its yellowish, plum-like fruit, is fragrant, ripens in late spring, and continues until early summer. The fruit is edible, and it has been established that it acts as a purgative, and as a sedative, to a much greater degree than as a stimulant. It does contain some stimulating hormones however.[24]

The maiden reports to her beloved at the end of the Song 'The mandrakes [Heb.dudha ´im] give forth fragrance'.[25] The season, therefore, is late spring or early summer. The only other Biblical context in which the fruit is mentioned associates its being found by Reuben in the field 'in the days of wheat harvest', which is consistent with its use here in the Song.[26]

The Genesis story unveils Rachel's belief that the fruit possessed some property which promoted procreation. Though Jacob loved her more than Leah, it was Leah's womb that the Lord had opened. In her barrenness, Rachel envied her sister, and saw in the mandrakes, brought home by Reuben to Leah, a means of encouraging her own conception. She said to Leah 'Give me, I

---

[21] Rev.14.15f. [22] Matt.3.12. [23] We may compare the incident in Ruth 3 when Boaz 'went to lie down at the end of the heap of corn' to guard it. Ruth came to lie at his feet, and on awakening, Boaz heard her say 'I am Ruth thine handmaid: spread therefore thy skirt over thine handmaid; for thou art a near kinsman'. How near a kinsman the Shulammite longs that her beloved might be is clear from her words 'Oh that thou wert as my brother . . .', Song 8.1. [24] Zohary PB 188f. [25] Song 7.13[14]‡. This is the Mandragora officinarum. [26] Gen.30.14a.

pray thee, of thy son's mandrakes'.[27] Leah seemed wiser by far! She insisted on having Jacob, if her sister was to have the mandrakes, and it was Leah who conceived and bore Issachar, and later, Zebulun, thus becoming the proud mother of six boys. No, the true secret of both the fruitfulness and the barrenness of the womb is with God. Notice, when 'the Lord saw that Leah was hated ... he opened her womb', and in His own good time 'God hearkened to her (Rachel), and opened her womb. And she conceived and bare a son and said, God hath taken away my reproach: and she called his name Joseph, saying, The Lord add to me another son'.[28] The passage of time had brought her to confess that He alone can add fruit to union.

In the Song, the inclusion of the mandrakes in the bride's appeal to her beloved, therefore, not only adds more colour to the late spring and early summer scenery, but designedly insists that the time is appropriate for the fruitful consummation of their love. Even nature harmonizes with the couple's hearts, and gives its Amen to the fact that there is 'a time to love'.[29] The context blazons this abroad by presenting a cluster of references to him as 'my beloved' [Heb.dodhi]. Also she promises 'There will I give thee my love [Heb.dodhay, plural, lit.loves]', following which she says 'The mandrakes [Heb.dudha˘im, plural] give forth fragrance'. The whole piece is climaxed as she says 'and at our doors are all manner of precious fruits, new and old, which I have laid up for thee, O my beloved [Heb.dodhi]'.[30] Israel's Beloved, her long awaited Messiah, is patiently awaiting this joyous day Himself. When the nation wakes up to this thrilling fact, she will exclaim 'I am my beloved's, and his desire is toward me'.[31] Do we not vibrate in harmony with Him whose 'desire is toward' Israel? The

---

[27] Gen.30.14c. The word [Heb.dudhay*] occurs five times in Genesis, 30.14(2),15(2),16, and once in the Song 7.13[14]. It is related to the word love [Heb. dodh] which occurs six times in the plural in the Song, and is used 33 times by the loved one to address 'my beloved' [Heb.dodhi]; for details see pp.45f, n.27–31. The Greeks called mandrakes 'love apples', and lauded their aphrodisiac powers, and their ability to facilitate conception.   [28] Gen.30.22ff.   [29] Eccles.3.8.
[30] Song 7.9,10,11,13 [Heb.dodhi, vv.10,11,12,14]; 7.12 [Heb.dodhay, v.13]; 7.13 [Heb.dudha˘im = mandrakes, v.14].   [31] 7.10[11].

word is a pregnant one. It is used in Genesis 3 of Eve after her sin. She heard the Lord God decree 'I will greatly multiply thy sorrow and thy conception; in sorrow thou shalt bring forth children; and thy desire shall be to thy husband, and he shall rule over thee'.[32] Thank God, the Suffering Servant has borne our griefs, and carried our sorrows, and those of Israel, and soon 'the pleasure of the Lord shall prosper in his hand'. His vicarious suffering as He bare the sin of many in the past, and His present intercession, guarantee that His desire which is toward His own people will be satisfied in the future. He will rule over Israel as their appointed King. Already, we respond to this, yet another of His appointed glories, and gladly sing:

> Our sympathies, our hopes are Thine,
>   O Lord we wait to see
> Creation all, below, above,
>   Redeemed and blessed by Thee.

---

[32] Gen.3.16. The word 'desire' [Heb.teshuqah*], apart from these two occurrences, is found only at Gen.4.7; see pp.281f, n.17f.

8

LIKE A WATERED GARDEN

SO FAR in the Song, we have made excursions into the forest, the
orchard, and the field. As we have done so, our itinerary has taken
us through very real scenes, and we have been encouraged to gaze
at the beauties of nature which have surrounded us. Our poet
guide has captured our attention, and created in us a greater sensitivity to what is so obviously the handiwork of God. Without
doubt, the hymn writer's mind had mused in the Song before he
penned those words to which we, too, respond:

> Heaven above is softer blue,
>   Earth around is sweeter green;
> Something lives in every hue
>   Christless eyes have never seen:
> Birds with gladder songs o'erflow,
>   Flowers with deeper beauties shine
> Since I know, as now I know,
>   I am His, and He is mine.

It has been particularly instructive, also, not simply to be baptized into such tangible beauty alone, but to ponder the figures mirrored in forest and field. The real scenery of life provides considerable imagery descriptive of life. External forms, however attractive, are more enhanced when read as symbols, similes and
metaphors of spiritual graces, and even as featuring typological
projections of salvation history itself. This our poet helps us to do.

An Enclosed Garden. For the moment, our guide departs from his own very real world, into the flights of fancy. He conducts us into a garden of delights, stocked with all kinds of aromatic plants, many of which are not native to his own land. Before we concentrate on the various plants we shall consider first the garden itself. The word [Heb.gan‡] describes an enclosed area, whether inside a wall or a hedge. By this means its facilities were secured[1] and set apart for its owner.[2] It would need some perennial source of water supply for irrigation purposes.[3] Often there were different types of trees featured in it, to provide fruit and shade for the owner. Additionally, flowers, herbs, and vegetables might be cultivated in it.[4] All was thoughtfully planned, carefully planted, and was to be developed and guarded.[5] Solomon claims 'I planted me vineyards; I made me gardens and parks, and I planted trees in them of all kinds of fruit: I made me pools of water, to water therefrom the forest where trees were reared'.[6] There was none more qualified than he to describe in such detail the endless delights of a garden.

In the Song, the garden features prominently.[7] Most of the word's occurrences are in the singular, where it is used of the maiden. This is clearly established in chapter 4. Her beloved first describes her as 'a garden shut up (enclosed)', then claims that she is for him 'my garden', whilst she encourages him to 'come into his garden'. He is delighted and ready to respond saying 'I am

---

[1] From the verb 'to surround, protect, defend' [Heb.ganan*], the subject of which is always the Lord, 2 Kings 19.34 = Isa.38.6; 2 Kings 20.6; Isa.31.5; 37.35; Zech.9.15; 12.8. The name of modern Jenin, at the S.E. entrance to the Valley of Jezreel, is the Arabic equivalent of the Hebrew for 'garden', and stands on the site of the Biblical Beth-haggan (translated 'the garden house' in 2 Kings 9.27); cf. the vineyard's protection, Isa.5.1f.   [2] The kings often had breathtakingly beautiful gardens surrounding their palaces, e.g. that of Ahasuerus, Esther 1.5, and Herod the Great, Jos. Wars 5.4.4; cf. also 'the garden of Uzza', 2 Kings 21.18, and 'the king's garden', 25.4; Jer.39.4; 52.7.   [3] Gen.2.10; Song 4.12,15. For a suggestive treatment of the similes of the 'wall' and the 'well' as the safeguard and the secret of fruitfulness respectively see CDP 60–63.   [4] Gen.2.8f; cf. the Garden of Gethsemane with its olives, John 18.1ff, also Ahab's proposed vegetable garden, 1 Kings 21.2.   [5] cf. Gen.2.8,15.   [6] Eccles.2.4–6.   [7] Song 4.12,15,16(2); 5.1; 6.2(2),11; 8.13‡.

come into my garden, my sister, my bride'.[8] For him, then, the maiden is set apart as his very own delightful possession.

Three times it appears to be used more generally, when it is found in the plural form. Clearly, these 'gardens' do not represent the maiden, as one of the instances makes patent. Her beloved says 'Thou art a fountain of gardens, a well of living waters'.[9] We might say of this instance that she is a well-spring of blessing to others. It is all but impossible to read this description of her without sensing what must be its only satisfactory parallel. There we learn the secret of such life-producing ministry. It is in the ascended and glorified Messiah, and in the descended Spirit of God. Could we have expected such a breathtaking promise through Israel to have been announced at any more appropriate feast than that of the Tabernacles? We recall those wonderful words uttered on 'the great day of the feast'. Jesus then 'cried, saying, If any man thirst, let him come unto me, and drink. He that believeth on me, as the scripture hath said, out of his belly shall flow rivers of living water'. John's inspired comment was 'But this spake he of the Spirit, which they that believed on him were to receive: for the Spirit was not yet given; because Jesus was not yet glorified'.[10] Even today, those that believe are intended to be 'a fountain of gardens' stimulating spiritual growth in those who belong to the Lord, and 'a well of living waters' to those in need of divine life.

The garden of all gardens for the Old Testament is the one with which man's beginning is associated.[11] It is, by way of location, the garden which the Lord planted 'eastward, in Eden'.[12] Then, by way of description, it becomes 'the garden of Eden', that is, the garden of delights.[13]

---

[8] Song 4.12,16(2); 5.1; 6.2a; cf. [Heb.ginnah] 6.11.　　　[9] 4.15; cf. 6.2; 8.13.
[10] John 7.37ff. Compare and contrast John 4. The well of living waters there represents 'the energy of the Spirit of God in our spirits, leading us to the enjoyment of God, in holy, intimate communion', CDP 62.　　　[11] Gen.2.8,9,10,15,16; 3.1,2,3,8(2),10,23,24.　　　[12] [Heb.(be = in) `edhen, Gen.2.8; cf. (me = from) `edhen, 2.10 and (qidmath = the east of) `edhen, 4.16. In these places the LXX transliterated Eden [Grk. `Edem].　　　[13] [Heb.gan `edhen], Gen.2.15; 3.23f, the word being derived from the verb 'to delight, luxuriate' [Heb. `adhan*], used of

The garden features in similes concerning Israel. Sometimes these emphasize the Lord's chastening judgments of the nation, and their cause.[14] More encouragingly, the prophets use it in connection with the idyllic conditions to be enjoyed by Israel in the future. The nation is seen as valleys 'spread forth, as gardens by the river side'. *Isaiah* predicts that when the Lord has comforted Zion, He will make 'her wilderness like Eden, and her desert like the garden of the Lord'. The promise stands: 'thou shalt be like a watered garden, and like a spring of water, whose waters fail not'. Then 'as the earth bringeth forth her bud, and as the garden causeth the things that are sown in it to spring forth; so the Lord God will cause righteousness and praise to spring forth before all the nations'.[15] For *Jeremiah*, the context of the new covenant with its regathering of the nation brings its Edenic hopes, 'and their soul shall be as a watered garden; they shall not sorrow any more at all'. *Ezekiel* continues on the theme, saying 'The land that was desolate is become like the garden of Eden'. *Amos*, too, speaks of the time when Israel 'shall plant vineyards, and drink the wine thereof; they shall also make gardens, and eat the fruit of them'.[16] On the one hand, the land itself will look Edenic, and on the other hand the people of God will be spiritually suited for this 'garden of God'. Nature and the nation are to become delightfully harmonized.

Passages like these must be significant for understanding the garden theme of the Song. The end purpose of the Lord for Israel, and through them, for the peoples of the earth generally, is latent at the beginning in the creation story, and will be patent at the end in the kingdom glory.[17]

The 'garden of Eden' has proved highly significant for Biblical theology. Isaiah set Eden in parallel to 'the garden of the Lord'.[18] The Greek Old Testament chose to replace the Hebrew word for

---

[13] *cont.* Israel's experience when they had entered Canaan and 'delighted themselves in thy (God's) great goodness', Neh.9.25. In these instances the LXX translated Eden [Grk.truphe = luxury, splendour], as also Joel 2.3; Ezek.28.13; 31.9,16,18; 36.35. [14] Isa.1.29ff; 65.3; 66.17; Lam.2.6; Joel 2.3.
[15] Num.24.6; Isa.51.3; 58.11; 61.11. [16] Jer.31.12; Ezek.36.35; Amos 9.14.
[17] Gen.2.4–25 and Rev.21.9–22.5. [18] Isa.51.3; see also 'the garden of God', Ezek.28.13; 31.9,16,18(2).

The photograph on the back cover is of the beautiful 'Madonna Lily' in one of Carmel's mountain valleys, May-time. It is used by the beloved to describe his loved one: 'As a lily among thorns, so is my love among the daughters', Song 2.2. See pp. 83–88.

1. Spring-time sunrise over the Golan Heights and the Lake of Galilee. Note the birds on the wing. See pp. 53–55, 209f.

2. 'I have compared thee, O my love, to a mare among Pharaoh's chariotry', Song 1.9. See pp. 55f, 191f.

3. Tutankhamun in his chariot on the field of battle – part panel of an Egyptian painted wooden chest.

2

3

4. 'I am black, but comely . . . as the tents of Kedar, as the curtains of Solomon', Song 1.5. A typical Bedouin tent made up of black goats' hair curtains. See pp. 59f, 190f.

5. A flock of sheep led by shepherd boys near Herodian in the Judean Desert. See p. 57f.

6. 'Beside the flocks of thy companions', Song 1.7. See pp. 191, 323.

garden, whenever 'Eden' was in view, with the transliterated old Persian word for park, pleasure ground, or garden [Grk. paradeisos].[19] The phrase 'garden of Eden' was then translated as 'the park, or garden of delights' [Grk.paradeisos tes truphes].[20] Consequently, within Judaism, some came to regard Paradise [Grk.paradeisos] as the name for 'the garden of Eden'. In the Jewish apocryphal books the name Paradise became identified with the abode of the righteous after death, for the garden of Eden, or delights, was surely reserved for them.[21] It was there, too, that they had access to the tree of life, a hope held out to the believing overcomer in Revelation 2.[22]

In the context of a detailed description of his loved one in the Song, we read 'Thy shoots are an orchard of pomegranates, with precious fruits'. The word for 'orchard' here [Heb.pardes], is also a loan-word from Persian. The king of Persia had the most beautiful gardens set apart for his own pleasure and satisfaction. They were stocked with all the glorious and good things that earth could produce, and were called 'paradises'. Most translate this single use of the word in the Song, as also its only other Old Testament use, as 'orchard'. Certainly, the Greek translation adopts a similar loan-word in each case also. As the word is being used as a metaphor for the unique attractiveness of the maiden, and the peculiar delight her beloved finds in her, the force of the word would be better brought out with its origins in mind. She is to him a veritable 'paradise of delight'. Darby obviously thought this when he translated the phrase 'Thy shoots are a paradise of pomegranates'. Recalling the Greek translation's adoption of the same Persian word for the 'garden' [Heb.gan] of Eden, and as a replacement for the loan-word [Heb.pardes] in chapter 4 of the Song, encourages our sensing the beloved's bold figure for his loved one as a 'paradise excelled'. With the parallels relating to

---

[19] Gen.2.8,9,10,15,16; 3.1,2,3,8,10,23,24; 13.10.   [20] Gen.2.15; 3.23,24; cf. Joel 2.3; Ezek.28.13; 31.9.   [21] e.g. 2 Esdras 7.36. There is some variety in its use: it may refer to Eden, to the waiting place of the righteous until resurrection, cf. Luke 16.22–31; 23.43, and even to the eternal home of God's people in 'the third heaven', Apoc. Moses 13.2f; cf. Paul's experience, 2 Cor.12.2f, later said to have been followed by Rabbi Aqibha, bT. Hag.14b.   [22] NT references to paradise are Luke 23.43; 2 Cor.12.2; Rev.2.7*.

the garden which we have considered, and those happy projections of the prophets adopting the same theme, we trace the
developing Messianic purpose towards its grand goal of 'paradise
restored'! In many instances the prospect of that future era, when
creation's groans will have ceased, appears to surpass what we
know of the original Edenic conditions. However, we are not to
forget that there was no sin in that happy pair originally. In the
kingdom age which is to come, creation's blessed condition will
reflect God's triumph in the reconciling and regenerating work of
His Son.[23] Yet that very kingdom, as glorious as it is, will be the
era when righteousness reigns, and when sin still exists, though
it be suppressed and judged. In the several cycles of the Song, the
'drama of redemption' pursues its divinely appointed course until
the saved nation blissfully enters the thousand year reign 'leaning
upon her beloved'. Already, in the present, the true Israel of God,
as a kind of firstfruits, is 'like a watered garden' to her ascended
and glorified Lord, as chapter 4 of the Song suggests.

An Abundance of Waters. Man's dependence upon water
necessarily resulted in a certain prominence being given to it in the
Bible, the story of which is largely cradled in that part of the Near
East where water is at a premium. As a result, figurative, symbolic,
and even theological uses of water in the Scriptures should be
noted. R. C. Walls proposes a fourfold analysis of the use of water
Biblically: it is found in 1) judgment/salvation contexts, 2) cleansing procedures, 3) the satisfying of physical/spiritual needs and
4) God-promoted fruitfulness and refreshment settings.[24]

In the climax of the Song we find the counterpart of the first of
these for 'Many waters cannot quench love, neither can the floods
drown it'. In two parallel though quite distinct parts of the Song,
the beloved, in describing the maiden's teeth, adopts the second
use of water by saying 'Thy teeth are like a flock of ewes . . . which
are come up from the washing'. But it is in the latter part of chapter
4 that the subject is most emphasized. Here the bride is lavishly
supplied for herself and is described as 'a spring shut up, a fountain sealed'. Her own enclosed garden has limitless, and yet

---

[23] Col.1.20–23; Matt.19.28; cf. Acts 3.19f.   [24] TWB 279ff.

untapped sources of blessing as proposed in the third sub-division of the subject above. And still there is more. She is 'a fountain of gardens, a well of living waters, and flowing streams from Lebanon'. Having been satisfied herself, she promotes fruitfulness in those gardens around her, life-giving waters may be drawn from her well, and perennial refreshment surges from her as flowing streams, as indicated in the fourth division of the subject-matter above.[25]

It is in the field of salvation history that the water theme is specially significant. Consider the Flood, also the Exodus event involving salvation and judgment at the Reed Sea etc. However, it is in the forecasts of eschatology that these images are developed most. Israel must yet enjoy the love of her God which the waters cannot quench nor the floods drown. Her Maker, who is her Husband has said 'as I have sworn that the waters of Noah should no more go over the earth, so have I sworn that I would not be wroth with thee, nor rebuke thee'. He is yet to respond to the question 'Where is he that brought them up out of the sea . . . that divided the water before them to make himself an everlasting name?'[26] Then all God's promises shall be fulfilled to Israel, and in particular His word 'thou shalt be like a watered garden, and like a spring of water, whose waters fail not'.[27] The bride is described as such a garden in the Song, and embodied these hopes already as her beloved king, who became her husband, described her.

Let the one who has been drawn to Jesus the Messiah, the Son of God, for salvation, and knows Him as the Lover of their soul now, realize that prayerful desire

> Like 'a watered garden',
> Full of fragrance rare,
> Lingering in Thy presence,
> Let my life appear.

---

[25] See Song 8.7 'waters/floods': 4.2; 6.6 'washing' re teeth, cf. 'washed' re feet, 5.3: 4.12 'fountain sealed/spring shut up': 4.15 'fountain/well/streams'. Consider also 'rain', 2.11, 'dew', 5.2, and 'pools', 7.4[5].   [26] Gen.6–8; Exod.15; Isa.54.5,9; 63.11f.   [27] Isa.58.11.

9

THE FRAGRANT PLANTS

OUR WORD 'orchard' is made up of two elements meaning 'garden yard'. It is used to describe an enclosed area stocked with fruit trees, usually of one variety. This contrasts dramatically with a typical garden or orchard adjoining an Arab home today. Perhaps the thing that is most characteristic of these is the tremendous variety of fruit trees, herbs and plants that feature in them. The lemon, orange, grapefruit, pomegranate, fig, and vine are almost certain to be represented. There may well be a tall and elegant date-palm and nut trees also. And still there will be more, plants in profusion among which are sure to be those herbs and spices which are the making of so many of the tasty dishes which are part of the daily fare.

Despite the delights that such a garden yields to the owner, the lover in the Song could not find in it enough beauties, fragrances, and fruits to express what his loved one meant to him. Alongside the home-grown produce, he imports luxury items from afar, in order to avoid having to confess that the half had not been told.

We have reviewed the trees used in simile already,[1] and also some of the flowers.[2] We shall enjoy with him now an itinerary among the aromatic plants in his paradise, designed to help us appreciate, not only the beauties, but also the fragrance of his loved one.

---

[1] See chap. 6.   [2] See chap. 7.

101

Henna. This is a tree-like shrub, reaching in height up to four metres. It belongs to the willow family.³ In the spring season it bursts into flower, covered with clusters⁴ of yellowy-white blossoms with a fine perfume. These have to be removed, and pressed out immediately, to prevent decay setting in, if the oil extracted is to be acceptable as an ingredient in perfume production.⁵ It is the leaves, and even the root of the shrub, however, which are most sought after. From these, once dried and crushed into powder and mixed with water, a sweet-smelling dye is produced which is extremely popular for tinting hair, colouring finger nails, and even dyeing clothes. The shrub grows in the Near East and as far away as India, and may be seen today in the Jordan Valley and on the Coastal Plain.⁶ It was known at En-gedi in particular when the Song was written.⁷

Henna [Heb.kopher*]⁸ is used only in the Song in the Old Testament. It was found in the oasis, garden, and field alike.⁹ When the maiden uses it as a figure of her beloved, we are to

---

³ Lawsonia inermis L., see Zohary PB 190.   ⁴ Song 1.14.   ⁵ An interesting and relevant archaeological discovery in Level 5 at En-gedi, Tel Goren on the western shore of the Dead Sea, confirmed that there was a flourishing perfume industry based there during the Single Kingdom period of the OT. There were groups of large barrels measuring up to one metre high, with a variety of utensils, implements, decanters, and perfume juglets, AOTS 224f, Mazar.   ⁶ cf. Jos. Wars 4.8.3.   ⁷ Song 1.14. See again p.79, n.73.   ⁸ 1.14; 4.13; 7.11[12]. The Hebrew word translated henna [kopher] has two homonyms with which it may be confused, or compared. Chap. 7.11[12] is an example of confusion. The usual English replacement here is 'in the villages' [for Heb.bakkepharim, see e.g. AV, RV, JND, NIV]. Visitors to Israel quickly learn that Capernaum, put on the map specially through the ministry of the Lord Jesus, is 'the village of Nahum [Heb. Kephar-Nachum], whereas Kaphr-Yassif in Western Lower Galilee is 'the village of Josephus', the birthplace of that famous first century Jewish historian. The Hebrew word for 'village' uses exactly the same consonants as the word for 'henna', and as the phrases preceding and following it read 'let us go forth into the field', and 'Let us get up early to the vineyards', it is more probable that we should translate the phrase in 7.11[12] 'lodge among the henna bushes', lit. cf. NIVmg, NEB. A word using the same consonants and which is used frequently in the OT, is translated 'ransom' [Heb.kopher], and its word-family usage relates to the place, price, and propitiatory work of atonement.   ⁹ Song 1.14; 4.13 and 7.11[12] respectively.

understand his beauty and fragrance in the setting of his fruit-fulness. 'My beloved is unto me', said she, 'a cluster of henna flowers in the vineyards of En-gedi'. This is the more remarkable when we recall that that oasis, served with tumbling waterfalls of fresh water, nestles on the very edge of the barren and desolate Dead Sea.[10] For him, henna is simply the first of a ninefold perfume of praise by which he expresses how enchanting she is to him.[11]

Nard. The natural habitat of the lowly plant 'spikenard'[12] is the slopes of the towering Himalayas in North East India. Nature has provided it with a coat of hairs above its roots[13] to protect its stem and leaves from cold and wind alike. It is an aromatic perennial herb, brightened with clusters of small flowers. In the past, 'it was prized as a source of fragrant oil, extracted from stem, leaves,[14] and root stock. This, along with other oils, was used in the production of the costly spikenard ointment, valued as a cosmetic and in the treatment of nervous disorders. The Mishnah confirms it to be a luxury item, and consequently forbade its use after the destruction of the Temple.[15] There is no longer a demand for it.

Spikenard [Heb.nerd*] is found only in the Song in the Old Testament, and is used solely in connection with the maiden.[16] In chapter 4 it refers to the plant itself, whereas in chapter 1 it designates the finished product, the ointment. In the former, her beloved compares her to this fragrant plant as but one of her pleasing attractions, one of her many fragrant and living graces. This is how he sees her. In the latter, the maiden, in speaking of her precious purchased perfume, indicates the attention she has given to preparing herself for him.

---

[10] Song 1.14. [11] 4.13c–14.
[12] Nardostachys jatamansi, Zohary PB 205. [13] The hairy covering which is similar to that of an ear of corn, prompted the name given it in Greek [Grk.nardostachys = nard + ear of grain, see AGD under 'stachus']. Feliks points out that the word for spikenard in the Mishnah Kerit, 6a [Heb.shibboleth nerd] has exactly the same meaning, Feliks SoS 26. [14] The Mishnah name for the oil [Heb.shemen foliaton] indicates that the oil is extracted from the leaves, Feliks SoS 26. [15] Tosef.Sot.15,9.
[16] [Heb.nerd*] Song 1.12; 4.13,14.

It would be impossible to leave this without considering the only other Biblical references to 'spikenard'. They are found in the New Testament, both in connection with the same incident in that momentous 'last week' leading up to our Lord's death.[17] The incident took place at Bethany. The same Mary who had fallen at her Lord's feet in deep sorrow at the death of her brother, Lazarus, and who had had him restored to her from the tomb, was at His feet once again. However deaf His disciples were to the Lord's predictions concerning His approaching death, burial and resurrection, she was acutely aware, in sympathy with His spirit, that He was at the threshold of these epochal events. It was not simply her Lord's words nor His works which had drawn her to such costly and adoring worship.[18] Undoubtedly, she had believed His forecasts of the approaching hour, and had bought genuine nard, because, being 'very costly', it alone would be suitable for His anointing.[19] It was His self-unfolding sacrificial love, as far as to death, which she knew to be imminent, and this was her opportunity to give to Him now that which there would be no occasion to give Him after the event.[20] In this instance, she served Him. The precious nard from afar, rather than the locally available olive oil from the Mount of Olives, expressed her sacrificial love for Him, and that worship which was due to her altogether lovely One alone. What He was to her caused her to pour out all that she was and had! How thrilled the Lord was to receive such sympathetic, and spiritually intelligent worship. He discerned and expressed that 'she hath anointed my body aforehand for the burying'. Shall He lack today?

Saffron. This plant [Heb.karkom†] appears only once in the Bible. Most identify it as the true saffron.[21] This grows wild in Israel, but is easily cultivable also. The Mishnah refers to fields sown with it. It develops from a corm, and is a very small plant having dainty, six-petalled, blue-lilac flowers. Each of these have three stamens, and produce many aromatic orange coloured

---

[17] (Spike) nard [Grk.nardos*], Mark 14.3; John 12.3.   [18] cf. Luke 10.39; John 11.32–44.   [19] John 12.3,5; the cost approached one year's pay for a labourer, cf. Matt.20.2.   [20] ct. the women who bought, prepared, and brought spices to anoint the Lord's body, but all too late, Mark 16.1–8; Luke 24.1–9.   [21] The Crocus sativus, Song 4.14† [= Grk.krokos].

stigmas. The latter are collected, dried and crushed for a seasoning and colouring agent in food and drink preparation.[22]

This flower is delicately beautiful and fragrant, a quite different addition to the beloved's descriptive range in the Song.

Calamus. The word [Heb.qaneh] is used in a number of ways in the Old Testament. Fundamental to all of these is the idea of something stalk or reed-like.[23] Calamus is its translation on three occasions, though in two further instances where it is rendered 'cane' the RV margin has 'calamus'.[24] Our primary concern is with an aromatic grass or reed which was imported from India, and possibly Arabia.[25] From this perennial a sweet-smelling substance was extracted which was much sought after for perfumes, cosmetics, flavouring, and even medicine.

The subtle compounding of one fragrant substance with another is all a part of the perfumer's art. The Scripture makes us familiar with this in connection with the production of the holy anointing oil. God's list of contents included four of the chief spices, among which 'sweet calamus' was to be one. This divinely appointed recipe was neither to be made up, nor to be used for any sphere other than God's house, and the priestly personnel who served in it. Solomon, by selecting such a range of the 'chief spices' to speak of the one dear to him, is already pointing beyond normal human attractiveness, to that beauty and fragrance which only God by His Spirit can put upon the one who is dear to Him. He has found already all of these elements of attractiveness in His own well-beloved Son, the Messiah, the Anointed One.

---

[22] Zohary points out that to obtain one gram of saffron stigmas 150 flowers would be required, PB 206.   [23] There are some 62 occurrences of the word [Heb. qaneh] in all. Its main uses are of 1) a 'stalk' of grain, Gen.41.5,22: 2) a 'branch' of the golden lampstand in the Tabernacle, Exod.25.31,32(3) + 20× more: 3) a measuring reed, Ezek.40.3 + 19× more: 4) a reed, e.g. Isa.19.6, also figuratively, e.g. 2 Kings 18.21. See also next note for another use.   [24] For 'calamus' see Exod.30.23 [Heb.qeneh-bhosem]; Song 4.14; Ezek.27.19 [Heb.qaneh]: for (sweet) 'cane' see Isa.43.24; Jer.6.20 [Heb.qaneh-hattobh].   [25] Known commonly as 'Ginger grass', Cymbopogon martinii, Zohary PB 196. Any one of three or four varieties could be meant. Cymbopogon schoenanthus grows wild today in the far Negev, Feliks SoS 25.

Cinnamon. The word [Heb.qinnamon*][26] designates a tree of the laurel family, native to Sri-Lanka, the East Indies and even Vietnam. The wild variety is bushy and evergreen, reaching up to 10 metres in height. Its inner bark contains an oil which is highly valued, and the bark was also used to flavour sweets, as an ingredient in curry powder, and in the incense and perfume industry.

In the Song, it is introduced to extend the range of expression used in extolling the loved one's fragrant appeal. Of course, the impure woman can use this very perfume, along with two others we are yet to consider, to further her clandestine pursuit of men. Having carefully prepared her programme of appeal, she shamelessly thrusts herself at her victim, saying 'Come, let us take our fill of love until the morning'.[27] There is none of this about the maiden in the Song. The beloved finds in her the moral counterpart of nature's perfumes, the fragrant graces exuding true purity.

Like the previous perennial which we considered (calamus), cinnamon is one of the ingredients of the holy anointing oil reserved for use in God's house, and by the priesthood.[28] He counts his loved one, in all her varied fragrance, as set apart solely for him, too!

Aloes. This term [Heb. ´ahaloth*] seems to identify a tall tree, as the masculine form of the word 'lign-aloes', is used in parallel with the fragrant and massive 'cedar trees' in Numbers 24.6.[29] This tree, commonly called 'eaglewood', is the source of a fragrant and resinous oil which is extracted from its timber. This is used

---

[26] Cinnamon [Heb.qinnamon* = Grk.kinnamomon*] is the Laurus Cinnamomum Zeylanicum. (Feliks SoS 24f, equates this with 'cassia' [Heb.qetsi ´ah, and qiddah = Cinnamomum cassia, Exod.30.24; Ps.45.8[9]; Ezek.27.19]. This is unlikely as in Exod.30.23f both spices, cinnamon and cassia, are separately identified as ingredients in the holy anointing oil). In the OT it is its character as a perfume that is specified, Exod.30.23; Prov.7.17; Song 4.14. In the NT it is clearly one of the much sought after items of trade, Rev.18.13.   [27] See Prov.7.1–27, especially vv.17f.   [28] Exod.30.23, where it is supplemented by the word 'sweet' [Heb.qinneman-besem].   [29] This is likely if the 'lign-aloes' [Heb. ´ahalim, masc*] of Num.24.6, which are clearly trees, are identical with that which is described by

still for spice and perfume. It grows in East Africa and North India.

In the Song 'aloes' occurs only in the beloved's descriptive catena concerning his loved one. It finds its closest parallel in Psalm 45 where the royal wedding garments are redolent with its fragrant perfume, mingled with myrrh as in the Song. The messianic significance of that Psalm is obvious. Once Balaam 'saw that it pleased the Lord to bless Israel', he exclaimed that Israel was 'as lign-aloes which the Lord hath planted'.[30] Each cycle in the Song must bring Israel closer to God's determined purposes of grace for her.

It must be remarkable to some that the only New Testament reference to 'aloes' has to do with our Lord.[31] If Joseph of Aramathaea, a secret disciple, had sought and obtained Pilate's permission to honourably bury the body of Jesus, then Nicodemus, who at first had approached Jesus by night, also contributed his part to that burial. He brought 'a mixture of myrrh and aloes, about a hundred pound weight'. Was not this act of daring devotion to the one they loved precious to God? Had He not already unfolded that this was His sovereign purpose for that body which He had prepared for His beloved Son?[32] Mary had ravished her Lord's heart by anointing His body in anticipation of His burial, and the house was filled with its fragrance. Now God would see to it that the tomb itself also would be filled, through this timely and fragrant concern for His beloved. Mary's one pound of spikenard, poured out by one who was looking beyond the tomb, must be more precious than this embalming with a

---

[29] *cont.* our feminine term. This seems to receive further confirmation in Prov.7.17, where the masculine form is found along with myrrh and cinnamon as in Song 4.14 where the feminine form [Heb. ´ahaloth*] is used; it is found elsewhere only at Ps.45.8[9] where it is linked with myrrh and cassia. The tree's technical name is Aquillaria agallocha, and is identified as the aromatic aloes.   [30] Song 4.14; Ps.45.8[9]; Num.24.6.   [31] John 19.38–42, for 'aloes' [Grk. ´aloe†], v.39. Some claim that the 'aloes' of note 30 was also used, along with myrrh, for embalming. Others propose that embalming aloes is Aloe vera, which is a plant rather than a tree. It was used widely in Egypt for embalming, and became cultivated in other countries of the Near East including Israel.   [32] Isa.53.9.

massive one hundred pounds of myrrh and aloes which was motivated by the desire to preserve the body in death,[33] rather than by the hope of an early resurrection. How that intimate fellowship which Mary had enjoyed over the years enriched, and made more spiritually intelligent, her gift of gifts. We shall see further the appropriateness of the introduction of this myrrh and aloes combination at the end of chapter 4 of the Song when we give attention to the significance of the third cycle of the book, which points to the first advent of the Messiah, and its ramifications for salvation history.[34]

Frankincense. This is the name [Heb.lebhonah*][35] given to a species of medium-sized shrub native to India, Arabia, and East Africa,[36] and to the gum which it produces. As with myrrh, whilst the gum does exude from leaves and twigs, the output may be multiplied by incising the stems of the bush; it is also bitter to the taste. Droplets of the resin are whitish when they initially solidify, are brittle and appear like so many glittering jewels. The resin was collected, and transported over the ancient trade routes to the ready markets for it. Because it was so highly and pleasantly aromatic when burned as incense, it was always in great demand. To this day, it is used in the more elaborate ceremonies of Christendom.[37] It was used medicinally also.

In the Song frankincense is used three times. In the last of these, the beloved introduces this fragrant shrub from far-off lands in plurality among the many others in his 'paradise garden', so as to assist him to exhaust the description of the delights he finds in his maiden. Notice the relationship to myrrh here: 'with all trees of frankincense, myrrh and aloes, with all the chief spices'.[38] The

---

[33] cf. John 11.44, also v.39; Ps.16.10; Acts 2.27f.   [34] See p.226.   [35] The word is derived from a verb [Heb.labhen] meaning 'to be white', which is used of moral, Ps.51.9; Isa.1.18, and ethical purity, Dan.11.35; cf. also the adjective [Heb. labhan] meaning 'white' describing the manna, Exod.16.31, and the wearing of white garments which signified joy and cheerfulness, Eccles.9.8. The word 'moon' [Heb.lebhanah‡] is from the same root, being used as a simile of the maiden's beauty in Song 6.10.   [36] The genus Boswellia, Zohary PB 197; more particularly Boswellia carterii, DNTT 2.293f.   [37] The resin known as Boswellia sacra, Zohary.   [38] Song 4.14.

other two references describe the fragrance associated with the king's palanquin, and designate the hill to which he temporarily retires. In each of these instances frankincense follows myrrh, is closely associated with it, and both are used in the singular: his palanquin is 'perfumed with myrrh and frankincense, with all the powders of the merchant', and he intends going 'to the mountain of myrrh, and to the hill of frankincense'.[39]

The Old Testament references to 'frankincense' outside the Song are instructive.[40] We learn first that it was one of the four ingredients used in the preparation of the most holy incense. This was an essential element in Israel's God-prescribed service, and regarding the incense it was to be 'holy for the Lord'.[41] The compounded incense, was to be burned each morning and each evening on the Golden Altar. Frankincense apart from other spices was to be put upon the meal offering, and specifically upon the meal offering of first fruits.[42] It was also to be placed upon each pile of shewbread 'that it may be to the bread for a memorial, even an offering made by fire unto the Lord'.[43] All of this demanded some provision for it storage in the Temple.[44] Yet, the Lord complains through Isaiah that His people did not bring Him what He had asked of them, frankincense included.[45] Conversely, all too often, because of the sin of God's people, the most detailed attention to these external demands as a formality could not avert God's determined judgment of them, a fact so often insisted upon by the prophets.[46] Ceremonial apart from obedience is not acceptable to God.[47]

The New Testament knows of only One who rightfully is linked

---

[39] Song 3.6; 4.6. In the former, it is clearly burned as a perfume.

[40] [Heb.lebhonah*] occurs 18 times in addition to the 3 in the Song; 17 of these are associated with its use in God's house.   [41] Exod.30.34. Note the addition of 'pure' [Heb.zakkah]; here it is paralleled by a summary term for the other 'sweet spices' [Heb.sammim].   [42] Lev.2.1,2,15,16; 6.15[8]: notice none was to be placed on the fine flour sin offering, 5.11, nor on the jealousy meal-offering, Num.5.15.   [43] Lev.24.7; note 'pure' [Heb.zakkah].
[44] 1 Chron.9.29; Neh.13.5,9.   [45] Isa.43.23.   [46] Jer.6.20; cf. Isa.66.3 and Jer.17.25; 41.5.   [47] cf. Ps.50.13f; Isa.1.11; Hos.6.6; Amos 5.21ff; Mic.6.6.

with frankincense. He is the One who was born 'King of the Jews'.[48] His fragrant life, an unfolding and dispensing which delights and satisfies God's holiness, qualified Him to offer Himself without spot to God. Apart from Him, who He is, what He is like, and all that He did for God and for us, creation must end in catastrophe. But He has come, He has lived, and He 'gave himself up for us, an offering and a sacrifice to God for an odour of a sweet smell'. In coming, living, dying and rising, He has become the yea to all the promises of God, providing at one and the same time a sufficient sacrifice and a sweet savour to God.

Looking off to the future, Isaiah longingly awaits the day when the glory of the Lord will have arisen upon Israel. Then 'nations shall come to thy light, and kings to the brightness of thy rising' ... and 'they shall bring gold and frankincense, and shall proclaim the praises of the Lord'.[49] What the magi did at the first advent of the Messiah, the kings are to repeat at His second advent, when 'he shall bear the glory'. This must be the grand climax of God's purpose for Israel and the nations.

Myrrh. This word [Heb.mor*] is one with which we are more familiar. It belongs to a thorny shrub or small tree, a species which is indigenous to Arabia, Ethiopia and Somaliland, and at one time featuring in the area of Jericho.[50] Naturally, it exudes a fragrant, resinous gum from its bark, branches and stems. The flow of this may be accelerated by making incisions in the bark. Surprisingly, the pleasant odour of the gum contrasts dramatically with its bitter taste. This explains the choice of 'myrrh' for its name, which means 'bitter'.[51] The word is extended to include also the gum

---

[48] Frankincense [Grk.libanos*], Matt.2.11, and Rev.18.13 where the future judgment on Babylon brings the merchants of the earth to tears.   [49] Isa.60.6.
[50] Myrrh [Heb.mor] refers to a genus of spices such as Commiphora abyssinica (Berg) Engl., Zohary PB 200; also Feliks SoS 23, and Trever IDB 3.478. Josephus associates it with the Jericho plain, Wars 4.8.3.   [51] For its sweet-smelling property see Song 5.5, 13. The meaning of the adjective [Heb.mar] is clear; its 39 occurrences emphasize bitterness. Recall that Israel named the waters 'Marah, for they were bitter', Exod.15.23, and Naomi's proposal that those who knew her should henceforth call her 'Mara: for the Almighty hath dealt very bitterly with me', Ruth 1.20.

which the bush produces. The resin eventually solidifies into a crystalline form, though this may be readily dissolved in oil for use in various compounded perfumes in which it was an important ingredient.[52] It is used as a soothing agent medicinally, and as a means of dulling the senses to lessen the effect of pain.[53] Then, it had a prominent place in the manufacture of cosmetics and perfumes.[54] In particular, it was one of the ingredients a double portion of which was required for the divinely appointed holy anointing oil used in God's house. Each of the four spices selected for this, myrrh included, belong to the category of the 'chief spices'.[55]

In the Song, myrrh has the chief place among the fragrances, being mentioned eight times.[56] Only two of these are concerning the maiden, and these both follow her beloved's visit to 'Myrrh Mountain'. Only then is he able to adopt myrrh in his description of her, and make her his own possession by 'gathering my myrrh with my spice'.[57] The remainder of the references all have to do with him. The first and last occurrences both describe him as she sees him. At the beginning he is to her 'as a bundle of myrrh (that is, a sachet of the crystallized perfumed gum) that lieth betwixt my breasts'. In this instance he adds to her his own peculiar fragrance as he is given his place in the midst of her affections. In the final use of myrrh, she describes the lips of her glorious, though absent one, as 'dropping liquid myrrh', as though fresh from the incised shrub itself.[58] A similar pairing of the solid and liquid forms is found in connection with Solomon's palanquin 'perfumed with myrrh and frankincense, with all powders of the merchant', in contrast to the

---

[52] For the solid form see Song 1.13 'a bundle of myrrh', and for the liquid form see Song 5.5 'my hands dropped with myrrh, and my fingers with liquid myrrh'. [53] Mark 15.23, consequently refused by our Lord.   [54] In Esth.2.12 it is used in a course of beauty treatment, in Ps.45.8[9] in the perfuming of clothes, and in Prov.7.17 for the perfuming of a bed to incite to lust.   [55] Exod.30.23; its proportions are matched only by the cassia, 500 shekels, among the four spice ingredients.   [56] Myrrh [Heb.mor*] is found at Song 1.13; 3.6; 4.6,14; 5.1,5(2),13: the only other OT references numbering four in all are given in notes 54 and 55. [57] 4.14; 5.1.   [58] 1.13; 5.13.

'liquid myrrh, upon the handles of the bolt' which had dropped there from the beloved's hands.[59]

The key to the whole theme, and to the book as a whole, is the reference in chapter 4.6. The words of her beloved are 'Until the day be cool, and the shadows flee away, I will get me to the mountain of myrrh, and to the hill of frankincense'. We must grasp the parallelism here, of mountain and hill, of myrrh and frankincense. Is it possible for us to miss, then, the significance of this piece of fragrant topography? The mountain and the hill are both in the singular, and have definite articles, so as to keep us from any generalization which the use of the plural in the book invariably suggests. Surely, there can be only one 'Myrrh Mountain' and 'Frankincense Hill'. It is Golgotha, which is presented here in symbol, see pp.178f. The gigantic proportions of the sweet-savour offering which is so precious to God is made tangible in 'mountain' and 'hill' alike. We are being pointed off to the Messiah who loved us 'and gave himself up for us, an offering and a sacrifice to God for an odour of a sweet smell'. He is indeed the sweet savour offering along with an accompanying meal offering which God has provided for Israel and the nations in the future, and for the Church in the present.[60] Myrrh reminds us of the Messiah's anointing, of the office He had, and of the work for God which He came to do among men. What sufferings this involved! How these sufferings have fitted Him officially to serve our needs even now, for He was made 'perfect (officially) through sufferings'. Frankincense reminds us of that holy incense which He caused to ascend for God's own pleasure at the cross. How precious He was to His Father then. Truly the great high priest of His people adds His sweet perfume to our prayers and praises still.

The wise men from afar presented myrrh (along with gold and frankincense) at the birth of Jesus, for the One they had come to worship was born to die. The shadow of Golgotha was cast as

---

[59] Song 5.5.   [60] Eph.5.2. The words 'offering' and 'sacrifice' [Grk.prosphora and thusia] are found together in reverse order in Heb.10.5, 8 (a quotation of Ps.40.6 [7, Heb.zebhach and minchah]) where they clearly refer to the peace and meal offerings respectively. Compare the application of similar sacrificial typology to the believers' giving in Phil.4.18.

far as to Bethlehem. Small wonder then that Joseph and Nicodemus, after His death, bound the body of Jesus in linen clothes, using some one hundred pounds of myrrh (along with aloes).[61] The word 'myrrh', describing the substance [Grk. smyrna*] occurs nowhere else in the New Testament, though, significantly, the verb [Grk.smyrnizomai = to be mingled with myrrh†] is used only once, and that in connection with the Golgotha scene. Before they crucified Him, 'they offered him wine mingled with myrrh: but he received it not'.[62] The theme points to the bitterness of Messiah's lot as 'the man of sorrows'. Throughout the course of His life He suffered, but all this reached its climax in His death. Frankincense was brought by the magi at the King's birth, so that, from the beginning to the end, His life was a sweet savour to His God. The two perfumes were blended in perfect proportions in Him who was acceptable to His God, both officially and personally. Thus He offered Himself without spot in devotion to God and out of love for us.[63]

Praise God for 'Myrrh Mountain' and 'Frankincense Hill'!

---

[61] Matt.2.11; John 19.39f.   [62] Mark 15.23.   [63] Consider the message sent by the glorified Lord to His church at Smyrna [Grk.Smyrna†, and Smyrnaios†]. The two words occur once only at Rev.1.11; 2.8. For the message read Rev.2.8–11. This was sent addressed to a church that was about to pass through suffering, in which it was called to be faithful even to death. The promise held out was 'the crown of life', and that the overcomer 'shall not be hurt of the second death'. Appropriately, the message came from 'the first and the last, which was dead, and lived again'. What balm it is to know such a wonderful Lord in the bitter experiences of life.

10

THE FRAGRANCE THEME

ALTHOUGH our consideration of fragrant plants in the Song has been quite extended, we must not lose the scent yet! One phrase in chapter 4.10 suggests a threefold conclusion for the theme. To appreciate the sense we shall quote the phrase which precedes the one with which we are particularly concerned. We read 'How much better is thy love than wine! and the smell (or, fragrance) of thine ointments (or, perfumes) than all manner of spices!' In this appreciative description of her, her beloved excels her best efforts in speaking of him. For her, his 'love is better than wine', whereas the little word 'much' added in his eulogy of her love, is surpassing. Her love utterly intoxicated him! She says of him 'Thine ointments have a goodly fragrance', but for him, her 'ointments' were much better 'than all manner of spices'. Her fragrance he found unspeakably overpowering![1]

However, we must concentrate on the three elements in our verse with which the perfumer is occupied in the practice of his art. They are, respectively, '**smell**' (or, fragrance), '**ointments**' (or, perfumes), and '**all manner of spices**'. The first of these expresses the end product, the fragrance produced from the perfumer's skilful blending of the other two, namely ointments and spices. We propose considering them in the reverse order.

---

[1] Song 1.2b with 4.10b, and 1.3a with 4.10c.

115

First then, we shall gather what we can of **'all manner of spices'** [Heb.besamim*].² The word is often used generically, to include a whole range of spices from different plants. Numbers of these were brought by the people so that 'the anointing oil' and the 'sweet incense' could be produced for their divinely appointed uses in the Tabernacle. We are reminded, too, that many of these were represented in the gifts which the Queen of Sheba and the kings of the earth brought to Solomon. Spices emit their own evidence of wealth.³ In the Song, it is obvious that such an embracive meaning alone will satisfy the word's use in some places.⁴ In two instances, the word is used to qualify some other specific spice having a specially appealing odour, when it is translated 'sweet'. We read of 'sweet cinnamon' and 'sweet calamus'.⁵ Thirdly, it is used specifically of the 'balsam tree'.

Balsam is a shrub at home in the heat, originating in the desert areas of South-West Arabia and Somaliland.⁶ Similar semi-tropical conditions obtain in the Jericho and Dead Sea area, and there is considerable documenting of the cultivation of balsam plantations there.⁷ As with frankincense and myrrh, a resinous balm exudes from its stems and branches spontaneously, but may be more

---

² The word* appears with three slightly different pointings [Heb.basam, see Song 5.1†, besem, see 4.10,14,16; 8.14‡, and bosem, see 5.13; 6.2‡].   ³ For the Tabernacle see Exod.25.6; 30.23a; 35.8,28, and for those responsible for overseeing them in the Temple, 1 Chron.9.29,30. For the queen's gifts see 1 Kings 10.2,10(2); 2 Chron.9.1,9(2), and those from kings see 1 Kings 10.25; 2 Chron.9.24. Spices represented part of Hezekiah's wealth, 2 Kings 20.13; 2 Chron.32.27; Isa.39.2. All kinds of spices were used when Asa was buried, 2 Chron.16.14. Spices formed an important part of ancient commerce, Ezek.27.22.   ⁴ Song 4.10,16; cf. their association with women's beauty treatment, Isa.3.24; Esth.2.12.   ⁵ Exod. 30.23c,d.   ⁶ Commiphora opobalsamum (gileadensis); note the shrub did not grow in Gilead, and is not to be equated with the proverbial 'balm [Heb.tsori*] of Gilead' referred to in Gen.37.25; 43.11; Jer.8.22; 46.11; 51.8; Ezek.27.17. Zohary PB 198f; Feliks PWB 256ff; ct. Trever 'Spice', IDB 4.431f.   ⁷ See Jos. Ant.14.4.1 'Jericho (where the palm grows, and that balsam which is an ointment of all the most precious, which, upon any incision made in the wood with a sharp stone, distils out thence like a juice)', cf. 4.6.1; 8.6.6; 15.4.2; also Wars 1.6.6; 1.18.5. See also Pliny NH 9.6; 12.54. See Schurer RV 1.288, 298 with n.36 for detailed documentation: 'and the most beautiful and fertile region of Herod's kingdom, the celebrated district of Jericho with its palm and balsam plantations'.

efficiently tapped artificially. The small drops of bright green balm adhere in clusters and change to a brown colour gradually. Once solidified they fall, and are collected. This balm bears the name of the shrub from which it is produced. The balm encourages the healing of wounds, and because the resin was pungent it was a much sought after ingredient in the manufacture of perfumes.

Having named eight specific odiferous plants in describing the one he loves, her beloved still feels the need to be less inhibited in expressing the range of her appeal. It is for this reason that he uses 'spices' generically concerning her. Her perfumes excel the effect of 'all manner of spices'. However the Song's descriptions are generally drawn from living things rather than from manufactured end products. So he calls upon the contrasting influences of the north and south winds to 'blow upon my garden, that the spices thereof may flow out', thus accentuating their diffusion.[8] We might well ask 'Who then is this, that even the wind(s) obey him?' How well he knows the delicate balance of cold and heat, rain and warmth, the blustering and even threatening north, and the gentle south winds.

When the maiden speaks of her beloved's cheeks as 'a bed of spices', she probably has in view the association of the word with the holy anointing oil. To her, he is the one who has been anointed 'with the oil of gladness above thy fellows'. He is the anointed one with 'the precious oil upon the head, that ran down upon the beard'. It is by means of his anointing that his cheeks are so fragrant to her.[9] When she unfolds to the daughters of Jerusalem that her 'beloved is gone down to his garden, to the beds of spices, to feed in the gardens, and to gather lilies', she is revealing where his interests lie. He is enchanted with gardens where the very constituents of his own fragrant anointing are found in multiplied beds of the living spices. The mountains are not the natural habitat of balsam, as we have seen, so a more general reference to 'spices' is to be preferred in the maiden's appeal 'Make haste, my beloved,

---

[8] Both of these references illustrate the generalizing use of 'spices' [Heb.besem], Song 4.10,16.   [9] 5.13; cf. Exod.25.6; 30.23; 35.28. For the Messiah's anointing see Ps.45.7[8] = Heb.1.9; Ps.133.2.

and be thou like a roe or a young hart upon the mountains of spices'.[10]

We have only two further references to the word in the Song. The translation 'with all the chief spices' in the first of these, superficially favours our acceptance of a general significance here too. Nonetheless, a careful consideration of the structure of the verses treating the group of spices in chapter 4.13b–14 militates against this. Notice the threefold grouping marked off by means of the repeated 'with' [Heb. `im]. These provide us with the literary lines of demarkation, supplemented by the use of the conjunction 'and'. We set this out, indicating also the uses of singular and plural:

Table 1

Plural	Singular
Henna(s)	
with (Spike)nard(s)	
	(Spike)nard
	and Saffron
	Calamus
	and Cinnamon
with all trees of Frankincense	
	Myrrh
and Aloes	
with all the chief balsams (spices)	

From this it appears that each of the items in the list were intended to describe a particular genus of aromatic plant, and the closing phrase should read 'with all the chief balsams', that is, those of the approximately one hundred varieties that are particularly resinous. There are nine separately identifiable odiferous plants in the list therefore.

---

[10] Song 6.2; 8.14.

One other mention of our word is found in the Song. In this instance it is the balsam resin that is intended, as the beloved rehearses his appropriation of the one he loves: 'I have come into my garden ... I have gathered my myrrh with my spice' (i.e. my balsam).[11] The spices of the Song have made their contribution to its emphasis upon fragrance, but here 'spice' may form an ingredient in a spiced wine as the context speaks of union and communion in terms of eating and drinking. We have an anticipation of the great messianic banquet in this. She expresses her unashamed joy as she anticipates bringing him, at last, to her mother's house when 'I would cause thee to drink of spiced wine'.[12] So much for the phrase 'all manner of spices'.

We should give some attention now to **'thine ointments'** [Heb. shemen]. The word occurs frequently in the Old Testament. It is literally 'oil', and is used sometimes to express the idea of 'fatness', prosperity etc. Rather more specifically, it means '(olive) oil', which is a very rich product indeed. Olive trees dominate the scenery of many parts of Israel. The attractive evergreen, ranging from 5 to 7 metres high, develops an ever-thickening, gnarled trunk, and has an extremely long life. The fruit is picked and crushed to obtain its precious oil. Olive oil was the chief fuel used for lighting. It was used medicinally. Unquestionably, olive oil in the service of God predominates in Old Testament usage, the pages of Exodus, Leviticus, and Numbers accounting for over one half of the references to the word. These include oil with which the house, its furniture, and personnel were anointed. Olive oil fuelled its lampstand providing light for service in the holy place. Its oil was an essential part of the sacrificial system. The cleansing procedures of the healed leper, and the God-appointed arrangements at the concluding of a nazirite vow, called for the symbolic use of olive oil. Prophet and king alike, as well as the priest, were anointed. Truly, the olive tree was the first choice for the honour of being king of the trees. Yet, when this was proposed it asked 'Should I leave my fatness, wherewith by me they honour God and man?'[13]

---

[11] Song 8.2.   [12] 8.2.   [13] Jud.9.8f.

The two references to 'ointment' in the Song focus attention upon another use of the olive's fatness. It provided the base for the production of a whole range of perfumes. Pure and transparent in character, golden in colour, penetrating and softening in effect,[14] it was the ideal agent for blending, extending, and preserving many types of fragrant substances. It was with pure oil that the perfumer began. In itself it is virtually odourless. With the addition of different spices however, a wide variety of fragrant perfumes could be produced. The 'ointment' of the Song refers to such skilfully and subtly blended end-products of the perfumer.

The maiden's opening eulogy regarding her beloved includes reference to the actual 'goodly fragrance' of 'thine ointments'. The plural here indicates something of the range of appeal that his scents make to her senses. But is there not something 'better than precious ointment'? Most certainly, and she finds this in the one she loves. For if 'A good name is better than precious ointment', then to her his 'name is as ointment poured forth'.[15] The play on words in the verse is obvious, where 'Thine ointments' [Heb. shemanekha] is matched by 'thy name' [Heb.shemekha]. The 'name' in Scripture is virtually a code-word representing the sum of all that can be known of a person, all those separate unfoldings which combine to tell him out. The name thus perfectly expresses all that the person is; not so much what he can do, or what he is officially, but rather who he is personally.[16] Now her beloved, as he had made himself known to her, was not simply as ointment, however precious that might be. He was himself 'as ointment poured forth' [Heb.shemen turaq], diffused abroad without restriction for the appreciation of those whose spirits were sensitive to his perfections, as their sense of smell would respond appreciatively to fine perfumes.

The only other reference to 'ointment' in the Song features in the beloved's description of his loved one. Once again we note how he excels her in his appreciation of the richly varied fragrance

---

[14] Oil prevented the desiccation of the skin in the hot Near Eastern climate. Perfumes and ointments were usually used after bathing, Ruth 3.3; 2 Sam.12.20; ct. 14.2.   [15] Eccles.7.1; Song 1.3(2).   [16] TBD 56ff.

she exudes. For him the smell of her ointments was much better 'than all manner of spices'.[17]

Lastly, we consider the word **smell** [Heb.reach] which, as a theme permeates the Song. The word, properly meaning 'breath', does not refer to the sense of smell but to the odour emitted or experienced. Generally it refers to the appealing and fragrant odours.[18] It is used eight times in the Song, more than in any other Old Testament book except Leviticus and Numbers. The Song adopts the word to describe the fragrance of plants, and forests,[19] and also of the maiden's garments, and even of her nose (or breath).[20] Finally, the pleasing fragrance of the beloved's perfumes, and those of the maiden, stimulates mutual praise.[21]

Of course, one needs a delicate sense of smell to appreciate the subtle and amazingly varied appeals of perfumes. Perhaps among the seeing, hearing, tasting and touching senses, all granted us so as to fit us for this physical and tangible world, the sense of smell surpasses all in the subtlety of its discrimination. The lovers in the Song have this delicate and discerning appreciation of their partner's fragrance, though the maiden only rises to this means of describing her beloved on one occasion.[21]

The very first association of the word is definitive for the bulk of Biblical usage. We read that 'the Lord smelled the sweet savour' when Noah, on his emergence from the ark, offered burnt offerings on the altar he had built.[22] In the Mosaic legislation the Lord said 'My oblation, and my bread for my offerings made by fire, of a sweet savour unto me, shall ye observe to offer unto me in their due season'.[23] There are 39 such uses of this virtually technical term in the sacrificial ritual of the Pentateuch, and Ezekiel supple-

---

[17] Song 4.10.　　　[18] Used of an objectionable smell in Exod.5.21, where it refers figuratively to Israel's reputation.　　　[19] Song 2.13; 7.13[14] and 4.11 respectively. Note the first 2 are used literally of plants, where a springtime setting is in view. In 4.11 it is used figuratively; cf. Hos.14.6[7].　　　[20] 4.11 of the maiden's garments; cf. Ps.45.8[9] of the king-bridegroom's garments; of the maiden's nose in Song 7.8[9].　　　[21] 1.3 of his, 1.12 and 4.10 of hers.
[22] Gen.8.21.　　　[23] Num.28.2 marg.

ments this array with another four references.[24] In all of these instances it is clear that the Lord could find His rest, His satisfaction and delight, only in the God-appointed offering made by fire and in that one who brought it desiring thus to make an atonement for his own deficiencies.

In the New Testament the equivalent word for 'odour' [Grk. osme*] is used sparingly yet significantly. Mary of Bethany anointed Jesus with very precious ointment and 'the house was filled with the odour'.[25] She was in the presence of the One whose name was to her 'as ointment poured forth'. That same One loved us 'and gave himself up for us, an offering and a sacrifice to God for an odour of a sweet smell'.[26] God led in triumph His servants and diffused abroad through their preaching 'the savour' of His knowledge. They became 'a sweet savour of Christ unto God, in them that are being saved, and in them that are perishing; to the one a savour from death unto death; to the other a savour from life unto life'.[27] Even the sacrificial practical support given by the Philippian church to Paul is described as 'the things that came from you, an odour of a sweet smell, a sacrifice acceptable, well-pleasing to God'.[28] This reminds us of that fragrant odour which best expresses the pleasing character of a sacrifice that was acceptable to God.[29]

The Old Testament daily burnt offerings, accompanied by their prescribed meal and drink offerings, pointed forward to that once-for-all offering which alone could truly satisfy, yea ravish the heart of God. Had it not been God's purpose in creating man that he should glorify God and enjoy Him forever? Who but the Messiah, the Son of God, has ever lived the life which glorified God upon the earth? In that body which God had prepared for Him, He

---

[24] Apart from the two references in n.21f, for the phrase 'sweet savour' [Heb.reach nichoach] see Exod.29.18,25,41; Lev.1.9,13,17; 2.2,9,12; 3.5,16; 4.31; 6.15[8],21[14]; 8.21,28; 17.6; 23.13,18; 26.31; Num.15.3,7,10,13,14,24; 18.17; 28.6,8,13,24,27; 29.2,6,8,13,36. Also in Ezekiel at 6.13; 16.19; 20.28,41. 'Smell' [Heb.reach] occurs totally only 58 times in the OT.   [25] John 12.3.   [26] Eph.5.2.
[27] 2 Cor.2.14,16(2).   [28] Phil.4.18.   [29] Note that 'sweet savour' in OT [Heb.reach nichoach] = NT [Grk.osme euodias; replaces Hebrew in LXX of e.g. Gen.8.21 etc.] at Eph.5.2; Phil.4.18. Also see 'aroma' [Grk.euodia*], 2 Cor.2.15.

grew in wisdom, stature, and favour with God and men, and found His delight in serving His God and Father. He alone could say 'Lo, I am come (In the roll of the book it is written of me) to do thy will, O God'.[30] Of Him alone could God say 'This is my beloved Son, in whom I am well pleased'.[31] In the life of His own Son, God found the true counterpart of that perfection typified in the meal offerings of the first covenant. How much more was needed if propitiation was to be effected for all those who could never minister to the heart of God as they ought. Yes, the Son who lived a holy life must crown that life by a vicarious death. The meal offering of His life must both precede and supplement the burnt offering of His death, whilst the drink offering, expressing His un-broken joy in God, must find its crowning outpouring at Golgotha. Small wonder that it was reserved for Him to say 'I glorified thee on the earth, having accomplished the work which thou hast given me to do'.[32] This was the one sweet savour offering toward which all others pointed, and in which they find their fulfilment. The believer's acceptance finds its guarantee, despite all the shortcomings even in his holiest attainments, and his reconciliation is effected, in the One who 'gave himself up for us, an offering and a sacrifice to God for an odour of a sweet smell'.

For those out of every generation of Israel who are precious to their God, there has been no other true basis of acceptance than this: that they should 'love the Lord thy God with all thine heart, and with all thy soul, and with all thy might'.[33] One alone could and has atoned for their deficiencies in meeting such a demand. Wonderful Messiah, the child born to them, the Son given to them, the One whose 'delight [Heb.haricho, lit. his scent (from reach)] shall be in the fear of the Lord'.[34] This Messiah, who has ministered such fragrant delight to His Father's heart, is to draw to Himself 'with cords of a man, with bands of love' a nation which will bring forth both the fruits and the fragrances in the promised kingdom of God. Soon He will put His own beauty upon them,

---

[30] Ps.40.7f[8f]; Heb.10.7,9.   [31] Matt.3.17; 17.5 and //'s; 2 Pet.1.17. The latter reference clearly establishes that the transfiguration scene anticipates the future Messianic kingdom.   [32] John 17.4.   [33] Deut.6.5; Matt.22.37; Mark 12.30; Luke 10.27.   [34] Isa.11.3.

and diffuse His own fragrance through them, for all to see and smell.[35] It is this most intimate and fragrant relationship, the historical course of which is attractively portrayed to us in the Song. Beyond the couple and the cosmetics, we scent the Christ and the covenant people in the purpose of God.

We pause for a moment to review this truly overpoweringly fragrant atmosphere of the Song. There is not its equal in such brief compass anywhere. We have considered the eight odiferous plants specifically named,[36] all of which display something of the variety and fullness of the Creator's handiwork. To these we have added a ninth, balsam, in this chapter. In these things we detect something of His own fragrance, and His desire to find satisfaction and delight reciprocated from the works of His hands. It would be surprising in the extreme were His new creation work to be lacking anything in the delight it brings to Him. In the Son of His love, the Beginning of this new creation of God, He has found all His delights. This Saviour God will not stop until He has brought many sons to glory, each with the beauty and fragrance of His Son displayed and diffused through them. Even now the fragrant graces of the Lover of our souls are savoured by Him, and by all around us, as we long for His presence and linger in it increasingly. Look up, then, and plead 'Make haste, my beloved, and be thou like to a roe or to a young hart upon the mountains of spices'.[37]

---

[35] Matt.21.43; Ps.90.17. [36] In chap. 9. [37] Song 8.14.

11

THE CYCLE OF THE SEASONS AND THEIR PLACE IN THE SONG

SEASONAL CHANGES affect the scenery of the land; fauna and flora alike being influenced immensely by them. There is need to consider, therefore, the cycle of the seasons in Israel, and how this is reflected in the Song. This, too, has its spiritual significance.

You will recall those majestic, and mighty words of God on the fourth day of Genesis 1. 'And God said, Let there be lights in the firmament of the heaven to divide the day from the night; and let them be for signs, and for seasons, and for days and years: and let them be for lights in the firmament of the heaven to give light upon the earth: and it was so. And God made the two great lights; the greater light to rule the day, and the lesser light to rule the night: he made the stars also. And God set them in the firmament of the heaven to give light upon the earth, and to rule over the day and over the night, and to divide the light from the darkness: and God saw that it was good. And there was evening and there was morning, a fourth day'.[1] The Spirit of God unfolds the three purposes in view in making the luminaries. First, they would divide day from night, for light and darkness are part of God's appointed order for His creation.[2] Second, they were to be for signs and for seasons and for days and years. Third, they were to give light.

---

[1] Gen.1.14–19. [2] Ps.104.20; also Gen.1.4f.

125

The words 'signs' and 'seasons' are found in numerous Old Testament passages. For our purpose, the word **signs** [Heb. ˋoth = Grk.semeion] related to these created bodies, points the observer to something beyond their external splendour. Through them we are to learn, and that knowledge is intended to influence our lives, and not merely to fill us with wonder. These great monuments to God's creatorial will and word, together with other phenomena within the field of nature, send their signals to us.

Perhaps the most common proof of this is expressed in our Lord's familiar words when challenged to show 'a sign from heaven'. He said 'When it is evening, ye say, It will be fair weather: for the heaven is red. And in the morning, It will be foul weather today: for the heaven is red and lowring'.[3] The rainbow in the cloud is another of God's appointed signs for 'it shall be a token [Heb. ˋoth] of a covenant between me and the earth'.[4] The cycles of the sun and the moon were unchanging, so that they became symbols of permanence.[5] Consequently, any extra-ordinary functioning conveyed its own message.[6] The thick darkness at Golgotha was a cause of terror to many, but also it was designed to teach the impenetrable character of the mystery of the Messiah's sacrificial suffering.[7] The events leading up to the over-throw of that universal rebellion against the purpose of God for His Christ, will be accompanied by startling and significant changes among the astral bodies. For God 'will shew wonders in the heavens and in the earth, blood, and fire, and pillars of smoke. The sun shall be turned into darkness, and the moon into blood, before the great and terrible day of the Lord come'.[8] After that terrible day, when 'The kingdom of the world is become the kingdom of our Lord, and of his Christ', the great lights will il-luminate a period of unsurpassed glory by their multiplied light. Then 'the light of the moon shall be as the light of the sun, and

[3] Matt.16.1ff.   [4] Gen.9.13, see whole paragraph, and for 'token' or 'sign' [Heb. ˋoth], vv.12,17.   [5] Ps.72.5, we have noted already that this is one of Solomon's psalms; 89.36[37]. Both psalms relate to the purpose of God to be established through the Messiah.   [6] Josh.10.12; 2 Kings 20.8–11//Isa.38.7. [7] See Matt.27.45–56//Mark 15.33//Luke 23.44–49//John 19.28–30.   [8] Joel 2.30f[3.3f]; cf. 2.10; 3.15[4.15]; Isa.13.10; 24.23; Ezek.32.7f; Amos 5.20; 8.9; Zeph.1.15; Matt.24.29//Mark 13.24f//Luke 21.25f; Acts 2.20; Rev.6.12f; 8.12.

the light of the sun shall be sevenfold, as the light of seven days, in the day that the Lord bindeth up the hurt of his people, and healeth the stroke of their wound'.[9]

The word **'seasons'** [Heb.mo˘edh] in Genesis 1 demands even more careful consideration with the interpretation of the Song in view.[10] The parallel term 'signs' seems to demand that we see more here than a reference to the divinely appointed seasons of the year. We are being directed to those sacred seasons appointed by God which are fixed by the moon's appearance, for, we read, 'He appointed the moon for seasons'.[11] The great lights of the heavens, among other functions, were to alert the people of God to those God-appointed occasions when they should come together in worship and praise.

The daily burnt offerings were the very basic divine appointment.[12] All calendars take account of days in arriving at their systematization. Not only the daily cycle, but also the annual cycle of the sun, with its two distinct equinoxes, provided the sacred year with its boundaries. Spring had its festival of the Passover/Unleavened Bread.[13] Autumn witnessed the celebration of harvest home, in that joyous festival of Tabernacles.[14] It is clear that these festivals are bound to the seasons, which in turn are vitally related to the unchanging cycle of the sun under the providential goodness of God. Firstfruits of the barley harvest were an essential part of the Spring festival season, and its availability was dependent upon the sun. Similarly, the ingathering of fruit was intimately related to the climax of the agricultural cycle.[15] The agriculturalist must be influenced by this annual cycle, and his concern will be, of necessity, with a solar calendar. The solar year

---

[9] Isa.30.29; 1 QH 7.24f; bT. Sanh.91b.   [10] It is derived from the verb 'to appoint' [Heb.ya˘adh]; the fem. noun meaning congregation [Heb. ˘edhah] refers to a company of people gathered by making an appointment; our word, the masc. noun 'season' [Heb.mo˘edh] may be an appointed time, though it mostly refers to an appointed place in the phrase 'the tabernacle/tent of the congregation', Exod.27.21 and often.   [11] Ps.104.19.   [12] Exod.29.38–42; Num.28.3–8. [13] Exod.12.6,14–19; 13.3–10: note here, 'it shall be for a sign unto thee ... Thou shalt therefore keep this ordinance in its season from year to year'; 23.15; 34.18; Lev.23.5–7; Num.28.16–25.   [14] Lev.23.34–43; Num.29.12–38; Deut.31.10–13. [15] Lev.23.10f,39; Exod.23.16.

is not an exact multiple of days, as our leap years constantly remind us.[16]

The moon, too, has an important place in Israel's sacred festival appointments. The new moon provided the opening marker for each month in the calendar, and this was celebrated by its own special sacrifices.[17] Further, the major festivals, which we have referred to above, commence at full moon in months 1 and 7 respectively.[18] We should note that the lunar month cycle is not made up of an exact number of days either.[19] This explains why Israel's months alternate between 29 and 30 days in duration.

God's sacred calendar, embracing the first seven months of Israel's year as God has appointed it, integrates both the solar and lunar 'seasons', that is, it is a luni-solar calendar. It was the Passover that decreed when the calendar was to commence for them. Exactly one hundred and seventy seven days, or six lunar months, lay between the opening of the Passover and the opening of Tabernacles each year.[20] With this the divine appointments for the nation were to be climaxed. From this it is obvious that there is an association between the cycle of nature and the salvation history of the nation of Israel. And as surely as nature runs its divinely controlled course, so there are divine appointments in the nation's experience. In referring to the former, the word 'providence' is often used. We must not allow this to cloud our understanding of what is involved. Our God is not only the creator of the universe, but He is also its almighty sustainer. The so-called 'laws of nature' are the ongoing evidences of our God's sovereign control of that which He has originated. However, in saying this we so often fail to glory in its comforting corollary, that the God

---

[16] There are 365.2422 days in a solar year, hence the addition of one extra day every fourth year. [17] Num.28.11-15 for the regular New Moon offerings, and 29.1-6 for the convocation at the beginning of the seventh month; cf. 10.10; Ps.81.3[4] for the blowing of the silver trumpets. [18] Unleavened Bread and Tabernacles commence on the 15th of the month. [19] There are 29.5306 days in a lunar month. Complications arise when the two calendars are combined, involving introducing a leap month periodically. [20] From the 14th Nisan/Abib to the 15th Tishri, our March/April to September/October; there are 190 days from the preparatory 10th day of the first month to the eighth day following Tabernacles in the seventh month.

7. 'Feed thy kids beside the shepherds tents', Song 1.8. Kids of the goats on Mount Carmel. See pp. 191, 323.

8. Solomon 'spake of trees from the cedar that is in Lebanon even unto the hyssop that springeth out of the wall', I Kgs. 4.32[5.13]. See pp. 65, 67f.

9. 'Be thou like a roe or a young hart upon the mountains', Song 2.17. Gazelles in the wilderness of Zin in the Negev.

9

10. 'I see an almond tree . . .', Jer. 1.11f. A flowering almond hastens on the incoming spring season.

11. 'The fig tree ripeneth her green figs', Song 2.13. See p. 70f.

10

11

12 & 13. 'Winter is past . . . the flowers appear on the earth', Song 2.11f, See 81f.

13

12

of our salvation is controlling the various phases, times, seasons, of the history of the race, and particularly that programme 'under the sun' to which Israel is essential. In unfolding a calendar which is only taken up with seven consecutive months of the year, and in insisting that the sacred festivals in this programme matched the major agricultural seasons, a divine mystery is made clear. On the one hand, as the King of the ages,[21] the whole time-scale of His purpose is under His sovereign control, yet there is a certain main thrust to history which is demonstrably His direct will. On the other hand, we learn that the creation over which man was given dominion at the beginning, is still bound up with him and his fortunes. As surely as the autumn crowns the hopes emerging at springtime, so the exodus of Israel from Egypt is a guarantee of their bountiful ingathering in the land which God has promised them. Granted that the God of Abraham, Isaac, and Israel has appointed a passover work with its associated resurrection firstfruits to the nation, then it must follow that the joy of ingathering, even their future kingdom glory, is equally assured. We might add that, when the glad day of 'harvest home' for all God's promises to the nation arrives, creation too, nature itself, will manifest the happy harmony enjoyed between God's redeemed people and the whole of His fair creation.[22]

We are reminded of something of this in those familiar lines

> Deep in the unfathomable mines
> Of never failing skill;
> He treasures up His bright designs,
> And works His sovereign will.
>
> Blind unbelief is sure to err,
> And scan His work in vain;
> God is His own interpreter,
> And He will make it plain.

Small wonder that man, in turning his back upon the true God, deified the heavenly bodies themselves. Israel was forbidden to follow the pattern of paganism in this.[23]

---

[21] Rev.15.3.   [22] Isa.11.6–9; Rom.8.20ff; Rev.22.1–5.   [23] Deut.4.19; 17.3; 2 Kings 21.3,5; Jer.8.2; 10.2; Ezek.8.16.

After Noah's sacrifice to the Lord when he had emerged from the ark, the Lord's merciful purpose for the earth is recorded. 'While the earth remaineth, seedtime and harvest, and cold and heat, and summer and winter, and day and night shall not cease'.[24] God's faithfulness in this respect is sung millennia later. The psalmist, desperately concerned that the sanctuary had been destroyed and that the adversary continued to reproach God's people, cried out 'O deliver not the soul of thy turtledove unto the wild beast'. In that same psalm the singer found great comfort in the fact that 'The day is thine, the night also is thine: thou hast prepared the light and the sun. Thou hast set all the borders of the earth: thou hast made summer and winter'.[25] We propose considering the cycles of time as they become apparent in the Song armed with some of this background.

The Luminaries in the Song

The great luminaries have their place in the Song. First, there is the **sun** [Heb.shemesh‡], its blazing summer heat scorching the skin of the maiden as she had to guard the vineyards of her mother's sons. Conscious of this now that the eyes of her beloved are upon her, she says, 'Look not upon me, because I am swarthy, because the sun hath scorched me'.[26] In the second use of 'sun' in our translation, another word for sun [Heb.chammah‡, lit. the hot one] is linked with that second great luminary, the **moon** [Heb. lebhanah, lit. the white one].[27] In describing the loved one's over-coming attractiveness, the onlookers say that she is 'fair as the moon, clear as the sun'.[28] The opening phrase of this sentence, 'Who is she . . .?' is one of several important punctuating refrains in the Song. The poem has no anti-climax. The couple are united at last. Both moon and sun here are being used as similes to describe the splendour of the Shulammite. Our attention is focus-ed on the dawn of a new day, a day in which the moon precedes the sun, the evening leads through to the morning. The history of

---

[24] Gen.8.22.   [25] Ps.74.19,17.   [26] Song 1.6.   [27] In the same word family are 'frankincense' [Heb.lebhonah, because of its whiteness, see 3.6; 4.6,14‡], and Lebanon [Heb.lebhanon, see 3.9; 4.8(2),11,15; 5.15; 7.4[5]‡].   [28] 6.10; cf. Rev.12.1.

Israel has followed this divinely appointed pattern, as has the story of mankind more generally. The beginning, when seen in the light of the predetermined end, is like the evening. But the light is a derived and reflected one at best, and a failing one at worst. The evening darkens into the blackness of night if the moon fails. And such will be the case when the tribulation, the great one, finally breaks upon this unsuspecting world. For 'The sun shall be turned into darkness, and the moon into blood, before the great and terrible day of the Lord come'.[29] Yet the bright purpose of God cannot fail. A remnant within the nation is to be a light in those dark times, and their trying days are to be bright with light when the sun of righteousness arises with healing in its wings.[30] An evident precursor of all this will be reflected in those who faithfully stand for their God in those desperate times. The Song reveals nothing of their tribulation distress however. It is concerned more with their yearnings for their God as they look forth 'as the morning, fair as the moon, clear as the sun', for the messianic age which will surely dawn.

The Song provides its witness to day and night also. Two of its uses of '**day**' [Heb.yom] direct us to the end of the period of light, as the shadows lengthen and eventually merge into darkness. The other three references focus our attention on specific 'days': that day of the king's espousals, which is 'the day of the gladness of his heart', and that day when the Shulammite's sister is to be spoken for.[31] When it is proposed that the couple move about and enjoy together the open countryside, it was so wise to 'get up early to the vineyards' so as to avoid the heat of the sun. Though true shepherds have a twenty-four hour concern for the flock, perhaps it is never more kindly and considerate than when it ensures that the flock is rested at noon in some welcome shade.[32] Still, '**night**' [Heb.laylah] must come, and for the Song it never appears to do so happily. In chapter 3 it is the maiden's restless period, when, as in a dream, she seeks her beloved.[33] Chapter 5 reverses all this, by recording the beloved's appeal that she might open up to him. He is outside, his head 'filled with dew', his locks 'with the drops

---

[29] Joel 2.31[3.4]; cf. Acts 2.20.   [30] Mal.4.2[3.20].   [31] Day [Heb.yom] Song 2.17; 4.6; 3.11(2); 8.8‡.   [32] 1.7.   [33] Night [Heb.laylah] 3.1; also 3.8; 5.2‡.

of the night'.[34] There is a certain 'fear in the night' for which even mighty men need equipment and expertise in order to safeguard the things which belong to the king.[35] Be assured, however, that 'cold and heat . . . day and night' are within the framework of the purpose of our God.

Seasonal Cycles in Israel

Emphatically, springtime and summer brighten the imagery of the Song, though neither is named in the book. In fact there is no separately identified spring season, nor for that matter autumn, in the Old Testament. As we saw in Genesis, God's promise at Noah's time was that 'summer and winter' should not cease. In the Song we have one reference to winter: 'For, lo, the winter [Heb.sethawt] is past', the only reference to that particular word in the Bible. Although there is no specific reference to 'summer' in the book, there is ample evidence that much of its story is set in that bright season. We need to clarify and establish this.

The winter[36] in Israel has certain distinct characteristics. It is primarily the period of rainfall. This illuminates the word of the beloved to his loved one 'For, lo, the winter is past, the rain is over and gone'.[37] The greater part of the annual rain falls between December and March. Apart from thoroughly soaking the ground, the downpours fill up the great underground reservoirs and man-made cisterns to meet the needs through a long dry summer season. This period of heavy rainfall is introduced and concluded by the early and the latter rains.[38] Without the early rains in October/November time the farmer would be unable to prepare the hard, dry soil by ploughing, and to sow the seed in hope. If the

---

[34] Song 5.2.   [35] 3.8.   [36] The usual word [Heb.choreph] occurs only 7 times.   [37] Song 2.11. See Lev.26.4; Deut.11.14; Ezra 10.9,13; Isa.4.6. In the NT the winter [Grk.cheimon] is referred to 6 times, though twice it is translated tellingly 'foul weather' and 'tempest', Matt.16.3; Acts 27.20. The word includes the ideas of winter and storm. Note that Judaism's 'Feast of Dedication' is a winter festival, John 10.22.   [38] *rain* [Heb.geshem], *former rain* = early or 'autumn' rain [Heb.yoreh or moreh, both derived from the verb yaradh, to come or go down, descend], *latter rain* = 'spring' rain [Heb.malqosh].

latter rains, which normally round off the wet season in March/April were to fail, the final maturing of the grain would be in jeopardy. To quote, 'In the Syrian year there are practically two tides of verdure, one which starts after the early rains of October and continues through the winter, checked by the cold; and one which comes away with greater force under the influence of the latter rains, and more genial airs of spring'.[39]

Winter is also the cold period in the land, though by European standards it would be counted relatively mild. On the coastal plain, frosts are virtually unknown, and even Jerusalem, perched up on the central mountain ridge, might have a flurry of snow for two or three days in a given year, but it does not amount to much. Strictly, the winter is cold relative to the temperatures that obtain in the summer, as the phrase 'cold and heat' suggests.[40]

It should be added that there are two transitional periods between 'summer and winter', though these are not to be equated with our 'spring and autumn'. During the April/May and September/October periods, very hot, dry and dusty winds blow across the land from the desert on the south-east. These are described as the 'east wind' Biblically, even the 'burning wind',[41] the discomforting and disastrous effects of which are well-documented. The humidity drops sharply, the temperature rises dramatically, and all who experience these periods, long that they might be short-lived. Their duration varies, usually between 3 and 14 days, though one extending for three weeks in 1982 was tremendously trying. The periods when these winds blow may be con-

---

[39] G. A. Smith, The Book of the Twelve I.109; also Hist. Geography 64ff.

[40] Gen.8.22. That the cold is felt is apparent, Ps.147.17, and men are glad to gather around the fire, Jer.36.22, as in the Mediterranean area more generally, Acts 28.2. The occasion when Peter warmed himself at the fireside in the courtyard of the high priest's house will be recalled, John 18.18//. This was at night, in Jerusalem, at the Passover season = late March/early April. Of course, in the hill-country there are differences between day and night temperatures of sufficient magnitude to cause one to feel the chill even when it is not winter. [41] *east wind* [Heb.ruach (haq) qadhim, sometimes qidhim alone] see esp. Gen.41.6,23,27; Exod.10.13(2); 14.21; Isa.27.8; Ezek.17.10; Jonah 4.8. For the *burning wind* [Heb.ruach zil`aphoth] as a figure of the Lord's judgment, Ps.11.6.

ceived as the by-product of the winter/summer seasons struggling with one another in order to survive or arrive.

The **summer** which Israel experiences is long, unbroken, and dry, lasting for five months, from May through to mid-October. The temperature only varies from hot to very hot. In 'the heat of the day' people seek out the shade,[42] and the climate generally encourages the outdoor life. Meals are eaten, and many of the domestic tasks are done outside the houses. Leisure time in 'the cool of the day' is pleasantly spent on the patio, or balcony under the sky's canopy.[43]

One specially refreshing mitigating blessing of this otherwise parched period, is the dews that settle upon the coastal plain, south-west slopes of Mount Carmel, and on the hills and mountains of Lower and Upper Galilee. This results from that heat, absorbed by the ground during the heat of the day, being returned into the atmosphere at the cool of the day by radiation, condensing moisture. Those thirsty folk who enjoy the huge, luscious, and most refreshing Galilee water melons, rarely pause to consider where this fruit obtains its flood of juice. They appear well into this dry summer season, and the best melons are never watered. It is the dew that drops its secret, serving the fruit with its gentle distillings in the nights. If the days are dry, the nights in numbers of areas are damp with dew, specially in the August/September period. This is important for the setting of Song 5.2.

The portal to this period is bedecked with a vast range of beautiful wild flowers and fields of waving barley. The air is filled with fragrance and the songs of the birds. As the weeks pass, the fruit trees burst their buds and blossom. The wheat is harvested, the fruit develops and at last is gathered in. It is then that the joy of labour crowned with the blessing of God is entered upon, when the farmer who has done the work is the first to partake of the fruit.

Seasonal Cycles in the Song

From this review of the pattern of the seasons in Israel, we are able to discern more clearly the several phases of the Song's

---

[42] Gen.18.1f.   [43] cf. 3.8.

development. Consider the seasons suggested by the scenery forming the backcloth of the drama from chapter 2.8 through to chapter 5. At the beginning of this the 'winter' season is mentioned, together with its accompanying rains. 'For, lo,' says her beloved, 'the winter is past, the rain is over and gone'. With the winter behind them, he appeals to her to 'Rise up . . . and come away'. He goes on to encourage her response by referring to the attractiveness of the season following winter, without actually naming it. 'The flowers appear on the earth; the time of the singing of birds is come, and the voice of the turtle (dove) is heard in our land'. He would transport her deep into the countryside where the wild flowers and the birds' chorus herald the coming summer. It has not arrived yet, but already its harbingers are in evidence. Similarly, the fig's unripe fruit protruded on the branches calling for the tree to clothe itself in new leaf as the winter passed. Early summer witnesses the vines in blossom, their beauty and fragrance appealing to the hope of a joyous vintage. At the close of chapter 2 then, we are full of the joys of spring and early summer.[44]

The similes and metaphors of chapter 4, however, are drawn, not so much from the potential of nature bursting forth in the spring, but from the benefits and fruitfulness of nature now realized. He refers to 'a piece of a pomegranate', her love is 'better . . . than wine', her orchard of pomegranates are 'with precious fruits'. It is her desire that her beloved should 'eat his precious fruits', and he speaks of having 'drunk my wine'.[45] The spices, too, are all matured, and are even gathered.[46] In all of this, we sense that we have been conducted through a complete cycle, from the winter that is behind us, through the bright and beautiful hopes of spring and early summer, on to the gathered, appropriated fruits at summer's end. We may note also the fact that the bridegroom's head is said to be saturated with dew at the opening of chapter 5.

We suggest that a similar progression through the spring and early summer, and then on to the fruits enjoyed, is to be found again from chapter 6 onwards. Her beloved proposes going down into the garden of nuts 'to see the green plants of the valley, to

---

[44] Song 2.11f; cf. 'the lilies' in 2.16. See v.13.   [45] 4.3,10,13,16; 5.1.
[46] 4.6,10,13,14,16; 5.1.

see whether the vine budded, and the pomegranates were in flower'.[47] Yet the descriptions of the woman he loves in chapter 7 introduce the similes of 'a heap of wheat set about with lilies', the palm tree with its cluster of dates, the clusters of the vine, the smell of apples, and the best wine.[48] That is, from the springtime and early summer promise, his love pursues its path to summer and the fruits enjoyed when the agricultural cycle is over. We might compare her responses as she proposes to her beloved that together they 'go forth into the field', that they might check 'whether the vine hath budded, and its blossom be open, and the pomegranates be in flower'.[49] In noticing that the 'mandrakes give forth fragrance', she maintains the early summer setting suggested by the flowering trees. For her, this cannot suffice however. She desires to give to her beloved 'all manner of precious fruits', and as these contain both those of the new season as well as old fruit she has laid up for him, it is obvious that the season for gathering fruit has now come.[50] Small wonder that she sees the climax of their union in his drinking 'of spiced wine, of the juice of my pomegranate'.[51] This reciprocation in their love cycle, is expressed by many similes drawn from nature's cycle from spring and early summer through to the joyous consummation at the end of the summer. It is as clearly and beautifully painted, though somewhat differently, in chapters 6–8 as it had been from chapters 2.8 to 5.

We need to consider now the opening poem of the book which terminates at chapter 2.7. It has been wise to deal first with the two larger units where the cycle of the seasons is treated in considerable detail. We are thereby better fitted to discover a similar development, if seemingly less emphasized, in the poem with which the Song opens also. It is to be observed that the poem is framed by an opening and closing reference to the maiden being brought into the king's chamber, and his banqueting house (lit. house of wine).[52] The use of a 'cluster of henna flowers' as a simile by which she describes her beloved, plainly sets us in the spring season.[53] Equally, the open air bower comprising the green sward for their couch, and the fragrant and majestic cedars and

---

[47] Song 6.11.   [48] 7.2[3].   [49] 7.3,8,9[4,9,10].   [50] 7.13[14].
[51] 8.2.   [52] 1.4; 2.4.   [53] 1.14; cf. 2.1.

junipers, assure us of the spring and summer setting. The same may be said of the use of the rose of Sharon and the lily of the valleys as metaphors here. As the summer progresses the shade of the apple tree is so welcome.[54] Yet the climax can hardly be reached without her finding that 'his fruit was sweet to my taste', while she is sustained by raisins and comforted with apples. She must be brought into his house of wine, where she finds that his banner over her is love.[55]

These several blocks of the book which we have reviewed show a remarkable similarity in their use of nature similes and metaphors according to the seasonal cycle from spring through to the autumn, as we would describe it.

Initially in this chapter, we were reminding ourselves of the sun and the moon's roles, specially in that divinely forged link between the developing agricultural season and the calendrical pattern of the Lord's annual sacred festival appointments. The several harvests delivering the boons of nature to the nation, are identified with the great spiritual blessings which have been delivered to, and which are even yet to be fully realized by the nation, through the sovereign grace of God. This may provide us with a key to understanding the arrangement of the Song's contents. We cannot accept that we have in this book a somewhat random collection of songs suitable for use at a wedding. Neither is it likely that the writer keeps returning to the beginning, folding back the page in order to retell the story before bringing it to its happy consummation. Even if there is behind the Song a tale of vacillating love, as the maiden blows hot and cold at the different approaches of her beloved, in a Near Eastern context this would never justify its place in the canon of sacred Scripture. If the divinely appointed calendar of Leviticus 23 provides the nation with an anticipation of its spiritual history, are we not to detect through these several seasonal cycles of the Song the progressive love affair between Israel and the great Lover of her soul? We shall propose therefore, an historical and eschatological understanding of the Song's recurring seasonal themes. This alone satisfies the sublimity of its

---

[54] Song 1.16f; 2.3.   [55] 2.4f.

language, the subtlety of its arrangement, and its suggestive spiritual climate.

We take our leave of the major motifs of the Song, reserving others for briefer treatment in the course of considering the text. The interpretation and structure of the book must be explored next.

Part 3

INTERPRETATIONS
STRUCTURE
KEYS

Contents – Part 3

12

SOME MODES OF INTERPRETING THE SONG OF SONGS

WE EMBARK NOW on the most notoriously difficult waters of the whole sea of understanding divine revelation. We do not propose doing more than outline the major options claiming to provide the only safe navigation through this text.

Broadly, the approaches to interpreting the Song fall into the following categories, although the permutations within each group are formidable.[1]

1. The Song as a Collection or Anthology of Love Songs. This proposal satisfies those who see no original connection between the several artlessly or even skilfully arranged love poems. More recently, that sense of connection which is apparent has been explained away as the work of a final editor's hand, now by means of an imposed dialogue pattern, now by juxtaposing small poetic units by means of catchwords and other repetitions as they came to his mind.[2] None who accept this view see any recoverable story in the Song, and they reject the possibility of single authorship.

2. The Song as a Traditional Cycle of Wedding Songs. In a comparatively recent Syrian wedding-week custom, an appropriate

---

[1] For a broad review see Rowley SotL 197–245. [2] A recent scholar adopting this approach is Falk LL; also e.g. Landsberger JBL 73 and Murphy CBQ 39. This is 'a council of despair' for Goulder Song 2.

and individually written series of love songs with a common theme, are sung throughout the marriage celebrations. For some, this provides the nearest parallel to the Song. In this, seven songs feature during the seven days of festivities known as the 'king's week'. The various participants in the Song are, in this view, to be related to those of the bridegroom (the king), the bride (the queen), and the various guests. However, attempts made to discover the seven separate songs in the Song have not met with too much success. Also the bride of the Song is not described as 'the queen' anywhere. Nineteenth century AD Syrian customs are too far removed in time from the Song to provide light on our approach to it.[3] The joyous occasion of the Cana marriage or those marriage celebrations of our Lord's parables know nothing of these customs.

3. The Song as a Drama. This approach has history more firmly on its side. The third century Church Father Origen seems to have originated this mode of interpretation, and he allocated the different responses of the Song to the two dominant persons of the piece assisted by a dual chorus. Another and more recent version based on the dramatic construction of the Song sees three chief characters in it. The plot is built around a love triangle, in which Solomon, the supposed voluptuous villain of the piece, snatches away a beautiful country maiden from her humble environment. His intention is to add her to his already well-stocked harem, ridding from her memory and desire her local shepherd lover. Despite all his attempts to dazzle her with splendour, and win her with wealth, she proudly refuses all Solomon's blandishments, remaining loyal to her lover. Eventually, the king admits defeat, and permits her to return to her country home and the one she loves. Here, then, are proposed a sovereign, a shepherd, and a Shulammite. Because of the supposed difficulty of equating the king and shepherd roles in one person, this approach appeared more attractive to some. Also, the moral of the story was thought to be more obvious, and the triumph of pure love over all attempts to corrupt or drown it are shown to be doomed to failure. Further, those embarrassing stanzas so seemingly blatant in their sexual expressions, are said to be what we might expect from one so depraved as

---

[3] See p.27,n.35.

Solomon became. Problems arise with this approach as rearrange-
ments of the text are often felt to be necessary to make things
clearer, and some of the finest poetic expressions are alleged to be
mere flattery to ensnare the unsuspecting maiden. Also, the
maiden's responses, when addressed, are assumed often to be
directed to her absent lover rather than to the speaker who
prompted her remarks, without there being anything in the text to
indicate this. In both of these approaches the drama is based on
real people, and a story/plot is seen developing through the
chapters. These elements at least are to be welcomed.[4]

4. The Song Viewed Literally. It must be admitted that most
modern commentators believe that the Song's intention is to
remove the veil from a human love affair so as to endorse the purity of true love alone. At best, this approach presents the Song as
structurally unified, and as a poetic expansion of the theme suggested by Genesis 2.23f. Most of the literary poetic parallels to the
unique Biblical form of the Song are found in Egyptian love poems.
We should not be surprised that Near Eastern couples, not to
speak of others further afield, would be found to adopt common
motifs in expressing their physical attraction toward and their love
for one another. But the very mass of such extra-Biblical material,
not to speak of the corrupting nature of the cultically based Canaanite and Mesopotamian love poetry, shows an unhealthy pre-
occupation with a subject given very limited space in the Bible. In
addition, the *differences* from the Biblical example that have been
noted by those who have made a study of such literature, which
in our judgment have received insufficient attention or have been
too cursorily dismissed, should warn us against limiting the purpose of the Song to what is concerned only with the natural and
physical. There were Rabbis who, being persuaded that the Song
was secular only, wished to exclude it from the canon. From the
end of the 4th century AD onward there have been Church leaders
who felt similarly.[5]

It should be noted also that the Song is unique within the

---

[4] See p.57,n.20.   [5] IDB (S) 836ff; most recently Carr Tyn.34ff. Questioning
canonicity, see Mishnah ῾Eduy.,5.3; Toseph.Yad.,2.14; for the Church Theodore of
Mopsuestia, and in the last century Reuss.

literary forms of the Bible, because there are dangers in making 'public', that which must be 'private' essentially in order to remain pure. Man and woman were given to one another in marriage by a good Creator at the beginning. Their union, their knowing one another at every level of their being, is all part of the highest provision of a loving Lord, and a means of their entering a world of complete intimacy. This intimacy must be safeguarded; it cannot become common property. Further, we should not read the Song against the love, courtship and marriage backcloth of modern Western culture. Biblical models alone must inform our approach and understanding. In Israel, a couple would have had little or no opportunity to get to know one another prior to their betrothal. All is designed to lead to lasting marriage and a rejoicing in the wife of one's youth alone. The marriage bed is to remain undefiled.[6]

The relationship of Adam and Eve had been designed to reflect a loftier union from the beginning. Pure love is a parable of divine purpose.[7]

5. The Song Viewed Allegorically. It has to be said that this mode of handling the Song is the most ancient of all, and has held the field over many centuries. The Jewish interpreters understood it to present the love relationship between the Lord and His people Israel, conceived as the King and His spouse. From the Church Fathers onward, Christians have been encouraged to see here a heart-moving view of Christ and His Church, the Lamb and His bride. A more personal development of this approach to the Song saw through it the Lord and the individual believer's love relationship. Allegorists are concerned with the smallest details in opening up the meaning of what they see as 'the mystery', for which they are not to be despised. However, the major problem the method creates is that often there is no consensus as to the significance of any one detail, so that there are as many interpretations as there are interpreters of it! It is as though they say 'Never mind what the writer says; listen, rather, to my understanding of the matter'. One has to listen carefully because each item treated means something totally different from what it is, and words lose their proper meaning. In many instances, the interpretation proposed is extra-

---

[6] Prov.5.15–19; cf. Song 4.12,15; Heb.13.4.   [7] Eph.5.31f.

Biblical and completely fanciful, as when, for example the loved one's eyes, 4.1, are for some Rabbis the Sanhedrin, and for the Church Fathers church teachers who give light to the body!

So many hymns, so much praise and worship, so much devotional literature, and so many sermons have stirred the hearts and enriched the spirituality of God's people as a result, that we may justly exclaim 'Long live this ministry!' We would make a plea, however, for due consideration to be given to the Song's place in the canon of Scripture when concerning ourselves with the meaning of the Song, rather than with the blessings derived from the present ministry of the Song. If there is divine light forthcoming from this approach, its Old Testament locus, its chief characters and scenery, should all conspire rather to our seeing the Lord and His covenant people Israel projected through it. In this century, a number of European scholars have treated the Hebrew text with great thoroughness, seeing in it an historical allegory, though it must be admitted without finding overmuch support of others for their views. In postulating a post-exilic dating for the Song, they saw it as providing great encouragement for the returned exiles. These sorely needed to be reminded of the love bond between the Lord and His people. The nation's history and prophecy alike as poetically unfolded in the Song was designed to give them fresh heart.[8]

6. The Song Viewed Typologically. Typology for one 'is a figure of speech that moves in time'; for another, in typology 'descriptions and language of God's previous redemptive actions are employed to describe his continuing redemptive activity'. It is, therefore, 'characterized by historical continuity'. For our purposes, the main difference between typology and allegory is that the latter may disclaim or see little need to deal with a historical

---

[8] The one NT use of the word 'allegory' [Grk. allegoria] indicates that for the Bible a true history may be allegorized, so as to bring out an extended meaning in that which happened. Isaac and Ishmael, Sarah and Hagar and the event concerning them are clearly historical, and yet the facts are made the vehicles of other truths, Gen.21.8ff; Gal.4.21–24,28–31. A recent succinctly stated objection to an allegorical approach to the Song rejects it because it 'does not itself claim to be an allegory, and nowhere offers a key to allegorical explication', Falk LL 63.

basis, while the former demands and deals with the historical facts for the proposed meaning. The leading characters would still represent the Church and Christ, or Israel and the Lord, as we have seen in the allegorical approach, but the foundation for this is found in a real love affair between Solomon and the Shulammite. The typologist is thus disciplined by the facts, what is actually stated and what this means. Only then does he come to see something larger projected by the facts and altogether consistent with them. Verses like those from Jeremiah specifically adopt the joyous marriage celebration as a figure of Israel's overflowing thanks at the Lord's return, and the restoration of His people. Then, as never before, they shall say 'for the Lord is good, for his mercy endureth for ever'.[9]

Much of evangelical scholarship today, in seeking to gain a hearing where more liberal views have held the field unchallenged for so long, has restricted itself within the armour of literalism. We cannot content ourselves with an inflexible accuracy, which threatens to remove that grand and conquering liberty which a literary, structural and spiritual understanding of Scripture brings in its train. We will not be robbed by those rules of exegesis which barely pay lip service to the several levels of Biblical understanding, and yield little place for the great areas of typological influence in the Word of God. Our God sovereignly controls, not only the great historical processes and their divinely appointed goals, but also the shaping and selecting of the records He has given us concerning these in a typological fashion. We must press on beyond an accurate explanation, mere scientific exactness, 1 Cor.2.13–16.

Regarding the Song, what are the facts? From what is written a tolerably clear story can be adduced. The Shulammite came from the Galilean village of Shunem [Arabic Sulam] on the slopes of Givat HaMoreh at the gateway to the Hulah Valley. We know that, something in the order of 100 years later, Naboth had a family vineyard on the opposite side of this Valley at the royal town of

---

[9] Jer.33.10f. The Catholic view is that the Song is essentially a parable, the point being the story itself. All the details, while given their proper meaning, provide an expansive commentary with Isa.62.5 as text, referred to by Murphy CBQ 11, 387–91.

Jezreel. We do not read of her father; her mother and her mother's sons (maybe her own step-brothers), together with her sister are mentioned. This Shulammite was her mother's special favourite, though she was none too popular with her 'brothers'. They pressed her into caring for the family vineyards, a part of which involved catching the jackals that would spoil them. Already she had the care of a flock.

The maiden met the king during one of his many itineraries to the North. It was a case of love at first sight. Her 'brothers' thought this was a preposterous infatuation on her side, and sought to keep her occupied to rid her mind of the affair. The king, rightly assessing the situation, approached her as a shepherd among other shepherds caring for the royal estates. She was doubly thrilled when she found that her royal suitor had come to where she was, and in a lowly role, simply to prove his own love for her. This shepherd was her sovereign after all. The very first panel or poem of the Song introduces him in both of these roles, as the sovereign and the shepherd. How they enjoyed one another's company now in the country, and now in the house of wine.

Perhaps this dual role is the most difficult for us to imagine. It has driven some to propose the three character interpretation of the Song. However, this is to ignore that so many of the great men of the Bible were shepherds primarily. In fact, from an Old Testament standpoint, one might expect a verse concerning the essential qualifications of leaders and kings to read 'but if a man knoweth not how to rule his own flock, how shall he take care of the Israel of God'![10] The kingly role is often described in shepherd terms, and Solomon's father David was taken by God[11] 'from the sheepfolds: from following the ewes that give suck he brought him,

---

[10] cf. 1 Tim.3.5.   [11] The verb 'to pasture, tend' [Heb.ra‾ah] often figuratively of the tending care expected of rulers, Ps.78.70ff; cf.2 Sam.5.2; 7.7//s 1 Chron.11.2 and 17.6; Jer.3.15; 23.2,4; Ezek.34.2,3,8,10,23(2); Zech.11.4,7(2),9, and also of the care of Israel's God, Gen.48.15; Ps.28.9; Isa.40.11; Mic.7.14; Ezek.34.13,14,15,16. Its participle is used figuratively of rulers, Zech.11.16, and the Lord is called 'my shepherd', Ps.23.1, and 'the shepherd of Israel', 80.2, and addresses the Messiah as 'my shepherd', Zech.13.7; cf. Mic.5.4; Matt.2.6; Rev.12.5; 19.15. For the 'shepherd king' theme in the OT see Bruce TiT 100–114.

to feed Jacob his people, and Israel his inheritance. So he fed them according to the integrity of his heart; and guided them by the skilfulness of his hands'. Perhaps even more to the point, the Messiah of Israel, the Son of God, travelled about the land unrecognized by most. He had come in the role of the good shepherd, and yet He was 'born King of the Jews'. Of the tribe of Judah, the Son of David, He came forth 'a governor, which shall be shepherd of my people Israel'. Travelling incognito, there were some who were given to see beyond the externals, and these 'beheld his glory, glory as of the only begotten from the Father'. Like the hymn writer and all who believe, the maiden here could sing 'The king of love my shepherd is'!

The lovers' spring and summer excursions, with all their varied delights, seemed to have terminated with the oncoming of winter. The relationship suffered a setback, a cooling down period, the cause seemingly to be laid at the maiden's door. Springtime saw her beloved appealing to her again to join him, and though there were inner conflicts the maiden at last brought her beloved home to her mother's house. Thoroughly overwhelmed by his love, which would not let her go, she left the country for the city, and shared with him the crowning day of his espousals. They were married.

Remarkably (or is it?), we find her next lethargic and unresponsive to his loving appeals. When, after some delay, she did respond, her beloved had disappeared, and her fruitless search for him in the city streets brought her into trouble. She shared news of her loss with a sympathetic group of ladies in Jerusalem, and after thinking aloud with them, came to realize where he would be found. Well, he appeared once again, as suddenly as he had disappeared, was spellbound with her beauty and told her so. She told him she was his forever, and both went off to the very scenes where their love was born.

After this further Galilean springtime and summer, in which the family rejoiced and even her sister was spoken for, they were lastingly fulfilled in one another.[12] Truly, 'love never faileth'.

---

[12] A recent scholarly work reads the Song as a progressing love story, written in the post-exilic period, and with the apologetic purpose of fostering the tolerant reception of those of other nations, Goulder Song 74–8.

It is not difficult to see why an historical love, betrothal and marriage, followed by a temporary marital problem, should be construed typologically. Solomon, a king 'in all his glory', and yet a humble shepherd for a season, was seen to anticipate the Lord Jesus, the good shepherd and the true Messiah. It is the Church as the Bride who knows Him as her Bridegroom, who experiences His love and owns Him as her Lord. Yet even a church apostolically planted, like the one at Ephesus, needed to be warned of leaving its first love! For others, the vacillations of the maiden, and the uneasy course of her experience, reflect the failure of many believers to realize fully the unchanging love of Christ in their lives. Have any of us remained quite the same after sitting down consciously 'under his shadow with great delight'? Praise God, it is not only the one described as 'the disciple whom Jesus loved' who knows that in Him 'a greater than Solomon is here'.

However, as Feliks has aptly expressed it 'Every great literary work lends itself to a literal and an allegorical construction, and, in essence, we accept the approach of the commentators who regard the Song as a single love story of sacred and secular significance alike, developing against the background of changes in the landscape and nature of the Land of Israel'. This explains the Song's choice for a place in the lectionary cycle on the Sabbath of the Passover week in Askenazi circles to this day. For Murphy, too, the question arises whether 'one may legitimately ask if modern hermeneutical concerns have not moved away from the old literal-allegorical polarization. It would be a bold claim to say that the literal historical sense exhausts the meaning of the Song of Songs. The history of its interpretation in both the Jewish and Christian tradition shows that the communities in which the book was received found other levels of meaning'.[13]

---

[13] See Feliks SoS 9; Murphy IDB (S) 837, para 5. In CBQ 39, 491f while himself interpreting it in the literal sense of human love, he agrees that Israel itself accepted the Song, preserved and canonized it, because they understood it to relate to the Lord and His people, with a meaning beyond the literal and historical. Witness too, for example, the interpretation of the Gospel records as historical and yet as rich theological/typological/spiritual literature.

There appears to be, therefore, an even stronger case for discerning Israel's Lord and King, and the nation He loves, mirrored in this story. Is He not their King and also the Shepherd of Israel? Has He not loved them, does He not love them still, will He not love them yet? Surely it must be so, for has He not said 'Yea, I have loved thee with an everlasting love: therefore with lovingkindness have I drawn thee. Again will I build thee, and thou shalt be built, O virgin of Israel: again shalt thou be adorned with thy tabrets, and shall go forth in the dances of them that make merry. Again shalt thou plant vineyards . . . the planters shall plant, and shall enjoy the fruit thereof. For there shall be a day, that the watchmen upon the hills of Ephraim shall cry, Arise ye, and let us go up to Zion unto the Lord our God. For thus saith the Lord, Sing with gladness for Jacob, and shout for the chief of the nations: publish ye, praise ye, and say, O Lord, save thy people, the remnant of Israel'.[14]

It is in this typological watered garden that virtually every tree and shrub, every flower and plant, every bird and beast, every gushing water source, finds its Biblical explanation to a degree not matched by any other approach. Certainly Solomon is here, but a greater One, the anointed King Messiah of Israel is also here. A real mother and the maiden are here, but these represent the nation which in turn produced that 'nation within the nation', the remnant, which has always embodied the realization of true fellowship with their God.

How we long for that appointed time to arrive when Israel's Bridegroom, King Messiah, will come to bring His nation Bride into the joy and peace which His love has planned for her since the foundation of the world. O that the day might soon dawn when all Israel will plead 'Make haste, my beloved'!

---

[14] Jer.31.3–7.

13

THE STRUCTURE OF THE SONG

FOR MANY the Song is a compilation of lyrics, each having love for its theme and adopting a variety of literary techniques in pursuing the subject. The individual songs or poems are not otherwise connected with one another, so that we are not to expect any unifying story or developing theme. What appears as design is little more than the art of the compiler in arranging the pieces by means of catchwords and refrains which were all part of the common stock drawn upon by all poets and lyricists alike. One scholar has recently refuted strongly this approach, writing 'the anthology view is only a counsel of despair: we are driven to it only if proposals of meaningful sequence fail to convince'.[1] Our reading of the Song has found a story that is sequential. Stylistically, it is apparent that one hand has been at work throughout. The hand is one though the voices are many. The composer of this Song has introduced periodic refrains in his score, indicating careful design and subtle arrangement in marking the several cycles of progress. We shall note some of the more important of these which act as interlocking literary links.

Regarding Design

Literary formulae marking off terminal points are planted

---

[1] Goulder Song 2.

151

deliberately throughout the Song. As an example the poet composer provides us first with three matching calls for quietness. The
phrase used is 'I adjure you, O daughters of Jerusalem ... that ye
stir not up, nor awaken love, until it please', and it occurs at 2.7, 3.5
and 8.4. This is the beloved's charge, and he is concerned that such
love be permitted to develop at its own pace and free of artificial
stimuli. There is indeed 'a season, and a time to every purpose
under the heaven ... a time to embrace, and a time to refrain from
embracing ... a time to love'. Each of these settings plead for a
pause, and provide the Song with its 'Selahs'.

Literary formulae marking commencing points are set also
throughout the Song. As an example we shall note three matching
questions regarding identity: '*Who is this (she)?*' The first and last
references, at 3.6 and 8.5, obviously open new panels, or better,
poems, following on as they do two of the pause pleas of the
preceding stanzas. The third reference, 6.10, appears to provide us
with yet another poem commencement marker. All three expect
the response 'It is his loved maiden'.

A repetition of the maiden's hearing the '*voice of my beloved*' at 2.8
and 5.2, alerts us to another panel or poem opening. We have
already noticed the formula of conclusion 'stir not up' at 2.7, so
that the reference to the 'voice' of her beloved at 2.8 is a formula
of commencement here. Studies of the Song generally agree that
chapter 5.1 is the central climax, where the union of the lovers occurs. Therefore, the 'voice of my beloved' refrain at 5.2 marks the
opening of another distinct panel or poem.

The major movements in the music of the Song therefore come
to their crescendos at 2.7, 3.5, 5.1, 6.9 and 8.4. This is confirmed
by the use of formulae of commencement at 2.8, 3.6, 5.2, 6.10, 8.5.
With these observations we are able to set out a simple analysis of
contents:

1.1	–	2.7	Poem 1
2.8	–	3.5	Poem 2
3.6	–	5.1	Poem 3
5.2	–	6.9	Poem 4
6.10	–	8.4	Poem 5
8.5	–	8.14	Poem 6

Further support for the boundaries proposed is provided by other repetitions. The ends of poems 1 and 5 are also marked off by the phrase '*His left hand . . . and his right hand*' which occur at 2.6 and 8.3. Poems 2 and 5 conclude with the maiden referring to '*my mother's house*' at 3.4 and 8.2. If the conclusion of Poem 2 has a paragraph describing the maiden's search for her lover, her meeting with the watchmen of the city, 3.1–5, and her eventual success in finding the one her soul loved, then Poem 4 has a similar if contrasting scene with which to open, 5.2–8. Here the beloved initially approaches her but her response is too slow. Only after he withdraws does she open the door, and search for him unsuccessfully and with some injury to herself from the hands of the watchmen. This inversion, and its significance for the development of the Song, we shall have to consider at some length later.[2]

Help in establishing the stanzas of these six poems results from noting other structurally important refrains. Specially useful here are the uses of the word '*fair(est)*' all of which eulogize concerning the beauty of the 'fairest of women'. Its appearance at 1.8,15(2),16; 4.1(2),7,10; 5.9; 6.1,4,6,10; 7.1 and 6[2,7] provides us with one excellent stanza opening formula, cf. also 2.10,13. Of course, others are necessary, but these create already a liberal sprinkling of the smaller poetic units of the Song. As one would expect, three of the references are followed by lengthier parallel descriptions of the maiden's beauty in virtually the same words. These expatiate upon her eyes (immediately following 'fair'), 1.15; 4.1, her hair, teeth, and temples, 4.1–3 and 6.5c–7, her neck, 4.4 and 7.4[5], and her breasts, 4.5 and 7.3[4]. By this means the stanza-breaks at 4.1, 6.4 and 7.1[2] are heavily endorsed. The use of two words translated '*come*', the first [Heb.halakh] used only in appeals here at 2.10,(13) and 7.11[12], belong to the opening of distinct stanzas. The second [Heb.bo´] at 2.8, 4.8, 16e and 5.1a is used at the commencement, and in 4.16b at the conclusion of a number of the stanzas.

Repeated formulae also may signal the end of certain stanzas, functioning as a kind of literary full-stop. Twice we hear the

---

[2] See chaps. 14, and 16.

phrase *'Until the day be cool* [Heb.puach = breathe, blow‡],[3] *and the shadows flee away'*, once upon the maiden's lips, 2.17, and once upon her beloved's, 4.6. In each case a stanza of the Song is being closed down by reference to the day's close, the cool evening time when the shadows lengthen and deepen into darkness.[4]

For most, the threefold expressions of possessing and belonging are more familiar. The maiden first claims that *'My beloved is mine, and I am his'*, 2.17. Precedence is given to that which is her gain; He is her possession. In 6.3 she expresses the inverse of this. She says *'I am my beloved's, and my beloved is mine'*. The pre-eminent place is here yielded to him and his interests. Finally she owns that *'I am my beloved's, and his desire is toward me'*, 7.10[11]. At last she is fully absorbed with him, and thrills in his overwhelming desire set *'upon'* her. Beyond this structural function, these phrases are clearly progressive. They give the lie to the view that there is no development observable through the Song. Table 2 opposite sets out the incidence of the phrases which we have seen to be structurally important. The two phrases with which the list is closed have not been mentioned and no doubt you will wish to consider their function also, together with other repetitions which you find helpful as you add to this collection. It is virtually impossible to escape the conclusion that we are in the company of a master of beauty in design.

Regarding Development

Apart from the very obvious progress in the maiden's apprehension of her beloved which we highlighted in the preceding paragraph, a development is apparent in the several panels or poems of the book. The more one is familiar with the contents of the Song as a whole, the more evident this will be. Keep reading it! Earlier, we noted that most find 5.1 an indisputable high point,

---

[3] The only other use of the word in the Song is at 4.16 where it is translated 'blow upon'; the winds there cause the many fragrant plants to exhale and diffuse their perfumes. Compare the phrase 'the day be cool' [Heb.sheyyaphuach hayyom] with 'the cool of the day' [Heb.leruach hayyom], Gen.3.8.   [4] For the shadows lengthening into the night see 'My days are like a shadow that is stretched out', Ps.102.11[12]; cf.109.23; 144.4.

Table 2

Words of Refrain	Chapter/Verse References							
	1	2	3	4	5	6	7	8
I adjure you					8			
stir not up		7	5					4
Who is this...?			6			10		5
Voice of my beloved		8			2			
His left ... right hand		6						3
My mother's house			4					2
house of wine		4						
king's chambers	4							
Sought and found			1–4					
and not found					6–8			
The watchmen			4		7			
Behold thou art fair,								
eyes doves	15(2)			1(2)				
Behold ... fair (masc)	16							
How fair (beautiful)				10			1,6	
Thou art (all) fair								
(beautiful)				7		4		
Thou fairest	8				9	1		
My fair one		10, 13						
Fair as the moon						10		
Hair, teeth, temples				1–3		5–7		
breasts				5			3	
neck				4			4	
Appeal – Come		10,13					11	
Come – general		8		8, 16	1			
Until the day cool		17		6				
I am my beloved's						3	10	
Possession –								
My beloved is mine		16						
Sick with love		5			8			
See if vine budded						11	13	

For Hebrew verse numbering in chap. 7 add one to that of EVV.

for there the couple are united in marriage. Consequently, the Song's six poems, fall into two major groups. Now we shall review the first three poems so as to follow the drift of the story until the marriage is consummated.

Poem 1, 1.1–2.7, opens with the maiden expressing her experience: 'He is kissing me (imperf) with the kisses of his mouth: for thy love is better than wine'. As it draws to its close, we hear her earnest appeal: 'Stay ye me with raisins, comfort me with apples: for I am sick of love'. She speaks of being brought into 'the king's chambers', of being in the king's presence when he 'sat at his table', and of his bringing her into 'the banqueting house'. Little wonder that she becomes increasingly overwhelmed! Although she speaks of herself, somewhat self-consciously, on an 'I am' note, it must be left to the one she describes as 'thou whom my soul loveth' to bring out her surpassing beauty. While others speak to her as 'thou fairest among women', it is her beloved who specially emphasizes her beauty by repetitive poetic parallelism: 'Behold, thou art fair, my love; behold, thou art fair'. The scene concludes with her describing his embrace in which she delights. Such love must be allowed to rest there undisturbed; it is too delicate and sensitive a thing to be subjected to further strong physical pressure and excitement or that more inward, psychological arousal.

Poem 2, 2.8–3.5, is quite different. It comes as a surprise that the curtain rises with such a dramatic change of scenery. Have the cold winter rains put a dampener upon the spring and summer love affair of Poem 1? Certainly, the initiative is taken by her beloved here. She is no longer in his banqueting house. She is even far removed from what he describes as 'our land'. First love has cooled. He must come bounding over mountains and hills to appeal to her. So we are called upon to listen to 'The voice of my beloved! behold, he cometh'. Seeing him as 'a roe or a young hart', she is made aware that something had happened to cause his sensitive love to be frightened off. Yet equally, she is warmed again to him as he appeals to her to rejoin him in a fresh cycle of love. 'Rise up, my love, my fair one, and come away' he pleads. Springtime is here certainly, but summer hardly seems to arrive. However, clearly there is development for if she is out of their land and behind the wall and can only be seen through the lattice at first, she is eventually back in their land, then in the city, and finally she brings him into her mother's house. If she hears his voice at the beginning, she holds him and will not let him go at the end. At least his initiative is matched at last by her seeking him. It is important for the developing theme of the Song to be most familiar with the closing stanza of this poem. The maiden describes a night scene when first, upon her bed in what may be a dream reverie, she longs for her beloved. Then, she determines to get up and go out into the city to find the one her soul loves. Following this she encounters the watchmen and asks after her beloved. Having hardly left them she finds him, clings on to him, and brings him to her mother's house. At last, with him in her arms, the call goes out for love to be allowed to pause at yet another peak: 'stir not up, nor awaken love, until it please'.

Poem 3, 3.6–5.1, is the most fragrant of all. There is a striking development throughout. It is opened with a question we have found to be important structurally: 'Who is this . . .?' It links this strongly with Poems 5 and 6 which commence with the identical phrase, and pursue in a more positive way the climax achieved at the end of Poem 3.[5] The opening stanza focuses upon Solomon's 'glory train' in which he transports her to the crowning espousals day. They travel up from the wilderness to Jerusalem. At the end her beloved is invited to enter his garden, that is, to enjoy all the fragrant charms of the one he loves, whom he describes as 'my garden'. The king's royal palanquin is redolent with myrrh and frankincense, yet her garden, though stocked with a breath-taking array of fragrant plants, only yields its precious perfumes under the alternate influences of the north and south winds. At the beginning the daughters of Zion are urged to 'Go forth . . . and behold king Solomon'. At the end it is the lovers who are urged to 'Eat . . . drink abundantly, O beloved (ones, plural)'. Thus the day of espousals leads up to the joyous and consummating feast of espousals. Throughout, her beloved excels himself in describing her beauty. She is 'fair', then 'all fair', and yet there is so much more he wishes to say. In his third use of 'fair' he explores a whole range of fragrant flora in a fantasy garden which must remain an incomparable love

---

[5] See Song 6.10; 8.5.

eulogy. It does not seem possible to reach a higher note in any song of human love.

The second major movement of the Song, to which another three poems are devoted, relates how the joy of the couple's union is restored after a tragic interruption.

Poem 4, 5.2–6.9, introduces what must be the most dramatic break in the course of the Song, more serious by far than that assumed at the opening of Poem 2. All appears to be overturned, and the radical change introduced at first seems to threaten the future of the whole relationship. The opening words, in fact the opening stanza are recorded so as to throw us backward to Poem 2. Both commence with a reference to the 'voice of my beloved', whilst Poem 2 closes with a 'sought and found' stanza and Poem 4 opens with a 'sought and not found' stanza. The inversion is designed, and is intended to emphasize the differences. That which was the climax of Poem 2 has become the commencement of Poem 4. And yet there is obvious development throughout Poem 4. If the maiden has lost her beloved at the opening, then she knows where he is to be found toward the end. Her beloved, though he is neglected and disappears at the beginning, is speaking well of her again at the end, even using some of the glowing descriptive terms of Poem 3.[6] 'Thou art beautiful, O my love'. She is unique, incomparable, 'the choice one of her that bare her'.

Poem 5, 6.10–8.4, again opens with the question 'Who is she (this) ...?', which carries us back in thought to Poem 3 which opens similarly. Happily, the whole poem is on a much more positive note, having outlived the break introduced by Poem 4 and its unexpected ramifications. The beloved is fascinated by his 'new look' Shulam-mite as a fresh descriptive vocabulary would indicate. Even the onlookers, who invariably introduce the opening question, speak of her as she looks forth 'as the morning (dawn), fair as the moon, clear as the sun, terrible as an army with banners'. The development is patent. Her 'dance of Mahanaim' draws forth a detailed description of her beauty from the onlookers. 'How beautiful (fair)' they ex-claim. The king himself, who is 'held captive in the tresses' of her

---

[6] cf. 6.5c–7 with 4.1–3.

158

hair, must add his own praise to theirs. He not only speaks of her beauty saying 'How fair and how pleasant art thou', but he would make her his own. If her beloved at the beginning goes down 'into the garden of nuts, to see the green plants of the valley, to see whether the vine budded, and the pomegranates were in flower', then at the end she says 'Come, my beloved . . . let us see whether the vine hath budded, and its blossom be open, and the pomegranates be in flower'. As they journey through springtime together, their love must surely be consummated at summer's end when he will enjoy 'all manner of precious fruits, new and old' which she has laid up for him. And yet she longs to conduct him to her mother's house, and to know the embrace of his arms there. This recalls the parallel instance of her bringing him to her mother's house at the end of Poem 2, as do the closing words 'I adjure you . . . that ye stir not up, nor awaken love, until it please'. Love has found a way to reach its goal; 'love never faileth'!

Poem 6, 8.5–14, rounds off the several poems of the Song, opening with the last occurrence of the question 'Who is this?' In this poem we are taken back in thought to Poem 1 where it all began. The mention of his mother here reminds us of her mother in Poem 1. Those 'mother's sons' who were incensed against her there, speak up for her sister here. Now she has a vineyard of her own, happy for Solomon to have his all while granting a double portion to those who care for it. Then, she was made to look after the vineyards of others to the detriment of her own. In following the various vicissitudes of their love relationship throughout the poems, it is obvious that 'Many waters cannot quench love, neither can the floods drown it'. At immense cost it has been purchased, her beloved's worth and unceasing work has produced and sustained it. Her closing appeal to him is 'Make haste, my beloved'.

Regarding Analysis

The straightforward route for the married couple to have taken together would have been for them to journey from Poem 3 through Poem 5 to Poem 6, that is, by following directly the three 'Who is this' sign-posts. This was not to be, because of the loved one's hesitation in responding to her beloved's plea. During the night hours he was left out in the cold. A kind of parenthesis in the progress of their love resulted, and until this had run its course she encountered unnecessary trouble from the watchmen, while gaining an opportunity to witness to the peculiar glories of her beloved as never before nor after. The positive programmatic presentation of their love is interrupted in Poem 4. It might help us to see this more easily by putting to one side Poem 4, so as to indicate its somewhat 'mark-time' character by this means. We may set this out as follows:

Poem 1	1.1 – 2.7	
Poem 2	2.8 – 3.5	
Poem 3	3.6 – 5.1	– Poem 4 5.2–6.9
Poem 5	6.10– 8.4	
Poem 6	8.5 – 8.14	

The chiastic structure of the five poems set out on the left above is designed to indicate not only the closer but the more distant associations which they have with one another. Poems 1 and 6 open with the maiden's initiatives. There are no set backs either. Poems 2 and 5 open with the beloved's initiatives, demanded because of their being apart from one another. Poem 3 is central to all, joyfully recording the consecration, consummation and celebration of their marriage.

Although Poem 4 disturbs the more delightful drift of the story, and therefore may be detached from the rest to point up the delay that has been introduced, the many links with the poems around it by means of catchword, strophe, and even stanza, prove its right to *a* place in the story. Salvation history proves that it has *the right* place in the story! More about that in chapter 14.

Regarding some of the obvious literary links, Poems 2 and 4 open with 'The voice of my beloved', and both contribute one of the 'possession formulae'. Specially, we emphasize that Poem 2 closes with, and Poem 4 opens with, a night scene, a bedroom scene, a seeking scene, a watchmen incident, and a success or failure conclusion.

Poem 3 and Poem 4 both feature a lengthy descriptive stanza of the loved one, forging a link between these two poems. The sixty warriors at the opening of Poem 3 are matched by the sixty queens at the close of Poem 4. In Poem 3 Solomon's mother crowns him on

14

15

The Jordan Valley, south of Lake of Galilee, showing meandering river and the mountains of Gilead
in the background. May-time.

15. A flock of goats on hillside. 'Thy hair is a flock of
goats that lie along the side of Mount Gilead', Song
4.1. See pp. 59f, 255.

16. 'Thy temples are like a piece of a pomegranate
within thy veil', Song 4.3. See p. 72f.

17. 'Thy neck is like the tower of David . . .
whereon there hang a thousand bucklers, all
the shields of the mighty men', Song 4.4.
See pp. 15.15, 276.

16

18. *View from the top of Mount Hermon (Anti-Lebanons) toward the Lebanon Mountains westward.*

   'Come with me from Lebanon, my bride . . .', Song 4.8. See p. 15.

18

19. *The Hula Valley with the peak of Mount Hermon in the background. May-time.*

   'Look from the top of Amana, from the top of Senir and Hermon', Song 4.8. See p. 56f.

19

20. *The Jericho oasis with the Dead Sea in the background. May-time.*

   'Where the palm grows, and the balsam which is an ointment of all the most precious', Jos. Ant. 14.4.1. See pp. 116–119.

20

the day of his espousals, whereas in Poem 4 her beloved notes that his 'love', his 'dove', is 'the only one of her mother'.

Poems 5 and 4 are bound together by means of the unique phrase used of the Shulammite as one 'terrible as an army with banners'. Here also both poems feature one of the 'possession formulae'.

For us, to suggest that 'the "design" of the Song may be the result of skilful compilation of many short poems rather than original structural unity' lacks all credibility.[7]

A Detailed Analysis[8]

Title, 1.1, 'The Song of songs, which is Solomon's'

POEM 1. HIS BANNER OVER ME WAS LOVE, 1.2–2.7

The maiden's desire, 'Let him kiss me ...', 1.2–4
The maiden's self-portrait, 'I am black ...', 1.5–6

{ The maiden's plea, 'Tell me ...', 1.7
The daughters (?) directions, 'Go thy way ...', 1.8

The beloved describes her, 'my love', 1.9–11

The maiden's soliloquy, 'While the king sat at his table ...', 1.12–14

{ The beloved speaks of her beauty, 'thou art fair, my love ...', 1.15
The maiden speaks of his beauty, 'thou art fair, my beloved ...', 1.16
The maiden describes their outdoor bowers, 'beams, rafters ...', 1.17
The maiden's self-portrait, 'I am a rose of Sharon ...', 2.1
The beloved describes her, 'a lily among thorns ...', 2.2

{ The maiden describes her beloved, what he was to her, 2.3–4
The maiden is overwhelmed by his love, in his embrace, 2.5–6

The beloved's charge (to D), 'stir not up, nor awaken love ...', 2.7

---

[7] Falk LL 66f. Probably the best scholarly case for design, unity of structure, and of authorship is that of Exum's ZAW 85, 47–79.   [8] A separate line is allocated each distinct contribution, generally a stanza. Strophes as parts of complete stanzas are linked together (generally in dialogues). Change of participant(s) is indicated by a single line space.

POEM 2. WINTER IS PAST, 2.8–3.5

{ The maiden's soliloquy, 'The sound of my beloved ...', 2.8–10a

{ The beloved's appeal, 'Rise up, my love ... come away', 2.10b–13
The beloved's appeal, 'Let me see thy countenance', 2.14

Conflicting family(?) claims, 'Take us the foxes ... that spoil', 2.15

The maiden's possession claim and command, '... mine, ... turn ...', 2.16–17
The maiden's account of her successful search, 3.1–4 the watchmen questioned

The beloved's charge (to D), 'stir not up, nor awaken love', 3.5

POEM 3. I AM COME INTO MY GARDEN, 3.6–5.1

The friends ask 'Who is this?' as royal train ascends to city, 3.6–11

The beloved describes her beauty, 'thou art fair', 4.1–5
The beloved's excursion 'to the mountain of myrrh', 4.6
The beloved's summary statement re her beauty, 'all fair', 4.7
The beloved's appeal, 'Come with me from Lebanon', 4.8
The beloved describes her love, 'How fair is thy love', 4.9–11
{ The beloved describes his bride, 'A garden shut up', 4.12–14
{ The beloved describes his bride, 'a fountain of gardens', 4.15
{ The beloved's call to the winds to diffuse scent, 'Awake ... blow', 4.16a–b

{ The spouse's invitation to her beloved to 'come into his garden', 4.16cd
{ The beloved's glad response, 'I am come into my garden', 5.1a–d
{ The friends' joyous encouragement, 'Eat ... drink ... beloved ones', 5.1e–f

POEM 4. THE CHIEFEST AMONG TEN THOUSAND, 5.2–6.9

{ The spouse's confession, 'I was asleep but my heart waked', 5.2a–b
{ The beloved's appeal, 'Open to me', 5.2c–e
{ Her excuse and belated response, 'I have put off ...', 5.3–5
{ Her fearful and fruitless search, watchmen beat her, 5.6–7

{ Her charge to the 'daughters ... if ye find my beloved, tell him', 5.8
{ They query her reason, 'What is thy beloved more than ...', 5.9

162

She describes her beloved to them in unequalled glorious terms, 5.10–16

⎧ They query his whereabouts, 'Whither is thy beloved gone?', 6.1

⎨ She knows where her beloved is to be found!, 6.2

⎩ She confesses their mutual 'belonging', 6.3

The beloved describes her unique beauty, 'Thou art fair, my love', 6.4–9
  daughters called her blessed, queens, concubines praised her

POEM 5. ALL MANNER OF PRECIOUS FRUITS, NEW AND OLD, 6.10–8.4

The friends' question, 'Who is this?', 6.10

The beloved's soliloquy, 'I went down into the garden . . .', 6.11–12

⎧ The friends' appeal, 'Return. . . O Shulammite', 6.13a–b[7.1a–b]

⎨ The Shulammite's question, 'Why will ye look upon . . .?', 6.13c–d[7.1c–d]

⎩ The friends' description of her beauty, 'How fair . . .', 7.1–5[2–6]

⎧ The beloved's description of her beauty, and purpose, 7.6–9a[7–10a]

⎨ The Shulammite's glad response, supplementing his words, 7.9b–c[7.10b–c]

⎩ The Shulammite expresses total commitment to her beloved, 7.10[11]

The Shulammite's appeal to him, 'Come . . . let us go', 7.11–13[12–14]

The Shulammite's strong desires for her beloved, 8.1–3

The beloved's charge, 'stir not up, nor awaken love', 8.4

POEM 6. MANY WATERS CANNOT QUENCH LOVE, 8.5–14

The onlookers' question, 'Who is this . . .?', 8.5a–b

The spouse's claim, 8.5c–7

⎧ The family appeal for the 'little sister', 8.8–9

⎩ The spouse has found 'peace' at last, 8.10

The king has his portion from his vineyard and from hers, 8.11–12

⎧ The beloved's appeal to his spouse, 'cause me to hear . . .', 8.13

⎩ The spouse's response, 'Make haste, my beloved . . .', 8.14

Some notes on the analysis

Identifying the different speakers throughout is important in the understanding of the developing scheme. Among the commentators there are various views regarding this, but the application of a few simple rules resolves most of the issues in the Hebrew text. Here, attention must be paid to the gender of the suffixes, to establish whether the pronouns are masculine or feminine. Again, the use of the second and third person singular in the same sentence may or may not have the same significance for the speaker or writer as it creates in the mind of the English reader. A case in point is the verse which reads 'Let him kiss me with the kisses of his mouth: for thy love is better than wine', 1.2. When the opening verb is translated as an imperfect and not a jussive, 'He is kissing me . . .', the switch to 'thy' indicates the words she spoke to him then. The switches in the use of singular and plural also have to be weighed. It must be said, however, that a Hebrew plural may be used to point up the glory or majesty of a thing, as in the phrase 'thy love(s) is better than wine', 1.2.

The preceding more detailed analysis of the Song results from the application of these rules, though there remain still a number of debatable identifications. Ponder these instances:

We have proposed that 1.8 is spoken by the 'daughters of Jerusalem', or some other group of friends or onlookers. Many see it as a response of the beloved himself to the maiden's plea in 1.7. We believe that the indisputable use of the phrase 'O thou fairest of women' by the 'daughters of Jerusalem' in all of its other occurrences, 5.9; 6.1, helps to settle the matter.

There appears to be no warrant for proposing that 1.17 is to be put into the beloved's mouth, as though it were his response to her words in 1.16.

The three almost identical main charges, 2.7; 3.5; 8.4, are to be understood as the beloved's responses, as the selection of the female creatures (lit. 'does and hinds') in the first two instances suggests.

In the light of 1.6 and 8.11f, it appears best to see the demand 'Take us the foxes, the little foxes, that spoil the vineyards; for our vineyards are in blossom', as expressing the conflicting claims upon the maiden of the 'mother's sons'.

It is best to construe that the threefold query 'Who is this?', 3.5; 6.10; 8.5, is voiced consistently by friends or onlookers.

Not all accept 7.1–5[2–6] as spoken by friends/onlookers, but the plural 'that we may look upon thee' and 'Why will ye (masc) look upon . . .', 6.13[7.1], together with the impersonal statement that 'the king is held captive', 7.5[6], call for this interpretation.

The Hebrew suffixes throughout 8.5c–6b clearly indicate that the spouse is the speaker, and not her beloved.

The unspecified speakers in 8.9f appear to be the 'mother's sons' of 1.6.

In the proposed analysis, each speaker's contribution is separately spaced from the other(s). The reader should prayerfully meditate upon them so as to suitably entitle them for himself, thereby assisting the memorizing process.

Regarding the Form and Distribution of the Stanzas

It is apparent from the analysis that the bulk of the Song records the thoughts of the hearts or the expressions of the lips of the beloved and his loved one. Consider first, therefore, the form of those stanzas in which they are involved directly, and second those in which others take part:

1. The man, the beloved, engages in (34 verses):

   (a) a monologue about his loved one, 6.8–9
   (b) numerous monologues to his loved one, 1.9–11;
   2.10b–13,14; 4.1–5,7,8,9–11,12–15; 6.4–7
   (c) soliloquys, 4.6; 6.11–12
   (d) a monologue to the winds, 4.16a–b
   (e) monologues to the daughters of Jerusalem, 2.7; 3.5; 8.4

2. The woman, the loved one, engages in (36 verses):

   (a) numerous monologues/soliloquys about her beloved,
   1.2–4,13–14; 2.5–6,8–10a,16; 3.1–4; 5.2a–b,4,6a–b; 8.3,11
   (b) monologues to her beloved, 1.7; 2.17; 7.9b–10[10b–11],
   11–13[12–14]; 8.1–2, 5c–7, 12
   (c) monologues about herself, 1.12; 5.5,6c–7
   (d) monologue to the daughters of Jerusalem, 1.5–6

3. Dialogues between the beloved and the loved one (15 verses):

   (a) Him about her, 1.15; 2.2; 5.1a–d,2c; 7.6–9a[7–10a]; 8.13
   (b) Him to her about himself, 5.2d–e
   (c) Her about him, 1.16; 2.3–4; 4.16c–d; 5.3; 8.14
   (d) Her to him about their love bower, 1.17
   (e) Her to him about herself, 2.1

4. The woman dialogues with others (11 1/2 verses):

   (a) in charging the daughters of Jerusalem, 5.8
   (b) with the daughters of Jerusalem about her beloved, 5.10–16; 6.2
   (c) with the daughters of Jerusalem about her relationship with her beloved, 6.3
   (d) with certain male onlookers/friends, 6.13c–d[7.1c–d]
   (e) with the mother's sons about herself, 8.10

5. Others dialogue with the woman (4 1/2 verses):

   (a) the daughters of Jerusalem with her, 5.9; 6.1
   (b) male onlookers/friends, 6.13a–b
   (c) the mother's sons with her about their little sister, 8.8–9

6. Other monologues (15 verses):

   (a) the mother's sons to her, 2.15
   (b) the daughters of Jerusalem to her, 1.8
   (c) onlookers/friends question re her and the cavalcade, 3.6–10
   (d) onlookers/friends to the daughters, 3.11
   (e) onlookers/friends questions about her, 6.10; 8.5a–b
   (f) onlookers/friends, to them both, 5.1e–f
   (g) male onlookers/friends to her, 7.1–5[2–6]

Only the title verse, 1.1, is not included in this review. It is instructive to observe that the beloved majors in speaking directly and appreciatively *to* his loved one, whereas she speaks *about* him much more than she does *to* him. The bulk of the poems are given to the couple's reciprocated endearing expressions.

14

FINDING THE KEYS

AS LONG AGO as the 10th century AD an outstanding Jewish sage wrote 'Know, my brothers, that you will find great differences in interpretation of the Song of Songs. In truth they differ because the Song of Songs resembles locks to which the keys have been lost'.[1] Formidable as it is to open a door with only one lock when the key is lost, the task is more daunting where there are a plurality of locks for which none of the keys are to hand! This does not appear to have deterred the army of locksmiths who have taken up the challenge. We have handled but a few of the keys produced.

The Song's score presents Solomon and one referred to once as the Shulammite. Poetically, delicately, and yet with an openness not matched elsewhere in the Bible, their love for one another and their marriage is described. All of this, we believe, was intended to be read literally and also with great purity of mind. Yet this marriage union, like so many others in the Scriptures, is given quite a lengthy place in the scheme of divine revelation typologically.

Typical Marriage Unions

The very first such union is shown to enshrine a 'mystery' which opens up the vista of our Lord's love for His church. God built

---

[1] Introducing his commentary on the Song. Saadia HaGaon lived 892–942 AD.

a bride for Adam, and then gave her to him. Adam and Eve are real enough we are assured, and the intimacy of their union is stated in literal terms, but the Spirit of God had greater, better things than this in view in granting the facts canonical place.[2] At considerable length we are informed when and how Isaac obtained his beloved Rebecca. It was after father and son together had gone to Moriah, and then had returned from its altar more precious to one another than ever. It was after Isaac's mother had died, too, that Abraham sent her servant on a mission to obtain a bride for Isaac. Clearly, it was his father's initiative then. When that expedition had been successfully completed we read that Isaac brought Rebecca 'into his mother's tent, and took Rebecca, and she became his wife; and he loved her: and Isaac was comforted after his mother's death'. Thus the Word of God has provided another suggestive anticipation of the One rightly described as 'the son of Abraham', that is, the Messiah as a greater than Isaac. In the next generation, a part of Jacob's life story is devoted to the circumstances through which he gained the wife he loved. Isaac his father, as concerned that he should not marry 'a wife of the daughters of Canaan' as Abraham was in his own case, sent Jacob away to Paddan-aram to obtain a wife from Rebecca's family circle there. It was in this way that Isaac saw that God would 'make thee (Jacob) fruitful, and multiply thee, that thou mayest be a company of peoples; and give thee the blessing of Abraham, to thee, and to thy seed with thee; that thou mayest inherit the land of thy sojournings, which God gave unto Abraham'.[3] God governed over Jacob's affairs, not least in leading him to Rachel whom he saw, he kissed, and 'Jacob loved Rachel'. Such was his love for her that 'he served seven years for Rachel; and they seemed unto him but a few days, for the love he had to her'. Compressed into the life-time of a family are the elements of Israel's long history as a nation. In Ruth's case, things are reversed. Her love for her mother, Naomi, after the loss of her first husband, drew her to her mother's

---

[2] Gen.2.21–24; cf. Eph.5.25–32.   [3] It is important to trace the husband/wife relationship's place in the divine purpose. They are to be 'fruitful, and multiply', to 'replenish the earth', to 'subdue it', to 'have dominion', and in Jacob's case 'to inherit the land', see Gen.1.28; 9.1,7; 28.3; 35.11; 48.4.

homeland, there to become the life partner of wealthy Boaz. He became her kinsman redeemer saying 'Ruth the Moabitess ... have I purchased to be my wife, to raise up the name of the dead upon his inheritance'. The glad response of the people was 'The Lord make the woman that is come into thine house like Rachel and like Leah, which two did build the house of Israel'. The messianic purpose was prospered by this means. Truly 'the time will fail me if I tell of' these and other historical marriages with typological significance.[4] Enough has been said to support Westcott's assertion that Biblical history itself is one vast prophecy.

Jewish Interpretation of the Song

Much of the Rabbinic approach sees the Song as an allegory unveiling the intimate and unique relationship of the Lord and the nation of Israel. Documentation for this interpretation exists as early as Rabbi Aqibha in the 2nd century AD. Like numbers of Christian expositors that were to follow him however, no detailed, consistent and consecutive application of the proposal was forthcoming at that time. It can never suffice to say that we should detect the history of the divine relationship with the people here; there must follow an indication of how this is to be discovered throughout the Song.

A detailed attempt at this is found later in the **Targum** which constructs a history of salvation following the chapters of the Song. One study of this saw five distinct movements. **First**, the Exodus from Egypt and the Sinai revelation and all that was bound up with the wilderness wanderings, 1.2–17, is climaxed by the conquest of their God-given inheritance, 2.1–3.6. **Second**, Solomon's Temple and its dedication, 3.7–4.1, together with the priesthood's acceptance, and ministry, into which the nation is invited as a suited bride, 4.2–5.1. **Third**, Israel's sin which resulted in the Exile, 5.2–7. During the exile she confessed to her prophets how much she longed after her God. In turn God expressed His concern for Jerusalem and its sages, whereupon the prophets aided her,

---

[4] Consider, for example Joseph and his Gentile bride Asenath, Gen.41.39–46, 50–52, and Solomon and his marriage to Pharaoh's daughter, 1 Kgs.3.1.

5.8–6.1. **Fourth**, their prayer was accepted, they returned from the exile, the Temple was rebuilt, and Israel's praise and dedication to God and His house, plus rabbinic teaching, assured their continuance, 6.2–7.10[11]. **Fifth**, the nation's dispersion throughout the Roman Empire, which causes them to look for the messianic fulfilment, the Messiah is commissioned and he teaches the nation the fear of the Lord and to await the final outcome of the end times battle before going up to Jerusalem, 7.11[12]–8.4. The resurrection of the righteous follows, and Israel will enjoy renewed intimacy forever, receiving a double portion as recompense for their devotion to the Torah. God must retire to heaven until He restores the land, city, and Temple again, 8.5–14.[5]

Saadia HaGaon's approach also traces the nation's history from the Exodus to the Messiah's coming. For him, there were eight stages. **The first two stages** bring Israel from Egypt to Sinai, and then to the spies report and the disciplining of God, 1.2–3.5, followed by the portable Tabernacle period, the nation's wanderings, and the place given Moses and Aaron among the people, 3.6–4.7. **Stage 3** brought Israel to Canaan's inheritance, the Temple, the two-kingdom division of the nation, Judah's special place and the festival pilgrimages, 4.8–5.1. **Stages 4 and 5** lead us through the collapse of the kingdom, exile and return, the rebuilt Temple and renewed covenant, 5.2–6.3, to a consideration of the people who had returned, 6.4–9. **Stage 6** reflects on the lengthy national dispersion when they have neither king, prince, nor sacrifice (Hos.3.4) but abide still for God, 6.10–7.9[10]. **Stage 7** is the most remarkable, for here he sees two Messiahs. First, the suffering of Messiah ben Joseph to be followed by the appearing of Messiah ben David. The joyous conditions through the nation's obedience and the presence of God among them is likened to the joy of the Bridegroom and his Bride, 7.10[11]–8.4. Finally, **Stage 8** sees the complete restoration of Israel, and the third Temple built, 8.5–14.[6]

---

[5] This summary does not do justice to the detail, where there is considerable stress on the Oral Law, see Loewe BM 170-3.

[6] Commentary in Hamesh Megilloth, ed. J. Kapah. Summaries in Pope SoS 95–102.

The Missing Keys

The latter attempt at an allegorical interpretation of the Song in terms of the nation's salvation history is more aware of the true structural divisions of the material. It also presents a two dimensional messianic perspective from a Jewish scholar of the 10th century AD! This is so near to, and yet so far from, the truth. The Old Testament messianic programme, however enigmatic, cannot be understood where the thinking mould, the preconceived plan, demands one climactic appearance of a vindicating, liberating, conquering King. God's revelation includes the portraits both of a suffering and a sovereign Messiah. The great sage has grasped this, solving the problem by assuming the emergence of two Messiahs. In that we believe that he was mistaken. The true solution is to be found in one Messiah who first appeared to suffer and die, and whom God then raised from the dead to take over eventually the administration and glory of His kingdom. A greater ruler than Joseph was promised, One who would be rejected by his own brethren out of envy, whose undeserved sufferings would take him beyond a prison into death itself. And yet, through that death He would conquer him that had the power of death, and through resurrection would become the guarantor of the redemption of Israel.

Following in the train of His ascension to heaven, the Spirit-empowered apostles addressed the nation with stirring words: 'Ye are the sons of the prophets, and of the covenant which God made with your fathers, saying unto Abraham, And in thy seed shall all the families of the earth be blessed. Unto you first God, having raised up his Servant, sent him to bless you, in turning away every one of you from your iniquities'.[7] The glorified Messiah was now speaking through His servants saying, with even more pathos than Joseph could muster 'be not grieved, nor angry with yourselves, that ye sold me hither: for God did send me before you to preserve life . . . to preserve you a remnant in the earth, and to save you alive by a great deliverance . . . ye meant evil against me; but God meant it for good, to bring to pass, as it is this day, to save much people alive'.[8] That ministry still continues though nineteen and a half

---

[7] Acts 3.25f.   [8] Gen.45.5,7; 50.20.

171

centuries have passed, during which the Messiah awaits patiently the day appointed for His second advent. In proposing a comparatively close link historically, between the suffering and reigning 'Messiahs' the great Jewish teacher was also in error therefore. The Messiah is now at the right hand of God; He is the one 'whom the heaven must receive until the times of the restoration of all things, whereof God spake by the mouth of his holy prophets which have been since the world began.[9]

Attempts to trace the Biblical history of salvation in the Song have seemed doomed to failure even where there is a messianic goal. However, once Jesus is seen to be the Messiah, His *two advents* to earth provide the keys to the locks of the Song which have been lost for so long! It was here that the allegorical application of the Song to Christ and the Church by the Church Fathers was found lacking. Any view of God's redemptive programme which does not embrace the summing up of all things in the Messiah, whether they be the things in the heavens, or the things upon the earth, will prove too restricted. All Israel must yet be saved; creation's groans must cease. The sympathies and hopes of the Song take us through the several phases of salvation history without missing a major milestone. The Messiah and His work is central to this, and must become its grand climax too.

Seeking and Finding

We must take an overview of part of the Song in more detail. It overlaps three of the panels or poems which we have already proposed. The two stanzas enclosing the piece, 3.1–5 and 5.2–8, open with a bedroom scene in which the maiden is made aware that she has lost the presence of her beloved. Her reaction in each case is to go out into the streets of the city to seek him. In both cases she is found by the watchmen of the city, though their reactions to her differ on each occasion. It is important to note this. In the first instance she addresses a question to the watchmen, 'Saw ye him whom my soul loveth?' She notes that she had no sooner left them than she found 'him whom my soul loveth'. In the second instance

---

[9] Acts 3.21; cf.Ps.110.1.

she called to her beloved, and he gave her no answer. Perhaps it was this 'disturbance of the peace' that drew forth a completely different reaction from the watchmen. She recalls that 'they smote me, they wounded me; the keepers of the walls took away my mantle from me'. The climax of the stanzas differs too. In chapter 3, having found her beloved, she holds him and would not let him go until he was brought into her mother's house, 'into the chamber of her that conceived me'. The charge follows 'that ye stir not up, nor awaken love, until it please'. In chapter 5, having not found her beloved, and having suffered at the hands of the watchmen, she charges the daughters of Jerusalem to look for him, and 'if ye find my beloved, that ye tell him, that I am sick of love'. Read these stanzas carefully, comparing and contrasting the details.

Who are the watchmen?

The word watchmen [Heb.shomrim‡][10] is used three times in our stanzas. Elsewhere in the Old Testament it describes those who keep guard of a person(s), property, or city. They were responsible for the maintenance of order and for security. The watchman of the city patrolled its walls and streets, specially at night and in times of seige. For the people of God, however, 'except the Lord keep the city, the watchmen waketh but in vain'.[11] Surely it was the prophets' function that could be aptly described in terms of the watchmen's responsibility. They were commissioned as watchmen by their God, as Isaiah who was told 'Go, set a watchman; let him declare what he seeth', or as was revealed through Jeremiah 'I set watchmen over you', or as Ezekiel heard 'Son of man, I have made thee a watchman unto the house of Israel: therefore hear the

---

[10] The verb [Heb.shamar] means to keep, preserve, protect, watch, guard, and is used in a variety of contexts. Kindred words are 1. [Heb.mishmar] used of setting a watch or guard, e.g. during Nehemiah's building operations, 4.9,22,23[3,16,17],cf.Jer.51.12, and 2. [Heb.mishmereth] of priests and Levites who kept God's ordinance, charge, sanctuary, 1 Chron.23.22; Ezek.44.8,14,15,16; 48.11, and of keepers of the watch, 2 Kings 11.6,7. A synonymous term [Heb.tsaphah in Song at 7.4[5]‡ = looketh] is also found at for example 1 Sam.14.16; 2 Sam.13.34; 18.24,25,26(2),27; 2 Kgs.9.17,18,20; Isa.21.5,6.   [11] Ps.127.1.

word at my mouth, and give them warning from me' [all Heb.tsaphah].[12] We hear the repeated cry 'Watchman, what of the night?' The question in the minds of those Edomites was 'How long will this dark night of trouble last before a new and better day dawns?' 'The watchman said, The morning cometh, and also the night: if ye will inquire, inquire ye: turn ye, come' [all Heb.shamar].[13] The watchman's ministry, however, was far from being one of unrelieved gloom. The psalmist who had cried to his God 'out of the depths' said 'My soul looketh for the Lord, more than watchmen look for the morning; yea, more than watchmen for the morning'. Isaiah predicts that 'The voice of thy watchmen! they lift up the voice, together do they sing; for they shall see eye to eye, when the Lord returneth to Zion'. And 'I have set watchmen upon thy walls, O Jerusalem; they shall never hold their peace day nor night: ye that are the Lord's remembrancers, take ye no rest, and give him no rest, till he establish, and till he make Jerusalem a praise in the earth'.[14] We submit, therefore, that the watchmen in the Song represent the prophets.

Why do these Watchmen react so differently?

The reaction of the watchmen in the two incidents in the Song cannot be arbitrary. Surely, the explanation is already anticipated in our consideration of the prophets' ministry. Granted that things were right, or reasonably so, between the people and their God, the nation had nothing to fear from their preaching and teaching. Provided that they were seeking the Lord genuinely the prophets would encourage their spiritual desires. To put it in terms of the Song, when the maiden asked them 'Saw ye him whom my soul loveth', she was not abused, ill-treated, humiliated by them. Rather, she found the one she sought immediately she left them. The positive role of the prophets was to point the nation to the Messiah, and to stimulate every spiritual yearning that had been produced in the breasts of those within the nation who panted after their God.

To apply this to that Messiah-conscious remnant to which we are

---

[12] Isa.21.6; Jer.6.17; Ezek.6.17; cf.33.2,6(2),7; Hab.2.1.   [13] Isa.21.11(2),12.
[14] Ps.130.6; Isa.52.8; 62.6.

introduced in the opening pages of our New Testaments, they had hardly left behind them the ministry of their prophets when they 'found him'! What had been written was beginning to come to pass, and the prayerful yearnings of the remnant were satisfied in the coming of their Messiah. They brought Him to *their* 'mother's house', the land of promise, Israel, even to *His* mother's house at Bethlehem, cf. Luke 1–2. 'Now all this is come to pass, that it might be fulfilled which was spoken by the Lord through the prophet saying, Behold, the virgin shall be with child, and shall bring forth a son, and they shall call his name Immanuel'. This was the One who was 'born King of the Jews' to whose birthplace the prophet had already pointed. For 'thou Bethlehem land of Judah, art in no wise least among the princes of Judah: for out of thee shall come forth a governor, which shall be shepherd of my people Israel'. Not only did a multitude of the heavenly host praise God saying 'Glory to God in the highest, and on earth peace'. All those who looked for the consolation of Israel as forecast in the prophets could, with Simeon, exclaim 'mine eyes have seen thy salvation, which thou hast prepared before the face of all peoples; a light for revelation to the Gentiles, and the glory of thy people Israel'. Anna the prophetess finding Him in the temple 'gave thanks unto God, and spake of him to all them that were looking for the redemption of Jerusalem'.[15] It is to the incarnation, the 'coming in' of Jesus the Messiah, the Son of God, that chapter 3 of the Song points us.

We are not surprised that, having come to the mother's house, many others have 'found him'. For example, having encountered Jesus after His baptism, it was Andrew who 'findeth first his own brother Simon, and saith unto him, We have found the Messiah'. Once Philip was found by Jesus, 'Philip findeth Nathanael, and saith unto him, We have found him, of whom Moses in the law, and the prophets did write'. In all of these instances the words 'seek, and ye shall find' are found to be true.[16]

We are left with the task of considering the *unsuccessful* attempt to find the beloved in chapter 5 of the Song. It is with this that the more heavy handed response of the watchmen is associated. Why? Surely, we are being directed here to the more negative ministry

---

[15] Matt.1.22; 2.2,6; Luke 2.30ff,36.　　　[16] John 1.41,45; Luke 11.9f.

of the prophets; to the thunderous voices of condemnation, and the unpalatable pronouncements of judgments. The inviolable city was to fall, the messianic hope enshrined in the Davidic covenant would appear to be abrogated, the nation would be dispersed. As Jesus expressed it in His Olivet Discourse 'There shall not be left here one stone upon another, that shall not be thrown down'. The explanation why this should be the lot of the nation had been made clear before He had uttered these terrifying words. Had He not said with a pathos not matched by any of the prophets 'O Jerusalem, Jerusalem, which killeth the prophets, and stoneth them that are sent unto her! how often would I have gathered thy children together, even as a hen gathereth her chickens under her wings, and *ye would not!* Behold, your house is left unto you desolate'.[17] In the past, the sin and departure of the nation drew forth the exposure, the expostulation, and the execration of the prophets. Yet its plight, its suffering, its humiliation and immense loss has never equalled that which it has endured for nearly 2000 years now. And still the nation, though miraculously preserved throughout the Diaspora and even in the Land, still lacks king, prince, and sacrifice. The only explanation for this is found on the lips of their own rejected and neglected Messiah. Of the One who 'came unto his own (place)' we read that 'they that were his own (people) received him not'.[18] For Israel, this is the tragedy of all tragedies. It has unleashed the divine judgments pronounced by the prophets, which have left her smitten, wounded, and stripped bare. Despite the tremendous achievements of the modern State of Israel, and though she knows the support of so many who endorse her divine choice, and love her because their God has set His love upon her, still she looks out upon a sea of hostility and upon nations bent upon her destruction. There are prophecies that still await their fulfilment, for the 'time of Jacob's trouble' is still to run its appointed course, and Jerusalem must fall before it knows its final salvation and redemption. There are those who, encouraged to do so by the words of the psalm, 'pray for the peace of Jerusalem'. That peace is to be ushered in by the *second advent* of 'the prince of peace'. That happy day was prophesied by the

---

[17] Matt.24.2; 23.37f.   [18] John 1.11.

Messiah who wept over His own city. He did not say simply, 'Ye shall not see me henceforth'. In grace He looked beyond the present, saying 'Ye shall not see me henceforth, *till* ye shall say, Blessed is He that cometh in the name of the Lord'.[19]

The two stanzas introducing the watchmen in the Song therefore touch upon the experience of the Israel of God, the nation within the nation, at the *eisodos* and then after the *exodus* of its Messiah at His first advent. In the former the peculiar appeal is made to the nation to whom 'a child is born ... a son is given', the coming into manhood of the One who is the son of David according to the flesh, and yet the eternal Son of God incarnate. This *'coming in'* [Grk. eisodos] is a miracle and a mystery. In the latter His miraculous coming into the world is matched by His equally miraculous departure from this world, His *'going out'* [Grk. exodos]. This was the grand topic of conversation between the Messiah and Moses and Elijah when they were seen in glory upon 'the holy mount'. It is Luke who tells us that they 'spake of his decease' [Grk. exodos = His 'way out' of this world back to the Father]. The Lord Jesus in John's record succinctly speaks of the two events, saying 'I came out from the Father, and am come into the world: again, I leave the world, and go unto the Father'.[20] These two matchless events form an historical *inclusio*, between which the first advent of Israel's Messiah follows its divinely appointed course. Between the two 'seeking' paragraphs of the Song, that same momentous period is poetically presented. The counterpart to the literal story in Song 3.6–5.1 is to be found in the public ministry of the Lord Jesus. It touches upon the drawing of a bride to Himself, how He brings her from the wilderness to His capital city, how He speaks to her heart before finishing His work which makes her all fair in His sight, and finally His most delightful description of her when He makes her His very own. All of this is to be considered in greater detail in chapter 17. Suffice it to say here, in our concern to provide the interpretive keys for the understanding of the Song typologically, that the great watershed of this poem is provided by Myrrh Mountain, which is given a dominating central place.[21] This demands our attention.

---

[19] Jer.30.7f; Isa.9.6f[5f]; Matt.23.39.   [20] Luke 9.31; John 16.28.   [21] Song 4.6. It is centrally located in Poem 3, 3.6–5.1.

Where and What is Myrrh Mountain?

The beloved's words are '. . . I will get me to the mountain of myrrh, and to the hill of frankincense'. The 'mountain' theme features often in the Song. Mostly the word appears in the plural form.[22] In one of these, the word 'hills' is found in synonymous poetic parallelism.[23] Twice only in the Song 'mountain' appears in the singular.[24] The first of these in 4.1 refers to Mount Gilead specifically. We should note that the route taken by caravans travelling to Jerusalem from Galilee in the New Testament period followed the course of the Jordon Valley near the foot of Mount Gilead. The second use of the word in the singular should be construed specifically similarly. Consequently, 'the mountain' and 'the hill' of 4.6 call for identification, as the use of the definite article also indicates. They refer to one and the same place. For the Targum it was Temple Mount, inside the city, from which the incense was the means of dispelling the powers of darkness. Rather we believe, in the purpose of God it has to be 'The place of a skull', Golgotha, outside though very near the city, where out of love the Messiah 'gave himself up for us, an offering and a sacrifice to God for an odour of a sweet smell'. It was the wise men that brought 'frankincense, and myrrh' to the babe of Bethlehem. With a view to alleviating His sufferings, others 'offered him wine mingled with myrrh' at the cross. Once He had died, two of His friends wrapped His body with 'myrrh and aloes'. Myrrh and the Man of Sorrows belong together. The fragrance of sorrows meekly borne had exuded freely from Him throughout the course of His life here. Yet the piercing at the cross only served to cause the myrrh to flow in still greater abundance. A greater than Joseph died at Golgotha of whom it could be said 'The archers have sorely grieved [Heb.marar] him'.[25] Myrrh Mountain is a monument of Messiah's suffering love, fragrant to His God, and sanctifying to all who shelter in its shadow. He still leaves its tokens on our unopened door handles! That which was bitter to His taste, is fragrant to the God of salvation, and to all who come to know Him. The very first

---

[22] [Heb.har*] in pl. Song 2.8,17; 4.8; 8.14.   [23] 2.8.   [24] 4.1,6.
[25] See Joseph's blessing, Gen. 49.22–26.

mention of myrrh informs us that it was the first of four spice ingredients in the holy anointing oil. It must be sufferings first, and even in the guaranteed glories that follow, the fragrance of those sufferings has a pre-eminent part in the Messiah's excelling royal priestly office. His anointing is to be with 'the oil of gladness above' His fellows.[26]

Frankincense Hill is Golgotha viewed from another angle. This spice, too, was bitter to the taste, but fragrant to the smell. It is last in the list of five spices to be prepared in equal quantities in the holy incense. Notice how these spices occupy the first and the last places in the lists respectively. They are the alpha and omega of the two ministries. What all-embracing imparted blessings there are in Him who bore the cross! The fragrant frankincense exuded freely throughout the life of our Lord, but flowed forth to excess when He was pierced on Golgotha's Hill. As the holy incense was essential for the priestly ministries in the sanctuary, so the fragrance of all the Lord's moral excellence equips Him perfectly for His representative role on His people's behalf. This streams through to all His own who draw near to God through Him. Yet His priestly, intercessory love, now flows out of all the acceptability of His own fragrant life and death.[27]

It was to Myrrh Mountain and Frankincense Hill that the Messiah must retire if He was to furnish His loved one with that spotlessness, and that fragrance which alone will suit her for Himself. He must gather the spices before she can be supplied with them. No man took His life from Him; He laid it down voluntarily and unreservedly. He 'gave himself up for us, an offering and a sacrifice to God for an odour of a sweet smell'.[28] Only after His visit to this mountain and hill can His loved one also become 'full of fragrance rare'. Eternal consequences issue from that momentous hour! This is in truth the pivot of the ages.[29]

A View from this Watershed

From a literary point of view, Poem 3, Song 3.6–5.1, conducts us

---

[26] Ps.45.6f[7f] = Heb.1.8f; for details re myrrh see pp.110–3,n.50–63.　　[27] For details re frankincense see pp.108ff,n.35–49.　　[28] Eph. 5.2.　　[29] Heb.9.26.

to the great watershed of the book, the consummation of the marriage of the happy pair. Typologically, too, the poem in anticipating the first advent of the Messiah and His return to heaven, together with all that is bound up with that, brings us to the watershed of the divine plan in salvation history. The peak is reached in 4.6 which points us to the place Golgotha, and the propitiatory work completed there. We should expect that the stanzas leading up to this would touch upon the Messiah's life and ministry, while the stanzas immediately following it would point us to His resurrection and ascension ministries. This we believe to be patent. Once this is grasped, we obtain a panoramic view of the typological perspective of the Song as a whole, and are able to review all of God's ways with the true Israel from beginning to end, from the patriarchs through to the Millennium. From the vantage point of the first advent in chapters 3 and 4 we can look backward to the beginning of God's love for the fathers, and the covenant He made with Abraham guaranteeing the end from the beginning. Looking forward from 5.1 we are able to trace the gracious and sovereign ways of God with the Israel of God in the present, and then finally to the time when His covenant with David is fulfilled to the nation in the Messianic Kingdom of God on earth. Our purpose in the following chapters is to briefly sketch this progress of the divine purpose, the love relationship between the Lord and the true Israel, in the six poems of the Song.

Part 4

THE PROGRESS
THROUGH
THE POEMS

Contents – Part 4

TRANSLATION OF THE SONG OF SONGS by O. L. BARNES

KEY: M = Male; F = Female; D = Daughters of Jerusalem
(with −) words not in Hebrew; [with +] our literal rendering

TITLE, 1.1. The most excellent Song of Solomon.

POEM 1, 1.2–2.7

F
1.2. {He is kissing me with the kisses of his mouth.}
Much better are thine affections [loves] than wine!
3. For fragrance thine ointments are exquisite;
Such ointment is thy name, causing the pouring forth of thyself,
Therefore have virgins always loved thee!
4. Draw me! After thee we are running;
{The king has brought me to his own apartments}
We are rejoicing and are joyful in thee,
We have cause to remember thine affections [loves] more than wine.
How rightly they have always loved thee!

* * * * * * *

F
5. Black am I, yet comely,
O daughters of Jerusalem:
As tents of Kedar,
As pavilions of Solomon.
6. Do not stare at me because I am dark,
Because the sun has so scorched [burnt] me:
My mother's children incensed one another against me,
They made me keep these vineyards;
My own vineyard I have not kept.

* * * * * * *

F
7. O do make known to me,
Thou whom my very being [+ soul] utterly loves,
Where thou art pasturing thy flock,
Where thou art making it lie down at noontide;
Lest I am as one languishing
Beside the flocks of thy companions.

D+
8. If thou knowest not,
O most beautiful among women,
Get thee forth by the footsteps of this flock,
And pasture these thy kids
Beside the shepherds' tents.

* * * * * * *

M
1.9. I to a mare among chariot-horses of a Pharaoh
Have oft likened thee, my love.
10. Unchangingly lovely are thy cheeks
With these circlets,
Thy neck with bead-rows.
11. Circlets of gold we are making for thee
With studs of fine silver.

183

F

12. {All the time the king was at his banquet,
    My spikenard was giving-forth its fragrance}
13. A bundle of precious myrrh is my beloved to me;
    Between my breasts he is passing the night.
14. A cluster of fragrant henna is my beloved to me,
    Midst the vineyards of En-gedi.

M

15. Behold, thou art beautiful, my love,
    Behold, thou art beautiful,
    Thy two eyes are (– eyes of) doves.

F

16. Behold thou art beautiful my beloved,
    As well as most lovely;
    Too, our union is flourishing,
17. Our trysting-places are well-established,
    Our bond of love most strong.
2.1. I am a narcissus of the plain,
    A lily of the valleys.

M

2. As a lily among the thorns,
   So is my love among the daughters.

F

3. As an apple-tree among trees of the wood,
   So is my beloved among the sons.
   Under his shadow
   I have constantly delighted and dwelt,
   And his fruit is sweet to my taste.
4. He has brought me into his house of best-wine,
   And his banner over me is love.
5. O keep on sustaining me with these raisin-cakes,
   Keep on refreshing me with these apples,
   Because stricken with love am I.
6. {His left hand is under my head,
   While his right hand affectionately embraces me}

M+

7. I have solemnly charged you,
   O daughters of Jerusalem,
   Like gazelles [+ does, f.],
   Rather like hinds of the field,
   Do not ye cause to disturb,
   Neither do ye yourselves awaken such love
   Until it pleases.

* * * * * * *

+ Barnes proposes speaker for 1.8 is male, and for 2.7 is female, see p.164.

15

POEM 1. HIS BANNER OVER ME WAS LOVE, 1.2–2.7

THE TWO OPENING POEMS of the Song are quite different from one another. In the first, 1.2–2.7, the love relationship develops happily, and first love nearness and dearness predominate. There are angry and demanding brothers who do not help. The maiden's introspection turns her attention in the wrong direction more than once. Even the hint of a mightier enemy, Pharaoh, is noted. Nonetheless, the general tone is happy and healthy emotionally. In the second poem, 2.8–3.5, there is a strange absence of that nearness which the earlier poem had led us to expect. Winter has followed the spring-to-autumn setting of the first poem. Initially, her beloved has to make all the advances. She is far away, and none too quick to respond to his appeals. Even when she has arrived in 'our land', danger and duty seem the order of the day. However, these at last produce an awareness of her beloved's 'absence' which 'makes the heart grow fonder'. In both of the poems any failures that are apparent rest with the maiden. Despite these, her beloved sees her satisfied in his love at the conclusion of each of the poems.

We shall consider Poem 1, 1.2–2.7, in order to pursue some of the elements of the salvation history theme there. Before we do this, we need to follow the drift of the actual love story suggested by the several stanzas. One general point. From the very beginning the thrill of love is known. It is to be noticed also that the opening and closing stanzas excel in the maiden's expressions of satisfaction with the love of her beloved.

The Thread of the Story

Perhaps one of the more peculiar elements in the story faces us most starkly here. In the very first stanza we hear the maiden speaking of the king, and then directly to him, about his many excellences. 'Draw me' she pleads. In the next breath, almost, she speaks to a shepherd she is anxious to find, saying 'Tell me, O thou whom my soul loveth, where thou feedest thy flock, where thou makest it to rest at noon . . .?' Of two solutions that have been proposed, the one insists that there are two distinct suitors before the maiden's eyes. The first is 'the king' who has carried her off from her country environment against her own wishes. Then, she introduces to us her lover, 'a shepherd' to whom she is determined to remain true, and who fills all her thoughts during her exile in the palace. The subtle shifts necessary in construing who is being addressed militate against this view. Also, the proposed rearranging of the text, and the plundering of the love poetry, which results from denying that much of it was a genuine expression of the affection of 'the king', is unacceptable.

Another more straightforward solution sees here a 'love at first sight' romance. The maiden first encountered her beau in the countryside. His 'glories' swept her off her feet, and she was enthralled. She became totally preoccupied with him, to the annoyance of her 'mother's sons', who had no sympathy with an 'infatuation' which, in their judgment, lacked all realism. Probably there was also an overdose of jealousy motivating their objections. Thoughts of a palace home and a station above them were to be put out of her mind. They were the more determined to prevent any further developments of her obsession, and at the same time ensure that she would be kept busy and out of the path of any royal itineraries in the future. The king grasped the situation of the one he admired so, and determined to return in a totally different guise. Laying aside his royal glory, he came as a 'shepherd', and she loved him even more for that. He sat down with the flocks, sheltering from the noon-day sun. His companions were shepherds caring for the royal estates. Like noble and wealthy Boaz, he was out in the fields. As with humble Ruth, the maiden was encouraged not to wander elsewhere, but rather to feed her kids 'by the shepherds tents'. She was as overwhelmed with his kindness as was Ruth who said 'Why have I found grace in thy sight . . .?' Our maiden said 'Look not upon me, because I am swarthy'. Attention to enforced duty had taken its toll. Yet for him, her subjection in this had made her the more desirable. The king of glory came, as the loving shepherd, to where she was. This was paradoxical but the more precious for that reason.

The whole poem appears to oscillate between the country and the city, the vineyards and the banqueting house, the sovereign and the shepherd. She needs to be conducted from one scene to the other so as to assure her heart, for she is overly self-conscious. This her beloved does with great sensitivity, responding to her initial request to him 'Draw me', and so accommodating himself to her every mood until she is faint with love and finally requests 'Stay (support) ye me'. The experienced attractions, responses, and triumphs over all obstacles, led to the attained rest of betrothal.

We may note that she

is drawn by him	is sustained by him
is brought into the king's chambers	is brought to the banqueting house
desires his kisses	enjoys his embrace

There is development elsewhere in the poem

she suffers from sun scorching	then she is under his shadow
she is slaving away in the vineyards	she is sitting down in his presence
we will run after thee	love is not to be disturbed

Throughout the poem we are listening generally to the voices of the maiden or of her beloved. For her, he is 'thou whom my soul loveth', and 'my beloved'.[1] For him, she is 'my love'.[2] He is heard in six of the verses only.[3] What the maiden has to say very

---

[1] Song 1.7: 1.13,14,16; 2.3.   [2] 1.9,15; 2.2.   [3] 1.9–11,15; 2.2,7. To assist in identifying the different speakers throughout this poem see the more detailed analysis of contents on p.161, and the translation on p.183f. There appears to be an interjected answer of certain unnamed onlookers, probably the daughters of Jerusalem, at 1.8.

much concerns herself as her many 'I', 'me' and 'my's' would indicate.[4] Also, she is more free to talk about him, than she is to talk to him.[5] Even when she addresses him, she is more taken up with 'thy love', 'thine ointments', and 'thy name', excelling most in her use of similes concerning what he is to her.[6] As for her beloved, however, he uses 'I' only twice, and there is a complete absence of the 'me' and 'my' syndrome apart from the endearing title 'my love' by which he addresses her. Further, in three of the five verses in which he speaks to her, he talks most approvingly of 'thy cheeks', 'thy neck', 'thine eyes'. For him, a general statement regarding her beauty, 'thou art fair', will not suffice.[7] Again, the maiden alone indulges in self-examination and description. What a lesson there is in all this. He was providing her (and us) with an example, to follow which is well-pleasing to God.

The Thread of Salvation History

We have already intimated that the Song's backcloth presents the ongoing love relationship between the Lord and the Israel that is dear to His heart. Though the scenery is changing constantly, we are not to miss the fact that the Lord is sovereign in that. In each phase of the nation's long history, He pursues His bright designs for her. In this first poem of the book we expect to begin at the beginning. Where did it all begin for *the embryo nation* if not with Abram? Did not Jacob along with his large family go down into Egypt? Was not a *nation* brought out of Egypt, which had become a house of bondage to them? Did not their God bring them in to a beautiful and fruitful *land*? And was not that God of glory who appeared to Abram at the beginning, ready to presence Himself among them in the *Temple*? With these questions in mind, we shall consider the poem.

Abram and the God of Glory, 1.2–4. This opening stanza has two strophes each climaxing similarly: 'therefore do the virgins love

---

[4] 'I' in Song 1.5,6(2); 2.1,3,5: 'me' in 1.2,4(2),6(4),14; 2.4(2),5(2),6: 'my' in 1.6,12,13; 2.3,6: 'mine' in 1.6. These do not include the use of 'my' in the titles of the poem.   [5] Note 'him', 1.2, 'he', 2.4, 'his', 1.2,4,12; 2.3(2),4,6(2).
[6] 1.2,4; 1.3   [7] His use of 'I' 1.9; 2.7. For specific description see 1.10,15. Contrast specially his words in 1.15 with hers in 1.16.

thee' and 'rightly do they love thee', vv. 3c, 4e. Both strophes open
with the maiden's 'me' however. In reflecting upon her own experience of His special favour, she is not unmindful of what he is
to others too. Observe this link between the one and the many.
Even in that setting where he kisses her 'with the kisses of his
mouth',[8] that is with intense fervour and love, she knows that
others have a part also. She knows his loves, his perfumes and his
name,[9] that is how he has unfolded himself to her. And yet for
that very reason, 'Therefore do the virgins love thee'. How attractive is her beloved's pouring forth of himself even to them! Again,
she says 'Draw me' but quickly follows it with 'we will run after
thee'. How breathtaking it is that the one who is kissing her, v.2,
is the king, and he has brought her into his very own chambers
amid great rejoicing, v.4.[10]

For the nation of Israel, 'Our father is Abraham', and they proudly
own 'We be Abraham's seed'. This giant among the patriarchs was
loved and called by the 'God of glory', being told of the wealthy inheritance God had in mind for him from the beginning. 'Get thee
out of thy land, and from thy kindred, and come into the land which
I shall shew thee'.[11] Truly, the King brought him into His chambers
and caused him to experience His love. Abraham alone is called 'my
friend' by God.[12] Think of the unfolding of the divine name to him
when he came into the land. Added to this unique relationship, God
promised 'I will bless thee, and make thy name great; and be thou
a blessing: and I will bless them that bless thee, and him that curseth
thee I will curse: and in thee shall all the families of the earth be
blessed'. God chose him and by His love drew him, and others
would run after Him! This is where the Song begins, and in it there
is an anticipation of the end. It is also where everything begins and
where everything will end for Israel.

---

[8] The imperfect would be rendered better not as a wish, 'Let him kiss me ...' but
as stating her present enjoyed experience 'He is kissing me ...'.   [9] Some consider these changes of pronoun as a feature of Biblical style only, and that the
maiden is meant throughout. We believe that a change of person(s) is marked by
these switches from singular to plural pronouns here.   [10] cf. Ps.45.15[16].
[11] John 8.39,33; Acts 7.2f; cf. Gen.12.1–3.   [12] The title uniquely Abraham's
'my (thy) friend' occurs in Isa.41.8; 2 Chron.20.7 [Heb. participle of ʿahabh, lit. my
loved one, vb. often in Song]; cf. Jas.2.23.

The Patriarchal History, 1.5–8. The opening stanza, vv.5–6, introduces a quite different note. The maiden is talking no longer to her beloved. She is aware of her swarthy appearance, and how this attracts the disdain of the daughters of Jerusalem. She opens up to them the paradoxical character of her attractiveness to her beloved. Black she may be, but she is comely[13] to him. If for some she is as unattractive as those black goats-hair tents, yet for him she is as beautiful as the tapestries which adorned Solomon's palace. Her lack of self-esteem is contrasted with the beauty her beloved sees in her. The difference is in the eye of the beholder which was able to penetrate more than skin deep. There are three factors which contribute to her present state, which are the sun, the sons, and herself. First, there are the scorching rays of the sun that burned as they 'looked upon' her; the heat is upon her from above.[14] Then there is the unexplained anger of the mother's sons, which led to their compelling her to slave away; the pressure is on her from family around her. Finally, there is a certain neglect on her own part from within. Notice the literal and metaphorical use of vineyards here.[15]

In the second stanza, vv.7–8, the shepherd and the flock image is drawn upon.[16]

In the course of salvation history Abraham's covenant was handed on to Isaac and Jacob, but neither of these were the equal of 'father Abraham'. With Jacob in particular, the history took many an unhappy turn. His sons, born to him when he was slaving away for the benefit of other family members in Aram, were the cause of considerable anxiety and sorrow to him. Joseph especially felt the brunt of jealousy and envious hatred when he spoke to his brothers of that glory which he foresaw for himself. Of course,

---

[13] There are three synonyms for beauty in the Song: 1. 'fair' [Heb. yapheh] beautiful, where the emphasis generally is upon the outward form, 1.8,15(2),16; 2.10,13; 4.1(2),7; 5.9; 6.1,4,10; verb [Heb. yaphah], 4.10; 7.1,6[2,7]‡: 2. 'pleasant' [Heb. na`im], bringing out the deeper and more inward loveliness and graciousness, 1.16; cf. 7.6[7]; cf. verb 1.10‡: 3. 'comely' [Heb. na`weh], refers to that which is suitable in every way, both inwardly and outwardly, 1.5; 2.14; 4.3; 6.4‡; see p.252.34; cf. verb na`ah 1.10; Ps.93.5; Isa.52.7*.   [14] 'scorched' [Heb. shazaph] means also 'look upon, see, glance', Song 1.6; Job 20.9; 28.7.   [15] See pp.77f.   [16] See pp.57ff, esp. n.17f; 21f; 27f.

190

being only half-brothers, his 'mother's sons', they took greater exception to the favours bestowed upon Joseph by a doting father.
All of this led to their rejection of his hopes (and theirs), and to his
banishment to unjustified toil and suffering. He might have said,
'My mother's sons were incensed against me, they made me
keeper of the vineyards; but mine own vineyard have I not kept'.
There were many unhappy experiences for Jacob and his family
which brought them down into Egypt. The old man confessed 'The
days of the years of my pilgrimage are an hundred and thirty
years: few and evil have been the days of the years of my life, and
they have not attained unto the days of the years of the life of my
fathers in the days of their pilgrimage'. And yet from another
standpoint, their troubles were all part of the divine discipline as
'the sun' that had scorched them from above. In fact, in Joseph's
words, 'ye meant evil against me; but God meant it for good . . .
to save much people alive'. God's purpose was epitomized in
Joseph's children. His firstborn he called Manasseh 'For, said he,
God hath made me to forget all my toil, and all my father's house'.
He named his secondborn Ephraim 'For God hath made me fruitful in the land of my affliction'.[17] They could truthfully confess 'I
am black', but to their God they were 'comely'.

On arrival in Egypt they owned that they were 'shepherds', and
were even made rulers over Pharaoh's cattle in the best of the land
in Goshen. The Lord's purpose and His presence was to be found
'beside the shepherds' tents' alone at that time. Incredible as it
might seem, it was Jacob who blessed Pharaoh, and Joseph who
became the then 'Saviour of the world'.[18]

The Exodus From Egypt, 1.9–11. The reference to Pharaoh provides the clear key for the historical association of the whole poem.
This in particular is the 'Exodus' stanza. In it the beloved speaks
glowingly of his loved one. It is as though we are listening in upon
the Lord's assessment of that nation dear to His heart on the spectacular occasion of their liberation, and the spoiling of their
enemies. Already, we have considered the simile of the 'mare

---

[17] The general background is found in Gen.28–35; 37–50; more particularly 47.9;
50.20; 41.51f.   [18] Gen.47.4–7,10,27; 50.20.

191

among Pharaoh's chariots'.[19] His chariots were drawn by pairs of stallions. The word used here is singular and feminine [Heb. susah = mare]. Not only does this description stress the incomparable beauty of the maiden, but suggests another thought altogether. One mare loose among Pharaoh's chariotry would produce complete chaos! The one would see the overthrow of the thousand: their enemies would 'come out against thee one way, and shall flee before thee seven ways'. With the Lord committed to them in their weakness, Pharaoh's proud army was thrown into disarray. Israel had to 'stand still, and see the salvation of the Lord'. On that day 'Miriam answered them, Sing ye to the Lord, for he hath triumphed gloriously; the horse and his rider hath he thrown into the sea'. Moses and the children of Israel sang similarly, and said 'Pharaoh's chariots and his host hath he cast into the sea'. The saved nation could sing 'we cried unto the Lord, the God of our fathers, and the Lord heard our voice, and saw our affliction, and our toil, and our oppression: and the Lord brought us forth out of Egypt with a mighty hand, and with an outstretched arm, and with great terribleness, and with signs, and with wonders'.[20]

If the simile of the mare highlights both the delights and dangers the beloved sees in his loved one, he also notes those simple things which add to her attractiveness. Her 'cheeks are comely with plaits (of hair)' and her 'neck with strings of jewels (perhaps beads)'. Her wealthy beloved is determined to have made for her 'plaits of gold with studs of silver'. How this is reflected at the time of the Exodus. As the nation left the land of Egypt, Israel 'spoiled the Egyptians' and were given 'jewels of silver, and jewels of gold, and raiment'.[21] At this point in the Song, therefore, we trace the thrilling and materially enhanced state of the Lord's people at the momentous 'Exodus event'.

Israel Enjoying the Promised Inheritance with her Lord, 1.12–2.7. The general change of tone is quite dramatic; all is calm as 'the king sat at his table' and as his loved one comes to sit down 'under his shadow'. The conflict is followed by communion. In the

---

[19] See for more detail on the 'mare' pp.55f,n.14f.   [20] Deut.28.7; ct. Isa.30.17; Deut.26.7f; Exod.14.13; 15.21,1,4.   [21] 12.35f; 3.22; 11.2f.

21

21. *'A garden shut up (inclosed) is my sister, by bride', Song 4.12. See pp. 94–97. The 'inclosed garden'
here is at Artas, south-west of Bethlehem.*

22. *A recreated 'Solomon's Pool' at Neot Kedummim, with date palms and cedars in the background.*

22

23. One of the traditional complex of 'Solomon's Pools', near Artas, south of Bethlehem. 'I made me gardens and parks, I planted trees in them . . . I made me pools of water', Eccles. 2.5f.

23

24

24. An ancient well with typical recreated winding gear (and a modern bucket!) at Neot Kedummim. See p. 98.

25. The source of the Dan River at the foot of the Anti-Lebanon mountains in the Hula Valley. 'Thou art a fountain of garden, a well of living waters, and flowing streams from Lebanon', Song 4.15. See p. 98f.

25

several stanzas the imagery and even the scene may change, but the lovers' appreciative dialogue continues unbrokenly.

The first stanza provides the necessary stimulus for their endearing exchanges, and in this she describes him, 1.12–14. The king that 'sat at his table' is her beloved. This suits well the 'banqueting house' setting of 2.4. His love has brought her into his own royal surroundings. It is here that her spikenard spreads its appealing fragrance for him. It is here that he lies in her embrace, so as to enhance her appreciation of his fragrance and beauty.

For the nation that was brought out of Egypt the promised land was the goal. Consequently, the wilderness finds no place here. The Song pursues the love relationship between the Lord and the nation precious to him. One of the quotations we have already had before us stating that 'the Lord brought us forth out of Egypt', continued with the words 'and he hath brought us into this place, and hath given us this land, a land flowing with milk and honey'.[22] It is with this 'kingdom of priests, and an holy nation' that the Lord has found His delight. It is to His land, and to His own special place in it that He has brought her. His table is the altar. It is there that the children of Israel were to present 'My oblation, my food (bread) for my offerings made by fire'.[23] At the altar her pure worship, her 'spikenard sent forth its fragrance'. Beyond an acceptable sacrificial death, faith rests and is redolent in the presence of the Living One.[24] The nation learned to appreciate affectionately her 'Beloved' as one whose own fragrance was found upon her. To her heart He was 'as a bundle of myrrh, that lieth betwixt my breasts'. She had proved Him as her Saviour from Egypt, and she knew also that 'In all their affliction he was afflicted . . . in his love and in his pity he redeemed them; and he bare them, and carried them all the days of old'.[25] In the prescribed sacrifices He made Himself so near to her heart, and these anticipate His own sacrifice.

The remainder of this opening poem introduces a dialogue between the couple in the love story. We shall follow these couplets of conversation, each supplying another stanza to the poem.

---

[22] Deut.12.8f. [23] Mal.1.7f; Num.28.1. [24] See for detail re 'nard' pp.103f, n.12–20 there. [25] Isa.63.8f. For detail re 'myrrh' see pp.110–13, n.50–63.

In the first of these her beloved opens the dialogue, 1.15, by using his favourite term of endearment, 'my love' [Heb. ra˘yathi].[26] We have seen that 'thou art fair' is a frequently used formula of commencement in the Song, where it is found more than in any other Old Testament book. Here, and most often, it is found on his lips, and the repetition gives it a certain emphasis. He even uses the word as yet another term of endearment for the maiden, addressing her as 'my fair one', 2.10,13. Her beauty fascinated him,[27] and he would arrest her attention in making the point. It is the loveliness, the beauty of women rather than of men, that is given more space in the Bible.[28]

Under the simile of a woman the nation's beauty in the eyes of her Lord is also found. Through Ezekiel he reminds the nation that she was 'exceeding beautiful'. The prophet is quick to point out the source of her attractiveness however: 'thou wast exceeding beautiful, and thou didst prosper unto royal estate. And thy renown went forth among the nations for thy beauty; for it was perfect, through my majesty which I had put upon thee, saith the Lord God'. It was not her natural inherited beauty that appealed to Him. She was not to look to her own people or her father's house if the King was to desire her beauty.[29]

Particularly here in the Song it is her eyes that drew forth her beloved's praise. Neither was there a veil on her eyes to limit either his appreciation of them, or her full appreciation of him and all that she had through the king's grace. For the nation too, the revelation of God spoken to the fathers through the prophets was 'pure, enlightening the eyes', and there was neither 'tradition' nor 'hardness' as yet. In contrast, the Midrash Rabbah proposes that the Sanhedrin are the eyes of the congregation! When the nation had eyes for Him alone, Moses' prayer that 'the beauty [Heb. no˘am] of the Lord our God be upon us' would surely be answered.

---

[26] Found at 1.9,15; 2.10,13; 4.1,7; 5.2; 6.4. For detail see p.45,n.25f.   [27] In all the verb and adjective [Heb. yaphah, yapheh] are found 16 times. The next highest incidence elsewhere occurs in Genesis, 9 times. For its importance structurally in the Song see p.155. As a superlative it is used of the maiden by 'the daughters', 1.8; 5.9; 6.1. It is used of the beloved only at 1.16, see n.13.   [28] cf. Rachel, Gen.29.17, Abigail, 1 Sam.25.3.   [29] Ezek.16.13f; cf. Ps.45.10f[11f].

The maiden reciprocates, 1.16–2.1. She opens with the same phrase to describe her beloved, but avoids its repetition by introducing a synonymous word. She says 'Behold, thou art fair [Heb. yapheh],[30] my beloved [Heb. dodhi], yea, pleasant [Heb. na˘im]'. Whilst she does not have her beloved's liberty in specifying his particular charms, her choice of the word 'pleasant', or charming, is certainly appropriate as it is used Biblically to describe men more frequently than women.[31]

Of the messianic king, the psalmist says 'Thou art fairer than the children of men; grace is poured into thy lips', and Isaiah promises that 'Thine eyes shall see the king in his beauty'. Already in the nation's experience, she was being given foretastes of this. And such foretastes led them to pray that they might enjoy His beauty unceasingly. With the psalmist they would say 'One thing have I asked of the Lord, that will I seek after; that I may dwell in the house of the Lord all the days of my life, to behold the beauty [Heb. no˘am] of the Lord, and to inquire in his temple'.[32] Surely, it is in this part of the Song that she is brought to the 'house', and soon she is overwhelmed by his love in 'the banqueting house'.

The maiden, however, becomes aware of the beauty of the inheritance into which she has been brought, and is thrilled because grace has made her an heir with her beloved. She speaks of 'our couch ... the beams of our house' [Heb. batteynu, plural], and 'our rafters'.[33] The open air spring scene, with its luxuriant growth and majestic shady bowers, mirrors the peaceful intimacy they were to enjoy together in 'the land'. The 'beams', the 'house' (or houses), the 'cedars', and the 'firs' (or cypresses) are all words closely associated with the Temple and the king's palace complex.[34] The plural which Darby translates 'houses' may be rather a designed plural of majesty referring to the house of all houses for the nation, the House of God. Conversely, it may point to the whole building complex on Temple Mount including the House of

---

[30] The only time this word is used of him in the Song.　　[31] Though see 7.6[7]. Women bear names derived from the root, Naamah, Gen.4.22; 1 Kings 14.21,31, and Naomi, Ruth 1.2,3 etc.　　[32] Ps.45.2[3]; Isa.33.17; Ps.27.4.　　[33] Verse 17 is not to be allocated to the beloved as in NIV.　　[34] For details concerning the cedars and cypresses see pp.66ff.

God and the king's houses, amongst which was 'the house of the forest of Lebanon'. God's king and his house and God's House were to be truly inseparable. Certainly, it was in God's House more than anywhere else that Israel appreciated their God, and all He had given them in love. Here they beheld 'the beauty of the Lord'.

Perhaps, too, appreciating something of the cedar-like majesty of her beloved's gracious sheltering of her, she would naturally reflect on her own lowliness. The insignificant 'rose of Sharon' and the 'lily of the (mountain) valleys' belong in the land, and are beautiful.[35] There is a sense in which this description of herself, therefore, is fitting. However, the maiden still does not appreciate the miraculous change that has been wrought in her through her elevation by her beloved.

It was no different with the nation. She was a kind of firstfruits of that still grander purpose when 'the desert shall rejoice, and blossom as the rose', and 'the glory of Lebanon shall be given unto it, the excellency of Carmel and Sharon: they shall see the glory of the Lord, the excellency of our God'. In that bright future guaranteed to the nation, God 'will bring forth a seed out of Jacob, and out of Judah an inheritor of my mountains: and my chosen shall inherit it, and my servants shall dwell there. And Sharon shall be a fold of flocks, and the valley of Achor a place for herds to lie down in, for my people that have sought me'.[36] The nation had a foretaste of this blessing of the Lord when they entered into the length and breadth of their God-given inheritance in the presence of their Beloved. The Lord wanted them to realize this, which we must pursue further.

Another stanza of their dialogue now opens with the beloved's estimate of her, 2.2. His loved one may be as a lily, but to him she is 'as a lily among thorns'. Her beauty in his eyes is set off the more conspicuously by the thorns which surround her.

---

[35] For details re these flowers see pp.82–87.   [36] Isa.35.1f; 65.10. This prophesied future bliss will reverse all the effects of the divine judgments which will precede it. Of these Isa.33.9 speaks: 'The land mourneth and languisheth: Lebanon is ashamed and withereth away: Sharon is like a desert; and Bashan and Carmel shake off their leaves'.

This is a specially appropriate simile for the nation brought into the land. Those thorns are evidence of the divine curse in creation, through the entry of sin into the human race.[37] When Israel came into her promised inheritance, they did not arrive at a paradise restored. That awaits the establishing of the future kingdom of God on earth. Yet, already that nation sheltered by blood from divine judgment at the Passover, and redeemed by divine power from Egypt, were seen with the beauty of the Lord upon them. This set them apart from the 'thorns' around them, which were destined for destruction.[38] The two grow together in the world now, as they did then. So it will remain until 'the end of the age', when the angels will gather all that offends out of the Messiah's kingdom.[39] How pretty, precious and pure His people were to their Lord in their land is accentuated by their distinctiveness among those who were to Him as obnoxious 'thorns'. If perfection had not been reached yet, if this was not their final rest, then at least it was a harbinger of it. We see how her beloved would draw her on to see herself as He saw her.

The maiden now responds to His loving words, 2.3–6. We have noted previously, 1.16, that her responses are influenced markedly by her beloved's expressions. So it is in verse three here. If he had assured her of the superlative beauty he saw in her in contrasting a lily with the thorns around it, then she will speak of him 'as the apple tree among the trees of the wood' in order to point up the pre-eminence of 'my beloved among the sons'.[40] Still, the towering distinction between them predominates. If she is the lowly flower, he is the loftier tree. If beauty and fragrance belong to her, then these plus the grander benefits of a protective and restful shade from the sun and a refreshing sweet fruit to sustain the eater, articulate his supremacy.

How true this is of Israel's Beloved and Lord. Of course, He was Israel's great protector, answering their plea 'Keep me as the apple of the eye, hide me under the shadow of thy wings'. David, the servant of the Lord said 'How precious is thy lovingkindness, O God! And the children of men take refuge under the shadow of

---

[37] Gen.3.17f.   [38] 2 Sam.23.6f.   [39] cf. Matt.13.24–30.   [40] For detail re the tree see pp.69f and notes.

thy wings. They shall be abundantly satisfied with the fatness of thy house'. Hence 'He that dwelleth in the secret place of the Most High shall abide under the shadow of the Almighty'.[41] But above all, He was their rest, and under His shadow they were able to enjoy all that He was in Himself. His shadow certainly was their defence, but here the nation found it a great delight. He was in truth 'a tree to be desired' for all that He was in Himself.[42] There was, and still is, rapture as well as rest for all that 'sat down under his shadow'. And to this there is the added boon that 'his fruit was sweet to my taste'. Israel's Lord was a veritable 'tree of life' to them. It is to be so also in the future when Israel's Messiah, 'a shoot out of the stock of Jesse, and a branch out of his roots shall bear fruit'.[43]

There was more yet. The nation was brought 'to the banqueting house' [Heb. beth hayyayin = house of wine]. This climax was reached in Solomon's reign, when the Temple was built, and the nation rejoiced in the presence of their God during that great dedicatory week and the feast of the Tabernacles which followed it. It was then that 'the cloud filled the house of the Lord', that 'the glory of the Lord filled the house of the Lord'. The Temple courts rang with his words 'Blessed be the Lord, that hath given rest unto his people Israel, according to all that he promised: there hath not failed one word of his good promise, which he promised by the hand of Moses his servant. The Lord our God be with us, as he was with our fathers'.[44] The words bring together the scope of our poem. It began with the nation's 'fathers', and particularly the Abrahamic covenant. At the beginning the initiative was with the God of Abraham, and the patriarchs could say 'The king hath brought me into his chambers'. We have been conducted then through the descent to Egypt and the national Exodus deliverance under Moses, and have followed the nation into the promised land. At last, we have arrived at the reign of the promised 'son of

---

[41] Ps.17.8; 36.7[8]; 57.1[2]; 63.7[8]; 91.1; 121.5; cf.Isa.4.6; 25.4; 32.2

[42] ct. Gen.3.6; also the suffering Servant of the Lord in whom the nation found 'no beauty that we should desire him', Isa.53.2. In the future the desire of nations shall come, Hag.2.7. For the Midrash Rabbah Israel's God was the apple tree as He gave the Law, which the nation delighted to sit under. [43] Isa.11.1.
[44] 1 Kgs.8.10f,56ff.

David', the one who bore the glory and built the Temple, epitomizing the hope expressed in the Davidic covenant. Truly, as the nation was overwhelmed with the evidences of God's faithful and lavish love as they met in His Temple, it was to them the crowning of all His gracious initiatives. They could sing 'He hath brought me to the banqueting house, and his banner over me was love'. The preposition [Heb. ῾el] in this phrase means that their God had caused them to come near, He had brought them near.[45] Their God was unable to rest until He brought them into fulness of joy, where they drank with Him the wine of gladness which 'cheereth God and man'. Solomon's joyous festival of dedication brought the nation to the Temple and the God-appointed festival of the Tabernacles. This happy 'harvest-home' feast is to find its true fulfilment when the nation is united and blessed under their Messiah in the future. Then, after having been 'a shadow from the heat' for His people, 'in this mountain shall the Lord of hosts make unto all peoples a feast of fat things, a feast of wines on the lees, of fat things full of marrow, of wines on the lees well refined ... it shall be said in that day, Lo, this is our God; we have waited for him, and he will save us: this is the Lord; we have waited for him, we will be glad and rejoice in his salvation'.[46]

It is now that the maiden is aware that 'his banner over me was love'. She knew herself to be distinguished in this way; she was his and he loved her. The conspicuous banners over the several tribes in the camp in the wilderness identified who they were, and provided the rallying centres for all that belonged under them. There, the nation was seen in its distinctive units, each of which had been assigned its place by God. In the Song, however, the only other Biblical context where the noun 'banner' [Heb. degel] is found, it is the Lord's banner, under which all of His people are united. God's love distinguished them from all others, and the nation realized this. Her great Lover was a standard bearer, exalted and conspicuous among ten thousand, and she rallied under His

---

[45] The phrase 'bring in to' is used often of Israel being brought into the land of promise, e.g. Exod.6.8; 23.23; Deut.4.38; 6.23; Neh.1.9.   [46] For the Feast of the Tabernacles in the scheme of divine appointments for the nation see pp.127ff, n.14,18,20,22; also Isa.25.6,9.

banner which was love. His was a victorious love, stronger than death, and she was His forever.[47]

The maiden appeals using masculine plural imperatives, 'Stay ye me with raisins, comfort me with apples'. Her appeal directed any that might be in a position to help her. The experience of her beloved's love had exhausted her, made her faint. What a contrast with her experience in 5.8 where she is faint through longing for his love which her own failure has caused her to miss. 'Hope deferred maketh the heart sick'.

For the nation, to whom else can they go for such love. Their God was the lover of their souls. And yet He was the only One who could support them when His love overwhelmed them.[48] There can be for Him no joy to surpass that of supporting His own people so that they might realize more of His love for them. Her plea would indicate that it was in His fruit, which was sweet to her taste, that she could be strengthened so as to realize His love to the full.

Now her beloved draws her nearer to himself. His arms are around her and she knows love's embrace. The nation, too, experienced such security and satisfaction as she heard her God whisper 'The eternal God is thy dwelling place, and underneath are the everlasting arms'. Precious to Him, Israel came to ex-

---

[47] For 'banner' [Heb. deghel*] apart from Song 2.4 only of 1) 'every man by his own' Num.1.52; 2.2,17,34:   2) of *Judah*, 2.3; of *Reuben*, 2.10; 10.18; of *Ephraim*, 2.18; of *Dan*, 2.25,31:   3) standard of *the camp* of the children of Israel, 10.14,22,25. Clearly the several military units are in view in the Qumran War Scroll. The verb [Heb. daghal*] is found at Song 5.10; 6.4,10; Ps.20.5[6]. BDB sees two different roots here, 1) 5.10 = to look, behold, hence 'looked at', 'conspicuous':   2) 6.4,10; Ps.20.5[6] = to carry or set up a standard. To propose two homonyms in the Song does not appear warranted. In the text above we have carried the 'banner' idea through the Song. The reference to 'chariots' and 'Mahanaim' in 6.12f[6.12–7.1] are also martial in tone. The national salvation history approach to the Song finds no problem with this. More recently, Gordis has connected all the occurrences in the Song with a word meaning 'see, look' [Akkadian dagalu], and understands 2.4 as 'his glance upon me is loving'. The passages where the verb occurs can be translated suitably from this root also.   [48] The word stay or support [Heb. samakh] is used of the Lord's upholding: cf. 'Thou wilt keep him in perfect peace, whose mind is stayed on thee', Isa.26.3. See also Ps.3.5[6]; 37.17,24; 51.12[14]; 54.4[6]; 119.116; 145.14.

perience 'his left hand' under her head, 'and his right hand' embracing her.

The poem ends with the beloved's charge, 2.7. There has been unnecessary uncertainty as to the speaker in this verse. The use of the female creatures 'the roes and ... the hinds of the field' (better does and hinds) indicate that it is the maiden's love that is not to be excited or incited until it is ready and willing for its next stage.[49] Each phase of God's programme for Israel must be consolidated in the hearts of those that are dear to him. Students of the divine purpose are to learn that 'there is a time to love'. How sensitive and considerate is the nation's God. He has drawn the nation to Him, developed their appreciation of Himself, and sustained them in His love from the time of the patriarchs until they experienced the glory of the monarchy and the Temple ministries. This is the first great sweep in the ways of divine love with Israel. Hence, He puts Jerusalem's daughters on oath here, and urges a circumspect restraint: 'stir not up, nor awaken love, until it please'. He still awaits patiently that day when all the plans of divine love for Israel will have been executed and 'he will rest in his love'.

---

[49] 2.7; 3.5; cf. 8.4. Regarding the distinction in usage of the does and hinds (fem. creatures) and the gazelle and young hart (masc. creatures, better roes and harts) in the Song see pp. 60–63 and notes.

BARNES' TRANSLATION

KEY: M = Male; F = Female; B = Brothers
(with −) not in Hebrew; [with +] our literal rendering

POEM 2, 2.8–3.5

F
2.8. My beloved calls!
　　See, he has come!
　　Leaping over the mountains,
　　Springing over the hills!
　9. My beloved is like a gazelle [+ roe, m],
　　Rather a fawn of the harts:
　　See him standing behind the wall,
　　Showing himself through the windows,
　　Appearing attractive through the lattices.

F+
10. My beloved spoke and said unto me:

M
　　'Arise thou my love, my beautiful,
　　And come away:
11. For see, the winter has past,
　　The rain has ceased, it has gone;
12. The flowers have appeared in the earth,
　　The time of singing has come,
　　And the call of the turtle-dove
　　Has been heard in our land;
13. The fig tree has mellowed her unripe figs,
　　And the blossoming vines have effused fragrance.
　　Arise thou my love, my beautiful,
　　And come away!'

* * * * * * *

M
14. My dove in clefts of the rock,
　　In a hiding-place, the bosom of the cliff;
　　Let me see thy face,
　　Let me hear thy voice:
　　For sweet is thy voice,
　　And lovely thy face.

B+
15. 'O catch for us the foxes,
　　Little foxes that repeatedly lay vineyards waste,
　　Even our vineyards' tender fruit.'

F
16. My beloved is mine and I am his,
　　He who finds delight among the lilies.
17. Ere cools the day,
　　And the shadows have fleeted past,
　　Return! Be thou my beloved, like a gazelle [+ roe, m.],
　　Rather a fawn of the harts,
　　Upon the mountains parting us.

203

F
3.1. Upon my bed during the night
    I earnestly sought the one
    Whom my very being [+ soul] utterly loves;
    I earnestly sought him
    Yet I found him not.
  2. I rise up immediately,
    And unceasingly am I going about in the city:
    In its streets and in its open places;
    Eagerly am I seeking this one
    Whom my very being [+ soul] utterly loves.
    Eagerly have I sought him
    But I have not found him.
  3. Came upon me the watchmen,
    The guards in the city:
    'This one my very being [+ soul] utterly loves, have ye seen?'
  4. Scarcely had I passed from them,
    When I came upon this one my very being [+ soul] so loves.
    {I have laid fast hold of him,
    Neither do I intend to release him
    Until I have brought him into my mother's dwelling;
    Even into the apartment of the one who conceived me}

   M+
  5. I have solemnly charged you,
    O daughters of Jerusalem,
    Like gazelles [+ does, f.],
    Rather like hinds of the field,
    Do not ye cause to disturb,
    Neither do ye yourselves awaken such love
    Until it pleases.

* * * * * * *

+ Barnes proposed speaker for 2.10–15 is female; we have allocated recorded words of male, 2.10b–13, to him. He also suggested 2.15 and 3.5 were spoken by the female.

16

POEM 2. WINTER IS PAST, 2.8–3.5

THIS SECOND POEM of the Song is surprisingly different from the one we have just considered. The earlier intimacy has gone, and *distance*, then a *sense of danger*, and even the *pressure of duty* separate the lovers until the very end. We must trace this.

The Thread of the Story

The maiden hears her beloved's appeals, but she is not in his arms. Following the zenith of their developing love affair in the previous dry and warm spring through to autumn, a wet, cold and uninviting winter had ensued. Seasons, times had changed. Further, the circumstances had changed. She was now far removed from her beloved's 'banqueting house', and when he bridged the distance she was still behind a wall, and a window stood between them. Even his wooing words were met with some hesitation on her part. Yet when he came to her he announced the amazing changes in nature which heralded the change of season. Spring was again in the air, and he took advantage of its timely and attractive features to re-invigorate their love relationship. The country scenery later gives way to that of the city, and at last she earnestly seeks and finds the one who had come looking for her. All reticence was gone, and she clasped him and would not let him go until she had brought him into her mother's house. Her beloved again charges the daughters of Jerusalem, to prevent any disturbance of the maiden's latest rest in her refound love.

There are other differences between this poem and the earlier one. Perhaps the most surprising is seen by contrasting the opening of Poem 1 with the closing of Poem 2. At first, the king brought her into his chambers, whereas, at last, she brought him into the chamber of her that conceived her. Equally, there are many contrasts to be observed within this second poem itself. Throughout, she soliloquizes. Despite the peculiarities of the poem all is brought to a happy conclusion.

We may note

He comes upon the mountains to her	She goes about the city seeking him
He knows where she is	She seeks help to find him
She hears him	She holds him
He looks in at the windows	She brought him into the house
She talks about him	She directs him once
He appeals to her 'Arise'	She determines to 'rise now'
He addresses her	She asks after him
He asks her to 'come away'	She tells him to 'Turn' aside

The Thread of Salvation History

The poem carries forward the Lord's and the nation's love story from the exile in Babylon, through the post-exilic centuries back in the land, and on until the incarnation of Israel's Messiah. If Poem 1 traverses some one and a half millennia through history, moving from theocracy to monarchy, from altar and tent to Temple and palace, Poem 2 covers some six hundred years when the nation was subject to Gentile powers. We shall trace its uncertain progress until 'the fulness of the time came, (when) God sent forth his Son, born of a woman, born under the law'.[1]

The Call for the Return from Exile, 2.8–13. At this point in the Song, the maiden recognized the sound of her beloved.[2] His very appearance appealed to her; for her he was like that attractive and agile male gazelle (the roe) or young hart. He had taken the

---

[1] Gal.4.4.   [2] The word 'voice' [Heb. qol], 2.14(2); 5.2; 8.13, is better 'sound' in 2.8,12‡; cf. 1 Kings 14.6 'heard the sound of her feet'.

initiative in coming to where she was.[3] Although she speaks three times of her beloved, she is slow to respond to him. And yet he persistently 'standeth behind our wall (of the building itself), he looketh in at the windows, he sheweth himself through the lattice', vv.8f.

Beyond *the maiden describing the initiative of her beloved*, we trace the divine intervention with a view to restoring the nation He loved to the land once again. The sound of His coming was to be heard as He came 'leaping upon the mountains, skipping upon the hills'. The exiles might have said 'How beautiful upon the mountains are the feet of him that bringeth glad tidings, that publisheth peace, that bringeth good tidings of good, that publisheth salvation; that saith unto Zion, Thy God reigneth! The voice of the watchmen! they lift up the voice, together do they sing; for they shall see, eye to eye, when the Lord returneth to Zion'.[4] All of this was part of His predetermined plan for them, and even the duration of their exile had been limited to 70 years in Jeremiah's prophecy. He said 'I know the thoughts that I think toward you, saith the Lord, thoughts of peace, and not of evil, to give you hope in your latter end'.[5] No distance was too great for Him, no obstacle too high or rugged; 'he cometh'. If Jeremiah prophesied this, then Daniel, having read the promise, confessed and prayed earnestly that God might fulfil His word.[6] Isaiah, too, forecast that every mountain and hill would be laid low, Babylon would fall, and Cyrus the Persian would be raised by the Lord to effect His loving purposes. He said 'He is my shepherd, and shall perform all my pleasure: even saying of Jerusalem, She shall be built; and to the temple, Thy foundation shall be laid'.[7]

The maiden now recalls her beloved's words to her, 2.10-13. Note the inclusio created by his word 'Arise [Heb. qumi], my love, my fair one, and come away'. We should note that there occurs in this poem for the first time in the Song a doubling of endearing terms by which he addresses his precious one. He leads the way in using

---

[3] For these beautiful creatures, and their love cycles which are so illuminating and appropriate for the love theme of the Song, pp.60-63, n.30-49.   [4] Isa.52.7f.
[5] Jer.29.11.   [6] Jer.25.11f; 29.10-14; cf. Dan.9.1-19.   [7] Isa.40.4; 44.27-45.7.

this means of drawing her. Twice he appeals to her as 'my love, my fair one'. How urgently he calls her to rejoin him and share in the joys of spring together. The rigours of the winter are over. And his scenic spring-season sketch brings Israel's countryside to life as the main positive element in his appeal.[8] Everything combines to accentuate the influence on her senses, whether seeing, hearing, smelling, tasting, or touching. This is the vast field into which he would draw her again, prepared by a kindly providence for their mutual enjoyment. This is 'our land' he avers. 'Arise . . . come!'

Can we miss the place that this has in the nation's experience of the untiring love of their covenant conscious God? We recall that this fresh initiative is set against the great spring festival, the Passover season, then it pursues its course through to the early summer period, Pentecost. For Israel, these have been associated always with their redemption from Egypt, and the revelation given to them subsequently at Sinai. Passover and the Feast of Weeks celebrated respectively the triumph of divine intervention, and the gift of the Torah bringing divine illumination.[9] Also, by the use of Exodus typology, the prophets forecast the return from the Babylonian Exile, and then the grander final redemption which will usher in the Messianic kingdom. The former of these is poetically presented in our stanza. Isaiah, particularly, anticipated the return from the exile in terms of a divine intervention and a stirring appeal to the people. He said, in effect, in so many passages 'winter is past'. 'Awake, awake, stand up (= our *'Arise'* [Heb. qumi]), O Jerusalem, which hast drunk at the hand of the Lord the cup of his fury'; he further cried 'Shake thyself from the dust; *arise* [Heb. qumi], sit thou down, O Jerusalem: loose thyself from the bands of thy neck, O captive daughter of Zion'.[10] It was to 'our land' that the Lord would woo His people once again. Cyrus, the king

---

[8] For detail re the flowers, pp.82–87, birds, pp.53ff, and fruit trees, pp.68–80.

[9] The NT has linked Pentecost with the descent of the Holy Spirit, and His ministries throughout the period when our Lord is building His Church, see Acts 2.1 RVmarg.   [10] Eschatologically, the word is important, see Isa.60.1 'Arise, shine; for thy light is come': Jer.31.6 'For there shall be a day, that the watchmen upon the hills of Ephraim shall cry, Arise ye, and let us go up to Zion unto the Lord our God'.

of Persia, was raised to facilitate the people's return confessing 'All the kingdoms of the earth hath the Lord, the God of heaven, given me'. His God-given charge involved encouraging them with the words 'Whosoever there is among you of all his people, his God be with him, and let him go up to Jerusalem, which is in Judah'.[11] The divine Lover's pressure on those longing for the return of His favour is before us at the period of this new exodus, this recurring Passover season.[12]

The nation had suffered a chilling setback. It was in 587 BC that the Southern Kingdom, Judah, had finally collapsed before the might of Babylon, and the last of those to be exiled were carried away. With Nebuchadnezzar 'the times of the Gentiles' had commenced, and the nation no longer had a king or a Temple. It was Jeremiah, the weeping prophet, who was commissioned by the Lord to speak to Judah in the run up to their exile. He reminded them that 'the stork in the heaven knoweth her appointed times; and *the turtle(dove)* and the swallow and the crane observe the time of their coming; but my people know not the ordinance of the Lord'.[13] Judah was insensitive in mind and conscience to the signs of the times, and the word of the prophet alike. Already Jeremiah anticipates the exile, and hears 'the voice of the cry of the daughter of my people from a land that is very far off: Is not the Lord in Zion? is not her King in her?' The question expects a re-sounding 'no'. From then on the Shekinah was absent from the Temple, the Lord had removed Himself from the midst of His people. How frequently Daniel, the prophet of the exile, refers to Him by the title 'the God of heaven'.[14] They confessed that they were as men that had watched the agricultural seasons come and go. 'The harvest is past', referring to the barley and wheat ingatherings from March/April to May/June, and despite the failure of these crops they still hoped against hope. Then they saw that 'the ingathering of summer fruits is ended', and these too had suffered a disaster. With what pathos they use a proverbial saying to suc-

---

[11] Ezra 1.2f; cf. 2 Chron.36.23.   [12] We may contrast the psalmist's plea for God to rise up on His people's behalf: 'O deliver not the soul of thy turtledove unto the wild beast ... Have respect unto the covenant', 74.19f.   [13] Jer.8.7.
[14] Dan.2.18,19,37,44; 'a God in heaven', 2.28; 'the Lord of heaven', 5.23; cf. Nebuchadnezzar's 'the King of heaven', 4.37.

cinctly describe the plight into which their sins had brought them. *'The harvest is past, the summer is ended, and we are not saved'.*[15] If this aptly describes their experience culminating in the exile, the encouraging contrast is supplied by our stanza in the Song. Their Beloved Lord visited them and spoke to the nation in exile saying 'lo, *the winter is past* . . . the time of the singing of birds is come, and the voice of *the turtle(dove)* is heard in our land', the latter being a distinctly summer visitor.[16]

The Post-Exilic Period in the Land, 2.14–17. Three different speakers are to be distinguished in the remaining verses of chapter 2. *Firstly,* we hear the beloved speaking to her, 2.14. As his dove she is no longer behind the house wall, though even there he was able to see her by peering through window and lattice. Now, back among the mountains of Judea, tucked away in those inaccessible 'clefts of the rock . . . and covert of the steep place', her beloved has to plead with her 'Let me see thy countenance, let me hear thy voice'. *Security* counted most with her now, and only *solitariness* could result. It was impossible for their love relationship to develop when *danger loomed large in her mind.* He gives her every encouragement to forsake her fears and enjoy his assuring company. He tells her 'sweet is thy voice, and thy countenance is comely' (note the inversion of the words here). To know what she was to him secured her from all fears.

Secondly, the change of tone and pronoun suggests a change of speakers again. The maiden's 'mother's sons' are the most likely candidates here, 2.15. They were insistent that she rid their vineyards of 'the little foxes' (jackals) which could so easily spoil their blossoming trees. This sounds strangely like those we have already encountered in 1.6. They urge meticulous attention to *the claims of duty* upon their sister. From what follows, we get the impression that she complied. We must turn to this.

Thirdly, the maiden's voice is heard, 2.16f. In the light of his actions and words to her, revealing how much she meant to him, she rests in the fact that he belongs to her. A certain *self-assuredness* has resulted from realizing the interest she has aroused in her beloved.

---

[15] Jer.8.20.   [16] Song 2.11f. For the distinctive features of the seasons and their importance for the development of the Song see chap.11.

Still, it is some evidence of advance that she feels sufficiently secure now to speak of his being her possession. She is satisfied. Because of the claims of duty upon her, however, she does not feel free to drop everything for him. There are things to be done which will take her through to the cool of the day when the shadows lengthen, and are finally swallowed up in darkness.[17] Consequently, her beloved must wait for evening and nightfall while she responds to the rigorous demands of her 'mother's sons'. And so she issues her orders to him: 'Until the day be cool, and the shadows flee away, turn, my beloved, and be thou like a roe or a young hart upon the mountains of Bether' (craggy, rugged, hence 'separation', RVmarg).

These closing verses of chapter 2 discriminatingly touch upon some of the elements of the inter-testamental period as it involves God and the nation. *The first* of these, suggested by the text 'in the clefts of the rock', is a certain 'Fortress Judea' mentality which resulted from the troubles of their past and the humanly precarious nature of their present. Already this is apparent in Ezra and Nehemiah. Clearly, the struggling community that had returned to the land were surrounded by implacable foes.[18] By Nehemiah's period in the land, there seemed little hope of liberty to enjoy the Lord and His things apart from tightening up security in the form of rebuilding Jerusalem's perimeter wall. They might have expressed it as Paul did centuries later 'we were afflicted on every side; without were fightings, within were fears'. However, the great leaders which God gave to the nation at that time, were not intimidated. They put their God and His interests and desires first, and surprisingly 'set the altar upon its base; for fear was upon them because of the people of the countries: and they offered burnt offerings thereon unto the Lord, even burnt offerings morning and evening'. They went on to lay the foundation of the second Temple, and they were 'praising and giving thanks unto the Lord, say-

---

[17] cf. Ps.102.11 'My days are like a shadow that is stretched out'; 109.23 'I am gone like the shadow when it is stretched out'; 144.4 'Man is like to vanity: his days are as a shadow that passeth away', all of which conduct us into the darkness rather than the light of the dawn as many construe it.   [18] Ezra 4–6; Neh.2–6.

ing, For he is good, for his mercy endureth for ever'.[19] Almost a century later, the wall they had built was not an end in itself for Nehemiah. The security that God had thus engineered through his exemplary spiritual leadership, freed the people to give to their God the glory due to His Name. They met in holy convocation, drank in His Word and were reduced to tears by it, and found great joy in obeying it. Its truth led them to praise Him as the Creator, and providential Sustainer. As they reviewed His gracious, good, faithful, and merciful ways with them, from Abraham through the course of their history, they were led to confess their sins and cast themselves upon His mercy again.[20] When their love for God poured itself out in these ways, they had no cause to fear. Like David, who had been delivered by the Lord from the hand of all his enemies, they could sing as one 'I love thee, O Lord, my strength. The Lord is my rock, and my fortress, and my deliverer; my God, my strong rock, in him will I trust; my shield, and the horn of my salvation, my high tower. I will call upon the Lord, who is worthy to be praised: so shall I be saved from my enemies'.[21]

Would that the nation had gone on in this glad and humble spirit in the presence of its God. Alas, as the centuries passed by, it rather became more embattled and besieged in outlook, *seeing everyone and everything as a threat*. A fine people turned in upon itself, the simplicity and boldness of its faith declined. The daring of the Maccabees is a specially bright exception here, but much of the apocryphal literature of the period indicates how far the majority had fallen. Apocalypses painted the hopelessness of the present, and longed for the better tomorrow which would follow in the train of terrifying judgments.

A *second characteristic* of the inter-testamental centuries was the emergence of those religious parties which dominated the Judaism of Jesus' day. The most important of these for the history of the nation is that of the Pharisees. Like the 'mother's sons' of the Song these were committed wholeheartedly to the 'estate', the vineyards in which they were determined to see fruit produced for their God. Their concern was to safeguard their exposed 'sisters', keep them

---

[19] Ezra 3.3,11.   [20] Neh.8–9.   [21] Ps.18.1ff[2ff] = 2 Sam.22.2ff.

from straying religiously and morally, alert them to the numberless 'jackals' that can spoil the vines, and generally to keep their 'sisters' fully occupied even at the expense of their attractiveness. The Torah, which is Israel's unique boon, and which was such a delight to the psalmist,[22] was turned into something quite different by means of their unquestionable zeal which was not according to knowledge. The New Testament records highlight the traits of the character and the religion of numbers of those who came into conflict with the living Lord and Messiah. Their case can be caricatured all too easily, and we are to be gladdened by the spirit of a Nicodemus made familiar to us through John's record. However, Jesus needed to insist that 'except your righteousness exceed the righteousness of the scribes and Pharisees, ye shall in no wise enter into the kingdom of heaven'. His concern for those bowed down under multiplied traditional religious demands caused Him to cry 'Come unto me, all ye that labour and are heavy laden, and I will give you rest'. He castigated some of His 'mother's sons' because 'they bind heavy burdens and grievous to be borne, and lay them on men's shoulders; but they themselves will not move them with their finger'.[23] *Religious duty* which proposes that the present time is not opportune for God's people to enjoy the presence of the Lover of their souls is ill-conceived and ill-directed.

In the third instance, therefore, we are not surprised to find the nation, satisfied with the divine guarantees and obvious commitment to her on the one hand, and yet not enjoying that intimacy with the Lord which He desires above all else. The national election was not only a fact; it was intended to be a thrilling and motivating truth. God was their God and they were His people. So, here in the Song, a glimpse of what He was for her, now assured her that He was hers, 'My beloved is mine'. This settled her timorous spirit, but it should never have encouraged a delay in her responsiveness. The great covenant formula in which the Lord says 'It is my people' is to be matched by their saying 'The Lord is my God'. There is a danger, however, in relegating to a place of secondary importance their own commitment to Him. In the thrill of that relationship on her side, 'I am his', nothing, either *'danger'* or *'duty'*, is to hinder

---

[22] Ps.19.7–14[8–15].   [23] John 3.1–15; Matt.5.20; 11.28; 23.4.

the realization of His nearness.[24] Yet sadly, throughout this period, a consciousness of what is absent rather than what is present predominates. The rabbis refer to the absence of the ark of the covenant, the fire which came down from God, the Shekinah glory as evidence of the divine presence, the Holy Spirit, and the priestly Urim and the Thummim.[25] The Lord is turned away 'upon the mountains of Bether'. She may be satisfied with the knowledge that He belongs to her, yet she is unconcerned in proposing that He should be away to the mountains of 'clefts, divisions, separation'. The path was to become even more rugged for their God, before He could bring His people into the blessings which His love had sovereignly determined for them.

The Incarnation of the Messiah, the Son of God, 3.1–5. When the maiden proposed that her beloved should leave her for a while, she did not expect his absence to prove quite so prolonged! Evening came, the shadows had lengthened into the darkness of the night, and she was left waiting. Night after night passed, as the use of the plural in verse 1 suggests: 'On my bed, in the nights I sought him whom my soul loveth' (JND). It was very much a bad dream to her. She determined to get up from her bed and actively seek him. The constraints of *danger* or *duty* did not exist for her now. After sharing her problem with the watchmen, her overwhelming sense of loss at the absence of her beloved, she found him and brought him home.

We have already established the key place this paragraph has in the developing drama of salvation history.[26] One or two matters

---

[24] The 'possession formulae' found on the maiden's lips, 2.16; 6.3; 7.10[11] reflect the nation's covenant consciousness in the light of God's expression of it. Responsibility is insisted upon in such passages as Deut.26.16–19; cf. Jer.7.23; 11.4. Notice the contrast in this connection between His words 'as he spake unto thee', and the covenant which 'he sware unto your fathers, to Abraham, to Isaac, and to Jacob', Deut.29.12f. The great irrevocable covenants, and not least the 'new covenant', provide Israel with the guarantees of those divine 'I wills' that nothing can take from her, e.g. Jer.24.7; Ezek.34.30f; 36.28; 37.23; Hos.2.23[25]; Zech.13.9. All of these verses accord God's claim upon them as His people the first place in the couplet. In Jer.31.33 the reverse is the case: 'I will be their God, and they shall be my people'. [25] bT.Yom.21b. [26] See chap.14, and specially pp.172–177.

need to be considered here. The sense of 'distance', 'darkness' and 'silence' between God and the nation percolates through the 'silent years' of the inter-testamental period. There was no prophet's voice heard, and a deep longing for God to intervene again was abroad among the true Israel. How easy it had been for them to lose touch with Him. It was to demand a very real effort to bring Him into their lives again. Those who were spiritual began searching for their God 'in the nights'.[27] If general darkness had settled upon the people, an awareness of just how much some of them were missing Him, was dawning on their souls. As Isaiah expressed it in another context 'With my soul have I desired thee in the night; yea, with my spirit within me will I seek thee early: for when thy judgments are in the earth, the inhabitants of the world learn righteousness'. Hosea also refers to a future day when 'the children of Israel return, and seek the Lord their God, and David their king'.[28] For the Israel of God at the opening of our era, the Lord was the one 'whom my soul loveth', and they knew that they could not be satisfied until they had found Him.[29] Their search[30] was an intensive one, urged on by a sense of personal loss. The cheering thing here was that their Beloved was sought and found.[31] As those panting after the Lord sought Him, the watchmen, that is the prophets who transmitted the promises and warnings to the nation on God's behalf, 'found' them. Without further explanation the burning question was put to those prophets 'Saw ye him. . .?' There was only one 'Him' for them! And upon leaving them, those seeking ones of the nation 'found him'. Historically, the discovery began when Mary 'was found with child of the Holy Ghost'. Everything was so much more tangible, and awe-inspiring when the shepherds at Bethlehem were told 'Ye shall find a babe wrapped in swaddling clothes, and lying in a manger'. Sure enough, when they came with haste, they 'found both Mary

---

[27] As a phrase only at Song 3.1,8; Ps.92.3; 134.1. As with David long before, they knew what it was to 'remember thee upon my bed, and meditate on thee in the night watches', though they did not have his peace in this, see Ps.63.6[7].
[28] Isa.26.9; Hos.3.5.   [29] The phrase occurs here at 1.7; 3.1,2,3,4‡. The word 'soul' includes all that she is essentially, herself as embodying her desires.
[30] 'sought' [Heb.baqash] at 3.1(2), 2(2); 5.6; 6.1‡.   [31] 'found' [Heb. matsa´] at 3.1,2,3,4; 5.6,7,8; 8.1,10‡.

both Mary and Joseph, and the babe lying in the manger'. God ensured, however, that Herod's cunning request of the magi that 'when ye have found him (the young child), bring me word again', was not satisfied. Initially, the incarnation of Israel's Messiah, Lord, and Saviour, was known to but a few. Yet those who were privileged to 'find' Him in those early days would not let him go. There were the Zecharias' and Elizabeths, the Simeons and the Annas who were looking and longing for God's redemption of His people, and these all 'found' Him. Happy people indeed! Trespassing beyond the silent years however, to that time after Jesus had come to John to be baptized, the circle expanded dramatically. Andrew ran off to Peter saying 'We have found the Messiah'. Philip sought out Nathanael and told him 'We have found him, of whom Moses in the law, and the prophets, did write'. It is to this momentous phase in the plan of God that the Song brings us here. The human mind cannot take it in. The One who was equal with God took upon Him 'the form of a servant, and was made in the likeness of men; and being found in fashion as a man, he humbled himself'.[32] Happily He was 'found' at this time. Tragically, this was not the case later in chapter 5. We shall consider the reason and the consequences in chapter 18.

This second poem of the Song, like the first, concludes with *the beloved's charge*, 3.5. God's redemptive plan for Israel in this phase has brought them out of the exile, and back to their God-given homeland where those in love with their God welcomed the Messiah when He came. We know of one who took Him into his arms saying 'mine eyes have seen thy salvation'.[33] They had been brought out of darkness, and were on the very threshold of that ministry of which Isaiah had written 'the people which sat in darkness saw a great light, and to them which sat in the region and shadow of death, to them did light spring up'.[34] Another great milestone along the highway of salvation history having been reached, the charge is 'stir not up, nor awaken love until it please'.

---

[32] Matt.1.18; Luke 2.12,16; Matt.2.8; John 1.41,45; Phil.2.7f.   [33] Luke 2.30.
[34] Matt.4.16 = Isa.9.2[1].

BARNES' TRANSLATION

KEY: M = Male; F = Female; O = Onlookers
(with −) not in Hebrew; [with +] our literal rendering

POEM 3, 3.6–5.1

O

3.6. Who is this [she] coming up from the wilderness
   Like pillars of smoke;
   Thoroughly perfumed with myrrh and frankincense,
   With every aromatic powder of a merchantman?

7. Behold! 'Tis Solomon's canopied-couch:
   Sixty mighty men are round about it,
   Of the mighty men of Israel.

8. Every one of them swordsmen,
   Thoroughly skilled at warfare;
   To a man his sword upon his thigh
   In case of alarm during the night.

9. Solomon the king made for himself a palanquin
   From wood of the Lebanon.

10. Its pillars he made silver,
   Its canopy gold,
   Its seat purple,
   Its midst being lavished [or aglow] with love
   From the daughters of Jerusalem.

11. Go forth and gaze with ecstatic-wonder,
   O daughters of Zion,
   Upon king Solomon,
   With the crown wherewith his mother proclaimed him crowned
   In the day of his espousal,
   Even in the day of his exceeding joy.

* * * * * * *

M

4.1. Behold, thou art beautiful my love,
   Behold, thou art beautiful:
   Thine eyes are (− eyes of) doves behind thy veil;

2. Thy hair is like a flock of goats
   That have spread down along mount Gilead;
   Thy teeth are like a sheared flock of sheep
   That have come up from the washing place,
   Each one of which is paired,
   And none are missing among them.

3. Like a line of fine scarlet are thy lips,
   And thy speech [or mouth] is comely;
   Like an open pomegranate is thy cheek
   Behind thy veil;

4. Like a tower of David is thy neck,
   Built up high;
   Many an eminent shield is hung thereon,
   All armour of the mightiest men;

5. Thy two breasts are like two fawns,
   Twins of a gazelle [+ doe, f.],
   That feed among the lilies.

6. Ere cools the day,
   And the shadows have fleeted past,
   I haste me to a mountain of precious myrrh,
   And to a hill of sweet frankincense.

217

M
4.7. Thou art altogether beautiful my love,
   Yes, no blemish is in thee!
 M
  8. With me from Lebanon, O bride with me,
   From Lebanon do thou come!
   Look ye from the top of Amana,
   From the top of Senir, even Hermon,
   From the dens of lions,
   From the mountains of leopards!
 M
  9. Thou hast completely ravished my heart,
   O bride mine own kin,
   Thou hast completely ravished my heart
   With one of thine eyes,
   With one shapely link of thy neck [spine].
 10. How thine affections [loves] have always excelled,
   O bride mine own kin,
   How thine affections [loves] have even surpassed wine!
   And the fragrance of thine ointments
   Far more than all perfumes!
 11. Pure honey thy lips are distilling, O bride!
   Honey and milk are under thy tongue,
   And the fragrance of thy garments
   Is as the fragrance of Lebanon woods.
 M
 12. A garden enclosed art thou,
   O bride mine own kin,
   A spring preserved,
   A fountain sealed.
 13. Thy shoots are a paradise of pomegranates,
   With fruit most delicious:
   Much henna together with much spikenard:
 14. Spikenard and saffron, calamus and cinnamon,
   Together with all kinds of trees of frankincense,
   Myrrh and aloes, with all the chief spices [+ balsams]:
 15. A fountain in the midst of gardens,
   A well, living waters,
   Very streams from Lebanon!
 16. +Arise O North wind, and come O South,
   Blow upon my garden,
   Diffuse abroad its perfumes. +
 F

   Let my beloved come into his garden,
   And eat its [his] choicest fruit.
 M
5.1. I have come into my garden,
   O bride mine own kin,
   I have gathered my myrrh with my spice,
   I have eaten my honey from the comb with my date honey,
   I have drunk my wine with my milk.
 O+
   Eat, O friends!
   Drink, yes drink abundantly, O beloved ones!

+ Barnes allocates all of 4.16 to female, and all of 5.1 to male.

17

POEM 3. I AM COME INTO MY GARDEN, 3.6–5.1

THE MESSIAH'S EISODOS has been poetically presented in 3.1–5; His Exodus climaxed by His ascension to heaven explains the differences in the record of 5.2–8. Between these two focii, we know that the whole of His wooing and winning ministry to the nation of Israel unfolded. In the Song, Poem 3, 3.6–5.1, is devoted to this phase of salvation history, and provides its vital pivot. Consequently, this whole poem is devoted to a span of a few years. Again, we trace first the actual course of the couple's joy in love.

The Thread of the Story

In considering the structure of the book, we have highlighted already the progress through this poem. How is the story developed? The lovers had been together in the Galilee at her mother's house. Her beloved arranges for her to be conducted in state to his palace in the capital city, Jerusalem. Can we wonder that the onlookers, amazed by the pageant, the fragrance and splendour of that cavalcade, asked 'Who is this?' The route from the north took them down the Jordan Valley, passing beneath the towering mountains of Gilead to the east. Arriving near Jericho, a remarkable oasis of palms in a barren wilderness, the royal procession began its ascent to the royal city. Fragrant matching palm-like pillars of smoke provided an accompanying canopy for the caravan as though marking a divine theophany. The cry goes out to the daughters of Zion that they might go out to meet the king and his

219

bride-to-be. The happy wedding day had arrived, 'the day of his espousals ... the day of the gladness of his heart', 3.6–11.

Would one expect the groom to have eyes for any other? No, she fills his vision, and he opens his first stanza of praise with the words 'Behold, thou art fair, my love; behold, thou art fair'. He describes her physical charms, which had been swathed in the incense clouds ascending from his carriage. Now he would go personally to get her a supply of those same fragrant substances, to enhance further her attractiveness, 4.1–6.

It is only after this excursion until nightfall that he returns to her, exclaiming with excelling and all embracive praise 'Thou art all fair, my love; and there is no spot in thee'. How easy it is to be in Jerusalem in body, and yet to be far away in mind and heart. 'Come with me', he cries. It is with him alone that she will find satisfaction and security, as she becomes as ravished with his charms as he is with hers, 4.7–9.

Her beloved now tastes the joys of her love, exclaiming 'How fair is thy love, my sister, my bride!' He goes on to describe her, using the similes of garden and waters. As the garden and spring 'shut up', he speaks of what she is for him alone. As a 'fountain of gardens, a well of living waters, and flowing streams from Lebanon' he has in view what she is to others. It would be by the quite different influences of the north and south winds upon his garden that all its well-stocked fragrances would be diffused abroad, 4.10–16b.

Such overwhelming love draws her to urge her beloved to 'come into his garden, and eat his precious fruits'. How quickly he responds: 'I am come into my garden, my sister, my bride: I have gathered my myrrh with my spice; I have eaten my honeycomb with my honey; I have drunk my wine with my milk'. Notice for him it is her fragrance first, and then the satisfaction he finds in feeding upon her. The pure delight and intimacy of pure love ranges over all the senses here. He hears, sees, smells, tastes, and touches.[1] Could others who knew something of what the lovers meant to one another wish anything more than that they should

---

[1] For *hearing* cf. 2.8,12,14; cf. 'voice' in 2.14; 5.2: *seeing* cf. the many detailed descriptions: *smelling* cf. 1.3,12f; 2.13c; 3.6; 4.10,11: *tasting* cf. 1.2; 2.3; 4.10f,16; 5.1; 6.2,3; 7.9,13[10,14]: *touching* cf. 2.6; 7.8[9]; 8.5.

'Eat ... drink abundantly, O beloved ones (plural)', 4.16c–5.1.

As we progress through 3.6–5.1 we notice a number of contrasting topics in the opening and closing stanzas:

> Caravan comes up from wilderness
> > The Beloved comes into his garden
> Pillars of incense freely arise
> > N and S winds needed to diffuse hers
> Call for Jerusalemites to go to meet
> > Call to lovers to eat and drink
> Climax in the day of espousals
> > Climax in the feast of espousals

The Thread of Salvation History

We propose that the counterpart to the literal story of 3.6–5.1 in the salvation history programme is to be found in the public ministry of the Lord Jesus, His last ascent to Jerusalem surrounded by His own disciples, His subsequent death and resurrection, and His ascension to heaven followed by the descent of the Spirit and the thrilling ministries of the Acts. Which elements of the Messiah's foundation-laying first advent and the more immediate ramifications of it are highlighted here?

The Public Ministry of Israel's Messiah, 3.6–11. The stanza dealing with this describes the ascent from the wilderness to Zion.

The opening question *'Who is this* that cometh up?' is not completely answered in the closing command 'Go forth, O ye daughters of Zion, and behold king Solomon'. For it is clear that although Solomon is the only one named in this stanza, and twice very officially and significantly 'king Solomon', yet he is bringing with him his bride-to-be. Compare specially 8.5 where the answer to the same opening question is more simple to infer from the fact that it is his Shulammite who is 'leaning upon her beloved'. That same one is being transported in state with her beloved from the wilderness to his capital city here. The remarkable change of *status* soon to be effected is suggested by this radical change of *place*.

The several strophes describe the diffused fragrance and

the crack troops providing the defending force of the royal caravan, vv.6ff, the sumptuously appointed 'coach' made by Solomon himself but enhanced by those who loved him, and the king's arrival in Zion suitably crowned for his wedding day, vv.9ff.

Notice, their journey is an ascent [Heb. ˋolah], a word taking in both a topographical and a timeless truth. The myrrh, frankincense, silver, gold and purple are appropriate to a king of glory's ascent but mark an all but unbelievable elevation for his Galilean bride-to-be. This king of glory is also a king of grace!

In this brief span the Song encompasses all that belongs to Messiah's service viewed externally, from His baptism in the wilderness to His final messianic entry to Jerusalem, the city of the great King. There is a designed contrast between the two locations.

The Qumran men had long since abandoned the Temple and city, rejecting the whole spectrum of religio-political parties which supported them, and had set up their now famous centre in the wilderness. Similarly it was a wilderness pulpit and baptistry to which the thundering ministry of John the Baptist drew the crowds. People did not go out to see either a reed shaken by the wind, or a man dressed like a duke. The wilderness was the only suited locus for the one of whom it was written, 'Behold, I send my (the Lord's) messenger before thy face, who shall prepare thy way before thee'. John was the 'voice of one crying in the wilderness'.[2] Was this not a call for the nation to repent, for they were heading in the wrong direction? Did it not remind them of their great exodus beginning when the Lord 'found him in a desert land, and in the waste howling wilderness; he compassed him about, he cared for him, he kept him as the apple of his eye'? Had not the Lord sought to recall them through Jeremiah, saying 'I remember for thee the kindness of thy youth, the love of thine espousals; how thou wentest after me in the wilderness, in a land that was not sown'?[3] It was there that Jesus went out to be baptized by John, and was tested over a period of 40 days, as the

---

[2] Matt.11.7–10; cf. 3.1,3; Mark 1.3,4; Luke 1.80; 3.2,4; John 1.23.
[3] Deut.32.10; Jer.2.2; cf. Ezek.16.35–38.

nation had been throughout 40 long years.[4] God had provided the nation with manna in the wilderness, and the Son of God, that came down as the bread of God from heaven, provided food for the 5000 in a desert place.[5] Small wonder that the crowd wanted to make Him king! It is not without significance, either, that the Lord's public ministry was based in Galilee largely, an area dismissed out of hand by the proud religious leadership. It was in 'The land of Zebulun and the land of Naphtali, toward the sea, beyond Jordan, Galilee of the Gentiles, the people which sat in darkness saw a great light, and to them which sat in the region and shadow of death, to them did light spring up'.[6] It was to the lost sheep of the house of Israel He came. And His ministry had caused a great stir among them, and had drawn many around Him.

However, now He was to 'come up out of the wilderness' and was en route to Jerusalem, the city of the great king. The route was upward. One always 'goes up' to Jerusalem. On numbers of occasions the Lord had ascended to Jerusalem during the course of His public ministry,[7] but it is concerning the last of these that so much detail is given us. The disciples, His loved ones, were with Him along with a multitude that followed Him, as they wound their way up from Jericho through the wilderness land of Judea. At last, leaving Bethany and Bethphage behind, the messianic king riding on a colt towards His capital city, came over the crest of the Mount of Olives. Along that palm strewn way the onlookers might well have asked 'Who is this?' Designedly, their Messiah had given them their answer in terms of the prophet Zechariah: 'Behold, thy king cometh unto thee ... lowly, and riding upon an ass'.[8] On Olivet, the caravan was joined by a great multitude which had come out from Zion to meet Him. These are the counterpart of those in the Song who are urged to 'Go forth, O ye daughters of Zion, and behold king Solomon, with the crown wherewith his mother hath crowned him in the day of his espousals, and in the day of the gladness of his heart'.[9] The mountain resounded as

---

[4] Matt.4.1//Mark 1.12f//Luke 4.1.   [5] Matt.14.13,15; Mark 6.31f,35; Luke 9.10,12; see also John 6.   [6] John 7.52; Matt.4.15ff = Isa.9.1f[8.23–9.1].
[7] John 2.13ff; 5.1ff; 7.2ff; 10.22f; 12.12ff.   [8] Zech.9.9//Matt.21.4f//John 12.14ff.
[9] Song 3.11.

'the multitudes that went before him, and that followed, cried, saying, Hosanna to the son of David: blessed is he that cometh in the name of the Lord; Hosanna in the highest'. 'Blessed is the kingdom that cometh, the kingdom of our father David'.[10] The emphasis on 'king Solomon' in our paragraph in the Song finds its counterpart here. And once it is stated there that it was 'Solomon', that is, the son of David.[11] Certainly, 'when he was come into Jerusalem, all the city was stirred, saying, *Who is this?*'.[12]

There are other suggestive contacts with the glories of the One who came to His own. Suffice it to say that the hints regarding who He is, and what He would do, represented in the gifts brought to Him at His birth, 'gold, and frankincense and myrrh', are found in reverse order in our paragraph in the Song.[13] First place now must be given to *myrrh* which speaks of His suffering on His people's behalf. He is on His way to Myrrh Mountain! The *gold* of glory was to follow as too the *purple* of imperial majesty, which point on to the grand goals yet to be achieved. The *frankincense* spreads abroad all His fragrant acceptability to God while the *silver* assures us of redemption won for His people. Despite all the infernal and human forces that pitted themselves against Jesus the Messiah, the Son of God, none could touch Him until His hour had come. He, and all those bound up with Him, are infinitely more secure than that caravan with its sixty mighty men in attendance. God truly had given His angels charge concerning Him and His own; there were twelve legions of angels available to Him should He choose to beseech the Father.[14]

The Messiah's Private Ministry with His Own in the Upper Room, 4.1–5. The bridegroom in the Song consistently sought to assure the heart of the one he loved. When he had brought her to his city he spoke tenderly to her, expressing what was in his heart. He tells her of a sevenfold physical attractiveness he found in her. His attention is centred largely upon her head, her face, as he describes her eyes, hair, teeth, lips, and temples, before making mention of her neck and breasts.

---

[10] Ps.118.25f = Matt.21.9 = Mark 11.9f = Luke 19.38 = John 12.13.   [11] Song 3.9,11; 3.7.   [12] Matt.21.10.   [13] Matt.2.11; cf. Song 3.8,10.
[14] Matt.4.6 = Ps.91.11f; Matt.26.53.

How truly this anticipates the assuring words of our Lord to His own disciples in that Upper Room in Jerusalem. If the crowds had been alerted and curious, He does not allow this to distract His attention from those who were His immediate concern. This is another instance of the divine ways with the nation of Israel. As He had spoken to the heart of the people in order to bring them out of Egypt at the Exodus, so He has determined to do again for Israel. He will yet 'bring her into the wilderness, and speak to her heart', and commands His servants 'Speak ye to the heart of Jerusalem'.[15] While He was in the world, as the true Servant of the Lord, Jesus spoke many gracious words, and always knew 'how to sustain with words him that is weary'. Yet the Lord's incomparable Upper Room ministry perhaps best expresses His selfless and kindly concern for His own. It was then that 'Jesus knowing that his hour was come that he should depart out of this world unto the Father, having loved his own which were in the world, he loved them unto the end'. 'Let not your heart be troubled' said He, 'ye believe in God, believe also in me'. They were a precious love gift to Him from His Father.[16] How fair they were in His eyes.

Consider the first of her charms to fascinate her beloved. We can hardly read this description of her eyes without contrasting those of Leah's, whose eyes 'were tender', soft, delicate, weak, lacking lustre and brilliance. We are immediately directed off to Rachel who 'was beautiful and well favoured', that is she had a fine figure and was good looking. In the Song, his loved one's eyes are black and lustrous, lively, capturing attention. Many suggest that he is referring to the pupils of her eyes when he remarks 'Thine eyes are (as) doves' [Heb. yonah]. Trace the developing use of this simile in the Song. At first her fairness is established by referring to her eyes alone: 'Thine eyes are (as) doves'. Now here, in chapter 4 he says 'Thine eyes are (as) doves behind thy veil'. At last, she describes his eyes similarly: 'His eyes are like doves' but adds 'beside the water brooks; washed with milk, and fitly set'.[17] This more complete description encourages the view that she sees his pupils as doves, along with those contrasting glistening whites

---

[15] Hos.2.14[16]; Isa.40.2; Gen.50.19ff.   [16] Isa.50.4; John 13.1;14.1.
[17] Song 1.15; 4.1; 5.12. See pp.53f, n.2–9 for detail.

of his eyes, the perfection of their setting comparable to the work of an expert jeweller. One aspect of the secret is brought out here therefore. In her pupils, he is to be seen; in their lustre, she brightly reflects him. To grasp his whole intention in the figure it is important to note that he speaks to her three times as 'my dove' [Heb. yonathi]. The reflection of what she was to him, expressed in this tenderest of terms, he finds in her eyes. Hence its primary place in what he intended as a full description, as indicated by his sevenfold selection. All that she is to him he sees revealed in her eyes, yet those eyes are within her veil. Whilst this may suggest a true modesty, and subjection on her wedding day, the veil has no place in the earlier or later references to her eyes.

Referring this to those surrounding our Lord at the end of His life, a better interpretation is forthcoming by connecting the veil with the limited understanding which even His own disciples had of their Lord and His work at that time. Like the case of the blind man who came to see things clearly only after a two-stage miracle, the disciples tended to see things through a veil until they met their Lord in resurrection, and later received the Holy Spirit so as to appreciate Him even more fully. For Israel 'until this very day at the reading of the old covenant the same veil remaineth unlifted; which veil is done away in Christ . . . But whensoever it shall turn to the Lord, the veil is taken away'.[18] In the future when the nation shall have turned to their Messiah, they shall exclaim 'then was I in his eyes as one that found peace'.[19] Nothing short of a divine miracle could bring sight to the blind, and many of the leaders in our Lord's day were as 'the blind (who) guide the blind'.[20] If no demon, nor man could open the eyes of the blind, Jesus could and did. This established the messianic character of his ministry; He alone brought 'recovering of sight to the blind'.[21] He gave sight to many, and to seven specific cases in particular.[22] One of these who was born blind, spoke up for Jesus and was put

---

[18] Mark 8.22–26; 2 Cor.3.14ff; ct. Gen.24.65.   [19] Song 8.10.
[20] Matt.15.14.   [21] John 10.21; 9.32; 9.6,11,14,15,17,30; Isa.42.7 cf. Luke 4.18; Isa.35.5 cf. Matt.11.5.   [22] Matt.15.30f; 21.14; Luke 7.21f; 14.13,21. Seven cases are found at Matt.9.27f (two men); 12.22(2); 20.30 (two men) cf. Mark 10.44,49 and Luke 18.35; Mark 8.22f; John 9.9.

out from the synagogue. Already, he could see things that the religious leaders could not see. He had proved for himself what the Lord was capable of doing. His conclusion was twofold. He said first, 'He is a prophet' and later, in His defence, 'If this man were not from God, he could do nothing'. The Lord was determined to bring that work to perfection, so that there would be no vestige of a veil left on his eyes. Finding the man he asked 'Dost thou believe on the Son of God?' The man asked 'Who is he, Lord, that I may believe on him?' The Lord answered 'Thou has both seen him, and he it is that speaketh with thee'. The man said 'Lord, I believe'. And he worshipped him.[23] The whole context provides a play on the literal and on the spiritual significance of sight and seeing.

In the Father's sovereign purpose, He has chosen to reveal His Son, the Messiah to the babes, whilst hiding this from the wise and prudent. How Peter establishes this fact for us. Whilst men did not know truly who the Son of Man was, the Father revealed to Peter that He is 'the Christ, the Son of the living God'. To this revelation from the Father, the Lord Himself added another concerning the great work that He was about to do.[24] Here was sight for both eyes! As with the blind man above, two aspects of the Person were perceived, and such balanced appreciation or understanding of our Lord is suggested by the two eyes. It is with this faculty of spiritual sight that our Beloved is concerned first, and particularly in those

---

[23] John 9.17,33,35–38. Eyes focus attention on the physical *faculty of sight*. Then the dullness or brightness of the eyes reflect the physical and emotional *state* of the person, Ps.38.10[11]; 19.8[9]. Emotional upset and sorrow may cause the eyes to flood with tears. Beyond all this, the eyes represent one's *perception*, ability to understand. Hence one can 'have eyes, and see not', Jer.5.21 etc. Conversely, when one sees so as to grasp or know a thing mentally, an *opinion or judgment* is arrived at, and the thing becomes acceptable or unacceptable 'in our eyes', cf. Jer.7.11; Song 8.10. When God intends to 'set mine eyes upon them for good' He means He is to *concentrate His attention* upon them for blessing, Jer.24.6; ct. Amos 9.4. In a person's eye their character and attitudes can be read, their secrets, and deep inward emotions, whether ill-will, jealousy, pride, arrogance, mockery, lustfulness, pity or humility. An *evil eye* may be one determining harm, or one revealing a niggardly, grudging spirit; ct. *the bountiful eye*, Prov.22.6. This wide range of metaphorical association indicates not only a certain vividness in expressing truths, but also just how closely physical, moral and spiritual realities identify.   [24] Matt.11.25ff; 16.16ff cf. v.21.

who, during His earthly life, were given eyes to behold His 'glory, glory as of the only begotten from the Father'. Only by beholding Him could they become more like Him, and the same is true for any of us!

Each of the remaining six elements need to be pondered in the light of the Gospel records. At least observe that if those who are His own must start with 'light', the seventh and concluding feature leads us to 'affection and love' where all must find its ultimate rest. The nation's 'breasts' are referred to in simile regarding Israel's unfaithfulness and spiritual adultery in Hosea and Ezekiel.[25] Here, there is no such unchastity; the spouse is before her beloved in all purity as he describes her. The dual nature of pure love is emphasized in the simile: two breasts, two fawns, twins of a roe [Heb. tsebhiyyah, doe]. The maiden is not the mother here, feeding the babe at her breast. She is the youthful espoused beauty, the graceful form of whose breasts is seen to be like the most graceful of the young creatures, set off as by a garland of spring flowers among which they feed undisturbed in un-molested safety. We are told elsewhere in the Song that her belov-ed is like a roe [Heb. tsebhi], and that he feeds among the lilies.[26] He finds his satisfaction and delight among them. Her breasts, then, are described as 'fawns (young males) that are twins of a roe [Heb. tsebhiyyah – female, better doe]'. Again, there is a reflection of himself developing in her.

We are reminded of that description of John as 'the disciple whom Jesus loved', and the fact that he is found, consequently, 'leaning upon Jesus' bosom'.[27] The idea of love, and the realiza-tion of it in a special intimacy through reciprocal affection, is what is suggested. If he is like a roe, and he feeds among the lilies, then her breasts are like (young) roes that feed among the lilies. Ponder the fact that 'as he is, even so are we in this world'. The balanced character of the affections of God's people is displayed when they revel in His love and seek to return it, but also when they love

---

[25] See Hos.2.2[4]; Ezek.23.3,21.   [26] He is 'like a roe' in Song 2.9, 17; 8.14, and he 'feeds among the lilies', 2.16; 6.3. For details on the gazelles etc, see pp.60–63 and notes.   [27] '*loved*' John 13.23; 19.26; 21.7; '*leaning*' 13.25; 21.20.

those whom He loves, and find their satisfaction where He finds His, 'among the lilies'.[28]

The Messiah's Sacrificial Death, His Reconciling Ministry, 4.6. Having spoken to the heart of his loved one, her beloved must leave her until the darkness has come. He must visit Myrrh Mountain and Frankincense Hill. He is to procure there all that she needs to become all that he desires.

How much more crucial was our Lord's mission which took Him to the cross on behalf of 'His own'. With great urgency He said to His disciples in the Upper Room 'Arise, let us go hence'. His hour had come, and He must wend His way to Golgotha in order to finish that work which God had given Him to do. For 'now once at the end of the ages hath he been manifested to put away sin by the sacrifice of himself'. In that momentous event, which has changed the course of history, men may be 'reconciled to God through the death of his Son'. And He gave Himself up 'an offering and a sacrifice to God for an odour of a sweet smell'.[29] It is this which is anticipated in Song 4.6. What followed this? Our poem provides us with a panoramic view from this salvific watershed.

The Post-Resurrection Ministry, 4.7–14. The New Testament records indicate that the Lord, having been raised from the dead, first gave to His own loved ones incontrovertible evidence of this fact over a period of 40 days during which He assured their hearts in His love. The stanzas here touch upon this as the beloved speaks of the absolute delight he finds in his bride now, v.7, the dangers from which he would have her flee, v.8, the ravishing character of her love, vv.9–11, and the thrill it is for him to know that she is for him alone as the garden and spring shut up, vv.12–14.

Notice, first, her beloved's superlative description of his loved one's fairness, or beauty now, v.7. No longer does he see her simply as 'fair'; rather she has become '*all* fair' to him. No doubt the improvement literally is to be found in those spices he has obtained for her at Myrrh Mountain. She is more fragrant to him now than ever before. Viewed in the salvation historical scheme, the secret

---

[28] For this balanced and dual nature of love's response to God's love see 1 John 4.7–21; cf. John 13.34; 15.12,17.   [29] Heb.9.26; Rom.5.10; Eph.5.2. For detail re Myrrh Mountain see pp.178f.

of this change effected in His own, is attributable to the Golgotha work which their beloved Messiah has completed on their behalf. His sacrifice of Himself had made purgation for sins, He had made 'propitiation for the sins of the people', the Messiah had been 'once (for all) offered to bear the sins of many', and by the will of God they had 'been sanctified through the offering of the body of Jesus Christ once for all'.[30] A better covenant, a new covenant had been established by Him and through His work, and in His resurrection He became its living guarantor and its mediator. Apart from the shed blood of Israel's Messiah and Lord, there could be no remission, nor could their conscience be cleansed 'from dead works to serve the living God'.[31] Hence His unique praise of those He loved: 'Thou art all fair, my love; and there is no spot in thee'. She could have sung:

> Clean every whit, Thou saidst it Lord;
> Can one suspicion lurk?
> Thine is a faithful word, and Thine a finished work.

Here, for the first time in the Song her beloved addresses her as 'my bride' [Heb. kallah‡], 4.8. What is more, all the uses of this word in the Song are concentrated in these few immediate stanzas.[32] It is the word usually used in referring to a bride at the very threshold of marriage, and is found paralleled with 'bridegroom' consequently.[33] This is so appropriate here, where the marriage appears to be consummated at 5.1. How perfectly it suits the spiritual experience of the Israel of God in the presence of their risen Messiah. They, as a kind of firstfruits, could have applied Isaiah's words to themselves then, saying 'I will greatly rejoice in the Lord, my soul shall be joyful in my God; for he hath clothed me with the garments of salvation, he hath covered me with the

---

[30] Heb.1.3; 2.17; 9.28; 10.10.   [31] Heb.7.22; 8.6; 8.8,13; 9.15; 12.24.
[32] Standing alone in 4.8,11; the combination 'my sister, (my) bride' in 4.9,10,12; 5.1. The word 'bride' is also used of the 'daughter-in-law', a family relationship also spiritually significant for Israel in connection with Ruth and Boaz, Ruth 1.6,7,8,22; 2.20,23; 4.15. See chap.2, esp. pp.26f on the subject of marriage. For the range of titles used for the 'bride' see Index.   [33] See Jer.7.34; 16.9; 25.10; Joel 2.16 in judgment contexts, and Jer.33.11 which is full of eschatological hope.

robe of righteousness, as a bridegroom decketh himself with a garland, and as a bride adorneth herself with her jewels'. Now He was with them on resurrection ground, the Lord rejoiced in His own, anticipating the complete fulfilment of the prophet's words 'as the bridegroom rejoiceth over the bride, so shall thy God rejoice over thee'.[34] Then her beloved goes on to describe his loved one as 'my sister, (my) bride', v.9. While the former term [Heb. ˊachothi] is found among the tender love expressions of Ancient Near Eastern vocabulary, it is peculiarly appropriate to describe that kinship link between the earliest Jewish disciples and their Beloved Messiah.[35] None of them appreciated at that time, however, that God was building a new Bride (note the absence of the possessive pronoun 'my' here) of which they were the founder members. This awaited God's fresh revelation through the converted rabbi Paul.[36]

The pleasures and satisfaction his bride brings to the beloved beggar description as he calls up the *taste* of wine, honey, and milk, and the *smell* of her perfumes, vv.10f. We may compare the occasions when the risen Lord appeared to the disciples. He assured them of His physical, bodily resurrection. He even ate the fish and 'honeycomb' set before Him.[37] What peace His presence and His words brought to them at last. The hearts of the disciples had to be thrilled and ravished with His love *privately* before they could become His glad witnesses to the nation and to the world *publicly*.

How precious the bride was to her beloved as 'a garden shut up ... a spring shut up, a fountain sealed'. She had been kept in her pure virgin beauty and freshness for him alone, v.12. And those loved disciples were beyond question the Messiah's own, uniquely

---

[34] Isa.61.10; also 49.18; 62.5. All of these passages deal with Israel's future blessing.   [35] 'sister' [Heb. ˊachoth], Song 4.9,10,12; 5.1,2; 8.8(2)‡; cf. 'my brother' [ˊach li], 8.1; see p.286, n.135f. It is used 1) literally of relationship of varying nearness, 2) metaphorically of Judah, Samaria, Jerusalem, Jer.3.7,8,10; Ezek.16.46 etc, and of wisdom, Prov.7.4. With the possessive 'my' it is four times in parallel with 'bride' as an endearing love term, cf. Tob.7.12,16; TDOT 1.188–193; TWOT 1.31f. In the NT [Grk. ˊadelphe] it is used 1) literally, Matt.13.56//Mark 6.3, 2) metaphorically, of sisters in the faith, Rom.16.1; 1 Cor.7.15; 9.5; Philem.2; Jas.2.15, and 3) spiritually, as those who are akin in spirit with the Lord, Matt.12.50//Mark 3.35.   [36] Eph.5.25ff; cf. 2 Cor.11.2f; John 3.29; Rev.21.2,9; 22.17.   [37] Luke 24.36–43.

set apart for Himself. Their very fear which they felt because they were His, had driven them behind the barred door 'for fear of the Jews'.[38] The garden was shut up for Him in more senses than one! Immediately He concerned Himself to bring them into the uninhibited experience of His love.

The bride heard her beloved speak of her as a veritable paradise of *fruits* and *fragrance* which he was *tasting*, and *smelling*, vv.13f. What delights the Messiah enjoyed in the presence of His own in those resurrection appearances, and what encouragements He whispered in their ears. They were His paradise of pomegranates, bursting with the potential of a multiplied harvest sweet to His taste; they were a garden stocked full of the most varied fragrant plants each a delight to His discriminating sense.[39] He found myrrh and aloes there, for the savour of His own burial was upon them. Their new life was not in themselves, for they 'were buried therefore with him through baptism into death: that like as Christ was raised from the dead through the glory of the Father, so we (they) also might walk in newness of life'. More was required to release all this potential for His delight and glory.

The Messiah's Ascent to Heaven; the Spirit's Descent, 4.15–5.1. As her beloved's longing to make her his own increases he speaks of the mighty release of her 'living waters, and flowing streams'. He urges those variable winds to blow upon his garden 'that the spices thereof may flow out'. His loved one readily responds, urging him to 'come into his garden, and eat his precious fruits'. With great delight he said 'I am come into my garden', taking her to wife as 'my sister, (my) bride'. This finds its counterpart when the ascended Lord sent the Holy Spirit, and the great Pentecostal union was forged. How else could the potential the Lord had always seen in His own be realized apart from their receiving the gift of the Comforter? Only then could it become true that out of their inward parts 'shall flow rivers of living water. But this spake he of the Spirit, which they that believed on him were to receive: for the Spirit was not yet given; because Jesus was not yet glorified'.[40] It

---

[38] John 20.19–23.   [39] For pomegranates pp.72ff, n.44–55. For fragrant plants/fragrance pp.101–124.   [40] John 7.38; 4.15. In the Acts the disciples

is only at this point of the Song, therefore, that her beloved says of her 'Thou art a fountain of gardens, a well of living waters, and flowing streams from Lebanon'. This is anticipating the great change effected at Pentecost in Acts 2, and the ever widening sphere of blessing marking the ongoing triumph of the early believers as they were equipped and filled by the Holy Spirit. The refreshing streams flowed out from Jerusalem to the uttermost parts of the world, from the 'garden' to the 'gardens'.[41]

The waters flowed out from within the community of believers, but the God of salvation history controlled the winds which blew upon them from without. The Acts notes a number of 'winds', both the cold and fierce northerlies and the warm and welcome southerlies. How the whole range of the affairs of the early witnesses and churches are seen to be under divine control. 'Blow upon my garden', commands the sovereign Lord, 'that the spices thereof may flow out'. The fragrances, which all represent the perfections of the Lord Himself as appreciated by God, are now found in His own people, and must be wafted abroad. Paul finely expresses this in an outburst of thanksgiving 'unto God, which always leadeth us in triumph in Christ, and maketh manifest through us the savour of his knowledge in every place'.[42]

In the Song, the marriage is joyously consummated at the conclusion of this poem. The beloved describes this in a sevenfold way. He says 'I am *come into* my garden, my sister, (my) bride: I have *gathered* my myrrh and my spice; I have *eaten* my honeycomb with my honey; I have *drunk* my wine with my milk', 5.1a–d. Here the two become one flesh, as he enters his garden into which she has invited him, and savours all the delights of her love. At this point all their well-wishing friends encourage them to enjoy one another's love to the full: 'Eat [Heb. ´akhal], O friends' they say, 'Drink [Heb. shathah], yea drink abundantly [Heb. shakhar], O beloved (ones)', 5.1e–f. This functions as yet another 'Selah' in the grand song of salvation. Also, these words highlight an extended metaphor, that of eating and drinking, adopted frequently in the

---

[40] *cont.* were instructed to wait for the promise of the Father and to be baptized in the Holy Spirit, 1.4f, cf. v.8; Luke 24.49.   [41] For the garden/water theme see pp.94–99 and notes.   [42] 2 Cor. 2.14; Song 4.16.

Song, though the use of these particular words is concentrated just here.[43] Well-being, fellowship, joy, harmony and even covenant making are bound up with their Biblical use. If his fruit is sweet to her taste and she calls for raisins and applies to sustain her in her love, then for him her lips drop as the honeycomb and honey and milk are under her tongue. If she links together his love and wine, then he more than reciprocates.[44] In fact, the Messiah, before leaving His disciples instituted the Lord's Supper so that He might be before them forever. 'Take, eat', He said, 'Drink ye' He insisted, for so He will yet do with them in His Father's kingdom.[45] How the glorified Lord and Messiah longs to be invited in to sup with His own even where the majority are unresponsive.

For the Israel of God of the first century AD, all was finalized for Him and His bride when, after His atoning death for her, He rose again and returned to heaven. His arrival there, and the descent of the Holy Spirit to earth, forged the eternal relationship with His own which even we Gentiles enjoy in the present. To express that in terms of the divinely appointed festivals programme, we have been conducted through the Passover season, 4.6, to the Pentecost season and all that follows in its wake, 4.15–5.1.

---

[43] Eat [Heb. ˊakhal], 4.16; 5.1(2)‡ cf. Acts 1.4 ARVmarg: drink [Heb. shathah], 5.1‡: drink abundantly [Heb. shakhar], 5.1‡.   [44] re food: her of him 2.3; cf. 5.16; 2.5; him of her 4.11,16; 5.1. Re drink: her of him 1.2,4; 2.4; him of her 4.10; 5.1; 7.9[10]; 8.2. On the occasion of the covenant making with Israel when Moses was joined by Aaron and his sons along with the seventy elders we read that 'they beheld God, and did eat and drink', Exod.24.11. Another word for feeding [Heb. raˋah] is really 'pasturing', sometimes with the flock in view, and in other instances used metaphorically, see pp.57f, n.17,21, and TWOT 2.852f.   [45] The eschatological supper is in mind beyond the Lord's Supper, Matt.26.29; cf. 22.1–14; Rev.19.9; Luke 14.15; 22.29f; cf. Isa.25.6; 55.1.

BARNES' TRANSLATION

KEY: M = Male; F = Female; D = Daughters
[with +] our literal rendering

POEM 4, 5.2–6.9

F
5.2. {I am sleepy but my heart keeps awake}
A call! My beloved knocks!

M
'Open to me, my love mine own kin,
My dove mine undefiled;
For my head is saturated with dew,
My locks with droplets of the night.'

F
3. 'I have already taken off my inner-garment,
How now should I put it on?
I have already washed both my feet,
How now should I re-soil them?'
4. My beloved had withdrawn his hand from the door-recess,
And I was deeply disquieted over him.
5. I arose to open to my beloved,
And my two hands dripped myrrh,
My very fingers liquid-myrrh,
From the lock handles.
6. I opened to my beloved
But my beloved had already departed, he had gone!

F
My inmost being [+ soul] longed to speak intimately again with him:
I earnestly sought him but I found him not,
I called him but he answered me not.
7. The watchmen found me,
The guards in the city;
As a consequence they smote me, they wounded me,
They took away my mantle from me,
Those watchmen of the walls.
8. I have solemnly charged you,
O daughters of Jerusalem,
If ye find my beloved
What ye must make known to him,
That stricken with love am I.

D
9. What is thy beloved more than any other beloved,
O most beautiful among women?
What is thy beloved more than any other beloved,
That thus thou hast solemnly charged us?

F
10. My beloved is radiant and ruddy,
Pre-eminent among ten thousand!
11. His head: fine gold of consummate excellence;
His locks: flowing, black as the raven;
12. His two eyes, like doves beside water-brooks,
Bathed with milk, set with perfection;
13. His two cheeks, like a raised bed of sweet-spice,
Prolifically growing aromatic herbs;
His lips: lilies, distilling liquid myrrh;

235

F
5.14. His two hands: rolls of gold,
   Perfectly set with chrysolite;
   His body: skilfully-carved ivory,
   Fittingly adorned with sapphire-blues;
  15. His legs: pillars of marble,
   Firmly supported on bases of finest gold;
   His bearing: as the Lebanon,
   Excellent as the cedars.
  16. His mouth: most sweet,
   Yes, he is altogether exquisitely lovely!
   This is my beloved, yes this is my friend,
   O daughters of Jerusalem!

D
6.1. Whither has thy beloved gone,
   O most beautiful among women?
   Whither has thy beloved turned aside?
   For now we also are eagerly seeking him with thee.

F
2. My beloved has gone down to his garden,
   To his raised-beds of sweet-spice,
   To find delight among the gardens,
   And to gather lilies.
3. I am my beloved's, and my beloved is mine:
   This one who finds delight among the lilies.

* * * * * * *

M
4. Beautiful art thou, O my love, as Tirzah,
   Lovely as Jerusalem,
   Awe-inspiring as an army displaying banners.
5. Cause thine eyes to turn away from me,
   For they have quite overcome me.
   Thy hair is like a flock of goats
   That have spread down along the Gilead.
6. Thy teeth are like a flock of sheep
   That have come up from the washing-place,
   Each one of which is paired,
   And none are missing among them.
7. Like an open pomegranate is thy cheek
   Behind thy veil.

M
8. Though there are three-score queens,
   And four-score concubines,
   Even virgins without number,
9. Unique is she, my dove mine undefiled;
   Unique is she of her mother,
   The choice one is she of her who bore her.
   Maidens have seen her and greatly eulogize her,
   Queens and concubines, even they loudly praise her.

* * * * * * *

236

18

POEM 4. THE CHIEFEST AMONG TEN THOUSAND, 5.2–6.9

SO FAR IN THE SONG we have traced the Lord's love relationship
with Israel from:

1. the period of the patriarchs, through the descent into and the
   eventual exodus from Egypt, and from thence into the promised
   land (chapter 15);
2. the return from the Babylonian Exile through the post-exilic
   period in the land, and up to the incarnation, the eisodos, of the
   Messiah (chapter 16);
3. the incarnation, the eisodos, through the public and more
   private ministry of the Messiah, to His sacrificial death at
   Golgotha, His private ministry to His disciples throughout the
   course of His resurrection appearances, and finally His ascension to heaven and the descent of the Holy Spirit with the consequent expanding divine blessing upon the early witness of
   His own from Israel (chapter 17).

This work had progressed through the centuries among God's
people, and He had never left Himself without witness to His saving grace thus far. Further, God's work had always been in the
hands of His servants in Israel, and even when the Messiah was
upon earth, He made it clear that He had been sent to 'the lost
sheep of the house of Israel'. When He sent out the Twelve to
prepare His way, He commanded that they too must go 'to the lost
sheep of the house of Israel'. For the disciples their sympathies and
hopes, as Jews, even after the resurrection were occupied very

237

much with their beloved nation. Addressing the risen Lord they asked 'dost thou at this time restore the kingdom to Israel?' The Lord chose not to answer their question directly. Rather, knowing the somewhat startling change in the Father's saving programme which was to unfold gradually before their eyes, He encouraged them to give themselves to the work of God unstintingly and without prejudice. He said 'ye shall receive power, when the Holy Ghost is come upon you: and ye shall be my witnesses both in Jerusalem, and in all Judea and Samaria, and unto the uttermost part of the earth'.[1] It was this latter part of this commission that latently contained the most surprises. Poem 4 of the Song that we are now to review deals with that period of the salvation history programme where the 'things hard to be understood' even for these Jewish apostles bring the early church to age, and sharpen its delineations of the glorified Messiah and Lord.

The Thread of the Story

The marriage of the lovers has been consummated at 5.1 as we have seen, so we might have expected no further lapses on the bride's part. The first stanza of this next poem therefore makes disappointing reading to us, and her attitude and lethargy when she heard her beloved's knocking and appealing proved a disaster, 5.2–8. It opens 'I was asleep, but my heart waked'. She is even beaten and wounded by the city's watchmen as she tries to find the one she should not have lost! Finding some women whom she assumes will be sympathetic, she seeks their help in locating her lost beloved, 5.9–6.3. Two probing questions from these crystallize her thoughts. Firstly, their 'What is thy beloved more than another beloved?' sets her at liberty to describe him as she has never done before. Her witness makes her yearn the more for him, and it develops a desire to seek him in the hearts of these 'daughters'. Secondly, their question 'Whither is thy beloved gone?' is most peculiar. One would have thought that if the bride knew where her beloved one had gone she would not have sought the aid of these 'daughters'. However, the greatest service that can be done for one smitten with a love problem is to draw out her heart and encourage

---

[1] Matt.15.24; 10.6; ct. Acts 1.6.

238

her to think aloud! Surely, the reason the bride was able to describe exactly where her beloved would be found, is the direct fruit of her uninhibited expression of all that he was to her, from head to foot. Because she knew who and what he was, and all that made him so utterly unique, she then knew where he would be. She can rest in knowing she belongs to him, and he to her as a result. Absence is over, distance is gone. The third stanza grows out of this one, 6.4–9. Her beloved speaks to her in appreciative and intimate terms, vv.4–7, some of which remind us of those he had used of her at the beginning of chapter 4. He opens with 'Thou art beautiful, O my love'. In other strophes he speaks about her, indicating how incomparable she is, 'the choice one of her that bare her', vv.8–9. What higher expression of true appreciation is to be found than in this man and his bride who count the other partner 'chiefest among ten thousand' or 'the only one ... the choice one', or the altogether unique one. The relationship has, on her side, reached a new peak of appreciation which is not equalled elsewhere in the Song.

We may notice

He says his head is filled with dew	She is brought to say his head is as most fine gold
His demand of her, 'Open'	His delight in her, 'Thou art...'
She is lying on her bed	She is like an army with banners
Her heart yearns at the sight of his hands	He is overcome with her eyes
Her appreciation of him – He is the chiefest	His appreciation of her – She is the choice one
Daughters do not know him	Daughters, queens, praise her

Some Inter-relationships

It is important to have grasped the inter-relationships between our opening stanzas here, 5.2–8, and the closing stanza of Poem 2, 3.1–5. Read again pages 171–180 if this is not fresh in your mind.

3.1–5	5.2–8

Comparisons

A night scene	A night scene
A bedroom scene	A bedroom scene
Aware of Beloved's absence	Eventually finds He has gone
Goes to look for Him	Goes to look and calls
Watchmen find her	Watchmen find her

Contrasts

She seeks him on her bed	He seeks entry from outside
No mention of dew	Refers to his dew-filled head
She questions watchmen	The watchmen beat, wound her
Finds her beloved	Does not find him
Clasps him, brings him home	————
He charges others	She charges others to find and
'Stir not love'	'tell him I am sick of love'
(Introduces His Incarnation	(Follows His Ascension
His 'Eisodos')	His 'Exodus')

The Thread of Salvation History

The Continuing Appeal of a Neglected Messiah, 5.2–8. Already we have considered the fragrant joy and out-flowing blessing marking the union of the Bridegroom and His Bride. The early chapters of Acts finely illustrate this as the disciples, indwelt, equipped and energized by the Spirit of God, fearlessly and appealingly took the message of the ascended Messiah to the nation. They encountered a changeable weather pattern, now the south winds warm with the blessing of God, and now the north winds of adversity, but these contributed to their expansion numerically, their enriching spiritually, and to the outflow of those graces precious to their Lord.[2] The death of Stephen in Jerusalem, however, signalled a certain hardening of attitudes, and what might appear as a fortuitous change of direction in the ongoing work of the Church. Chapter 5.11 is the first unchallenged use of the word 'church' in Acts, and along with 8.1,3 it refers to the Jerusalem church of Jewish believers. Now, the history goes on to trace the expansion and opposition pattern as the Word of the glorified Lord is spread to 'the uttermost part of the earth'. It is this period to which our poem belongs. How was it that the Church which began at Jerusalem, and which, initially, made all its progress among Jewry, later became predominantly Gentile in composition? What explains the fact that the majority of the nation did not respond to the appeals of a Messiah whom they left out in the cold? Is Israel presently totally set aside, not knowing anything of the glories of the One who died and rose again? Does God speak

---

[2] cf. the conditions and 'climate' of Acts 2–7 along with Song 4.13–5.1.

to the heart of the Jew today? Our poem provides us with some helpful answers to questions like this. The maiden in the opening poems represents that part of the nation which realizes God's love. The spouse here represents that Israel of God of the present, those who actually experience, and reciprocate in measure the love which their God pours upon them. We shall trace the history of this precious remnant here.

These opening stanzas highlight the problem poetically. Israel could never say that she was left in ignorance concerning her resurrected Messiah. He took the initiative, 'in the night' of His rejection. He made her hear His sound, His urgent knock at her door, His personal and heart-directed appeal, 'Open to me'. He reminded her of all that she was to Him in multiplied terms of endearment 'my sister, my love, my dove' with which she was already familiar.[3] He went further and introduced a new term, 'my undefiled',[4] to attract her on to a purity far exceeding anything with which she had concerned herself already. The nation which sought after a righteousness, a holiness according to the demands of their Holy God was altogether different from the defiled Gentile. Hence, even here she points out to her Beloved 'I have washed my feet; how shall I defile them?' There was so much more needed yet however. If she was to be His loved one, commitment to Him whatever the personal cost, was essential. He was the one Lord and Master who could keep her feet clean.[5] For this reason, He sought to draw her with the most moving of words, in which He told her in her ease 'my head is filled with dew, my locks with the drops of the night'. Notice this uncharacteristic presentation of Himself. He would point up the contrast in their circumstances,

---

[3] 'my sister' would teach the 'blood and flesh' relationship which the Messiah had with the nation, for 'our Lord hath sprung out of Judah', 4.9,10,12; 5.1,2. Note this vital link which the only reference outside of Poem 3 establishes with our Poem 4; see Heb.2.14f; 7.14: 'my love' refers to her as the object of His heart's choice, Song 1.9,15; 2.10,13; 4.1,7; 5.2; 6.4: 'my dove' touches upon her gentleness, loveliness, acceptability, and singleness of heart, 2.14; 5.2; 6.9 see pp.53f.
[4] 'my undefiled' [Heb. tammathi] only at 5.2 and 6.9 in the Song, forming an inclusio (with 'my dove') for the poem. His all seeing eyes, as the great High Priest with the Urim and the Thummim (from same root as our word), saw what His grace would put upon her, and her fruit to sanctification, Rom.6.22.   [5] John 13.3–11.

and His own undesirable lot in the night, in order to move her. Was He not hinting also at both the boon and the demand of her being His?

This type of loving overture from a Messiah, on whom the gentle and refreshing dew of the Spirit rested, was sung to those who were comfortable and self-satisfied. The voice did not move her. And yet, as the nation had been warned earlier, it was now that she was being offered mercy. 'Today if ye shall hear his voice, harden not your hearts'.[6] Praise God, His hand did move her: 'My beloved put in his hand by the hole of the door, and my heart was moved for him', v.4. The sight of His hands caused the light to dawn upon the two He had met on the Emmaus Road. Was it only the way He broke the bread; did they not see that those hands were nail-pierced?[7] Certainly here, two stages are apparent. At first it was the sight of His hands that made her rise up to open the door, but then 'upon the handles of the bolt' He had left a substance from His hands, 'liquid myrrh', v.5. Opening to Him meant that her 'hands dropped with myrrh' too! Her Beloved obtained that myrrh from His bitter experience at Golgotha, but something of the bitterness of His experience was now upon her who was moved, though too slowly, for Him. The ramifications of this she discovered quickly. 'I opened to my beloved; but my beloved had withdrawn himself, and was gone'. If her heart [Heb. me`im] had been moved when His hand had appeared, her soul [Heb. nephesh] failed her at His disappearance, v.6.[8] There was a definite sevenfold response on her part: her heart was moved, she rose up, her hands dripped with the liquid myrrh He had left behind Him, she opened the door, her soul failed her, she sought for and called after her Beloved. But the delay proved disastrous. What an unfolding of the mystery of the government of God. On the one hand, 'Isaiah is very bold, and saith, I was found of them that sought me not; I became manifest unto them that asked not of me'. On the other hand, Jesus had said 'Ye shall seek me, and shall not find me'.[9] So in the Song, she sought without finding

---

[6] Heb.3.7–11; cf. Ps.95.7–11.   [7] Luke 24.30ff.   [8] heart, lit. = inward parts [Heb. me`im‡] is used here to represent the seat of strong emotions inwardly, she yearned for him; in 5.14 it is used of the body or belly externally: soul [Heb. nephesh‡] is used in the Song of feelings, appetites, passions, emotions in connection with love at 1.7; 3.1,2,3,4, and of deep desire, 5.6.   [9] Rom.10.20, the Lord's pleadings and the nation's rebuffs were all foreknown and within God's purpose; Isa.65.1; John 7.34,36.

Him, and called but He did not answer. This is quite different from Song 2.10 where her Beloved had 'answered'; here He does not [Heb. `anah, same word in both places though not with the same nuance‡]. Her troubles were multiplied when the watchmen found her, for 'they smote me, they wounded me ... took my mantle from me', v.7. The Old Testament prophets had warned of the impending trouble if the nation did not respond to the pleas of their God. Daniel had forecast that 'the anointed one (Messiah) (shall) be cut off, and shall have nothing: and the people of the prince that shall come shall destroy the city and the sanctuary'. Jesus Himself had warned that 'the days shall come upon thee, when thine enemies shall cast up a bank about thee, and compass thee round, and keep thee in on every side, and shall dash thee to the ground, and thy children within thee; and they shall not leave in thee one stone upon another; because thou knewest not the time of thy visitation'. Numbers of the preachers sent to the Jewish audiences of the Acts, heralded the same solemn warnings against those failing to respond to the message of grace. The writer of Hebrews conveyed the Spirit's warning to his own generation likening it to 'the day of the temptation in the wilderness, wherewith your fathers tempted me by proving me, and saw my works forty years'. God had said that such a generation were not to 'enter into my rest'.[10] The Beloved derived no pleasure from seeing the one He loved illtreated and abused. Yet His very absence and her troubles were a part of His faithfulness to her, and in His sovereignty He used these very means to bring her to Himself. God's ways in government and grace may appear strange, but they are inevitably successful. The ways of God with Israel in the present is developed in detail in Romans 9–11. It is the subject projected through the poetry of our poem.

The purpose of God can never fail. Though Israel, His chosen and favoured people, have passed through many tragic experiences for almost two millennia, and for most of that time have not lived in their national homeland, yet He has been blessing in a special way a remnant of them. Isaiah had anticipated this, crying out that 'if the number of the children of Israel be as the sand of

---

[10] Dan.9.26; Luke 19.43f; Heb.3.8–11 = Ps.95.7–11.

the sea, it is the remnant that shall be saved', and again 'Except the Lord of Sabaoth had left us a seed, we had become as Sodom, and had been made like unto Gomorrah'.[11] It is sovereign grace that has determined the salvation of the remnant in the present. God has not cast away His people. Paul, like the other Jewish founder members of the Church are the proof of this. As in Elijah's day, God even now has 'seven thousand men, who have not bowed the knee to Baal. Even so then at this present time also there is a remnant according to the election of grace'.[12] In the light of this, the righteousness which Israel sought, and still seeks, she has failed to obtain, while 'the election obtained it'. This is the Israel of God today. If for the nation there has been a tremendous opportunity lost, yet for those who come to realize their loss, despite the troubles into which it has brought them, there is predetermined blessing. Our poem pursues this subject also.

The Enhanced Appreciation of the Remnant Drawn After Him, 5.9–16. This stanza is distinct from, yet closely linked to the one following it. It addresses itself to the question raised by the daughters of Jerusalem 'What is thy beloved more than another beloved?' It leads naturally to their second question 'Whither is thy beloved gone?' In each case there is an answer from 'the fairest among women'.

Perhaps no stanza of the Song has attracted so much devotional attention as the first of these. It has no equal among those portions in which she describes her beloved. Because of this fact, the special relevance to the Israel of God today should be obvious. The nation has always awaited its promised Messiah, but has never grasped the greatness of Who He is, nor the peerless majesty which belongs to Him officially. The Israel of God of the present, the 'remnant according to the election of grace', has appropriated Him in all His glory and majesty. These are 'Israelites indeed', who, out of loss and trouble, are brought to the feet of the One they own as 'My Lord and my God'. In turning to Him, their veil has been taken away. For them, the Messiah 'hath been made a minister of the circumcision for the truth of God, that he might confirm the promises given unto the fathers'. To them, He is not only the

---

[11] Rom.9.27,29 = Isa.10.22f; 1.9.   [12] Rom.11.4f; 1 Kings 19.18.

prophet and priest, but 'the Christ, the Son of God'. They may have known previously a Messiah 'after the flesh, yet now (say they) we know him so no more'. They see Him as 'the image of God' and know 'the glory of God in the face of Jesus Christ'.[13] It is to a glorified and absent Messiah that she bears such eloquent witness here, gripping the attention of other 'daughters of Jerusalem' in the process. Could you equal her appreciative and loving attention to detail as she describes her Beloved from head to foot? He becomes precious indeed to the one who believes, and all who do so become part of 'an elect race, a royal priesthood, a holy nation, a people for God's own possession, that ye may shew forth the excellencies of him who called you out of darkness into his marvellous light'.[14] This she gives herself to do here.

To the question 'What is thy Beloved?' her answer is 'A greater than Solomon'. Through this testimony drawn from the lips of Solomon's loved one to some of her interested contemporaries, we trace the adoring witness of those Jews who come to appreciate that Jesus is the Messiah, the Son of the living God. How different these believing ones are from their own kinsmen for whom 'he hath no form nor comeliness; and when we see him, there is no beauty that we should desire him'. For the present day believer in Jewry, their Messiah and Lord has form, comeliness, and beauty; He has more glory, and wisdom than their most glorious and wise king. They would be able to describe Him in specific and detailed terms, vv.11–16a, framing their portrait in wide-ranging general terms, vv.10,16b, and answering the enquirers' opening question 'What is thy Beloved?' with an adoring and almost breathless 'This is my beloved [Heb. dodhi], and this is my friend [Heb. re‎`i]', v.16c.[15] His glories beggar description.

---

[13] Rom.15.8; 2 Cor.5.16; 4.4,6; 3.16.   [14] 1 Pet.2.7,9f, hence she now obtains mercy.   [15] 'beloved' [Heb. dodhi] is the usual term by which she refers to him, see pp.45f: 'friend' [Heb. ra‎`yah, fem.] is his most used endearing term for his loved one, see p.45; only here does she use the masculine form [re‎`ah] of him, 5.16, though onlookers adopt it in the plural once to refer to them both, 5.1e‡. It is another instance of reciprocity in the descriptive terminology chosen by the pair. Spiritually this is suggestive, for she is to Him what she finds He is to her at the end! 'Friend' is used of a husband, Jer.3.20, and even of illicit sex partners, Jer.3.1; Hos.3.1.

What do we learn from her concerning her glorified Messiah in all His completeness? *Primarily* He is 'white' [Heb. tsach]. The root means 'to be cloudless, and hence to be dazzling, bright, splendid'; in the portrait here we are reminded of our Lord's appearance on the Transfiguration Mount when 'his garments became white as the light', 'glistering, exceeding white; so as no fuller on earth can whiten them', 'white and dazzling'.[16] It was the cloudless splendour of His holiness which set Him apart from all others, whether at His birth when the One born was to 'be called holy, the Son of God', or throughout His public ministry when He was addressed so often as 'the holy one of God'. Here He is seen in all the resplendence of His holiness in heaven now, the One who is 'holy, guileless, undefiled, separated from sinners, and made higher than the heavens'.[17]

Secondly she describes her Beloved as 'ruddy' [Heb. ˊadhom]. The contrast is as remarkable as it is vivid. The very word here takes us back in thought to the first man, Adam. In this we grasp the primary thought here. The Holy One is the Human One too, and the attribute that radiates His deity is matched by that which displays His humanity. This One has proved Himself to be the antitype of the ram skins dyed red which covered the Tabernacle in the wilderness. Though the nation's sins 'be red like crimson, they shall be as wool' through Him and His work. His consecration to His God, as far as to death, has provided the Israel of God with an antidote for her failure in that total devotion to her God which alone will satisfy Him.[18] Again He lives to supply her with a better 'water of cleansing' than Israel knew through the ashes of the red heifer.[19] Here, particularly, it is that insistence on His glory as the Last Adam, the Second Man, that is before her wondering eyes. The Messiah who died for her sins, is the same One who rose again in fulfilment of the Scriptures. He is the living Guarantor of a future kingdom on earth, one in which He will be seen to be

---

[16] Matt.17.2//Mark 9.3//Luke 9.29 all of which anticipate the age of kingdom glory, 2 Pet.1.16–18.   [17] Luke 1.35; 4.34; Heb.7.26; cf. Isa.6.1ff.   [18] Isa.1.18; Exod.25.5; 26.14; 35.7,23; 36.19; 39.34. How He longs to see His own reflecting Himself as Zion's Nazirites who 'were purer than snow, they were whiter than milk, they were more ruddy in body than rubies', Lam.4.7.   [19] Num.19.2; Heb.9.13f.

greater than great king David, of whom it was said that 'he was ruddy', and whose son He is after the flesh. The Son of David is also
the Son of Man. This is the Man in God's own image to whom all
has been committed, and to whom the Israel of God is attracted.[20]

Thirdly, He is to her 'the chiefest among ten thousand'. The
word 'ten thousand' [Heb. rebhabhah] is the farthest that the mind
stretches in general in the Bible. The women in Israel sang 'Saul
hath slain his thousands, and David his ten thousands', that is,
David was the super-warrior, the pre-eminent captain of the army.
There, military prowess and victory over enemies is in view. No
foe, nor even the pestilence shall destroy the one who knows the
Lord as his refuge for 'A thousand shall fall at thy side, and ten
thousand at thy right hand; but it shall not come nigh thee'. In the
Song however it is pointing us off to the pre-eminence of the
ascended and glorified Messiah in the throne room of heaven. It
is true of Him now, as of the Ancient of Days, that 'thousand
thousands ministered unto him, and ten thousand times ten thousand stood before him'. Round about the throne were many
angels, 'the number of them was ten thousand times ten thousand,
and thousands of thousands; saying with a great voice, Worthy is
the Lamb that hath been slain to receive the power, and riches, and
wisdom, and might, and honour, and glory, and blessing'. He has
been highly exalted, and given the name which is above every
name. He is now 'far above all rule, and authority, and power, and
dominion, and every name that is named, not only in this age, but
also in that which is to come'.[21] This One is the 'chiefest', 'marked out by a banner [Heb. daghal]'.[22] He is the unique rallying centre for all the redeemed, clearly distinguishable and set above all
others, and thus is beyond comparison, 'that in all things he might
have the pre-eminence'. In these three general descriptive terms
which she uses of Him in verse 10 we learn *what He is essentially*,
'white', *what He became and shall ever be*, 'ruddy', and *what He has
been made* consequently, 'chiefest'.

---

[20] 1 Cor.15.3,20–28,45ff.　　[21] 1 Sam.18.7; Ps.91.7; cf. 3.6[7]; Dan.7.10; Rev.5.11f,
the One who 'came from the ten thousands of holy ones: at his right hand was a fiery
law unto them' in Moses' time, Deut.33.2, is seen among His heavenly entourage
here: Phil.2.9; Eph.1.21 RV marg.　　[22] See pp.199f, n.47. Gordis SoS, proposes
here derivation from a word meaning 'see', hence 'conspicuous'.

There is just one more general phrase she uses of her Beloved, and with which she closes this stanza; 'yea, he is altogether lovely', v.16b. Again she sees in Him what the nation as a whole fails to see. For them, 'when we see him, there is no beauty that we should desire [Heb. chamadh] him'. We have seen that she did sit down 'under his shadow with great delight [Heb. chamadh‡]' when she came into her God-given inheritance, 2.3. But here, now that her Beloved is all glorious and exalted in heaven, she chooses an intensive plural from the same root [Heb. machamaddim‡] to embrace all his lovelinesses. He is in sum total 'delightfulnesses' to her, and she needs no other in addition to Him. She might have used the words of the psalmist 'Whom have I in heaven but thee? and there is none upon earth that I desire beside thee'.[23]

We turn to the specific details of her description, 5.11–16a. Notice how she loses sight of herself completely as she considers her Beloved, and speaks well of Him. As the hymn expresses it:

> Worthy of homage and of praise,
> Worthy of all to be adored;
> Exhaustless theme of heavenly lays,
> Thou, Thou art worthy, Jesus, Lord.

Darby has pointed out that when the Beloved speaks of the features of the bride He speaks to her assuring her of His delight in her. However, when she describes His features, she speaks of Him to others, not to Him as if to approve Him. He fills her wondering eyes. Nothing less than a full-length portrait will begin to do justice to His tenfold loveliness. There is no deterioration here, from His golden head to His golden feet, vv.11,15. How different this is from the imposing image which Nebuchadnezzar saw in his dream concerning the succeeding Gentile world empires, the head of which was gold, but the feet were iron and clay. Three different words for 'gold' are used in these verses, which express the glory of *His head*, v.11 [Heb. ketem paz], *His hands*, v.14 [Heb. zahabh], and *His feet*, v.15 [Heb. paz].[24] Contrast the hymn

---

[23] Isa.53.2; ct. Ps.73.25.   [24] 'pure gold' [Heb. kethem], 'fine gold' [Heb. paz], 'gold' [Heb. zahabh], see pp.339f.2.

248

writer's words regarding His head, hands and feet:

> See from *His head*, *His hands*, *His feet*,
> Sorrow and love flow mingled down;
> Did e'er such love and sorrow meet,
> Or thorns compose so rich a crown?

She is gazing on her Lord in glory, and expressing that which she sees to those with an ear to hear. His head, His locks, His eyes, His cheeks, His lips, His hands, His body, His legs, His aspect, and His mouth are described in turn.[25]

Finally, her descriptive masterpiece is rounded off with the words 'This is my beloved, and this is my friend, O daughters of Jerusalem', v.16c–e (see note 15).

Where is the Messiah Engaged Today?, 6.1–3. The question raised and answered in these verses has been solved for the Israel of God beyond all controversy. After all, they have found Him and know where He is and what His concerns are. To the question 'Whither is thy beloved gone?' the one who had been seeking Him replies 'My beloved is gone down to his garden ... to feed in the gardens, and to gather lilies'. The daughters of Jerusalem had been so attracted by her description of her Beloved, that they enquire of her which way He turned [Heb. panah‡] for they wish to 'seek [Heb. baqash] him' with her, v.1. In the Song, only the Beloved is the One who is sought for.[26] How strange that they should expect

---

[25] For some detail see Appendix 3, pp.339ff.   [26] 'seek' [Heb. baqash‡] used of the *maiden or bride* seeking her beloved, 3.1(2),2(2); 5.6, and of the *daughters of Jerusalem* seeking him with her, 6.1: 'find' [Heb. matsa´‡] used of the maiden finding or hoping to find her beloved, 3.1,2,4; 5.6; 8.1, of *the daughters* charged to find him, 5.8, of *the watchmen* who find the maiden, 3.3; 5.7, of *the maiden* as one who 'found peace', 8.10. The theme is theologically significant. Regarding 'seeking', 1). it often refers to the positive attitude of one *'seeking the face of God'*, e.g. 'When thou saidst, Seek ye my face; my heart said unto thee, Thy face, Lord, will I seek', Ps.27.8(2): *'seeking the Lord'*, 105.3: *'seeking God'*, e.g. 69.6[7]: *'seeking thy name'*, 83.16[17]: specially in *summons to worship*, 1 Chron.16.10,11; cf. Ps.105.4; Exod.33.7; 2 Chron.11.16; Ps.27.4. 'Let all those that seek thee rejoice and be glad in thee: let such as love thy salvation say continually, The Lord be magnified',

her to know, as she had turned to them for assistance in her own quest! They infer that one who knows her Beloved this well, is bound to know where He is likely to be. How true that is spiritually.

They are proved right. Expressing *what* He is to her has revealed *where* He is, v.2. She knows where His interests lie. Although He is 'high and lifted up' in His present exaltation, yet such is His love for 'His own' that He will be 'gone down [Heb. yaradh][27] to his garden' when conditions are right. She has come to see herself as He had described her; she is His garden, 4.16c. This garden together with its spice beds is how He saw 'His own' after His resurrection and ascension. It is the beds of spices in His garden that are His first delight. It suggests His own fragrant graces which are produced in her by the Holy Spirit.

She has become aware that her Beloved has other interests now. His condescending grace has brought Him down 'to feed in the gardens, and to gather lilies'. The subject of the garden has been considered in some detail in chapter 8. We must notice that the only uses of the plural 'gardens' are in 4.15, 8.13 and our verse here. This cannot be without significance. His garden, in the singular, clearly refers to the Israel of God, those from the nation who are His, the 'remnant according to the election of grace'. The 'gardens', in the plural, include all those out of every nation who have a place in the larger 'paradise of God'. The hesitation on the part of the favoured nation to open up to the Messiah after His

---

[26] *cont.* Ps.40.16[17]; 70.4[5]: 2). it is used of approaching the Lord to obtain favour when there are specific problems, 2 Sam.21.1; 2 Chron.20.3f: 3). in repentance, 2 Chron.7.14; 'afterward shall the children of Israel return, and seek the Lord their God, and David their king', Hos.3.5; cf. 2 Chron.15.3f; Amos 5.4ff; Zeph.2.3. Of particular relevance to the subject for the Song, 'I will go and return to my place, till they acknowledge their offence, and seek my face: in their affliction they will seek me earnestly', and 'They shall go with their flocks and herds to seek the Lord; but they shall not find him: he hath withdrawn himself from them', Hos.5.15,6. See also pp.172f. For 'find' see p.311.   [27] 'gone down' [Heb. yaradh‡], in Song 6.2 so that the two's and three's that meet in His Name may know His presence in the midst, in 6.11 to overview the developments which prepare for His second advent. It is used frequently in connection with *divine manifestations, theophanies*, e.g. Gen.11.5,7; 18.21; Exod.3.8; 19.11,18,20; 34.5; Num.11.17,25; 12.5; 2 Sam.22.10.

resurrection and ascension, has only proved to be to the widening of the circle of blessing as He has embarked upon a world-wide mission. He has given the divine increase to the planting and watering ministries of His servants. We expect to find such descriptions as 'the churches of Christ', 'the churches of the saints', but it must have come as something of a shock to hear of 'churches of the Gentiles'. The 'church at Jerusalem' is one thing, but what of 'the church of God which is at Corinth'? The assembly at Corinth is spoken of in simile as 'God's husbandry',[28] it is cultivated soil indeed. The spouse here, therefore, sees her Belov-ed 'feeding',[29] a great shepherd word, finding that which satisfies Him among the numberless companies of His people throughout the world. For the first time too, she notices that He will be gone down 'to gather [Heb. laqat][30] lilies'. These represent the in-dividuals in whom He sees the beauty of lowliness and divine grace. Previously she had been aware that He was to be found 'feeding among the lilies'. Now He gleans from the fields of the world. James, the Lord's brother, grasped the same truth after hearing Peter, Barnabas, and Paul speak of God's remarkable ways, and 'what signs and wonders God had wrought among the Gentiles by them'. So 'James answered, saying, Brethren, hearken unto me: Symeon hath rehearsed how first God did visit the Gen-tiles, to take out of them a people for his name'. Even Caiaphas' word was made to have a prophetic ring to it for those with ears to hear: he knew 'that Jesus should die for the nation'. The apostle John was given to see much more than this, wonderful though it is. He knew that Jesus' death was 'not for the nation only, but that

---

[28] Rom.16.16; 1 Cor.14.33; Rom.16.4; Acts 8.1; 1 Cor.1.2.   [29] 'feed' [Heb. ra`aht]. Where does he feed?, Song 1.7: among the lilies, 2.16; 6.3, and in the gardens, 6.2. See also in the Song 1.8; 4.5. The verb is used often in a figurative way of a ruler, e.g. Jer.17.16; Zech.10.2; 11.16; 13.7.   [30] 'gather' [Heb. laqatt] 6.2 = to pick, gather up. Often of *the manna* in the wilderness, Exod.16.4,5 etc. Specifically of *gleaning*, Ruth 2.2,3,7,8,15(2),16,19,23. Animals *grazing*, Ps.104.28, has led some to suggest that her beloved is depicted as a gazelle in 6.2, and the parallels of feeding and grazing are warranted. The salvation history connection suggests that 'gathering' be maintained, and the context does not warrant reverting to the simile of the gazelle in vv.1f.

he might also gather together into one the children of God that are scattered abroad'.[31]

Knowing *where* He was, and *what* He was doing, only made her the more confident that she belonged to Him. The extension of His salvation and blessing universally were the necessary corollaries of the greatness of His Person which she had come to appreciate. Jew and Gentile alike now are the objects of His love. She had been led to see that Israel is the nation 'of whom is Christ as concerning the flesh', and yet He 'is over all, God blessed for ever'.[32] His disciplines of grace had taught her to put His prerogatives first therefore, as her claim indicates. She sees now that 'I am my beloved's, and my beloved is mine', v.3; ct. 2.16.

What the Israel of God is now to the Messiah, 6.4–9. Those from among Jewry who believe that Jesus is the Messiah, the Son of God, know that 'neither is circumcision anything, nor uncircumcision, but a new creation. And as many as shall walk by this rule, peace be upon them, and mercy (though they be of the uncircumcision), and upon the Israel of God' (who are of the circumcision). Being found in an Old Testament book, it is the latter particularly who are before the Beloved in our stanza. How does He describe this 'new creation' among Jewry? 'She is the choice one of her that bare her'!

Firstly, He speaks to her, vv.4–7. We may summarize His description with His opening words 'Thou art beautiful, O my love, as Tirzah, comely as Jerusalem'. We note the reappearance of the often used punctuating word 'beautiful' [Heb. yaphah‡].[33] The word is paralleled here by 'comely' [Heb. na'wah*],[34] as her Beloved multiplies words again to speak to her heart adequately. His choice of similes is particularly instructive. Both of the cities mentioned

---

[31] Acts 15.12ff; John 11.51f. When the Lord comes into the air, the Church will be gathered together to Him, 2 Thess.2.1. At the second advent of our Lord another gathering of the elect is to take place, Matt.13.48; 24.31; Mark 13.27; Luke 3.17; ct. Matt.13.28ff.   [32] Rom.9.5.   [33] See p.153.   [34] 'comely' [Heb. na'weh*], an adjective used of the maiden here, generally 1.5; 6.4//'beautiful', and specifically of her face, 2.14, and her mouth, 4.3. It is used figuratively of Jerusalem as a comely woman, Jer.6.2//'delicate' [Heb. me'unaghah]. It is translated 'seemly' when used of praise, Ps.33.1; 147.1. See also Prov.17.7; 19.10; 26.1.

were elevated and attractive in themselves. The former belonged
to the tribe of Joseph (Ephraim), whilst the latter was actually in
the inheritance of Benjamin. These were the two sons granted to
Rachel, the wife whom Jacob loved. The Lord opened Rachel's
womb to bring about Joseph's birth, whereas Rachel died after her
hard labour resulting in Benjamin's birth. Joseph was born outside
the land, whereas Benjamin was born in the land. Jerusalem was
already the united kingdom's capital in Solomon's day. As the
psalmist glowingly described it 'Beautiful in elevation, the joy of
the whole earth, is mount Zion, on the sides of the north, the city
of the great king'. Soon after Solomon's death, when the kingdom
was divided, the northern kingdom, variously known as the house
of Joseph, Ephraim, and Israel, chose Tirzah as its first capital
city.[35] Both of the cities were the choice of kings, and stood out in
their surroundings, providing us with appropriate similes of corporate splendour. By bringing them together, Solomon was led to
anticipate the beautiful oneness of God's people in the eyes of her
Beloved, despite all the external divisions which spoil it to this day.
The balancing beauty of concern for her own God-given portion on
the one hand, as illustrated by the selection of Tirzah, and concern
for God's own portion on the other hand, as suggested by the inclusion of the city which He had chosen to place His Name there,
should be pondered. What a rich heritage is associated with her.

The third simile of verse 4 is yet another emphasizing her

---

[35] In this connection, there is considerable profit to be gained from a study of Tirzah [Heb. Tirtsah = pleasure, beauty*]. The word is derived from the verb 'to be
pleased with, to accept favourably' [Heb. ratsah]; cf. noun 'favour, acceptance'
[Heb. ratson]. Both words are used often of God's favour to His people, and His
acceptance of their sacrifices. He not only so speaks of 'my servant, whom I uphold;
my chosen, in whom my soul delighteth', but we are told that 'the Lord taketh
pleasure in his people: he will beautify the meek with salvation', and that 'In an
acceptable time have I answered thee, and in a day of salvation have I helped thee',
Isa.42.1; Ps.149.4; Isa.49.8 = 2 Cor.6.2. It is one of the cities, Josh.12.24;
1 Kings 14.17; 15.21,33; 16.6,8,9(2),15,17,23; 2 Kings 15.14,16 named after the five
daughters of Zelophehad, see Num.26.33; 27.1; 36.11; Josh.17.3, the seventh
generation from Joseph; note the association of cities and women, Isa.54.6; Rev.21.
Two great principles regarding the God-given inheritance of His people are

corporateness, presenting her 'terrible as bannered hosts', RV marg. This again seems to take us back in thought to the camp in the wilderness where all the tribes were united around their Lord in the midst. What an awe-inspiring sight His hosts were when He was in the midst of them. Of Edom, Moab and the Canaanites alike it was said 'Terror and dread falleth upon them; by the greatness of thine arm they are as still as a stone; till thy people pass over, O Lord . . . which thou hast gotten. Thou shalt bring them in, and plant them in the mountain of thine inheritance, the place . . . which thou hast made for thee to dwell in, the sanctuary, O Lord, which thy hands have established'.[36] This is like the promised inheritance to which He is bringing them, and shows how the glorified One sees those who own that they are His.

Apart from His description of the eyes of the one He loves in verse 5ab, the remainder of the similes He uses concerning her are similar or identical to those He has used before in chapter 4. Consider the two sevenfold portraits:

4.1–7	6.4–7
————	1. beautiful as Tirzah
————	2. comely as Jerusalem
————	3. terrible as bannered hosts

---

[35] *cont.* demonstrated in this family, of which this city is a physical embodiment: 1). the daughters' faith articulated in their appeal that their father's inheritance should be secured to them, looked to God to safeguard their family inheritance. This was called for because their father had died in the wilderness, undoubtedly through sin, without leaving behind him a son and heir. If there was no written title up to that time in *law*, God's *grace* saw to it that faith which counted upon Him when there was no legal claim, would gain its own reward. 2). This decision of grace resulted in a fresh problem to do with inheritance however. Should Zelophehad's daughters marry outside of their tribe, what had been *secured for the family* would become *lost to the tribe*. The chiefs of Manasseh therefore insisted on some safeguard so as to maintain all that had been allocated by lot under the control of God's disposing sovereignty. This plea too, was upheld. For archaeological light regarding Tirzah see specially EAE 2.395–404 De Vaux; and for the information derived from the Samaria Ostraca, Aharoni LB2 356–369 and MBA 137.   [36] 'terrible' [Heb. ʾayom*] 6.4,10; Hab.1.7; cf. [Heb. ʿemah] of terror inspired in their enemies through them, Exod.15.16.

254

1. eyes doves behind thy veil
2. hair as a flock of goats
   along side of mount Gilead
3. teeth like flock newly shorn
   come up from washing
   every one hath twins
   none bereaved
4. lips like a thread of scarlet
5. temples piece of pom-
   egranate behind thy veil
6. neck like the tower of David
7. breasts like two fawns

4. turn away thine eyes for
   they have overcome me
5. as a flock of goats along
   side of Gilead
6. like flock of ewes
   come up from the washing
   every one hath twins
   none bereaved
   ——————
7. as piece of pomegranate
   behind thy veil
   ——————
   ——————

Being arrested initially by His loved one's threefold splendour, by features which she had not displayed before, He returns once again to speak more particularly of her eyes which overcome Him as He looks at her. How effectively does the Israel of God plead when her eyes are turned upward to her Lord. Her loving desire for Him glows in her eyes, her love is communicated in a look. The word 'overcome' [Heb. rahabh‡] meaning to storm, or assail, indicates something of their influence upon Him. The man ensnared by the ill-advised promises he had made, is urged to 'importune (the same word) thy neighbour'. We are reminded of the success gained by that one who went to his friend at midnight seeking three loaves. It was 'because of his importunity' that he returned with all that he requested.[37] Certainly, there was no veil upon her eyes now, for she had turned to her Lord, and the divine revelation was completed too (ct. 4.1).[38]

The Lord pronounced through Balaam that He saw no 'iniquity in Jacob, neither ... perverseness in Israel', for in the Tabernacle He saw His favoured ones sheltered under the eleven goats' hair curtains. They were covered by the value of the sin offerings of the many goats slain. Here the Lord saw His loved one's hair covering her, and it was 'as a flock of goats'. His bride was not only *submissive* to Him, but was *sheltered* through the efficacy of His substitutionary work.[39]

---

[37] cf. regarding the rich young ruler how that 'Jesus looking upon him loved him', Mark 10.21. See also Prov.6.3; Luke 11.8.   [38] 2 Cor.3.13–16.   [39] Num. 23.21. The goat is frequently associated with the sin offering.

She had perfect and clean teeth also. The Israel of God have responded to His word, 'Except ye eat the flesh of the Son of man and drink his blood, ye have not life in yourselves. He that eateth my flesh and drinketh my blood hath eternal life; and I will raise him up at the last day. For my flesh is meat indeed, and my blood is drink indeed. He that eateth my flesh and drinketh my blood abideth in me, and I in him'. Feeding upon Him is the God-appointed means of growth in grace and in His knowledge even today.[40]

Finally, we come to the pleasure that 'His own' are to Him in their fruitfulness. The unlimited potential and power for service is to be tapped from the hem of our great High Priest's garment as He serves in the true sanctuary in heaven. There the pomegranates were represented in the presence of God.[41] And yet the Lord now finds His loved one's fruitfulness opened up to Him for His satisfaction. He appreciates it to the full even if for others it is still veiled. Meditate on these things which He speaks winsomely to His own.

Secondly, and to conclude the poem, *her Beloved speaks about her*, 6.8–9. The One whom God has appointed Heir of all things is to be surrounded by those who have been blessed by Him. Each will fill the place appointed. Small wonder that Paul bows his knees 'unto the Father, from whom every family in heaven and earth is named'. These tiers of divine blessing could be represented by the sixty queens, the eighty concubines, and the numberless virgins here. But to the heavenly Bridegroom there is one who is incomparable. She is unique. Those who come to know Jesus, the Messiah, the Son of God now, are peculiarly precious to Him. They belong to that election of whom it is said that God 'chose us in him before the foundation of the world'. Of our Beloved we read that 'he came and preached peace to you that were far off (Gentiles), and peace to them that were nigh (Jews): for through him we both have our access in one Spirit unto the Father'.[42] Israel has many advantages as the nation separated from all others by God. It was with her fathers that God made irrevocable covenants. Not only

---

[40] John 6.53–56.   [41] Exod.28.33ff; cf. Matt.9.20ff//.   [42] Eph.3.14f; 1.4; 2.17.

256

6. 'There is hope for a tree . . . that it will sprout again', Job 14.7. Another fine example of the Biblical use of the botanical motif featured at Neot Kedummim, near Modi'im. See pp. 119f. For the simile applied to the re-sprouting of Israel. See Isa. 6.13.

27. Close-up of a walnut tree in early summer.

28. Close-up of the tender vine budding in the spring-time.

29. The pomegranate tree in flower in the spring-time.

'I went down into the garden of walnuts . . . to see whether the vine budded, and the pomegranates were in flower' Song 6.11. See pp. 72ff, 76–80, 264f.

27

29

2

the illustrious few, but many of her sons and daughters will know the eternal blessing of their God. But there are some of Israel, those who have identified themselves with their rejected Messiah and Lord, who have found themselves more blessed than they could have imagined in their wildest dreams. The future guaranteed to them as 'a remnant (of their nation) according to the election of grace' through God's sovereign grace alone, surpasses any hope declared in the Old Testament. These are beloved for the Messiah's sake,[43] to whom they gladly confess that they belong. They belong to the city which is at the same time the Bride![44] It is not surprising that He says of her 'she is the only one of her mother; she is the choice one of her that bare her'.[45] The mother, of course, is Israel, but out of that nation has come this choice one, 'the Israel of God'. Amongst Israel's blessed, these are supremely blessed. While the Messiah is whispering this of her already, a wondering universe will acknowledge soon that the half had never been told them. In that day bright with glory, the daughters, the queens, and the concubines alike will call her blessed indeed, and praise her.[46] How the Israel of God needs to know this precious truth when its faith is tested by persecution, and they are so often despised and rejected by their own nation and families. Here, then, is her Beloved's response to her. To Him there is only one like her: 'my undefiled . . . the choice one'! She had been brought to know Him as utterly incomparable too, though this did not come to her without loss and pain.

> Hast thou seen Him, heard Him, known Him?
> Is not thine a captured heart?
> Chief among ten thousand own Him,
> Joyful choose the better part.

---

[43] For the enhancement of the Messiah's personal and official glory see the use of the title with the article (the Christ in English) in Ephesians, TBD pp.130f. [44] Rev.21.1–22.5. [45] 'one' [Heb. ˘echadh] indicates magnificent, incomparable to her mother here, but often has the connotation of uniqueness by virtue of divine election as with Abraham, Isa.51.2; Ezek.33.24, and Israel, 2 Sam.7.23// 1 Chron.17.21. Her beloved's use calls for both levels of meaning. See TDOT 1.197f, Lohfink. The adj. 'choice' [Heb. barah], 6.9,10‡, is derived from the verb 'purify', and 'choose' (though only in the participle) [Heb. barar], and EVV have 'pure' in margins consequently. Note the beloved's association of 'my undefiled' with it in 6.9. [46] cf. Leah, Gen.30.13, and the ideal woman in Prov.31.28f.

BARNES' TRANSLATION

KEY: M = Male; F = Female; O = Onlookers
[with +] our more literal rendering

POEM 5, 6.10–8.4

O
6.10. Who is this [or she] coming forth herself like dawn;
Beautiful as the moon,
Bright as the sun,
Awe-inspiring as an army displaying banners?

* * * * * * *

M
11. Into a nut-garden I went down
To seek-out among tender shoots by the stream,
To find if the vine had budded,
Or the pomegranates had blossomed:
12. I had not realized
My desire had already given me
Chariots [multitudes] of my willing people.

* * * * * * *

O
6.13. Return! Return! O Shulammite!
[7.1] Return! Return! For we are looking unto thee.

F +
What see ye in the Shulammite?
What looks like a choral-dance of two camps.
O +
7.1. How beautiful thy feet look in fine sandals,
[2] O prince's daughter!
The graceful curves of thy thighs
Are like artistic ornaments;
A work of the hands of a master craftsman.
2. Thine inward-part is a mouthed goblet,
[3] Lacking no transporting delight.
Thy belly is a standing sheaf of wheat,
Draped in white lilies.
3. Thy two breasts are like two fawns,
[4] Twins of a gazelle [+ doe, f.]
4. Thy neck is like a tower of fine-ivory.
[5] Thine eyes are clear pools in peaceful reflection
Beside the gateway of a city well-peopled.
Thy nose is like a peak of the Lebanon
Facing toward Damascus.
5. Thy head upon thee is like the Carmel;
[6] Indeed, the hair of thy head, like purple thread,
Holds a king captive in the locks thereof.

* * * * * * *

259

M
7.6. How thou dost ever excel,
[7] Yes, how thou dost continually afford pleasure,
    O love, in all refined delights!
 7. This thy stately bearing has always been likened to a palm tree,
[8] And thy two breasts to its fruit-clusters.
 8. I soliloquized; 'I am climbing-up into a palm tree,
[9] I am plucking fruit among its topmost branches.
    For now indeed thy breasts are
    As vine-clusters,
    And the fragrance of thy person [+ nose, breath]
    As choice apples.
 9. Thy very speech [+ mouth, palate], like the best wine'

F +
[10] Flows from [+ to or for] my beloved freely;
    Gently moving the slumbering [or silent] lips.
10. I am my beloved's,
[11] And toward me is his desire.

        * * * * * * *

F
11. Come! my beloved, out to the country.
[12] We must stay in the villages [+ among the henna bushes];
12. For we must get early to the vineyards,
[13] We are seeing if the vine has budded,
    The grape-blossom burst forth,
    Or the pomegranate flowered.
    There am I giving to thee my love [+ loves]!
13. The love-fruits have effused fragrance,
[14] And within our reach is every kind of delicious fruit,
    Fresh as well as dried [+ new as well as old];
    My beloved, I have treasured these up for thee!
F
8.1. O that one might give thee as a brother to me,
    Who suckled my mother's breasts!
    Meeting thee in the street, I am kissing thee:
    Then certainly none are despising me.
 2. I am leading thee, I am bringing thee
    Into my mother's dwelling,
    {Fully teach thou me!}
    I am causing thee to drink of choice spiced wine,
    From sweet juice of my pomegranate.
 3. {His left hand is under my head,
    While his right hand affectionately embraces me}
M +
 4. I have solemnly charged you,
    O daughters of Jerusalem:
    How can ye cause to disturb,
    Or how can ye yourselves awaken such love
    Until it pleases?

        * * * * * * *

+ Barnes proposes the whole of 6.13 spoken by a chorus, 7.1–10 complete by the male, and 8.4 by the female.

19

POEM 5. ALL MANNER OF PRECIOUS FRUITS, NEW AND OLD, 6.10–8.4

IN THIS POEM there are two movements toward the grand goal. In the first of these all leads up to the beloved's desiring his loved one and his coming to her, 6.10–7.10[11]. The second records her glad response to him and her desire for their unbroken enjoyment of life together, 7.11[12]–8.4.

The Thread of the Story

In the first movement, the Shulammite is barely heard. There are a series of inter-woven appreciative descriptions of her by sympathetic onlookers,[1] and by her beloved.[2] However, two brief responses of the Shulammite provide us with the major divisions of the stanzas.[3] The general tone is martial in character.[4] In the second movement,[5] apart from the last verse the Shulammite speaks throughout. Initially, she urges her beloved to come away from the crowd to the privacy of the countryside,[6] and then expresses her wish that he were her brother so that she could demonstrate publicly her love for him without embarrassment. She would bring him, with a view to his complete acceptance, into her mother's house and family circle.[7] Both now being satisfied in the realization of reciprocated love, her beloved insists again that love

---

[1] Song 6.10,13a,b,d[7.1a,b,d]; 7.1–5[2–6].   [2] 6.11f; 7.6–9a[7–10a].
[3] 6.13c[7.1c]; 7.9b–10[10b–11].   [4] cf. 'army', 'chariots', 'two camps', 'tower',
6.10,12,13[7.1]; 7.4[5].   [5] 7.11[12]–8.4.   [6] 7.11–13[12–14].   [7] 8.1–3.

261

is to be allowed to take its rest just there.[8]

We may note that

Opens on a martial note	Ends on a peaceful note
He comes down to see	She wants him to join her in seeing
He is alone	She says 'come let us...'
He leaves his house	She brings him to her mother's house
His soul set him among his people	She knew his desire was toward her
She is dancing	He insists that love be not stirred
He is held captive in her tresses	She is held in his arms

The Thread of Salvation History

The previous poem 5.2–6.9, focused our attention upon the Israel of God in the present, while the glorified Messiah is absent and is sharing His Father's throne in heaven. This period as it affects Jewry is specifically in view in Romans 11. *Paul answers the question* there 'Did God cast off his people?' with a resounding 'Perish the thought!' He, like all Jews who come to know Jesus as their Messiah and Lord, gives the lie to such a view. Yet he confesses that it is but a 'remnant' who come into the blessings reserved for the 'election of grace' in the present time.[9] *Another vital question* there is, that if God has not finished with 'his people' entirely, could it be that the nation as a whole has stumbled so as never to recover? Is their national cause, their election because 'they are beloved for the fathers' sake',[10] lost irretrievably? Many today reject a future kingdom of God on earth, and that Israel is to be restored to divine favour as His earthly administrative centre. For these, the nation can hope for no more than to be incorporated into 'the people of God' at the end of this age, after which the eternal state will follow immediately. Paul gives a resounding 'no' to this also. For him, though Israel has 'fallen' now, there is a time yet to come glowingly described as 'their fulness'. 'For I would not, brethren, have you ignorant of this mystery, lest ye be wise in

---

[8] Song 8.4.   [9] Rom.11.1–10.   [10] 11.28.

your own conceits, that a hardening in part hath befallen Israel, until the fulness of the Gentiles be come in; and so all Israel shall be saved: even as it is written, There shall come out of Zion the Deliverer; he shall turn away ungodliness from Jacob: and this is my covenant unto them, when I shall take away their sins'.[11]

This glad day when Israel's covenant keeping God shall say 'it is my people' and they shall say 'The Lord is my God' is the subject of poem 5. Phase one in this demands that:

A REDEEMER SHALL COME TO ZION, 6.10–7.10[11]

What are some of the features that obtain 'in that day'?

Israel Terrible as a Bannered Host, 6.10. Earlier her beloved had compared her to a mare among Pharaoh's chariotry.[12] This directed us to the exodus of Israel from Egypt, and the startling means which God used to bring about the rout of her enemy. The description of her by a group of appreciative onlookers here is quite different. *Firstly*, it is how others are seeing her now, and *secondly* it is the more elevated and awesome as it is combined with similes of the dawn, the moon and the sun.[13]

We, too, might well ask 'Who is she?' as we have observed the re-emergence of the nation in its homeland. This is a sign indeed. Israel is one of the 20th century indicators that 'the day is approaching' when the prophetic clock is to be started once again. None could gainsay that, apart from many other spectacular achievements of the modern state of Israel, one that particularly has called forth more wonder than any other is her remarkable military capability and prowess. Many within the nation and in other nations, on the occasion of the lightening success marking the so-called six day war, were convinced of an almost supernatural element providing the only satisfactory explanation. Surely the image of the present Israeli state is so dramatically different from that of her dispersed and persecuted forefathers through the

---

[11] See Rom.11.11–27; cf. Isa.59.20f; Jer.31.31–34.   [12] Song 1.9.   [13] 6.10; ct. v.4 where it is her beloved who so describes her. While it is only the glorified Lord who sees the Church in this way now, for many it will be much more apparent in Israel before the Lord comes.

last 20 centuries that contemporary startled onlookers might well ask the question 'Who is she?'

Were we in a position to see things as God sees them, from heaven's vantage point, we would be startled even more. For when John saw the great sign in heaven, it involved seeing Israel as God did, and being assured, not only of His future *protection* of her, but of His future grand *purposes* for her. John the seer saw the nation without the martial trappings, focusing upon her heavenly resplendence alone.[14] This more spiritual and divine image is still strangely absent from that privileged nation chosen 'to shew forth the excellencies' of the God who had called her.[15] Who is able, apart from her God, to bring about this even greater change for which the sympathetic onlooker waits? The Scriptures assure us that the world will yet see the emergence of such a nation, a resplendent and awesome host in harmony with her God that will be the harbinger of the hoped-for 'morning without clouds'.[16]

The Advent of Israel's Messiah, 6.11–12. Nothing short of a divine intervention on Israel's behalf can establish her as the blessing which God intends her to be in the midst of the earth. Verses 11 and 12 direct us to the coming of Israel's Lord and Messiah. These are *His* words,[17] and our hearts thrill in harmony with our Lord's as we anticipate His second advent when He will come down. 'I went down into the garden of nuts,[18] to see the green plants[19] of the valley,[20] to see whether the vine budded, and the

---

[14] Rev.12.1f; cf. Gen.37.9ff. The 3½ years of dearth, or even of birth pangs find no place in the Song. The 'day of Jacob's trouble' is needed to purge out the rebels, and refine the nation, but contributes nothing to the 'love relationship' story, ct. Zech.13.7ff or Isa.58. [15] 1 Pet.2.9. [16] 2 Sam.23.4. [17] Pace RSV; Living Bible. [18] 'Walnut' [Heb. ´egozṭ], see p.74. [19] The word 'green shoots' [Heb. ´ebhṭ] in the plural indicates how all of them are precious to him. Compare the kindred word [Heb. ´abhibh] referring first to the green ears of barley, the firstfruits, Exod.9.31; Lev.2.14, then to the month when this appeared, the great passover month Abib, set apart to commemorate the Exodus, Exod.13.4; 23.15; 34.18(2); Deut.16.1(2). [20] The word for 'valley' [Heb. nachalṭ] refers to a wadi, or water course, which may be a rushing torrent in the rainy season but be quite dry in the summer. It is used specifically of the Kidron Valley, as of other stream beds, 2 Sam.15.25; 1 Kings 2.37; 15.13; 18.40; 23.6(2); Jer.31.40. In our passage it is associated with a 'garden'. John describes the Kidron as a 'winter

pomegranates were in flower'.[21] With what patience He has waited[22] the appointed 'time to love', the springtime through to early summer. It is like a re-enacted exodus event in more ways than one. Then the Lord said 'I am come down to deliver them'. As a result of His intervention 'Terror (the same root as the word 'terrible' used of His loved one here) and dread falleth upon them (their enemies) . . . till thy people pass over which thou hast purchased'.[23] David, too, in a personal way, had experienced the Lord's parting of the heavens so that He might scatter his enemies.[24] Yet, Israel is still guaranteed the literal advent of her Lord and Messiah to give effect to all of His gracious and loving promises to her. How long, Lord?

We cannot remain unmoved when we read the words of the beloved's only soliloquy in the Song. In bold words he reveals his own deep inner emotions when he went down.[25] Believers often sing of 'the love that brought Thee (the Lord) down to earth to die on Calvary'. We do not meditate sufficiently on that love which will bring Him down for His own people when He comes again.

---

[20] *cont.* torrent' [Grk. cheimarros†], 18.1, and associated it with a 'garden', Gethsemane, north of the city of David. The 'king's garden', Neh.3.15, was at the south of the city of David, and was developed by Solomon and was well-known to him. Robert observes that this valley is known to the Arabs as Wadi al-Joz [Heb. ´egoz] which means 'Walnut Valley'. Note that this valley is at the foot of the Mount of Olives, upon which the returning Lord's 'feet shall stand in that day' so that 'it shall cleave in the midst thereof toward the east and toward the west, and there shall be a very great valley' [Heb. ge´ gedholah, not our word], Zech.14.4.
[21] For 'vine' and 'pomegranate' see pp.76-80, 72ff respectively. Note that the word 'budding' [Heb. parach‡], 6.11; 7.12[13], is used of Israel and its land in eschatological contexts, e.g. Isa.27.6; 35.1f; Hos.14.5,7[6,8]; Ps.72.7; 92.12f[13f]. This bursting into life after winter's 'death' is like a resurrection life, as already typically set forth in Aaron's rod that 'budded', Num.17.8[23], and in the ornaments of the Tabernacle and Temple, Exod.25.31,33(2),34; 37.11,19(2),20; Num.8.4 (of almonds) and 1 Kings 7.26,49 = 2 Chron.4.5,21 (of lilies).
[22] cf. 2 Thess.3.5.   [23] Exod.3.8f; 15.16ff. In both of these contexts, the fact of Israel's being brought out of Egypt is followed by reference to their being brought in to the land of promise.   [24] 2 Sam.22.10 = Ps.18.9[10].   [25] The word 'soul' [Heb. nephesh‡] is used by his loved one elsewhere in the Song, 1.7; 3.1,2,3,4; 5.6. He was the one whom her soul loved. Only here, 6.12, is it used of the overwhelming desire his love for her produced in him.

That Israel, His loved one, to whom He will come down and with whom He will thrillingly identify, He describes as 'the chariots [Heb. merkabhah‡][26] of my princely people'. He can no longer rest 'until her righteousness go forth as brightness, and her salvation as a lamp that burneth'.[27] A most significant truth emerges. The Israel which, through its religious adulteries and sins, had been disowned by God as 'Not my people' [Heb. lo ̄ ̄ammi], is here described glowingly as 'my people' [Heb. ̄ammi].[28] This fulfils the promise that 'in the place where it was said unto them, Ye are not my people, it shall be said unto them, Ye are the sons of the living God'. God will yet say to them which were not 'my people', 'Thou art my people; and they shall say, Thou art my God'.[29]

The adjective 'princely' or 'willing' [Heb. nadhibh‡] further enriches the revelation here. The word is used of those who are princely in rank, true nobility. The Song so describes his loved one just two verses later: she is addressed 'O prince's daughter' [Heb. bath-nadhibh†].[30] Also, it is used of those moral qualities of mind and character, true nobleness, in which God delights: 'the noble deviseth noble things; and to noble things doth he stand'.[31] It is also utilised to describe that person who is willing, inclined, or impelled to do a certain thing. The verb and noun are used

---

[26] Solomon's reign familiarized the nation with these, 1 Kings 10.26, and with the horses and horsemen essential for them, 4.26[5.6]. See, in simile, reference to the mobile lavers of his Temple too, 7.33. The war chariot is what is in view (cf. the modern equivalent used by Israel's army, their tank called the 'merkabhah'), as in Song 1.9[Heb. rekhebh‡]. Compare a word derived from the same root translated 'seat' [Heb. merkabh‡], 3.10.   [27] Isa.62.1. The display of the Shulammite's beauty in Song 7.1–5[2–6] reflects this purpose of divine love.
[28] Hos.2.23[25]; 1.9.   [29] This description 'my people' [Heb. ̄ammi] is used very frequently throughout the whole OT from Exod.3.7,10 to Zech.13.9 [in Hebrew Bible to 2 Chron.7.14]. It is used by the Lord often to accentuate the waywardness of those so priviledged as 'my people'. How quickly this was followed by the bright promise 'Yet the number of the children of Israel shall be as the sand of the sea', Hos.1.9–11[2.1–3]; cf. Isaiah's ministry under the title 'Comfort ye my people', 40.1; 51.16; 52.6; 63.8; 65.22. We recall the immense cost to make Israel's restoration possible, for of the Servant of the Lord it was said 'for the transgression of my people was he stricken', 53.8.   [30] cf. Num.21.8 of Israel's princes in 'the Song of the Well'.   [31] Ps.32.8(2)JND.

frequently of volunteering, offering to God freely, and of the freewill offering itself.[32] The most significant parallel for our passage is found in Psalm 110, which gives expression both to the present exaltation of our glorified Lord, and to His subsequent return to the earth in power in order to take over its universal administration. The One who is David's Lord, and to whom the LORD Himself said 'Sit thou at my right hand, until I make thine enemies thy footstool', is yet to send forth 'the rod of thy strength out of Zion'. Then, we are told 'Thy people offer themselves willingly [Heb. nedhabhah] in the day of thy power: in the beauties of holiness from the womb of the morning, thou hast the dew of thy youth'.[33] It is to the coming from heaven of David's Lord, when He is to be joined gladly by those holy volunteers of His people, that we are directed here in the Song. Should any doubt the feasibility of that which will change the whole character of universal administration, let the words of that same psalm banish all questioning, for 'The Lord hath sworn, and will not repent, Thou art a priest for ever after the order of Melchizedec'.[34] The oath of the God that can never lie doubly guarantees the coming of the One who shall reign as the greater than Melchizedec from Jerusalem, the King of righteousness, the King of Peace, and the Priest of the Most High God. Happy that people who join forces with Him!

Israel's Conversion and Celebration, 6.13[7.1]. The Hebrew text here provides us with a truer division of the chapters. The closing verse of chapter 6 in the English Versions forms the opening of

---

[32] The adjective in our passage is used of the 'willing-hearted' who contributed so freely for the construction of the Tabernacle, Exod.35.5,22. David the penitent pleads that 'a willing spirit' might sustain him, Ps.51.12[14]JND. The verb is used of those who volunteered for the army of Deborah and Barak, people and princes alike [Heb. nadhabh], Jud.5.2,9. David was overwhelmed at the response of the nation with the Temple project in view 'But who am I, and what is my people, that we should be able to offer so willingly after this sort?', 1 Chron.29.14; cf. vv.5,6,9(2),17(2). The noun [Heb. nadhabhah, fem.] is used, for example, of the gifts for the Tabernacle, Exod.35.29; 36.3, and for the Temple, 2 Chron.31.14, and for the free-will offerings at the Passover, 2 Chron.35.8, at Pentecost, Deut.16.10, and at Tabernacles, Ezra 3.5. Compare also the Bible name Nadab, Exod.6.23; 1 Kings 14.20.   [33] Ps.110.1–3; cf. the Lord's promise to His people 'I will love them freely', Hos.14.4[5].   [34] Ps.110.4.

a new stanza continuing to 7.5[6].

First, there is the fourfold call to the Shulammite. It is to the voices of sympathetic onlookers that we listen once again.[35] They wish to see her in all her uniqueness and glory, and hence their fourfold call to her to 'Turn back' [Heb. shubhi]. How often this occurs throughout the Old Testament. It has many nuances, one in particular having to do with the nation's spiritual relations with God. On the one hand, *negatively*, Israel is to be smitten down by her enemies 'because ye are turned back from following the Lord, therefore the Lord will not be with you'.[36] Conversely, and *positively*, the nation is challenged frequently to turn back to God, to seek Him penitently.[37] Solomon had made the plea so familiar to the whole nation on the occasion of the dedication of the first Temple which he had built.[38] The 'all Israel' which is yet to be saved in a day 'shall return'. Hosea prophesied that 'the children of Israel shall abide many days without a king, and without a prince, and without sacrifice'. This is the situation even to this day. Beyond this, however, the same prophet looked forward to the 'afterward', when 'the children of Israel (shall) return, and seek the Lord their God, and David their king, and shall come with fear unto the Lord and to his goodness in the latter days'.[39] Isaiah was assured that the ransomed and redeemed of the Lord 'shall return', a 'remnant shall return'. He named his first son signifi-

---

[35] Note the masculine plural 'ye' addressed to them by the Shulammite in 6.13c[7.1c], which rules out the call to 'Return' being either the word of her beloved or of the daughters of Jerusalem.   [36] Num.14.43, relating to their refusal to enter the land of promise because they believed the false report of the spies. Even Solomon himself was warned against turning away from following the Lord, 1 Kings 9.6.   [37] Many of the orthodox in Israel today urge the secularist majority to return to the religion of their fathers, the Rabbinic Judaism they so zealously represent. The phrase they use means 'to make return' [Heb. chazar bithshubhah]. To call the nation to a godly repentance, never to be repented of, means far more than this. It is all too easy to cause people to 'return, but not to him that is on high', Hos.7.16. Rather, it is essential to create that sense of sin and departure from God which will lead them to say 'Come, and let us return unto the Lord for he hath torn, and he will heal us'. 'O Israel, return unto the Lord thy God; for thou hast fallen by thine iniquity', Hos.6.1; 14.2[3]; cf. 12.6. Translated as an absolute religious term it means 'Repent'.   [38] 1 Kings 8.33,35,47f.
[39] Hos.3.4f; for 'seek' [Heb. baqash] see p.249, n.26.

cantly, thereby making him a living sign of this very truth. Shear-Jashub [Heb. she´ar yashubh, the latter word is a verbal form of our word 'return'] means 'a remnant shall return'.[40] Be assured: there will be those in that day who shall look with wonder upon the nation which responds to its God and returns!

Why is his loved one here, and here only, called the Shulammite [Heb. shulammitht]? One suggestion sees in it a reference to the family home of Solomon's loved one; she was a native of the Galilean village of Shunem [Arabic = Sulam]. The modern village, which still marks the location, nestles on the southern slope of Givat Hammoreh, and looks out on the luscious Jezreel Valley. The article appearing before the word hardly demands the rejection of such a proposition.[41] This maiden, more than David's Shunammite Abishag, or that Shunammite so familiar to us through the records of Elisha's ministry, was to Solomon *the* Shulammite, 'the only one', 'the choice one'.[42] This may well be helpful in setting the scene of the story, but it does not begin to exhaust the significance for the Song.

To place the names Solomon and Shulammite side by side in Hebrew suggests another meaning immediately.[43] For those onlookers, and for the loved one herself, she is the 'Solomoness'! She is his, she is one with him, his name is hers, another subtle pointer to their existing marriage alliance.

There is even more than this to be understood here in connection with the outworking of salvation history. The love relationship between the Lord and Israel at this stage in His programme has in view not only their oneness, but the particular blessing revealed when Israel knows herself and is known at last as 'the Shulammite'. For the millennia of the nation's long history, the people have greeted one another with the many sided 'Shalom'. It embraces so much more than 'Peace!'. It includes that blissful state when all fears and their causes have been removed, when all is peaceful and secure, when there is nothing lacking, but rather there is a realization of completeness, wholeness, health, perfect well-being, and

---

[40] Isa.7.3; 35.10; 51.10; 10.21f.   [41] Pace Rowley AJSL 56,'39,84–91.
[42] 1 Kings 1.3; 2.17,21f; 2 Kings 4.8–37; 8.1–6.   [43] [Heb. Shelomoh and Shulammith, the latter being the feminine form of the former].

the contentment that flows from this. Such grand results are impossible apart from the sacrificial basis for them in the 'peace offering', which effects complete reconciliation. The Messiah, her divine Beloved, has already provided for this, though Israel as a nation has not yet apprehended it. Until He is accepted there can be 'no peace, saith the Lord, unto the wicked'. Thank God, Israel is soon to 'look upon me whom they have pierced',[44] and to confess that it is by means of the chastisement which the Servant of the Lord endured that the nation has gained 'our peace'.[45] When she confesses Him 'the Lord our righteousness',[46] Israel will own herself and be owned as the Shulammite, displaying all that her Beloved is in Himself. She is to be the one who has 'found peace' [Heb. shalom].[47]

It was upon such a one that these sympathetic observers would 'look' [Heb. chazah‡].[48] This is not related to the word translated 'to see' in verse 10[Heb. ra'ah‡].[49] While it is used of the physical faculty of beholding with the eye, as primarily it is here, it is the word often employed of the seer's ecstatic vision. In fact, the word 'seer' [Heb. chozeh] is derived from the same root. Apart from the 'return' of Israel none will see realized in her that which God's seers were given to see concerning her. How joyfully Isaiah could cry 'look [Heb. chazah] upon Zion, the city of our set feasts: thine eyes shall see Jerusalem a quiet habitation, a tent that shall not be removed, the stakes whereof shall never be plucked up, neither shall any of the cords be broken. But there the Lord will be with us in majesty, a place of broad rivers and streams . . . For the Lord is our judge, the Lord is our lawgiver, the Lord is our King; he will save us'.[50] It is for a sight of these evidences of the Lord's blessing in the nation at peace, that the Song is appealing.

---

[44] Isa.48.22; cf.57.21; also Zech.12.10.   [45] Isa.55.5; cf. the Lord's very first word to His own in resurrection, 'Peace be unto you', John 20.19,21.   [46] Jer. 23.6; 33.16.   [47] Song 8.10; cf.Isa.62.2, 'the nations shall see thy righteousness, and all kings thy glory: and thou shalt be called by a new name, which the mouth of the Lord shall name'.   [48] Song 6.13[7.1](2)‡.   [49] This is used eight times in the Song, 1.6; 2.12,14; 3.3,11; 6.9,11; 7.12[13]‡ and is translated 'look' in 1.6. Another word for 'looketh' [Heb. shaghach‡], meaning to gaze or stare, is found in 2.9.   [50] Isa.33.20ff; cf.54.2; ct. her enemies wish 'let her be defiled, and let our eye see its desire upon Zion', Mic.4.11.

If *confession* leads to this, then *celebration* is to follow. The Shulammite is taken aback by their desire to look upon her. However, she is no longer self-conscious as she had been at the beginning, when she had said 'Look not upon me because I am swarthy', 1.6. She asked merely in which role they wish to look upon her, 'as upon the dance of Mahanaim?' The proposal satisfies completely the onlookers, who appreciatively describe her graceful and beautiful form as she dances to celebrate her joyous fulfilment.[51] It may be that the specifically named dance, which translated means 'two camps', suggests the antiphonal character of the song they sing to the accompaniment of timbrels as she dances, moving between the two lines of spectators. Such spontaneous responses suitably express the joy and thrill at the couple's soon-to-be-realized reunion, which reflects the fulfilment of God's loving purpose for Israel.[52] For Israel is yet to dance, the arrival of the new covenant era ridding the nation once for all of those inhibitions caused by centuries of troubles and sorrows. She will confess 'Thou hast turned for me my mourning into dancing'.[53] Jeremiah speaks of this. The nation is set dancing as she realizes that the Lord has loved her with 'an everlasting love'. Describing the saved nation as the virgin of Israel whom the Lord will build again, he writes[54] 'Again shalt thou be adorned with tabrets, and shall go forth in the dances of them that make merry'. The psalmist

---

[51] See generally the 'dance' theme [Heb. machol, masc., and mecholah, fem., 6.13[7.1]‡]. The word is derived from a verb [Heb. chul] meaning 'to whirl, twist, dance, even writhe', in which latter sense it is often used of birth travail, Isa.26.18; 54.1. It is used with the noun of dancing in Jud.21.21. See also the Psalm titles, 53.[1]; 88. [1, Heb. machalath*], and the place named Abel-mecholah, lit. 'dance meadow', Jud.7.22; 1 Kings 4.12*. The word family is characteristic in contexts of joyous celebration, Jer.31.13, involving company singing and even musical accompaniment. For the description of the Shulammite's beauty as she danced see Song 7.1–5[2–6].   [52] cf. 1 Sam.21.11[12](2), where the Philistines say of David 'did they not sing one to another of him in dances, saying Saul hath slain his thousands, and David his ten thousands', also 18.6; 29.5. The dance is an expression of victory, triumph. It is at the Exodus from Egypt, in 'the song of the sea', that the word first occurs, Exod.15.20, expressing God's praise in word and act. [53] Ps.30.11f[12f]; ct. Lam.5.15.   [54] Jer.31.3f; see the whole paragraph, vv.1–9 and v.13.

focuses upon the same scene when the nation is to sing a new song, exhorting 'Let Israel rejoice in him that made him: let the children of Zion be joyful in their king. Let them praise his name in the dance: let them sing praise unto him with the timbrel and harp'. Only then will 'everything that hath breath praise the Lord'.[55]

Again, the word 'Mahanaim' is itself suggestive for the eschatological interpretation of the Song. Apart from its use here, the actual word refers only to a place east of the Jordan Valley in Gilead, and near to the Jabbok River. Its naming is associated with the occasion when Jacob met with the angels of God as he returned to the land after many years of absence. Concerning the incident we read 'And Jacob said when he saw them (the angels), This is God's host [Heb. machaneh, singular]:[56] and he called the name of that place Mahanaim [Heb. machanayim, dual]'.[57] The play on the words is apparent, and Jacob understood the angels of God joining him and his 'host' as a divine encouragement and guarantee. There were two hosts now, so that he could face the future perfectly at peace. This was an essential preliminary to that changing of his name from Jacob to Israel at Peniel. Such, too, is the change expressed in the joyous dance of Mahanaim in the Song. Israel's host and God's host are now in happy concert in the Land.

Israel Beautified with God's Salvation, 7.1–5[2–6]. The psalm to which we have already referred concerning God's people praising 'his name in the dance', went on to say 'For the Lord taketh pleasure in his people: he will beautify the meek with salvation'. It is 'the meek', we recall, who shall 'inherit the earth'.[58] The beauties of the Shulammite which the onlookers admiringly describe here, therefore, are the several features of the Lord's

---

[55] Pss.149.1ff; 150.6, see v.4 for reference to 'dance'.   [56] There are many references to 'host' and 'hosts' in the OT. The dual, however, is reserved for the place which came to be a Levitical city in Gad subsequently, Josh.13.26,30; 21.38[36]; 2 Sam.2.8,12,29; 17.24,27; 19.32[33]; 1 Kings 2.8; 4.14; 1 Chron.6.80[65], Map ref.214177. Joshua was so thankful to, and became a worshipper of, the One who described Himself as 'captain of the host of the Lord', 5.14f.   [57] Gen. 32.1f.   [58] Ps.149.4; 37.9; Matt.5.5.

beautifying Israel, his people, with salvation. They scan her beauties from her feet to her head and hair.[59] It is as though they are arrested by the Lord's created masterpiece built upon earth, and from the earth upwards. The change from Isaiah's description in the most repulsive terms of the nation's sin and its consequences through divine chastisement, is certainly dramatic. 'From the sole of the foot even unto the head there is no soundness in it'.[60] Now, the Israel saved at the Messiah's second advent, with her sins all forgiven, is seen in a tenfold attractiveness from the sole of her foot to the crown of her head. Here it is the prince's daughter being described, one now noble in rank and made noble in her character. She has been made to 'sit with princes'.[61] This is how the nation is to appear when she is about to enter upon her princely prerogatives granted her by the Lord. All reflects the change from the Jacob of Mahanaim to the Israel of Peniel. Only thus can she show forth the excellencies of Him who called her out of darkness into his marvellous light.

Akin to this is the closing touch of the description, where her hair is said to be 'like purple'.[62] The admiring onlookers do not adopt the 'flock of goats' simile here, which directs us to the divinely provided covering for the nation derived from the hair of the animals used for the sin offering. Rather, they are attracted particularly by the colour of her covering, the colour belonging to rulers and imperial splendour. If ever a woman's long hair was a 'glory to her'[63] it is this one's. She is submissive to her Lord, and yet displays his regal glory which He has put upon her.[64] How fitting that 'the king is held captive in the tresses thereof'.[65] The overpowering and almighty love of Israel's Lord has first swept Him among His princely and willing people, and then has bound Him to her in the many strands of glory His grace has put upon her. At His first advent He had gone to the cross submissively out of love for the nation, being bound as their 'sacrifice with cords, even unto the horns of the altar'.[66] Here, at His second advent, that nation will have identified with His sufferings at last and

---

[59] Song 7.1–5[2–6].　　[60] Isa.1.6.　　[61] 1 Sam.2.8; cf. Ps.113.8f.　　[62] Song 7.5b[6b]. She is never called 'queen', ct. 6.9; 'the queen in gold of Ophir', Ps.45.9[10]. [63] 1 Cor.11.15.　　[64] cf. Ps.90.16f.　　[65] Song 7.5c[6c].　　[66] Ps.118.27.

become sharer of His glories. Isaiah's prophecies are to find their fulfilment concerning the nation, for 'his glory shall be seen upon thee' and 'Thou shalt also be in the hand of thy God . . . and as the bridegroom rejoiceth over the bride, so shall thy God rejoice over thee'.[67] Consider then, a tenfold beauty which the law could never have produced.

Thy Feet [Heb. phe͑ amayikh], 7.1[2]‡. The Talmud connects the feet with the three annual pilgrimages which the faithful were to make to the divinely appointed festivals at Jerusalem. The verb from which our word is derived is used of 'being impelled'.[68] It is better to see here, therefore, a hint concerning that time when righteousness is to go before the nation making their 'footsteps a way to walk in'. Their walk is then to be ordered 'in thy (God's) word'.[69] The fact that her feet are shod in sandals reminds us that grace has caused them to return 'home', and they have experienced a new 'exodus event' when 'men shall go over in shoes'. Like the returning prodigal, Israel's feet will be supplied with sandals as they were at the beginning. The nation is yet to carry the good news far and wide 'shod with the preparation of the gospel of peace'.[70]

Thy rounded thighs [Heb. chammuqey yerekhayikh], 7.1[2]; ct. 3.8‡. What a contrast to Jacob who limped upon his thigh.[71] How different this 'prince's daughter' who has sprung from his loins. Have we not arrived at that joyous Messianic era when 'the lame man (shall) leap as the hart'? To the shapeliness of her thighs is added the comparison of them to jewels, stressing both their beauty and their preciousness. The divinely bestowed glories of each of the tribes is seen in her, as earlier they found a place upon the breastplate of the nation's high priest.[72] Such a transformation would be totally impossible apart from the work of an artist, the divine Master Workman. The blessed nation here has been through the hands of her God, who is described often as 'my, his, our or your Maker', for nothing short of divine skill is able to produce a suited partner to share His glory.[73]

---

[67] Isa.60.2; 62.3,5.   [68] [Heb. pa͑ am], Jud.13.25.   [69] Ps.85.13[14]; 119.133.
[70] Exod.12.11; Isa.11.15; Luke 15.22; Isa.52.7; Eph.6.15.   [71] Gen.32.31[32], 25[26](2); Isa.35.6; cf. Acts 3.8. Here she is portrayed as wholly faithful to her husband; ct. the unfaithful wife upon whom the curse of God fell, and whose thigh fell away, Num.5.21,22,27.   [72] Exod.28.17–21.   [73] e.g. Job 32.23; Isa.17.7; 51.13; Ps.95.6; cf. Eph.2.10; 4.15f; Col.2.19.

Thy Navel [Heb. sharrekh], 7.2[3]†. Another contrast with her earlier condition is brought out here. For 'in the day thou wast born thy navel [Heb. shor*, a kindred word] was not cut'.[74] But if in His incomparable pity and compassion her God said then 'live', and bedecked her externally so bountifully that her 'renown went forth among the nations for thy beauty: for it was perfect through my majesty which I had put upon thee',[75] then He will create her attractiveness in a more personal and permanent form in a future day. For Israel, this dramatic change only awaits her acknowledgement of Him in all her ways, when she shall fear the Lord and depart from evil. This will prove to be 'health to thy navel, and marrow to thy bones'.[76] The Lord's masterly touch will produce the perfectly formed naval of the nation's new birth, a rounded bowl in which no joy is lacking either for her God, or for the nations that look on.[77]

Thy Belly [Heb. bitnekh], 7.2[3]†. The word here bears two major meanings. On the one hand it is used of the stomach, either externally or internally, and on the other hand it describes the womb as the organ of procreation. Here the external form of the Shulammite's stomach is described as 'a heap of wheat', indicating its attractive colouring and shapely full proportions.[78] Eschatologically, she is seen after 'harvest home', fruit of the corn of wheat which had fallen into the ground and died.[79] Nothing of the day of Jacob's trouble features here. Threshing and winnowing were all behind her; she had realized the Festival of Weeks at last. As in Ruth's case, she appeals to her Beloved, her Kinsman-Redeemer, when the threshing is all over.[80] In herself she reflects what her Lord intends to do for His land, when He makes peace in her borders, and makes her large with His blessing when He fills her with the finest of the wheat.[81] There will be no need of a security fence or wall around the threshing floor with its treasured 'heap of wheat' in that day. Rather, a girdle of lilies, so attractive to her Beloved, will adorn with beauty and purity that fulness which all will then see in her. At last it will be found true of her too that 'righteousness shall be the

---

[74] Ezek.16.4.   [75] Ezek.16.14; see vv.1–14.   [76] Prov.3.6ff.   [77] Jud.9.13.
[78] See 'Wheat', pp.88f, n.20–23.   [79] John 12.24.   [80] Ruth 3, esp.v.3;
Joel 2.23f; see Lev.23.15–21; Num.28.26–31 re Festival.   [81] See Ps.147.14;
Hos.14.5ff[6ff].

girdle ... and faithfulness the girdle of (her) reins'.

Thy Breasts [Heb. shadhayikh], 7.3[4]; 4.5.[82] The juxtaposition of
the belly and breasts here calls to mind those blessings pronounced
by Jacob upon Joseph. Whilst the patriarch could speak of such
blessings, it was the Almighty who was the source of them. 'The
Almighty, who shall bless thee, with the blessings of heaven above,
blessings of the deep that coucheth beneath, blessings of the breasts
and of the womb'.[83] Recall that it is the onlookers who are describing so appreciatively the Shulammite here. How they embody
Isaiah's exhortation 'Rejoice ye with Jerusalem, and be glad for her,
all ye that love her: that ye may suck and be satisfied with the breasts
of her consolations; that ye may milk out, and be delighted with the
abundance of her glory'.[84] At last the onlookers see and describe
her beauties in the very terms which her Beloved had used of her.
They were satisfied with her consolations now fully matured in her,
and in that abundance of glory now divinely bestowed upon her.

Thy Neck [Heb. tsawwaʼrekh], 7.4[5].[85] She has a tall, slender and
stately neck. The days of the hardened or stiff-necked obstinacy of
the nation's past are now over.[86] Israel's decorated neck as she left
Egypt is not in view, nor the strongly defended neck of those the
Messiah drew to Himself during his first advent and then thrust out
to boldly face His opponents.[87] Here her beautiful neck is seen as
ivory, the very material from which the body of her Beloved was
formed.[88] That is, she is seen in that imperishable glory made over
to her through His death and resurrection on her behalf. Only thus
can she be fitted to share in His reign of peace and glory, anticipated
already in Solomon's 'throne of ivory', and in those 'ivory palaces'
of the 'Song of loves'.[89]

Thine Eyes [Heb. ʼeynayikh], 7.4[5]. Her beautiful eyes are so

---

[82] A particularly emphasized theme in the Song, see the 8 refs: 1.13; 4.5;
7.3,7,8[4,8,9]; 8.1,8,10‡.   [83] Gen.49.25.   [84] Isa.66.10ff.   [85] For 'neck'
see 1.10; 4.4; 7.4‡.   [86] Deut.10.16; Neh.9.16,17,29; 2 Kings 17.14; 2 Chron.30.8;
ct. Ps.75.5[6]. For the adj. see Exod.32.9; 33.3,5; 34.9; Deut.9.6,13; 31.27.   [87] See
on 1.10, p.190; cf. the early disciples, who were called upon to face so much opposition to the spread of the gospel, e.g. Stephen, Acts 7; Prisca and Aquila, Rom.16.4;
and Paul.   [88] Song 5.14.   [89] 1 Kings 10.18; 2 Chron.9.17; Ps.45.8[9].

arresting.[90] The Rabbis rightly observe that the miracle of giving sight to the blind was reserved for the Messiah.[91] Before He takes up the reins of universal government He is to open the eyes of the blind, and the depth of perception marking the nation then is aptly described in terms of deep pools. Their longsighted vision, and regal oversight is suggested in the comparison with the reservoirs 'in Heshbon, by the gate of Bath-rabbim'. This Ammonite royal city which lay on the east of the Jordan, was taken by Israel under Moses, and was settled by Reuben/Gad,[92] prematurely as it appears. This part of the nation, before proving the wisdom and bounty of their God in the land He had initially allocated to them to the west of Jordan, would 'reign as kings' before the time.[93] That privilege and responsibility had been reserved for the nation in the future. This simile hints at the extended boundaries from which she not only looks out, but to which she becomes a God-appointed blessing as the 'daughter of multitudes' [Heb. Bath-rabbim].

Thy Nose [Heb. ʾappekh], 7.4,8[5,9]‡. She has a distinctive nose. Again a far-reaching overview[94] from the Anti-Lebanon mountains toward Damascus implies the expansiveness of the renewed nation. There are dangers lurking there no longer.[95] She proudly oversees the land of Abrahamic proportions, looking toward the east still! We may compare David's kingdom when 'he put garrisons in Syria of Damascus: and the Syrians became servants to David, and brought presents'.[96] Damascus is yet another royal city adopted in the descriptions of the Shulammite's new-found splendour. She shares with her Beloved that subtle sense of discrimination which is an essential ingredient in the administration of the kingdom of God

---

[90] See pp.225–228, esp. n.21, and pp.254f.   [91] 2 Kings 6.20(2); Isa.35.5; 42.7; Ps.146.8. Consider the Messianic claim latent in the miracles of Jesus, especially those seven specific cases in which He gave sight to the blind, Matt.8.22–26; 9.27–31; Mark 8.22–26; John 9.1–7; Matt.20.29–34//'s, and the general remark in Matt.21.14, His closing miraculous Messianic appeal. Contrast the spiritual blindness of Israel in part in the present, Rom.11.7,10, cf. v.25.   [92] Num.21.25; 32.37; Josh.13.17,26; 21.39.   [93] Josh.22.19; cf. 1 Cor.4.8.   [94] [Heb. tsaphah, not the word used for watchmen in 3.3; 5.7], cf. the kindred word [Heb. mitspeh = watchtower] Isa.21.8; 2 Chron.20.24; cf. 'the Hivite under Hermon in the land of Mizpah', Josh.11.3.   [95] ct. Song 4.8; cf. Isa.35.9.   [96] 1 Chron.18.6.

when 'his scent shall be in the fear of the Lord'.[97]

Thy Head [Heb. roshekh], 7.5[6]. Her head is majestic. We have seen earlier that the remnant of the nation in the present 'which is according to grace' describes her glorified Messiah as having a head of 'most fine gold'. The onlookers see the saved Israel of the future with a head 'like Carmel'. If her eyes and nose in this description have been directed east-ward, her head is likened to this most splendid and attractive mountain on the western Mediterranean coast. Regarding the wilderness, Isaiah pronounces that in the Messianic era 'the glory of Lebanon shall be given unto it, the excellency of Carmel and Sharon'. Jeremiah, too, speaking of that same future day tells of Israel being brought 'again to his pasture, and he shall feed on Carmel. . . . In those days, and in that time, saith the Lord, the iniquity of Israel shall be sought for, and there shall be none; and the sins of Judah, and they shall not be found: for I will pardon them whom I leave as a remnant'.[98] Carmel's beauty and fruitfulness is proverbial, and aptly portrays something of Israel's crowning glory in the Shulammite here.

Thy Locks [Heb. dalath roshekh], 7.5[6]. Her hair is evidently her glory. We have noted already its imperial colour, truly becoming to one who is a 'prince's daughter'. Purple was prominent in the king's palanquin by which he had transported his loved one to Zion for the day of his espousals.[99] Her hair captivated Him, displaying as it did her willing and loving subjection to Him as Head. As her Redeemer He had drawn her to Himself 'with the cords of a man, with the bands of love'. Now her returning Messiah King is held captive by her tresses.[100] The onlookers may admire her, but His delight is in her, and with the joy of the bridegroom over the bride, her God shall rejoice in her again.[101]

This is the catalogue of beauties and glories which the sympathetic onlookers see in that nation saved through the tribulation period, and which draws her Beloved Messianic King to herself. This is that election which is 'beloved for the fathers' sake', the 'all Israel' to be saved when 'There shall come out of Zion the Deliverer'.[102] It is to

---

[97] Isa.11.3marg.   [98] Isa.35.2; Jer.50.19f.   [99] Song 3.10.   [100] cf. 6.12 where his soul set him among the chariots of his princely people.   [101] Isa.62.4f.   [102] See Rom.11.25–28.

the Beloved's description of her that the Song now turns.

Israel Strongly Desired by her Messiah, 7.6–9a[7–10a]. Clearly, verse 6[7] opens a new stanza; her beloved's exclamation 'How fair' [Heb. mah-yaphith] is a commencing formula with which we are very familiar in the Song.[103] The beloved senses the inadequacy of any one term to describe his delight in her, adding 'how pleasant [Heb. mah-na‾amt][104] art thou, O love'. This is no description of love in the abstract. Rather, the Shulammite is herself the very object of his immeasurable love; we might capture its force better by adding the personal pronoun, translating 'my Love'. When Israel will be saved she comes to realize that her Beloved '*loved* me, and gave himself for me'. Then she will be ceaselessly thrilled in experiencing that '*he loves* me'! The sweet [Heb. na‾im] psalmist had sought one thing, 'to behold the beauty [Heb. no‾am] of the Lord'. The nation had desired more, even that 'the beauty [Heb. no‾am] of the Lord our God be upon us'.[105] Now the nation's returning Messiah, her Beloved, finds just such spiritual beauty produced in her. The Targum, with some insight, comments on this; 'Said King Solomon, How beautiful you are, O assembly of Israel, at the time when you bare the yoke of my kingdom . . .'. It is disappointing that it continues 'at the time when I chasten you with afflictions for your guilt, and you receive them with love, and they seem in your sight as delights'. In the context it is obviously her beloved who finds a plurality of 'delights' in his loved one, his daughter of delights [Heb. batta‾anughim]. Mirrored in this for the nation is that future day when 'The Lord thy God is in the midst of thee, a mighty one who will save: he will rejoice over thee with joy, he will rest in his love, he will joy over thee with singing'.[106]

If the onlookers' admiring gaze swept upwards from the Shulammite's feet to her head, her beloved's delights are differently orientated. It is her graceful stature[107] which arrests his attention, and which he likens to 'a palm tree'. Not inappropriately, it is Psalm 92,

---

[103] For the 'fair' theme [Heb. yaphah] see p.190, n.13, and pp.229f.   [104] cf. 1.16. Note the translations '(my) love', JND, 'my loved one', NEB, 'beloved one', RSV.   [105] 2 Sam.23.1; Ps.27.4; 90.17.   [106] Zeph.3.17; cf. Isa.65.19.   [107] Ps.92 title[1], vv.12–15[13–16].

'A psalm, a Song for the sabbath day' which, having first recorded the destruction of their enemies, says 'The righteous shall flourish like the palm tree: he shall grow like a cedar of Lebanon. They that are planted in the house of the Lord shall flourish in the courts of our God. They shall still bring forth fruit in old age; they shall be full of sap and green; to shew that the Lord is upright; he is my rock, and there is no unrighteousness in him'.[108] That millennial sabbath rest which remains for the people of God will not dawn until the nation which is to be saved may be truly described by her Beloved as the 'palm tree'. The many notices of the palm tree motif in the artistic decoration of Solomon's Temple provides the historical inspiration for the simile selected here. We should not be surprised to find the palm dominant in Ezekiel's millennial Temple also, Psalm 92 linking the spiritual significance of this with the righteous nation which is to be 'planted in the house of the Lord' and is to 'flourish in the courts of our God'.[109] In that happy day, the righteous nation will be a monument to the fact that 'the Lord is upright . . . there is no unrighteousness in him'. What a victory of divine grace that will be. The emphasis on merit, self-righteousness, and even 'the righteousness which is in the law' will have been abandoned. Like Paul, Israel will be found in Him (her glorious saving Messiah), not having a righteousness of her own, even that which is of the law, but 'that which is through faith in Christ, the righteousness which is of God by faith'.[110]

For her beloved, too, her breasts are as clusters of fruit. By means of this simile he is not describing their youthful and graceful beauty, but rather their maturity and abundant fruitfulness.[111] Like dates, her fruit was sweet and nutritious to his soul. Every impression she

---

[108] As with the church, 'the measure of the stature of the fulness of the Christ' is the fruit of a God-raised ministry among the nation, leading to a growing up, cf. Eph.4.13.　　　[109] For Solomon's Temple see 1 Kings 6.29,32(2),35; 7.36; 2 Chron.3.5. For Ezekiel's Temple see 40.16,22,26,31,34,37; 41.18(2),19(2), 20,25,26. For detail concerning the palm tree see pp.74.ff, n.58–62.　　　[110] Phil.3.9. [111] ct. 4.5//7.3[4]. The word for 'cluster' [Heb. ʾeshkol‡] is used in the Song for a cluster of henna, 1.14, of clusters of dates, 7.7[8], and of clusters of grapes, 7.8[9]; Num.13.23 and esp. Isa.65.8ff.

makes upon him creates deep desires within him, so that he determines to make her his own. Note his repeated 'I will'. He would
'climb up into the palm tree', and take hold of its fruit-bearing
stalks. The time of his patient waiting is over now. The apprehen-
ding of the saved nation by its Messiah and Lord is in view here.

It remains for him to appeal to her: she must become all that he
desires her to be. We read 'I said, Let thy breasts be ...',
vv.7b–9a[8b–10a].[112] As with Paul, the nation is to be encouraged
to apprehend that for which her Beloved has apprehended her.[113]
He longs for more than mere potential in her now. It is not the vine
in the budding and flowering stages that He seeks, but He would
handle and taste its abundant fruitfulness. Hence His desire that her
'breasts be as the clusters of the vine'. If the smell of her nose is to
be 'like apples', she must have found His fruit sweet to her taste
first. He would scent the fragrance of His fruit in her. Only as she
had found His love 'better than wine', and drunk deeply at His banqueting house, would her 'mouth (be) like the best wine', absolutely
superlative.[114] In the beloved's love, longing for satisfaction in the
sphere of all the senses, we read the longings of Israel's Messiah for
His people's reciprocated love.

Israel Responds to Messiah's Love, 7.9b–10[10b–11]. It is at this
point that the Shulammite breaks in, being unable to restrain herself
any longer. She assures her beloved that her kisses, being as the best
wine, shall go 'down smoothly for' him.[115] Such would be the in-
toxicating effect of the lovers' kisses that it would transport them into the dream world of sleepers, where they sleep yet their hearts
would be awake with desire.[116] It was her wish to pause there, and
to take in all that this meant to her overwhelmed heart. 'I am my
beloved's, and his desire is toward me'. Never before had she reached such heights![117] There had been a selfish element always in her
desire previously, a hangover from the fall where Eve's desire to

---

[112] 'I said' [Heb. ʿamarti] used in the sense 'to say in the heart', indicating what he
has in his mind, what he thought, cf. Gen.20.11; 26.9; 44.28; Exod.2.14; Num.24.11;
Ruth 4.4.   [113] cf. Phil.3.12.   [114] cf. Song 6.11; 2.3; 1.2; 2.4.
[115] 'Beloved' [Heb. dodhi] is used only of the male lover in the Song establishing
that this is the Shulammite's interjection here.   [116] cf. 5.2.   [117] ct. 2.16; 6.3.

her husband was with a view to having the dominant role in their relationship. Not so here. Neither was her beloved's desire *over her* dominantly, but it was *unto her* distinctively and uniquely. All this anticipates Israel becoming her Lord's Hephzi-bah, when His delight will be in her.[118] On this lofty note, having apprehended His love fully, and responded to it, the first movement of this poem concludes. She is totally absorbed with him.

We have arrived at the second great movement in this poem. If phase one has seen the Beloved Redeemer come *to* her, then in phase two she urges Him to come *with* her and never to part from her.

A NATION SHALL LONG FOR ITS LORD, 7.11[12]–8.4

Her voice is heard constantly here. What are the Shulammite's expressed desires?

Her Call for Unbroken Fellowship, 7.11–13[12–14]. Throughout this stanza the Shulammite alone speaks to her beloved. Appealingly, she addresses him: 'Come, my beloved'. It was because they were apart at the opening of Poem 2 that her beloved had called upon her to 'Rise up, my love ... and come away'.[119] That poem ended with her bringing him to her mother's house. Now, toward the close of Poem 5, it is the Shulammite who appeals to him, using the very same word 'come', the section ending again with her bringing him to her mother's house. In both cases it is the coming of Israel's Messiah to His own place that is projected. In Poem 2 He comes by way of lowly incarnation, His first advent. In Poem 5 we have the confirmation of His more glorious and consummating second advent. Notice too that previously she has often spoken in

---

[118] Note 'desire' [Heb. teshuqah] occurs only at Gen.3.16; 4.7 and Song 7.10[11]*. In the Genesis references it is construed with the preposition 'to' [Heb. ´el], in the Song with 'upon', 'toward' [Heb. ´al]. Both Genesis instances express a similar spirit, one of dominating over. Conversely, the Shulammite finds her beloved's loving and undivided attention resting upon her. See too Isa.62.4.   [119] 2.10,13. The verb 'come' [Heb. halakh] frequently shares with another imperative thereby increasing the warmth of the appeal.

the first person singular, but now the first person plural alone will suffice. 'Let us', she pleads. She has come to think His thoughts and to share His interests, and consequently she calls upon Him that they might share a wide range of mutual joys. That which *concerned* him in 6.11 now *attracts* her in 7.12[13]. 'Come, my beloved, let us go forth [Heb. yatsa´] into the field',[120] where those beautiful hinds of the field have their home. With the national hope in view, this refers to that land flowing with milk and honey where the blessing of God causes the vine and pomegranate to flower. All points to the glad time when the Lord shall have come to reign, and creation itself will reflect the harmonious relations established between the people and Himself, and between the heavens and the earth.[121] The psalmist devotes a 'new song' to this in which he says 'Let the field exult, and all that is therein; then shall all the trees of the wood sing for joy; before the Lord, for he cometh'.[122] God's word shall have gone forth and it will make the earth bring forth and bud; it will have accomplished that which He had purposed. Consequently Israel 'shall go out [Heb. yatsa´] with joy, and be led forth with peace: the mountains and the hills shall break forth before you into singing, and all the trees of the field shall clap their hands'.[123]

Further, she proposes 'let us lodge [Heb. lun, = spend the night, 1.13; 7.11[12]‡] among the henna bushes' [Heb. kaphar].[124] In Poem 1 which depicts the nation after first entering the land, she

---

[120] 'go forth' [Heb. yatsa´] in an imperative literal sense in 1.8; 3.11, and as an appeal in 7.11[12]; ct. fig. use of heart 'failing', 5.6‡. A great exodus event word, e.g. Exod.13.3,9,14,16; Deut.4.37; Ps.136.11. She takes it up to urge Him to join her in the inheritance into which she has come. [121] 2.7; 3.5. It is obvious that this proposed countryside retreat, the field, cannot refer to the Exile as the Targum suggests. [122] Ps.96.1,10–13. Note that David incorporates the text of this psalm within an outburst of praise and thanksgiving as he brought up the ark of the covenant to Zion. This was symbolic of the Person and Presence of the divine King, and anticipates the glad period when 'The Lord reigneth', 1 Chron.16.31. [123] Isa.55.10–13. [124] Lodging for the night in a plurality of villages cannot be right. There are several quite different Hebrew words using the letters k.p.r. including the meanings 'village', 'atonement', and 'henna'. In 4.13 the plural translated 'henna' is pointed identically to our word in 7.11[12] [Heb. kepharim], see NIV marg; NEB.

had compared her Beloved to a cluster of henna flowers. Poem 3 unfolds her Messiah's first advent in the land, where He describes her fragrance by means of henna.[125] Here in Poem 5, which brings us to the very threshold of the Messianic age, their fellowship among the henna bushes amid scenes of restored nature, serves to enhance their appreciation of each other.

An enthusiastic early morning start would bring them to the vineyards where they could see 'whether the vine had budded, and its blossom be open, and the pomegranates be in flower'. Beauty and fragrance point on to the blessing of harvest for the latter rains had come, and the floors were full of wheat already, and it was only a matter of time before the vats would overflow with wine and oil. Joel, in promising such days, addressed the land as well as the people, saying 'Fear not, O land, be glad and rejoice; for the Lord hath done great things ... Be glad then ye children of Zion, and rejoice in the Lord your God'. He added boldly that land and people would also know the Lord with them. 'And ye shall know that I am in the midst of Israel, and that I am the Lord your God, and there is none else'.[126] Can we wonder at the Shulammite, picturing the saved nation, appealing for her Messiah and Lord's fellowship in the setting of the land of Israel, now attractive with nature's new beauties? For the Lord will have brought forth 'a seed out of Jacob, and out of Judah an inheritor of my mountains: and my chosen shall inherit it, and my servants shall dwell there'.[127] Diaspora days will be over forever. It is just 'there' in the land, that she will give Him her loves [Heb. dodhay]'. Nothing short of a plural of excellence could begin to express the range and abundance of love which she desired to give to her Beloved, and to Him only. Her 'loves' were at last a more worthy reciprocation of His 'loves' which had been better than wine from the very beginning.[128] The season was right; the time to love had come!

There is an evident play on words here. The Shulammite would 'give' [Heb. nathan] her 'loves' [Heb. dodhay] and the 'mandrakes' [Heb. dudha'im] would 'give forth' [Heb. nathan] their

---

[125] Song 1.14; 4.13.   [126] See Joel 2.21–27; cf. Haggai who includes figs, grapes and olives as indicators of the restored favour of God, 2.19.   [127] Isa. 65.9; cf. Hos. 2.15[17].   [128] Song 7.12[13]; cf. 1.2.

fragrance.[129] Even the very storehouses were overflowing to the doors, packed full with 'all manner of precious fruits [Heb. meghedh] . . . which I have laid up for thee, O my beloved'.[130] She had treasured up all for him alone. No longer were her love, charms, fruit, to be withheld from her beloved.

Long since as a nation Israel has had the God-given treasures of the 'old'. But until now the nation has not 'been made a disciple to the kingdom of heaven', and as a result the 'old' has not profited. Even for those disciples from Emmaus the 'old' still remained stored up awaiting the light brought by the presence of their Messiah when He, 'beginning from Moses and from all the prophets', provided them with an incomparable exposition 'in all the scriptures' of those 'things concerning himself'. He is the key to all, and the objective of that broad, Biblical, Christologically orientated survey which He gave was 'that they might understand the scriptures'.[131] This is to become the saved nation's portion at their Messiah's second advent. What exhaustless treasures the nation and its returning Messiah are to share together. When she has taken hold of the fruit of the new covenant, which has brought her to a renewed heavens and earth, with a new spirit and a new heart, all will be completely different.[132] Significantly for our passage, she will be called by a new name, Hephzi-bah, and her land is to be called Beulah 'for the Lord delighteth in thee, and thy land shall be married'.[133] At last the nation will come to understand all things concerning her Beloved Messiah and the kingdom of heaven. Not until then will she bring forth out of her treasure 'things new and old'.[134]

---

[129] For the facts and suggestive associations of the mandrakes pp.89ff.

[130] After the mandrakes incident in Gen.30, the Lord opened Rachel's womb, and she gave birth to Joseph [Heb. = he will add]. In Moses' blessing of Joseph only are there other notices (5×) of the excellent or choice things of nature [Heb. meghedh], the gifts of God, the Lord's blessing of His land, see Deut.32.13–16 with Song 4.13,16; 7.13[14]*.   [131] Luke 24.27,45.   [132] For the new covenant see Jer.31.31; Heb.8.8,13; 9.15; 2 Cor.3.6; and for the present Lord's Supper association see Matt.26.28//Mark 14.24//Luke 22.20//1 Cor.11.25. For the new heavens and earth relative to Israel see Isa. 65.17; 66.22; for the new spirit and new heart, Ezek.11.19; 18.31; 36.26.   [133] Isa.62.2,4f.   [134] Matt.13.52. Much is recorded about old and new things, but the phrase 'new and old' in that order is found only in the Song and Matt.13; ct. the order and meaning of Lev.26.10.

Her Desire for Uninhibited Pure Love Fulfilled, 8.1–4. The last stanza of our poem opens with what may appear at first to be a peculiar request. Literally rendered it reads 'Who will give you as a brother to me?', v.1a. There are numerous Biblical instances of the idiom with which the phrase opens. It invariably expresses a strong desire.[135] She wanted to express spontaneously her affection for her beloved, which is shameful conduct in the extreme in a Near Eastern situation. She saw the only solution to her problem, the loving desire to kiss him wherever they met, in his being virtually 'a brother to me' [Heb. ˘ach li]. None would find any impropriety in her openness with one of her near of kin, v.1c,d.

The Messianic implications of all this should be obvious. The saved nation of the future is to be surprised beyond her wildest dreams when she finds in very truth that her Maker is her Husband. What glory that brings to their relationship! Yet she is also to come to realize that her Messiah is her near of kin too, 'as a brother' in order to be a kinsman redeemer indeed. At last the extent of divine grace will dawn upon her, for her divine Husband is a man, Immanuel, God with her, and her Messiah has sprung from her own mother, Israel. He was indeed the human child born, as well as the divine Son who was given. He truly had sucked the breasts of her own mother, Israel. How slow the nation has been in recognizing Him! It was as the climax of His first advent, with His redeeming work all complete, that He had frequently addressed her as He described her charms as 'my sister, my bride'.[136] Finally, in the context of His second advent, her wish that He were 'as a brother', seemingly impossible of fulfilment, is realized in her Beloved Messiah as He, in turn, finds in her a sister and marriage partner. Compare here the Messiah, after His second advent, speaking of the saved nation as His 'brethren'.[137]

Now she would be free to lead her beloved, unreservedly, into her mother's house, v.2a.[138] Five times in the Song she speaks of her

---

[135] See BDB 678f.   [136] Endearing terms, see 4.9,10,12; 5.1 [Heb. ˘ achothi khallah]. At last he is to her 'as a brother to me' [Heb. khe˘ ach li].   [137] Matt. 25.40.   [138] The human parent who bore her, Song 6.9, and suckled her, 8.1 (for the Messiah see Ps.22.9[10]), the one who had unquestioned authority over her house, 3.4; 8.2, the one with sons incensed against her daughter, 1.6, though herself considering her daughter as choice, unique, 6.9. Her beloved's mother travailed in bringing him forth, 8.5; cf. Isa.7.14; Rev.12.1f, and was a queen-mother, Song 3.11.

mother. Beyond the human parent who suckled her (and him) stands the metaphorical mother Sarah, Israel, Jerusalem and Bethlehem Ephrathah.[139] It is to her house that the saved nation yearns to bring her Beloved Messiah. Only then will that privileged nation 'Rejoice . . . with Jerusalem, and be glad for her . . . (and) suck and be satisfied with the breasts of her consolations . . . and be delighted with the abundance of her glory'. Israel's God shall comfort them 'As one whom his mother comforteth, so will I comfort you; and ye shall be comforted in Jerusalem'.[140]

In that grand eschatological era her Beloved Lord Himself will instruct her. The New Translation has captured the meaning in the words 'thou wouldest instruct me' [Heb. telammedheni], v.2b.[141] When the nation's Maker is her Husband, then 'all thy children shall be taught of the Lord, and great shall be the peace of thy children'. Happily the nation's desire will be, 'guide me in thy truth, and teach me; for thou art the God of my salvation; on thee do I wait all the day'.[142] She will enjoy yet another blessing of the new covenant when 'They shall teach no more every man his neighbour . . . for they shall all know me'.[143]

At last that blessed period suggested prophetically in the annual Feast of the Tabernacles will arrive. The vine will not be budding only, neither will the pomegranate be simply in flower as was the case in 7.12[13]. At that season the fruit for the winepress will have been gathered home, and God will say 'thou shalt be altogether joyful'.[144] The joyful nation will call upon her Beloved Messiah 'to drink of spiced wine, of the juice of my pomegranate', v.2c,d. A kindred word to that translated 'spiced' here is used of both the holy anointing oil and the incense which gave forth a 'perfume' in the Tabernacle. Suggestively, another form of the word describes her beloved's cheeks which she describes as 'a bed of spices'.[145] How the fragrance of her Beloved Messiah adds spice to her joy which

---

[139] The more important passages for the metaphor are Hos.2.4–7[6–9]; 4.5; cf. 10.14; Isa.50.1(2); 51.2f; Ezek.16.3ff; 19.10–14,2; 23.2.   [140] Isa.66.10f,13.   [141] cf. RV marg.   [142] Isa.54.4f,13; Ps.25.4f; cf. Isa.48.17. The same root [Heb. lamadh] features in all these references.   [143] Jer.32.33.   [144] Deut.16.13ff. [145] 'Spiced' [Heb. reqach], Song 8.2†; 'perfume', 'spice mixture' [Heb. roqeach], Exod.30.25,35; 'spices' [Heb. merqachim], Song 5.13†.

she wishes Him to drink in at last. The word rendered 'juice' [Heb. ˋasis‡] refers to that which has been pressed out, and is translated 'sweet' or 'new wine' in passages describing the kingdom age when 'in that day . . . the mountains shall drop down sweet wine'.[146] We pause to note again the perfect harmony which is to exist between creation itself and the blessed, fruitful and joyful nation when the Messiah comes, and the messianic banquet begins.

The Messiah of Israel has been waiting long for this glad moment. He already spoke of it in that dark night preceding His awful suffering at Golgotha. He had gathered His own disciples around Him to keep the Passover with them before He suffered. During the course of that meal He instituted the Lord's Supper. In taking the cup He said 'Drink ye all of it; for this is my blood of the covenant which is shed for many unto the remission of sins. But I say unto you, I will not drink henceforth of this fruit of the vine, until that day when I drink it new with you in my Father's kingdom'.[147]

Not until that glad day can the nation know her Beloved's warm and strong embrace for which she longs. Then 'His left hand should be under my head, and his right hand should embrace me', v.3. An anticipation of this had been given to the nation in Solomon's reign of glory when the nation had been brought into 'his banqueting house'.[148] What had been realized in part and in type then, is to become the saved nation's portion when she is in the arms of the 'greater than Solomon'.

When that overwhelming climax shall have been reached, her Beloved will charge solemnly all those who have waited, longed and prayed for the peace of Jerusalem, because the need for such an intercession will be a thing of the past. The refrain in verse 4 is grammatically different from that of the parallels in the Song,[149] and should be rendered interrogatively. Darby captures it well with part of his rendering 'Why should ye stir up, why awake . . .'.

---

[146] Joel 3.18[4.18]; cf. Amos 9.13.   [147] Matt.26.27ff; cf. Mark 14.23ff and Luke 22.15f,20.   [148] Song 2.4–6.   [149] In 2.7 and 3.5 an adjuration formula is used [Heb. ˋim . . . weˋim]. In 8.4 a prohibitive construction is used [Heb. mah . . . wemah], meaning 'Why do you . . .?' as at e.g. Exod.14.15 and 17.2(2); see BDB 553, 2b. It has the force of 'Do not . . .'.

30

30. *'Return, return, O Shulammite', Song 6.13[7.1]. The village of Sulam (Shunem) nestling at the foot of the Hill of Moreh at the entrance of the Harod Valley, March-/April-time. See p. 268ff.*

31. *'Thy belly is a heap of wheat set about with lilies', Song 7.2[3]. Threshed and winnowed wheat adjacent to an olive grove near Tubas at June time. See pp. 88f, 275f.*

32. *'Let thy breasts be as clusters of the vine', Song 7.8[9]. Mid to late summer-time. See pp. 76–80, 280f.*

32

31

33. *'Thy stature is like to a palm tree, and thy breasts to clusters', Song 7.8[9]. Fine specimens of fruit-laden date palms at the south end of the Lake of Galilee. See pp. 74f, 279ff.*

The time of love's good pleasure has finally arrived. His partner is silent and rests undisturbed in His love, as the Lord does in His.

The great stepping stones toward this messianic goal at the second advent were:

1. Solomon's reign of glory with its magnificent Temple.
2. The period of the first advent of the Messiah when He came to the mother's house.

Only at these points and at their climax in 8.4, where the Messiah's second advent is in view, is this type of refrain adjuring the daughters of Jerusalem found therefore.[150] By this literary device, we are alerted also to these phases in the history of the nation and in the programme of the God of Israel. It is to be observed, however, in the final reference the adjuration is no longer qualified by the phrase 'by the roes, and by the hinds of the field'. When the messianic goal is reached finally, the delicate nature of the lovers' relationship will be a thing of the past. The nation's timidities and fears will be gone for ever, and she will rest assured in her Beloved's love without fear of disturbance. She will be able to say then 'as for me, thou upholdest me in mine integrity, and settest me before thy face for ever. Blessed be the Lord, the God of Israel, from everlasting to everlasting. Amen, and Amen'.[151]

---

[150] Song 2.7; 3.5; 8.4.   [151] Ps.41.12f[13f].

BARNES' TRANSLATION

KEY: M = Male; F = Female; O = Onlookers; B = Brothers
[with +] our literal rendering

POEM 6, 8.5–14

O

8.5. Who is this [or she] coming up from the wilderness,
Leaning hard on her beloved?

* * * * * * *

F +

Under this apple tree I enamoured thee,
Here thy mother travailed with thee,
Here, having travailed, she brought thee forth.

6. Set me as a seal upon thy heart,
As the armlet upon thine arm,
Because love is as strong as death,
Inexorable as the grave is fervent love;
Its flashes are flashes of fire,
A consuming-flame of Jah.

7. Many waters have no power to quench such love,
Neither can flood-waters sweep it away.
If a man gives all the wealth of his house
In such love, [+ as the instrumental means of such love] +
Will it be utterly despised of him? +

* * * * * * *

B

8. Our sister is immature,
And there is a lack about her breasts.
What are we doing about our sister
In the day that she is sought in marriage?

9. If she has been a wall,
We are building upon her a turret of silver,
But if she has been a door,
We are securing over her a board of cedar wood.

F

10. I am a wall,
And my breasts like the very towers thereof!
Because of this I have ever been in his eyes
As one come to perfection [+ peace]!

* * * * * * *

291

F
8.11. Solomon had a vineyard
    Occupied by many people.
    He entrusted this vineyard to certain husbandmen;
    Each one bringing in lieu of its fruit
    A thousand pieces of silver.
12. My own vineyard is before me:
    The thousand silver-pieces are for thee, O Solomon,
    And two-hundred for those husbanding its fruit.

            * * * * * * *

M
13. Thou dwelling amidst the gardens,
    Those like-minded are attentive to thy voice.
    O do allow me to hear it!
F
14. 'Come quickly, my beloved!
    Yes, be thou like a gazelle [+ roe, m.],
    Rather a fawn of the harts,
    Upon the mountains of fragrant spices'.

            * * * * * * *

Barnes allocates vv.5c–7 to the female in accordance with the Syriac against the Hebrew MT masculine suffixes. His translation of the last sentence of verse 7 is:

        In exchange for such love,
                 It is being utterly despised of him!

We believe it is rendered better as a question.

Also the use of 'shalom', peace, in verse 10 is important to retain although 'perfection' may bring out one of its nuances.

20

POEM 6. MANY WATERS CANNOT QUENCH LOVE, 8.5–14

CHAPTERS 6.10–8.14 clearly fall into two poems each opening with the question 'Who is she?' or 'Who is this?' [Heb. mi-zoth in both cases]. The contrasts in the tone of the two poems are apparent.

Poem 5	Poem 6
He goes down to the garden	She comes up from wilderness
He was caught up in chariots	She is leaning on his arm
He is held captive by tresses of her hair	She asks to be set as seal on his arm
Both to see if vines flourish	The vines' fruit allocated
Two armies	Two sisters
Others see her neck like an ivory tower	She describes her breasts as a tower
He goes to the garden of nuts	He is on fragrant mountains

As we have observed already, the three uses of 'Who is this?' in the Song,[1] conduct us along the direct route of the couple's love relationship.[2] Equally, when this is seen to mirror the love relationship between the Lord and Israel it becomes clear that Poem 4 (5.2–6.9) functions as an historical aside in the flow of this programme. Prophetic purposes as such pursue their path from the first through to the second advent of the nation's Messiah, taking

---

[1] Song 3.6; 6.10; 8.5   [2] See esp. pp.159f.

293

no account of the present church period. It is to the final sealing of the couple's relationship that Poem 6 brings us, and for the nation, it reflects that grand messianic age when she will enjoy her Messiah's love and the blessedness and bounty of His kingdom.

The Thread of the Story

Poem 6 is no mere unconnected and disjointed appendage to an otherwise subtly developed poetic masterpiece as some suggest. Rather, the ten verses gather together numbers of the actors with whom we are familiar already, while bringing in the grand finale on a refreshingly new and triumphant note. *First*, there is the excited question of admiring friends, v.5a–b, *followed by* the loved one's description of the beginning of their human love, its sublime features and originating divine cause. Such true love can never fail, vv. 5c–7. *Then* the brothers' concern for their little sister's well-being and future happiness, vv.8–9, draws out the loved one's confession of her own faithfulness and her beloved's consequent favourable view of her, v.10. *This leads her to* remark on Solomon's wise administration of his possessions and her own determination that he should have all that she might rightly describe as her own, vv.11–12. True love yields its all to the one beloved. *Finally*, the appeal of her beloved, v.13, is matched by her call for him to come to her quickly, v.14.

There are three brief interjections of the loved one here,[3] the first two of which are followed by asides regarding love and the beloved Solomon respectively, vv.5c–7,10, and the third refers more to herself, vv.11–12.[4] This sets apart the closing two verses from the rest, another distinctive feature of these being that they are introduced by an appeal on the lips of her beloved, v.13, the only occasion he speaks in this closing poem. Others crowd around and pay attention to her voice, but, now that she and all that she has are his, he desires most to hear from her something only for him. Her glad response is 'Make haste, my beloved'.

Here, then, are the friends, her beloved's mother, her own brothers, her younger sister, the keeper-tenants, along with the chief actors, the loved one and her beloved, amid the changing

---

[3] Song 8.5c–6a,10,12.   [4] 8.6c–7,11.

scenes of the ascent from the wilderness, the shade of the apple tree, the fruitful vineyards, the delightful gardens and the now spice-laden mountains.

The Thread of Salvation History

The Song does not concern itself with the tribulation troubles of Israel. The nation, depicted as the woman in Revelation 12, is to flee as borne by eagle's wings into the wilderness, to a place prepared of God, where she is to be sustained throughout the last twelve hundred and sixty days (3½ years) of Daniel's seventieth week.[5] Apart from the Lord alluring her, bringing her into that wilderness, and speaking to the nation's heart, there is no hope. But the Lord is committed to do this, and Hosea remarks that He will use the disciplining experience to bring her to Himself once again. Only thus can He remain consistent to His own character and confirm His faithfulness to His own covenant. He says 'And I will betroth thee unto me for ever; yea, I will betroth thee unto me in righteousness, and in judgment, and in lovingkindness, and in mercies. I will even betroth thee unto me in faithfulness: and thou shalt know the Lord'.[6] To effect this there is to be heard 'The voice of one that crieth, Prepare ye in the wilderness the way of the Lord, make straight in the desert a high way for our God'. A veritable Elijah ministry is to be heard among them once again, calling the nation to God as John the Baptist did as forerunner of the nation's Messiah at His first advent.[7] What shattering changes are to be brought about when the question is asked concerning Israel's coming Lord, 'Who is this that cometh from Edom, with dyed garments from Bozrah?' The consoling answer for His own must be 'I that speak in righteousness, mighty to save'. As has been noted, the Song does not concern itself with that day of vengeance which is in His heart, but rather with 'the year of my redeemed (which) is come' at last. The nation must 'make mention of the lovingkindnesses of the Lord, and the praises of the Lord, according to all that the Lord hath bestowed on us; and the great goodness toward the house of Israel, which he hath bestowed on them according to his mercies, and according to the multitude of his lovingkindnesses'.[8] It is not surprising, then, His loved one

---

[5] Rev.12.3–6,14–17. [6] Hos.2.14,19f[16,21f]. [7] Isa.40.3; Mal.3.1.
[8] Isa.63.1,4,7; see whole passage.

is leaning upon His arm at the end.

The wilderness experience however, is a stepping stone to the blessings of the kingdom age to come. The Lord has decreed that He 'will give her her vineyards from thence'. 'Again shalt thou plant vineyards upon the mountains of Samaria: the planters shall plant, and shall enjoy the fruit thereof'. In fact, 'they shall fill the face of the world with fruit'.[9] The Song reaches its climax with the positive blessings into which the 'all Israel' that shall be saved is to be introduced by her Deliverer Messiah. And yet, the apple tree, the loved one's appeal to her beloved, the brothers, and the vineyards including her own, reappear from the very first poem. The beginning envelopes the embryo of the end, and so it must be in the ways of God. If the human love story behind this is crowned with 'a happily ever after' conclusion, then the saved nation's experience surely is to surpass all this.

Israel Comes Out of the Wilderness, 8.5a,b. Small wonder at the excitement evident when the loved one of the Song appears 'from the wilderness'. Neither are we surprised to read subsequently of the fruitful vineyards which belong to her Beloved and to her. The dramatic change which the sympathetic onlookers see in her, calls forth their startled 'Who is this . . .?' In 3.6 she had been brought in state, ascending from the wilderness to her beloved's capital city. Here she ascends once again, more closely and dependently linked with him. Earlier she may have asked others to support [Heb. samakh] her with raisins as she was overcome with his love, but this is the only occasion she is seen leaning [Heb. raphaqt, here in the reflexive meaning 'to support oneself'] upon his arm. As though to emphasize the point this verb appears nowhere else in the Old Testament. She is not only aware of where He feeds His flock and causes them to rest, nor does she appear having the divine Shepherd's rod and staff to comfort her now.[10] She leans upon a living Person who has divine ability to support her. Already the daughters of Jerusalem had owned him as peculiarly hers, '*thy* beloved', in chapter 5. Here again the friends see her special relationship in describing him as '*her* beloved'. He is this for the nation

---

[9] Hos.2.15[17]; Jer.31.5; Isa.21.6. [10] Song 1.7; Ps.23.4.

brought up into her divinely promised blessings directly by Himself, her Deliverer Messiah who gives her 'her vineyards from thence', when for her sake He 'comes out of Zion'.[11]

Israel Speaking to Her Messiah, vv.5c–7. There is no part of the Song so frequently misinterpreted as this one. The pronominal suffixes of the Hebrew text are all clearly masculine throughout these verses. Yet commentators generally construe the words as uttered by the beloved to his loved one, finding support for this in the Syriac text. However difficult it may appear, we must interpret the verses according to the Hebrew text as the words of the loved one to her beloved; the female is addressing the male.

Her opening claim, v.5c–e. This is perhaps the most surprising of all. Addressing her beloved she says 'Under the apple tree I awakened thee: there thy mother was in travail with thee, there was she in travail that brought thee forth'. It is patent that she sees herself as stimulating his arousal, and that the setting where all began at least in this final stage was under the apple tree, which in turn had been his very birthplace where his mother had delivered him. To grasp what is involved we need to recall the review of the love cycle of the harts and the hinds considered in some detail previously.[12] The beloved's swift response to his loved one's appeal is likened to that of the hart upon the mountains in the very last verse of the chapter we are now considering. We have noted already that the young fawn lives under its mother's care until maturity, after which it leaves for the herd of male harts. Only when the mating season arrives does the hart move again, seeking its female mate. Once its hind is found it woos and then flees from her, only to be chased in turn by the hind. The cycle initiated by the hart is that of approach, attraction, appeal, then absence. This is reciprocated by the hind and finally their union is effected at the very place of his birth, where they, in turn, breed their young.

In our verse, therefore, we are conducted to the climax of the couples' love relationship. She has fully responded to the earlier loving overtures of her beloved, and has come to him. He who

---

[11] Rom.11.26f; cf. Isa.59.20; 40.9ff.   [12] See esp. pp.60–63.

had sought her and who had awakened her interest in him, is in turn aroused by her seeking him in response to his love. We should expect, therefore, that their final union is set in the very context of his birthplace. The couple whose love cycle opened with his visit to the Galilee, are united finally in Judea.[13]

How are we to understand this eschatologically? As the incarnate Messiah our Lord sprang out of Judah. Micah had said 'But thou, Beth-lehem Ephrathah, which art little to be among the thousands of Judah, out of thee shall one come forth unto me that is to be ruler in Israel; whose goings forth are from of old, from everlasting'. It was out of Israel as concerning the flesh that the Messiah came. His mother, the nation seen as ensuring the continuance of the purpose of God, the woman of Revelation 12, brought forth the man-child there who was to rule all the nations. This one said 'the Lord hath called me from the womb; from the bowels of my mother hath he made mention of my name. . . . And now saith the Lord that formed me from the womb to be his servant, to bring Jacob again to him, and that Israel be gathered unto Him. . . . It is too light a thing that thou shouldest be my servant to raise up the tribes of Jacob, and to restore the preserved of Israel: I will also give thee for a light to the Gentiles, that thou mayest be my salvation unto the end of the earth'. God even addressed Him as the very embodiment of all that the nation was to be to Him: 'Thou art my servant; Israel in whom I will be glorified'. He would give Him 'for a covenant of the people, to raise up the land'.[14] This vital association of the Messiah with both nation and land may explain her earlier description of Him 'as the apple tree among the trees of wood'. It is with a view to the realization of her messianic hopes that the true among the nation are yet to seek out the One who had first sought them. They are to come to their land, to the land of His birth, and cry out to Him. Psalmists and prophets alike daringly call for the Lord to 'awake' [Heb. `ur]. One says 'Awake, why sleepest thou, O Lord? Arise, cast us not off for ever'. For another He is to 'Awake, awake, put on strength, O arm of the Lord; awake, as in the days of old, the generations of

---

[13] e.g. pp.186f; cf. Song 3.6–11. Isa.49.1,5f,3,8.

[14] Heb.7; Mic.5.2; Rom.9; Rev.12;

ancient times'. When the right conditions obtain in His people, we are not surprised to hear Him say 'Or ever I was aware, my soul set me among the chariots of my princely people'. He is aroused by what He sees in her. He responds to the nation's 'Arise, O Lord, into thy resting place; thou, and the ark of thy strength'. He is to come and dwell in the midst of His own people. Then 'the Lord shall inherit Judah as his portion in the holy land, and shall yet choose Jerusalem. Be silent, all flesh, before the Lord: for he is waked up out of his holy habitation'. If earlier He knew the time was not yet ripe and had said 'stir not up nor awaken love until it please', her time had come at last. She will hold back no longer: she must stir and awaken Him.[15]

Her earnest plea, v.6a,b. She continues to address her beloved using now the simile of the seal [Heb. chotham] to articulate specifically what she desires him to do for her. The verb appears in 4.12‡ and means there 'to seal up or shut'.[16] Its more primary significance however is 'to affix a seal'. In verse 6 the noun 'seal' [Heb. chotham*][17] is used referring to the typical Israelite name seal made out of some hard stone, often pierced with a hole and being worn around the neck on a cord, or occasionally worn on the finger in the form of a ring. The spouse, in using the seal as a simile of herself, recognizes something of the royal dignity which she

---

[15] Ps.44.23[24]; Isa.51.9; Song 6.12; Ps.132.8; Zech.2.13[17]; Song 2.7; 3.5; 8.4 where 'stir up' = po`el and 'awake' = hiph`il of the same verb. [16] cf. the enforced action of Darius after Daniel had been cast into the lion's den 'and the king sealed [Aram. chatham†] it with his own signet, and with the signet of his lords; that the purpose might not be changed concerning Daniel'. [17] The word occurs 14 times, 6 of these referring to the engravings of the tribal names upon the precious stones on the high priest's breastplate and shoulders of the ephod. These were 'to be stones of memorial for the children of Israel', see Exod.28.11,21,36; 39.6,14,30. Seals as such might have human or animal forms on them, along with a name and some indication of the royal or official dignity of the owner, Gen.38.18 [cf. 'signet', Heb. chotemeth†, v.25]; 1 Kings 21.8; Jer.22.24; Hag.2.23; in similes, Job 38.14; 41.15[7]*. Roller or cylinder types have been found also which their owners either carried on neck bands or cords, cf. Gen.38.18,25; Song 8.6. Seal rings, of course, were worn on the finger, Gen.41.42; Hag.2.23; Jer.22.24, see IDB 4.254–9 Tufnell. When such a seal was affixed for example on a document it gave to it official legitimation.

now has as belonging to Him. A few of the many personal seals that have been found in Israel were inscribed with the words 'wife of . . .'. She pleads then that she might be as a seal on a cord about his neck, and as a signet ring upon his arm, and be his wife indeed forever. Nothing short of this, the evident unique relationship to him personally as chosen and taken by him, dear to his heart, and with a public dignity bestowed upon her as she is seen on his arm, would suffice now. In the Lord's words to Zerubbabel we are assured that He will do this, for He has said 'I will make thee (lit. set thee, put thee [śamtikha kachotham, virtually the same Hebrew as in Song 8.6]) as a signet: for I have chosen thee'.[18]

Clearly, the simile expresses the privileged relationship which the Lord intended to re-establish between the Davidic leader of His people and Himself.[19] The saved nation will enjoy such loving and lofty privileges when she is identified with her Messiah at last, after His arm, the symbol of His strength, and the instrument of His deliverance has been revealed. This age must yield to that age which is to come!

Her logic based on the love that cannot fail, vv.6.c–7. The opening word 'For' [Heb. ki] introduces her well-supported case for the plea she has just made. It is not of her own love that she speaks, but of love generically, and particularly as she had experienced it through him. If she now loves him, it is because he had first loved her, and had accommodated himself to her different moods to bring her to true love at last. Neither does she offer a definition of love: who could provide one? Rather, she describes numbers of its facets which had produced in her the confidence to make her plea. What is it about love that creates such boldness in her?

Firstly, there is the strength [Heb. ʿazz] of love. Usually this word is used of one of the Lord's essential attributes, that might which He exerts on behalf of His people and against all who oppose them. Then, He is described as the source of that strength which His

---

[18] Hag.2.23. See TDOT 5.263–9, Otzen.   [19] ct. the Lord's plucking off Coniah of Judah though he was 'the signet upon my right hand', and giving him over to Nebuchadnezzar, Jer.22.24.

people need in the vicissitudes of life.[20] Here only is it used to describe true love, which is also divine in its source. As the Targum has it, 'strong as death is the love of Thy Divinity'. It is the strength of its irresistible call that is symbolized. But why is love spoken of only comparatively in the verse? It is said to be 'strong as death' [Heb. khammaweth], that power which we can neither withstand nor deny. It is its unbreakable power, its irresistible strength, humanly speaking, that lends to the comparative phrase a superlative quality, as though to say that 'love is extremely strong'.[21]

Secondly, there is the unyielding, obdurate [Heb. qasheh‡] character of jealousy. Perhaps the appearance of the word 'jealousy' [Heb. qin'ah‡] in this context disturbs us at first. Let it be said immediately that jealousy has both a positive and a negative significance. It is the former that is meant here. It refers to that ardent love, that consuming zealous affection which will brook no rival, and which demands undivided devotion from its object. Israel's God so describes Himself: 'I the Lord thy God am a jealous God'. He is 'the Lord, whose name is Jealous'.[22] We may compare the zeal for God's house which consumed the Messiah while He was in the world. The strength of total emotional involvement with another, of burning zeal for one's partner in love, is in view in the Song. This is to be jealous *for* someone rather than to be jealous *of* someone. That zealous love is unyielding; it will neither give up its relentless claim upon nor its vehement commitment to the one it has embraced. Gone are the days when the nation will say 'where is thy zeal [Heb. ῾ayyeh qin῾athekha] and thy mighty acts? the yearning of thy bowels and thy compassions are restrained toward me'. His had been an unchanging jealous love from the beginning, and at last she will apprehend the might of its relentless grasp.[23]

It was indeed 'cruel [Heb. qasheh‡ = unyielding, inexorable,

---

[20] Strength [Heb. ῾oz] is one of the Lord's attributes, e.g. Ps.96.6, seen in action in the best interests of His people, e.g. Exod.15.13, so as to cause them to confess Him as their strength, e.g. Exod.15.2, to call upon Him to exert it on their behalf, e.g. Isa.51.9, and to make it the theme of their praise when He does, e.g. Ps.68.34[35].
[21] See VT 3,209–24, Thomas.   [22] Exod.20.5; Deut.5.9; Exod.34.14. The Messiah cannot tolerate a rival either, 2 Cor.11.2f.   [23] Ps.69.9[10]; John 2.17; Isa.63.15.

here // `azzah] as Sheol'. In this, love's strength being compared with Sheol is appropriate too. Its 'hand' can be forced to release a soul only by the exerted might of God.[24] True married love cannot let its partner go, how much less the Lord His people? 'How shall I give thee up, Ephraim? how shall I deliver thee, Israel?'[25]

Thirdly, 'the flashes thereof are flashes of fire'. The radiance of love assumes its brightest proportions when tangibly displayed by the presence of the Lord Himself. It was 'in a flame of fire' that the Angel of the Lord appeared first to Moses. Then, by means of a 'pillar of fire', 'a light of fire', the Lord evidenced His presence among His people and directed them. Its greatest glory will be when 'the Lord will create over the whole habitation of mount Zion, and over her assemblies, a cloud and smoke by day, and the shining of a flaming fire by night'.[26]

Love, in fact, is 'a very flame of Yah' [Heb. shalhebheth yah]. Here only in the Song does the divine name Yah appear. For this reason, some construe it as one of the standard idioms to convey a superlative sense, as for example the AV translation 'a most vehement flame'.[27] We believe it to be in keeping with the enigmatic character of the Song that here, at last, the key to its understanding should surface. Yah, the One who is, and whose absolute existence in terms of this title was hymned first at the beginning of His ways with the nation, in their exodus from Egypt,[28] will be there at the end, when His unchanging,

---

[24] Death and Sheol regularly appear in synonymous parallelism, e.g. Ps.6.5[6]; 16.10; 18.5; 49.14[15]; 89.48[49]; Prov.5.5; 7.27; Isa.28.15. Strictly, *death* affects the body, whereas *Sheol* is the abode of departed souls, and is distinct from Gehenna, the lake of fire and endless torment. Through His victorious resurrection, Jesus has the keys both of *death* and *Hades* [Grk. `ades equivalent of Heb. She`ol], Rev.1.18. Paul asserts therefore, the guaranteed resurrection of the saints in 1 Cor.15.55. He finds OT support for this from Hos.13.14 construed as a divine guarantee of eventual almighty intervention on Israel's behalf. Consider this passage in connection with the phase of the nation's experience reached in Song 8.6.   [25] Hos.11.8f.
[26] Fire [Heb. `esh‡] attends the divine appearances, Exod.3.2; cf. Gen.15.17; Exod.13.21f; 14.24; cf. Num.9.15f; Ps.78.14; Isa.4.5.   [27] For the 'use of divine names as superlatives' see AJSL 44, '28/9, 212f, JPM Smith; also Gordis, SoS pp.26,99.   [28] Hebrew title [Yah] occurs some 50 times, and first at Exod.15.2 in the Song of the Sea, which is itself cited at Ps.118.14 and Isa.12.2.

everlasting love will shine forth more brightly than ever. Of course, love does emanate from the Lord Himself, He is its true source. As the apostle has it, 'love is of [Grk. ˊek = out of as a source] God; and every one that loveth is begotten of God, and knoweth God'.[29] The point here rather appears to be that the union of Yah and Israel when He comes in glory to her, will be the brightest display [Heb. shalhebheth‡ = flame][30] of love she will ever have experienced. Love is theophanic, for God is love.

If to this point she has been concerned more with what love is positively, she now goes on to establish further its invincibility negatively.

For *fourthly*, 'Many waters cannot quench love, neither can the floods drown it', v.7a–b. There is a marked parallelism between the terms waters [Heb. mayim rabbim] and floods [Heb. neharoth] here, and death and sheol in verse 6. If love is as strong as death, and jealousy is as unyielding as sheol, then many waters cannot quench it neither can the floods drown it. Jonah could speak of being cast into the depths, into the heart of the seas, of the flood or river being around him, and of God's breakers and billows going over him, yet how the Lord his God brought his life up from the pit. David could describe the bands of death [Heb. maweth] having encompassed him, and the torrents [Heb. naharey] of Belial making him afraid, and yet of the Lord drawing him out of great waters [Heb. mimmayim rabbim].

Isaiah also weaves together the same words as those in the verse in the Song in a surprisingly similar way. In a great salvation oracle,

---

[28] *cont.* All but seven references, Exod.15.2; 17.16; Song 8.6; Isa.12.2; 26.4; 38.11(2) are found in the Psalms where it occurs frequently in the phrase 'Hallelujah = Praise ye Yah' (always at the beginning or end of a psalm). As an abbreviated form of Yahweh it finds its special niche in poetry and song, and 'seems to express His absolute rather than His continuous existence', JND translation on Exod.15.2 note s. It forms part of the combination titles *Yah Yahweh*, Isa.12.2; 26.4, and *Yah 'Elohim*, Ps.68.18[19], and is found in parallel with other divine titles such as *Yahweh*, Ps.106.1; 111.1; 112.1; 113.1; 135.1; 146.1; 148.1; 149.1, *God*, 150.1, *our God*, 147.1, *the God of Jacob*, 94.7, and *'Adonay*, 130.3.   [29] 1 John 4.7, see vv.7–10.
[30] cf. kindred word for 'flame' [Heb. lehabhah] used symbolically of the Lord's presence at Exod.3.2; 13.21; Isa.4.5.

the Lord that created Israel said 'Fear not for I have redeemed thee; I have called thee by thy name, thou art mine. When thou passest through the waters [Heb. ki-ta`abhor bammayim], I will be with thee; and through the rivers, they shall not overflow thee [Heb. ubhanneharoth lo`yishtephukha]: when thou walkest through the fire, thou shalt not be burned; neither shall the flame kindle upon thee. For I am the Lord thy God, the Holy One of Israel, thy saviour. ... Since thou has been precious in my sight, and honourable, and I have loved thee; therefore will I give men for thee, and peoples for thy life'. What assurance Israel is to draw from the love of God for her. As their kinsmen in law He is to redeem them, name them, and be with them and keep them through their day of trouble as He had been with those favoured three thrown into Babylon's fiery furnace. He will be their Saviour and will ransom them. Notice that it is God's unchanging love that guarantees all this to the nation. What will He not bestow, as He has said of them 'the Lord loveth you'? In a similar vein the believer glories in the fact that nothing, not even death itself, 'shall be able to separate us from the love of God, which is in Christ Jesus our Lord'.[31]

However, the Jonah and David passages to which we have made reference bear strong messianic overtones, as also does that other Davidic psalm which records 'the waters are come into my soul [Heb. bha`u mayim `adh-naphesh]' and 'I am come into deep waters [Heb. ba`thi bhema`amaqqey-mayim], where the floods overflow me [Heb. weshibboleth shetaphatheni]'. The urgent plea follows 'let me be delivered ... out of deep waters [Heb. mimma`amaqqey-mayim]. Let not the waterflood [Heb. shibboleth mayim] overwhelm me, neither let the deep swallow me up; and let not the pit shut her mouth upon me'. In anticipating Golgotha, did the Messiah not say 'I have a baptism to be baptized with; and how am I straitened till it be accomplished'.[32] The greater than David could say more meaningfully, the earth having shaken and trembled, 'He sent from on high, he took me; he drew me out of many waters'.[33] Messiah's love for His God and His people was

---

[31] Isa.43.1-4; Deut.7.8; Rom.8.38f.   [32] Jon.2.3,5,6[4,6,7]; Ps.18.4,16[5,17]; 69.2,14f[3,15f]; Luke 12.50.   [33] Ps.18.16[17].

tried to the utmost, but it firmly endured. He exhausted all the wrath of a sin-hating God, He bore sin away, He blotted out the handwriting of ordinances, He put sin away by the sacrifice of Himself. The might of the devil and all his hosts was smashed, disannulled once for all, by the almighty One whose love took Him into Golgotha's dark depths. The waterflood did not overwhelm Him, those many waters could not quench His love, that most supreme expression of it. It was there that 'love endured its last', and uniquely demonstrated that love 'endureth all things. Love never faileth'.[34] That same almighty One is soon to take up the love initiative once again for Israel, and 'in his love and in his pity' He will yet redeem them. In that matchless new covenant era enjoyed by those who will have 'found grace in the wilderness', they will prove the truth of His words 'I have loved thee with an everlasting love'. Neither can he 'rest in his love' before that glad day.[35]

Fifthly, we understand the victorious nature of love here. The final phrase reads 'If a man would give all the substance of his house for love, he (it) would be utterly contemned', 8.7c,d. Perhaps the first question to resolve here is whether 'he' or 'it' is the better translation of the latter part of the verse. The Hebrew [lo] can be read legitimately either way. If 'he' were to be adopted, then it is the 'man' that is in view; if 'it' then it would be 'all the substance' that would be meant. The latter should be accepted in our judgment; the AV, JND, NIV and RSV translators opted similarly. The remainder of the verse is usually taken to mean that love simply cannot be bought. Real love is not mercenary. A man's offer of money for love would be utterly scorned.[36] Many who take this to be the meaning, see the loved one as rejecting altogether the blandishments of the incalculably wealthy Solomon in favour of the true love of her poor shepherd suitor. We have already dismissed the claims of this love triangle interpretation. The whole phrase needs reconsidering Biblically.

It must be said, initially, that the custom of paying a 'bride price' is neither condemned or contemned by the peoples of the Ancient Near East. Biblically, this practice is documented and illustrated.[37]

---

[34] 1 Cor.13.7f.   [35] Jer.31.3; Zeph.3.17.   [36] As Falk LL 105, and Goulder
SoS 66 most recently.   [37] See p.25.17f.

Such a payment was never construed as a payment 'for love', that is to gain or win it. Neither were those gifts [Heb. mattan derived from the word 'give' = nathan in our verse] for the bride's parents and the bride herself spurned. Further, the Lord presents His claim for Israel, His bride or wife, in terms of purchase. Out of quite distressing circumstances, Hosea was instructed to 'Go yet love a woman ... even as the Lord loveth the children of Israel. ... So I bought [Heb. karah = get by trade, buy] her to me'. The extent of God's love for His people is seen in what He has paid to make her His own. Through Isaiah He has said 'I am the Lord thy God, the Holy One of Israel, thy saviour; I have given [Heb. nathan] Egypt as thy ransom [Heb. kaphar], Ethiopia and Seba for thee. Since thou hast been precious in my sight, and honourable, and I have loved thee [Heb. we͐ani ͐ahabhteykha]; therefore will I give [Heb. nathan] men for thee, and peoples for thy life'.[38] Jesus the Messiah, in speaking of the kingdom of the heavens likened it to 'a treasure hidden in the field; which a man found and hid; and in his joy he goeth and selleth all that he hath, and buyeth that field'. Extending the description further He said 'the kingdom of heaven is like unto a man that is a merchant seeking goodly pearls: and having found one pearl of great price, he went and sold all that he had, and bought it'.[39] The Proverbs, in eulogizing wisdom, encourage all to 'get wisdom: yea with all thou hast gotten (though it cost all you have, NIV) get understanding'. Again, 'wisdom is better than rubies'.[40] On the verse in the Song the Targum commends rather than contemns the man who gave all the wealth of his house to buy wisdom in the Exile promising 'I will restore to him double in the world to come, and all the spoil taken from the camp of Gog would be his'. For the Midrash Rabbah, the unquenchable love is God's, and the Torah is the treasure precious enough to warrant giving up all one's wealth.

These more positive contributions touching on the subject suggest another interpretation of our verse altogether. It would be better translated as a rhetorical question rather than as a statement.

---

[38] Hos.3.1f; cf. the happier case between Boaz and Ruth: 'Moreover Ruth the Moabitess ... have I purchased to be my wife', Ruth 4.10. See also Isa.43.3f. [39] Matt.13.44f. [40] Prov.4.7; 8.11.

The sense is captured in a paraphrase such as 'Assuming that a man were to go to the extreme lengths of giving all the wealth of his house in or with love as the instrumental means [Heb. ba͏̄ ahabhah], would this costly expression of love be utterly scorned, and remain unreciprocated?'[41] Surely love never fails. The Messiah has gone to greater lengths than this however. Though He was rich yet for our sakes He has become poor. The Son of God 'loved me, and gave himself up for me'. 'Hereby know we love, because he laid down his life for us'.

True love, divine love, motivated the nation's Beloved, not only to give all His substance, but to give Himself for His loved one. This is love which beggars all human description. It is only a matter of time before the saved nation will find its own way of reciprocating her Messiah's love. Israel too, will realize that 'we love, because he first loved us'. The costliness of the ransom guarantees that it will achieve its end.

If the loved one is incapable of defining love, at least she can describe it in action. She has seen it in her Beloved as in none other. He has demonstrated love's strength, its unyielding character, its brightest and most glorious display, its unquenchable nature and finally its unquestioned victory through costly sacrifice.

What of Diaspora Jewry?, 8.8–10. Establishing the speaker(s) in these verses is difficult. It is possible, for instance, that we are listening to the loved one addressing the beloved on behalf of her younger sister. Confident in her own acceptance by him, she suggests that what is a concern to her is surely now a concern for him too. 'Both of us need to think through our position regarding this family member of mine!' The beloved one himself even might be anticipating her unexpressed concern for her sister, indicating that her interests are really his as well now.

---

[41] BDB, p.90 III.3, under the entry for the Hebrew preposition [be], understands it as referring to the instrumental means by which an act is accomplished citing Gen.30.16; Exod.34.20; and in connection with betrothal, 2 Sam.3.14, and buying, 24.24. For instances where the peril or cost of one's life is involved see 2 Sam.23.17; 1 Kings 2.23. In each of these cases it is the word to which the preposition is attached which indicates the means, which supports the interpretation offered. However, in the Song's case BDB suggests that it [Heb. be] refers to the preceding phrase 'all the substance of a man's house'.

It seems better however to construe this as a little intrusion prompted by the re-established union of the loved one and her beloved. Attention is now switched from them to her brothers and their little sister. Some take the little sister to be the Shulammite herself. A cursory examination of the loved one's descriptions in the Song will demonstrate the impossibility of this. This is not 'the heroine of the Song'! In fact, those who equate the loved one and the little sister, are forced to propose an earlier and 'more suitable' place in the Song for this incident. Surely, it is better to accept that this 'little sister' refers to a younger and less developed sister who has not featured in the Song until this time. The loved one, the older sister, contrasts herself with the description given of the younger sister here. In the actual story, the brothers, who in the Near East, in the absence of a father, are responsible for their sisters, appear to have learned from their negative and mistaken handling of their older sister's affairs. They determine to have a real concern for their younger sister's best interests, so as to present her spotless and handsomely bedecked to the one who seeks her hand in marriage.

Viewed allegorically and historico-eschatologically, the prophet Ezekiel has used the 'sister relationship' to describe Israel's past divided and sinful condition before the Lord, and God's sovereign purpose to bring the national 'sisters' back into happy and holy covenant relationship with Himself once again. It is evident in Ezekiel's allegory that Jerusalem (representing Judah, the two-tribed Southern Kingdom), is being contrasted, in the light of her additional favours, with Samaria (representing Israel, the ten-tribed Northern Kingdom) and Sodom (representing Moab?) both of whom had already fallen under the consuming judgment of God. Judah, too, would be judged. But all was not to be irrevocable doom and gloom. The Lord said 'Nevertheless I will remember my covenant with thee in the days of thy youth, and I will establish unto thee an everlasting covenant. Then shalt thou remember thy ways, and be ashamed, when thou shalt receive thy sisters, thine elder and thy younger (sisters): and I will give them unto thee for daughters, but not by thy covenant'.[42] This provides the best

---

[42] Ezek.16.60f, see whole chapter. Observe contrast between my covenant and

interpretive assistance in connection with our verses in the Song.

The blessings of the Messiah's return, reunion and the experience of His intimate love, are to be enjoyed by that nation in the land to which He is coming. The desires and affections of 'Israel in the land' will have been brought to maturity, and are to find their complete satisfaction in the love of their Beloved Messiah at His coming. This is expressed in terms of the loved one's description of herself in verse 10. There is no 'if' here as she speaks confidently of her moral impregnability; she has maintained her purity, unseduced by all who would have breached it. Further, her affections, represented by her breasts, are evidently fully developed; she is in truth thoroughly mature and suited to her Beloved. This is her glory, as she exclaims 'I am' [Heb. ˘ani] now as always, emphatically and unequivocally, 'a wall, and my breasts like the towers thereof'. That is, she stands before Him as one who has kept herself for her Beloved, impregnable, set apart, separated for Him.

If this is the testimony of the older sister, the Leah as it were, the firstborn, and the first to experience union in marriage, what of the 'younger', the 'little sister' [Heb. qetannah], the Rachel of this piece, who for us represents the Israel of the Diaspora?[43] Those responsible and concerned for her, the brothers, were aware that she was not as developed and ripe for marriage as the older sister. Their little sister 'hath no breasts'. Yet, they anticipated her maturing, and her eligibility 'in the day when she shall be spoken for', that is when her hand would be sought in marriage.[44]

Most understand the proposed responses of the brothers as in opposition to one another. The 'wall' is taken to represent the

---

[42] *cont.* thy covenant. The Song takes no account of the blatant sins of the nation, nor of the Lord's matching judgment through which Israel as a whole is to pass at the end. See also Ezek.23.4,31.   [43] In Gen.29.16,18, the same word [Heb. qatan, an adj. which may mean small, unimportant, young or younger] is used. It refers to a younger sister in Jud.15.2; Ezek.16.46. A cognate adj. [Heb. qaton] is used of Ephraim as the younger brother, Gen.48.19. This is found in parallelism with 'small' [Heb. tse˘irah] in Isa.60.22, the latter term being used of Rachel in contrasting her with the firstborn [Heb. bekhirah] Leah, Gen.29.26, and of Ephraim as the younger in Gen.48.14.   [44] cf. 1 Sam.25.39 where David sent and spake for Abigail.

strong moral defences of a virtuous woman, and the 'door' is then contrastingly referred to the sister's openness and vulnerability to seduction. The older sister's adoption of the first of these metaphors to express her own chastity has lent support to this view. However, if this were true, the brothers' response 'in' or on the day [Heb. bayyom] when approached for their younger sister's hand would be belated indeed! It is better, therefore, to interpret the two 'if' clauses positively, either as representing two distinct possible end-products of their sister's maturing, or as being in apposition rather than in opposition to one another, the two clauses supplementing each other to provide a total description. We prefer the former of these, basing our choice on the fact that the older sister, the loved one, claims that she fulfils the 'wall' metaphor completely. Could it be that the younger and less mature sister is to supply the 'door' element which may suggest her contact with the nations generally and thus complement and complete all that the saved nation of Israel is to be for their Lord and for men?

It was Israel's Messiah that comprehended all the Law in just two commandments. For Him, the criteria that count are love for God and love for men, though the 'great and first' of these is the former. The brothers, like that scribe who answered Jesus discreetly in grasping what is acceptable to the divine Suitor, are here 'not far from the kingdom of God'. This anticipates just one metaphorical presentation of Israel's millennial ministry, relating to the city which has 'a *wall* great and high; having twelve *gates* ... and names written thereon, which are the names of the twelve tribes of the children of Israel'.[45]

The responsible ones become the rewarding ones, bedecking their younger sister with silver or cedar as her conduct and commitment require. True love Godward will have kept her securely *separated* to Him, and her walls would have been continually before her God.[46] When her Beloved asks for her, they will enrich her with a conspicuous display of silver, token of realized redemption. True love manward would have prevented her becoming *isolated*, though remaining separated. Proper accessibility out of love for

---

[45] Matt.22.37–40//Mark 12.29ff; Luke 10.27; Lev.19.18; Deut.6.5; Rev.21.12.
[46] Isa.49.16.

others will have its own reward in cedar cladding. This glorious
and fragrant wood from Lebanon, is fit for palace and sanctuary
alike, and glorifies suitably the chaste love of this incorruptible one
also who now has the beauty of her Messiah upon her, 5.15.

Isaiah 60 provides a most suggestive parallel eschatologically. In
that future day when violence shall no more be heard in the land,
'thou shalt call thy walls Salvation, and thy gates Praise. ... Thy
people shall be all righteous, they shall inherit the land for ever;
the branch of my planting the work of my hands, that I may be
glorified. The little one [Heb. qaton] shall become a thousand, and
the small one [Heb. tse‾irah] a strong nation: I the Lord will hasten
it in its time'.[47]

Because of the strength of her love, maintaining herself
altogether for her Beloved Messiah, His loved one becomes aware
of what she is in her Beloved's eyes. The word 'Then' [Heb. ‾az]
has a temporal significance, though the word here is more likely
to bear a logical meaning, 'Therefore, thus'. The loved one is saying 'Because I am a wall, therefore I became and continue to be in
his eyes as one that found peace'. At various times she had
earnestly sought Him, and eventually found Him. But here the
seek and find theme reaches its climax.[48] She finds [Heb. matsa‾]
quite unexpectedly 'peace' [Heb. shalom]. Not infrequently, the
verb used is associated with 'grace' or 'favour' [Heb. chen], and
some of these relate to men who find favour in the eyes of God.
For example, Noah, prior to the outpouring of God's judgment on
the world generally, 'found grace in the eyes of the Lord'.[49] Only
here in the OT is the word 'peace' linked with the verb. This is a
particular blessing for the nation at the end.

There can be no peace for the wicked.[50] In the Song, even the
loved one has had to face incessant demands and dangers
throughout. There have been her incensed and overbearing

---

[47] Isa.60.18,21f. [48] For seek and find [Heb. matsa‾, nine times in Song] theme
see pp.172f,249f. [49] To 'find favour in the eyes of' [Heb. matsa‾
chen be‾eynay] God, is often found, Gen.6.8; Exod.33.12,13(2),16,17; 34.9;
Num.11.11,15; Jud.6.17; 2 Sam.15.25; Prov.3.4; cf. Gen.18.3; ct. esp. 'When a man
taketh a wife, and marrieth her ... if she hath found no favour in his eyes',
Deut.24.1. [50] Isa.48.22; 57.21.

brothers, a mighty Pharaoh, fears which cause her to retreat to the mountain ledge for safety, little foxes that threaten the vines; there are fears of the night, and roaming lions and leopards, and the watchmen who handle her roughly. We are reminded of one of the quite vociferous political movements in modern Israel whose desires are encapsulated in their slogan 'Peace Now!' [Heb. shalom `akhshav]. The Psalmist urged the people to 'Pray for the peace of Jerusalem' and longed that 'Peace be within thy walls'.[51] If it is not 'peace now', we are assured that it is to be 'peace then'. Israel, whose national greeting has always been 'peace' [Heb. shalom], must discover it and truly realize it at last. Apart from her greater than Solomon [Heb. shelomoh] she can never do so. He is the giver of peace.

The Messiah, before He was parted from His own and returned to heaven, bequeathed peace to those who found Him during His ministry on earth; 'my peace', He said, 'I give unto you'. During His absence from them they would experience tribulation, but He said 'in me ye may have peace'.[52] However, He cannot be content until, in His eyes, *the nation* 'finds peace' also. She is so much more to Him than 'mine own familiar friend' [Heb. `ish shelomi, lit. man of my peace] of Psalm 41. She is His Shulammite [Heb. shulam-mith] by name, and in experience is to become the receiver of peace. This is the climax of God's ways with the nation, when the covenant relationship is realized in a *land* of peace. 'And the work of righteousness shall be peace; and the effect of righteousness, quietness and confidence for ever. And my people shall abide in a peaceable habitation, and in sure dwellings, and in quiet resting places'. The Lord has pledged 'neither shall my covenant of peace be removed'.[53] As He rightly estimates things, 'in the eyes of her Lord' (Targum), she finds peace. As Jeremiah puts it[54] 'The people which were left of the sword found grace in the wilderness;

---

[51] Ps.122.6f.   [52] John 14.27; 16.33.   [53] Isa.32.17f; 54.10. Peace is associated emphatically with the Messianic period, Ps.72.3; 85.8–10[9–11]; Isa.54.13; 55.12; 66.12; Hag.2.9.   [54] Jer.31.2. Read the whole chapter with the two sisters in view. Notice that *the whole nation* is in mind in v.1, then *the Northern Kingdom* more particularly in vv.2–22, *the Southern Kingdom* in vv.23–26, and finally *the two are brought together* in the good of the new covenant through the sovereign grace of 'the God of all the families of Israel', vv.27–40.

312

even Israel, when I went to cause him to rest'. Her beloved is entirely complacent in her, and she is brought to her divinely intended fulfilment, completeness, soundness, prosperity, contentment, and harmony with God, with nature and the nations.

The Millennial Administration of the Kingdom, 8.11–12. For some, these verses provide the death knell to the view that Solomon is also the Beloved one of the Song. The bold contrast here between the king's right to administer his own possessions, and the girl's right to her own person would be completely vitiated, it is argued.[55] Quite why this should be is not clear, unless one is already committed to an interpretation of the Song which denigrates Solomon.

What is patent in the verses is that Solomon has a vineyard quite distinct from the vineyard which is the personal possession of the loved one. Further, it appears clear that although the loved one has the right of possession of her own vineyard, she gladly yields it all to Solomon. In fact she gives willingly to him that return which he demands of others, and provides also a liberal double tithe for her stewards. How different from her beauty-destroying drudgery of earlier days, and the demands of duty, which interfered with or intruded into their developing personal relationship. Now she was happy to place all that she had materially at her beloved's disposal, whilst ensuring that those who maintained it on her behalf were more than amply rewarded. Hers was his. This left her free to realize the thrill of being her 'beloved's' and of experiencing that 'his desire was toward' her. She, too, was his for ever. She might have expressed it in those well known words:

> All that I am and have, thy gifts so free
> ... O Lord for thee
> My ransomed soul shall be ... something for thee.

The formal re-introduction of Solomon's [Heb. shelomoh] name here suits the preceding stanza's climax in the word peace [Heb. shalom], and reminds us of the administrative heights to which love had brought the loved one. Isaiah provides an explanation regarding the rental demanded here. He forecasts that because of

---

[55] e.g. Carr SoS Tyn. p.173.

Judah's sin 'that every place where there were a thousand vines at a thousand silverlings, shall even be for briars and thorns'. In the Song the double use of the number one thousand [Heb. ˘eleph] is a suggestive pointer to the Millennial reign of the greater than Solomon. This is that glad period throughout which Satan is bound, and cast into the abyss 'that he should deceive the nations no more until the thousand years should be fulfilled'. Synchronously, those sharers in the first resurrection live and reign with Christ for a thousand years.[56] How suggestively we are brought to the very threshold of the kingdom of God upon the earth.

The vineyard that Solomon had was 'in Baal-hamon' [Heb. bebha˘al hamon], a place not referred to elsewhere in the Bible. It is mentioned in what is probably a Maccabean period apocryphal book, where it is associated with Dothan. An ancient ruin heap [Khirbet Balama] just south of modern Jenin, some four or five miles north of Dothan, and identified with Biblical Ibleam (Map. ref. 177–205), is the most likely place in Israel. As this is far from certain, it is not improbable that the vineyard in question lay somewhere outside of Israel proper, and its name might even suggest this. The name Baal-hamon means 'lord, or master of a multitude'. As it is being contrasted in the Song with the loved one's vineyard, clearly in the land of Israel and representative of it,[57] we would opt for somewhere in the more extended domains of Solomon, that is in Gentile territory then under his control. The verses thus bring out the universal character of Messiah's rule when God gives Him 'the nations for thine inheritance, and the uttermost parts of the earth for thy possession'.[58] As the rightful owner of the whole world, He gives [Heb. nathan] it out to those who are responsible to Him as stewards [Heb. notrim, participle of verb natar[59]]. He will look to them for an unbroken acknowledgement of His rights throughout His thousand year reign. In that day 'the wealth of the nations shall come' to Israel. They are to know Israel's Messiah in the role of peaceful administrator of the multitudes, their Lord, in fact as 'King of kings and Lord of lords'.[60]

How different it is to be for His loved one, the nation saved and

---

[56] Isa.7.23; Rev.20.2ff.   [57] cf. and ct. Isa.5.1ff.   [58] Ps.2.8.   [59] See 1.6(2); 8.11,12‡, meaning nurturers.   [60] Isa.60.5; Rev.19.16.

having its own inheritance, the land of promise. She can say of a truth 'My vineyard, which is mine [Heb. karmi shelli, adding a certain emphasis to her claim] is before me', and as such is the object of my attention. At last it will be Israel's,[61] and yet for that nation her Beloved Himself will be more to her than all that His love has bestowed upon her. She will yield to Him all that she has for the duration of His one thousand year reign; 'thou, O Solomon, shalt have the thousand'. In that day the Messiah will take under His government for God, the nations and His loved one Israel, summing up the things in the heavens and upon the earth in Himself. Then will be displayed what is 'the riches of the glory of his inheritance' of which He has taken possession by means of His saints.[62] In that happy millennial day Israel is to become what God had designated them from the beginning in the wilderness, 'a kingdom of priests, and a holy nation'. Isaiah writes of them in that day 'But ye shall be named the priests of the Lord: men shall call you the ministers of our God: ye shall eat the wealth of the nations, and in their glory ye shall boast yourselves. For your shame ye shall have double; and for confusion they shall rejoice in their portion: therefore in the land they shall possess double: everlasting joy shall be unto them'.[63] Instead of the Levite receiving the tithe, and in turn tithing that tithe to the priest, the nurturers of God's vineyard in that day, 'those that keep the fruit thereof' shall receive 'two hundred' or a double tithe. This is the blessing of the firstborn indeed!

Final Appeals – Longing for Communion and Union, 8.13–14. For the first time in this poem the voice of the beloved is heard appealing to his loved one, v.13. The Song fades away with an urgent appeal from the loved one to her beloved, v.14. The setting is the countryside, whether cultivated or more wild. They are away from the madding throng, a word or a leap away from communion and union.

The loved one is addressed as the one who characteristically dwells [Heb. hayyoshebheth, the feminine participle suggesting her normal residence] 'in the gardens'. The garden motif is domi-

---

[61] For the motif of the vineyard and Israel's past failure see Ps.80.8–11[9–12]; Isa.5.1–7.   [62] Eph.1.10,18.   [63] Exod.19.6; Isa.61.6f.

315

nant in the Song. When it is used in the plural it does not refer to the loved one herself. Here she dwells amid all those beautiful gardens her beloved has so ably and tastefully made for himself. She enjoys the beauties he has made. Earlier, these were the very places in which she was sure that he was to be found, where he found his delights.[64] She was in the right place. These multiplied gardens suggest an expansion of the range of Edenic conditions that obtained at the beginning. This is more than paradise restored! All those nations around Israel will find blessing mediated through her in fulfilment of the terms of the covenant made with Abraham in whom 'all the families of the earth (shall) be blessed'. What is more, in that day 'many peoples shall go and say, Come ye, and let us go up to the mountain of the Lord, to the house of the God of Jacob; and he will teach us of his ways, and we will walk in his paths: for out of Zion shall go forth the law, and the word of the Lord from Jerusalem'.[65]

There were those who were his companions at the beginning, and now there are those who are her companions,[66] and they were attentive to her voice. This cannot satisfy her beloved, neither the Messiah whom he portrays. His plea to her, therefore, is 'cause me to hear it (your voice)', as it had been when she had withdrawn herself to the rocky clefts earlier.[67] There were dangers in her isolation previously. He now gently urges her to consider Him before all others. It is not her daily recitations of the Shema˘ for which He longs, but for a spontaneous and warm expression to be given to her love for Him.

Her response is quick, as it is urgent. Earlier she had encouraged Him to turn and go to the mountains of separation. Then she had appealed to Him to come with her. Finally, now she begs Him to hasten to her upon the mountains of spices.[68] Her Beloved has been elevated on those spice-laden mountains made fragrant by

---

[64] See pp.94–98, where n.7 lists all the references in the Song. The instances of the plural are important here 4.15; 6.2; 8.13.   [65] Gen.12.3; Isa.2.3; Zech.14.16.
[66] The word companion, friend [Heb. chabher] occurs at 1.7; 8.13‡; cf. Ezek.37.16,19 where Israel is described as Judah's companions, and the tribes of Israel are said to be Ephraim's companions.   [67] Song 2.14.   [68] 2.17; 7.11[12]; 8.14.

His own presence. Her Lord is the One who treads on His high places, sure-footed and strong as He comes to His loved one. He has heard her 'How long?' in the many times of her distress, but soon He is to arise and say 'Behold, I come quickly'. The One who is 'the root and the offspring of David' has said 'Yea: I come quick-ly'. Surely your response must be 'Amen: come, Lord Jesus'. The personal return of the One 'whom the heaven must receive until the times of the restoration of all things' is that climactic event for which Israel still waits unconsciously.[69]

---

[69] Rev.22.12,16,20; Acts 3.21.

Part 5

IN
CONCLUSION

21

THE MYSTERY OF MILLENNIA IN METRE

IN SUMMARY, Solomon is the one divinely named Yedidiah, Beloved of Yah, the builder of the Temple, and the bearer of the glory. His wisdom was proverbial, and quite unsurpassed. The one who became his wife in the Song was 'the only one of her mother' and absolutely special to him. With great sensitivity and taste he paints the picture poetically of their developing relationship. The appeal of the varying sounds is enriched with the music of the lovers' voices. The beauty of the scenery is surpassed only by that of the lovers' form. The fragrance of the scents match the subtle delights they sense in one another. The sweetness and satisfaction of fruit and wines are excelled by the savour of their mutual love. And still there is a thrill reserved for the physical contact with the tangible beauty that surrounds them which must pale before their intimate union with one another. In a tangible world beautified by the master Creator's hand, true love alone will hear, see, smell, taste and touch, extending fully all of its God-given senses with great gladness of heart. We have sought to bring out something of this dimension in the Song's poetry on the plane of the story of their own love for one another. Another level, interpreting their genuine love relationship so as to warn and instruct us, has been developed by many modern commentators but has been given no space in this book, although of course, we agree that there are lasting lessons to be gained by all lovers here.

We have opted to devote most space to the deep mystery which

321

we understand Solomon to have seen projected through the wonderful love relationship between him and his loved one, namely the nation's varying experience of God's love which cannot fail. Already this was suggested in the queen of Sheba's words to Solomon. 'Blessed be the Lord thy God, which delighted in thee, to set thee on the throne of Israel: because the Lord loved Israel for ever, therefore he made thee king'. For Solomon, a typological and allegorical 'mystery' was revealed in this. Obviously, he was not able to identify each phase of salvation history. So much of this remained future and rather more general than specific to him. He contented himself with recording, as the Spirit prompted him, the several thrilling and tortuous elements en route to the triumph of divine love. With the divine library of history and prophecy now complete, we are able to trace the major milestones in the long haul of salvation history through to its grand climax in the kingdom of God. It is our purpose to reiterate the several staging posts in that journey through the millennia, so as to assist in discerning the whole sweep of God's ways with His beloved and chosen people Israel.

FROM THE PATRIARCHS TO THE MONARCHY, 1.2–2.7

We must start where it all started for the chosen nation. In pursuit of the divine purpose God's choice became evident in His call of Abraham. The poetry expressing the realization of this loving purpose opens the Song, 1.2–4, which we have entitled **Abram and the God of Glory.** Among the patriarchs, none equalled Abraham in his enjoyment of intimate personal relations with his God. He is described uniquely as 'Abraham thy (God's) friend', and the Lord Himself speaks of him as 'Abraham my friend'. In both instances the participial form of the verb 'to love' [Heb. ʿahabh, which has such a large place in the Song] is used, so as to underscore that he was the loved one characteristically to his God. God appeared to him, drew him, directed him, shielded him, communed with him, encouraged him, and consequently God was more to him than his only son Isaac. He had tasted for himself God's love and found it 'better than wine', and had come to savour the fragrance of God's 'name'. The King had brought him 'into his chambers' entailing blessing for his progeny too: 'we will be glad and rejoice in thee'. How 'rightly do they love thee'.

From Abraham onward the general Primeval History had given way to the more specialized attention to **Patriarchal History,** Gen.12–36. This whole period introduces the great fundamental elements of God's inexplicable and irrevocable choice and call, followed by His covenant with Abraham and the fathers. The unfolding revelation of God becomes preciously personalized. He made Himself known as 'the God of Abraham, and the God of Isaac, and the God of Jacob'. The history of the latter becomes mysteriously merged with that of Joseph. Joseph more than others of his family circle could say 'My mother's sons were incensed against me', and the enforced neglect of his personal vineyard resulted. Yet still the One whom his soul loved was to be found where the flocks were, and 'beside the shepherd's tents' in Goshen. Did not the brethren confess to Pharaoh that in contra-distinction to the Egyptians 'Thy servants are shepherds, both we, and our fathers'? To find her Beloved Lord, the fairest of women was to feed her flocks 'beside the shepherds' tents' therefore. If the Lord was to be found among men anywhere at that time, it would be along with this whole family of Jacob which, in the controlling providential love of God, had descended into Egypt, Gen.37–50. This is poetically presented in Song 1.5–8.

All of this is preparatory to Israel's victorious **Exodus from Egypt**, Exod.1.1–15.21, to which the Song devotes 1.9–11. Israel as the beautified mare looks on as Pharaoh's chariotry comes to an ignominious end. Little wonder that the nation triumphantly sang on that occasion 'unto the Lord, for he hath triumphed gloriously: the horse and his rider hath he thrown into the sea. The Lord is my strength and song, and he is become my salvation: this is my God and I will praise him; my father's God, and I will exalt him'.

The promises given to Abraham included both a seed and an inheritance. The intention of the God that brought them out of Egypt was to bring the nation in to the land of promise. The exodus was to issue in an eisodos! The long wilderness experience was not essential to the divine programme though necessitated by the faithlessness of the people. As is usual in the Song, this sorry interlude is given no space. The exodus is followed immediately by poetry drawing its imagery from the promised land. We have entitled this series of stanzas **Israel Enjoying the Promised Inheritance**, 1.12–2.7. This is set largely in the beautified countryside, first flowering and then fruiting through the spring and summer seasons. They are back in the vineyards, among the henna flowers, seeing the doves, now in the forest, and now on the Sharon plain, noting the lily in the mountain valley, even the lily among the thorns, and then bounding on to the end of summer to taste its sweet fruit, and its flowing wine. What a delightsome land! There the nation's divine King sat at His table, surely a hint at the commemorative passover meal with its circle of feasters around the Host, calling to mind the great redemptive event which brought them together. The King found His loved one becomingly fragrant. On her part, as the freed nation she 'sat down under his shadow with great delight, and his fruit was sweet' to her taste. He was incomparable, and He had brought her into His 'house of wine', the Temple, under the conspicuous banner of His love. It was here that she drank in deeply the joy of knowing Him. From Theocracy through to Monarchy there were always those who were as a lily among thorns to the Lord. These He brought to be overwhelmed by His love and to rest in it, 2.7. The Song does not unfold the division and disaster which led to the end of Monarchy and the Exile.

THE RETURN FROM EXILE TO THE ADVENT OF MESSIAH, 2.8–3.5

The major parts of this piece are so different from one another that it might be simpler to see it as two distinct poems. In the first he comes to her, 2.8–17; in the second she finds him, 3.1–5. In the first the imagery is largely drawn from the countryside; the second is set in the city. The stream of salvation history, however, flows on through the post-exilic period, which is described significantly from another viewpoint as the inter-testamental period, until it reaches its next great divinely appointed goal, the fulfilment of prophecy in the advent of the Messiah.

The Nation's Beloved Lord Visits her in Exile and speaks to her saying 'Rise up, my love, my fair one, and come away. For, lo, the winter is past'. The chilly silence is over, and the Lord woos her with attractive descriptions of the springtime 'in our land'. Notice not only His land, or her land but 'our land'. What condescending mutuality!, 2.8–13.

Unfortunately, those who returned never rose to the same heights of intimacy with their Lord. **The Nation became Obsessed with its Dangers and Duties**, with the nagging demands for separation and service, which kept her apart from Him despite His expressed desire to see her face and hear her voice. He is dismissed to 'the mountains of separation', 2.14–17.

It was when the nights came that she realized how much she truly missed Him. And how many dark nights there were for those of the nation who responded to the divine call to come back to their homeland. Persians, Greeks and Romans, not to speak of Samaritans, added to the darkness, and made that part of the nation more aware of her Beloved's absence, and thereby increased her own restlessness. She could find no rest without her Lord with her. At last, when Her Beloved Lord's absence could be tolerated no longer, she went out to seek the One whom her soul loved. She addressed her problem to the prophets who were the guardians of the hope bound up with God's city. No sooner had she left them, than she found the Lord whom her 'soul loveth'. **At last she had Him with her**, for the Messiah had come to the 'mother's house' of those who yearned for His coming. Those loved of the Lord could rest again in the overwhelming experience of His restored favour realized by His presence 'with them', 3.1–5. The child was born, the Son had been given. They were to 'call his name Immanuel; which is, being interpreted, God with us'. At Matthew 1–2 and Luke 1–2 we can pause once again in the onward march of divine initiative. God had 'sent forth his Son, born of a woman, born under the law, that he might redeem them which were under the law'.

THE MESSIAH'S MINISTRY AND THE SPIRIT'S MISSION, 3.6–5.1

Without controversy, we witness the marriage consummation here. For her King it is 'the day of his espousals'. For His loved one, drawn to Him out of the nation, there is the unique thrill of hearing

Him say 'bride' six times. The detail of this climactic part of the Song, and of salvation history, has been advanced in chapters 14 and 17. We shall highlight the several stanzas in which the poet traces the route to this wondrous union.

Messiah's Public Ministry, from Wilderness to Jerusalem. From the time of the herald's voice calling the nation to repentance and pointing them to the Messiah, up to the time when the Messiah Himself emerged from the wilderness for His final ascent to His capital city, many were embraced by His love. They formed that caravan making its way to Jerusalem, and which was welcomed by those who came out from the city to meet their King 'on the day of his espousals', 3.6–11.

Messiah's Private Ministry, in the Light of the Upper Room. The favoured few, who kept that last passover with Him before He suffered, were representative of all 'his own which were in the world' whom 'he loved . . . unto the end'. He used the occasion to speak to their hearts, and still continued after challenging them to 'Arise, let us go hence', 4.1–5.

Messiah's Sacrificial Death, His Reconciling Ministry. His once-for-all work at Golgotha is the veritable pivot of all the ages. Myrrh Mountain looms large in God's salvific purposes, and Frankincense Hill spreads its fragrance to the heights of heaven and the lowliest of earth. Once in the consummation of the ages, the Messiah appeared to put away sin by the sacrifice of Himself, 4.6.

Messiah's Post-Resurrection Ministry, the Forty Days with His Own. With sin and sins all removed, and removed for ever, the Messiah for the first time may say 'Thou art all fair, my love'. What a pristine standing! But there is more yet. He may also describe His loved one as '(my) bride'. What an unchanging and unbreakable union! His reassuring words are supplemented with a call to her to 'Come with me' from all that would constitute real danger to His loved one, 4.7–8. He expresses all His delights in her as He sits down to enjoy the honeycomb with her. He is no spirit, 4.9–11. He expatiates on her preciousness to Him, His very own 'garden shut up'. Of course, she must not remain 'shut up'. All of this belongs to those memorable forty days, when He provided His own with the incontrovertible evidence of His bodily resurrection, 4.12–14.

Messiah's Ascent to Heaven; the Spirit's Descent to Earth. It was to the advantage of His own that the Lord should go back to heaven. Only thus would the Comforter come. This is now before us in the Song. The one whom He had described as 'a garden shut up' for Himself, has to become 'a fountain of gardens' in order that the 'living waters' might flow to the whole world. Fair winds and foul would breathe upon them but thus His fragrance would be spread abroad. With the descent of the Spirit He could say 'I am come into my garden, my sister, (my) bride'. All who would wish the Beloved Messiah and His Bride well should happily respond 'Eat, O friends; drink, yea drink abundantly, beloved ones!', 4.15–5.1. Yet another phase, fundamental to all others in the divine plan of salvation, is completed.

THE ISRAEL OF GOD DURING MESSIAH'S ABSENCE, 5.2–6.9

The Continuing Appeal of a Neglected Messiah. The King installed upon His Father's throne in heaven did not cease to knock on the nation's door, as the history of Acts establishes. He had Israel engraved upon the palms of His hands, and appealed to her to 'Open to me'. It was the sight of His nail-pierced hand that moved her always, even if this proved too late to prevent her disappointment at His disappearance. This has brought upon the divinely loved nation the troubles predicted by God's faithful prophets. Throughout nearly two millennia now, it has been proven indisputably that 'they are not all Israel, which are of Israel'. Praise God, there are many of the nation who have 'sought him', 5.2–8.

The Enhanced Appreciation of the Remnant Drawn After Him. In seeking their Messiah, that 'election of grace', which find Him, acknowledge Him to exceed all the fame they have expected in their promised Messiah. So in the Song, by confessing her deep longing for Him, she is brought to surprise herself with her head to toe description of His divine and personal glories. Those of Israel who come to such a glowing appreciation of their glorified Messiah are the true 'Israel of God' in the present period. No previous group in the nation's long history has ever known such glorious heights of divine love. The 'Israel of God' today declare Jesus to be both Lord and Christ saying 'This is my beloved, and this is my friend, O daughters of Jerusalem', 5.9–16. May their witness draw many of their nation to enquire after Him!

Where is the Messiah Engaged Today? This secret is with those who confess Him as the 'altogether lovely one'. How ready they must be to tell others who enquire after Him. The 'Israel of God' must be ready to give their answer. 'My beloved is gone down to his garden', that is He is now 'with us', the saved ones of the nation who own Him as our glorified Lord in heaven. This is not all of the truth however. She quickly adds that He has gone 'to feed in the gardens, and to gather lilies'. The One who laid down His life for the sheep said 'other sheep I have, which are not of this fold: them also I must bring, and they shall hear my voice; they (Jews and Gentiles who accept the Good Shepherd) shall become one flock, one shepherd'. Truly the 'Israel of God', in which God's present purposes of grace for the nation continue, rejoices in the universal breadth of divine love. As she says, 'I am my beloved's, and my beloved is mine' and yet also 'he feedeth (his flock) among the lilies', 6.1–3.

What the Israel of God is Now to their Messiah. Those from the nation of Israel who believe that Jesus is the Messiah, the Son of God, know that 'neither is circumcision anything, nor uncircumcision, but a new creation. As many as walk by this rule, peace be upon them, and upon the Israel of God (who believe from among the circumcision)'. In this OT book, the Messiah describes what these out of the nation are to Him. For Him 'she is the choice one of her that bare her'. Those who know His love and reciprocate it now when the majority reject Him, are quite the choicest children which the divinely favoured nation has ever produced. He uses practically the same similes to describe her in this stanza, as He had used of those who became disciples during the days of His flesh. His delight is in her, 6.4–9.

WHEN THE MESSIAH COMES THE SECOND TIME, 6.10–8.4

'For yet a very little while, He that cometh shall come, and shall not tarry'. The Lord's love for Israel demands this.

A Redeemer Shall Come To Zion

The Nation will look Stunningly Bright. John adopts the description 'arrayed with the sun, and the moon under her feet, and upon her head a crown of twelve stars' to convey something of the nation's splendour. The dramatic change impresses the onlookers who ask 'Who is this?' The nation must be back in her land, an awesome force to contend with before the Lord returns, 6.10.

Messiah will Come Down for Her. Nearly two thousand years have elapsed since He 'went up' to heaven. Soon that same Beloved One will say 'I went down into the garden of (wal-)nuts'. How He longs for the evidence of fulfilled prophecy's springtime in Israel once again. When He comes back to Walnut Garden at Jerusalem His long patient love shall contain itself no longer. It is then that His people 'offer themselves willingly' to Him and the transformation will be as immediate as it will be remarkable. Willing people will be princely people too!, 6.11–12.

Israel's Conversion and Celebration. Many voices will appeal successfully for her to 'return to the Lord'. Only thus can the nation become the King's suited companion. When she does 'return to the Lord', she will dance uninhibitedly and joyously, 6.13[7.1].

Israel Beautified with God's Salvation. The psalmist's prayer will be fulfilled 'in that day': 'let the beauty of the Lord our God be upon us'. She will be seen as the prince's daughter which she has become. All onlookers will glowingly describe her, and it will be obvious why 'the king is held captive in the tresses' of her hair, 7.1–5[2–6].

Saved Israel Strongly Desired by Her Messiah. She is to be the one in whom He finds then all His delights. He will take her to Himself and be satisfied, 7.6–9a[7–10a].

Israel Readily Responds to Her Messiah's Love. What sweet relief it will be for the nation when she comes to know that 'I am my beloved's, and his desire is toward me', 7.9b–10[10b–11].

329

A Nation Shall Long For Its Lord

Israel Calls for Unbroken Fellowship with Her Messiah. 'Come, my beloved,' she says, 'let us go forth into the field'. She will desire to be alone with Him. She has reserved the experience of her love for Him, 'all manner of precious fruits, new and old'. How wise a 'disciple to the kingdom of heaven' she will become at last. These are truly new covenant joys which they will enter into together 'in that day', 7.11–13[12–14].

Israel's Desire for Uninhibited Pure Love. The nation's longing for public and general acceptance of the peculiar relationship which exists between herself and her Messiah is to be satisfied. On the other hand, she desires to know the love of the Messiah which passes knowledge, and to give to Him those fresh joys belonging to the kingdom which will be an unbroken festival of Tabernacles for them. When this happy conclusion is reached, she will rest in her Messiah's love as He at last shall 'rest in his love, he will joy' over her with singing, 8.1–4.

MILLENNIAL DAYS, 8.5–14

It is difficult to imagine a more vivid contrast than that suggested by the opening and closing words here, 'the wilderness' and 'the gardens'. Surely, this anticipates that unparalleled change to be brought about when 'the creation itself also shall be delivered from the bondage of corruption' and its groans will have ceased for ever.

Israel Comes Up from the Wilderness to the Land. Israel is to experience another, and greater exodus event climaxed in her entering the promised inheritance. The Lord's paradoxical word through Hosea will be fulfilled at last: 'I will allure her, and bring her into the wilderness, and speak to her heart. And I will give her her vineyards from thence'. True, the nation must be brought into the wilderness before this can happen, and yet it will be through that experience that she will be found 'leaning upon her beloved'. Total dependence is the route to dominion. What an ascent! The change in the nation will surprise the world, 8.5a–b.

Israel Speaks to Her Beloved Messiah of Divine Love. Apart from it she could not have 'awakened' Him. Because of its strength she could never be separated from Him. His unyielding love is to her 'a very flame of the Lord'. Its costliness to Him she can no longer despise, 8.5c–7.

What of Diaspora Jewry? For the little sister, too, there must be a 'day when she shall be spoken for'. The Messiah must first 'come out of Zion' as Deliverer, yet He is to 'turn away ungodliness from Jacob', the twelve tribed nation, as a whole. He shall commission 'his angels . . . and they shall gather together his elect from the four winds, from one end of the heaven to the other'. 'In that day' the Messiah's loved one shall be 'as one that found peace', 8.8–10.

The Millennial Administration of the Kingdom. The Messianic King, more glorious by far than Solomon, will administer the fruitful earth for the thousand years committed to Him. The very name of His vineyard describes Him as the 'Master of a Multitude'. The nations are to own their responsibility as his stewards. His own nation, enriched in her own promised land, will yield her bounty gladly to her Beloved Messiah. It shall be His for the duration of His reign, 8.11–12.

The Lovers' Insatiable Longing for Communion and Union. Israel in those blessed times will dwell in the midst of the nations. They will hearken to her voice 'for out of Zion shall go forth the law, and the word of the Lord from Jerusalem'. Certainly, 'the companions hearken for' her voice, but Israel's Messiah also will ever plead 'cause me to hear it'.

For the nation's part, she cannot bear His absence. It is as though she pleads 'Even so, come!' 8.13–14.

With this our longing hearts concur, for 'I Jesus have sent mine angel to testify unto you these things for the churches. I am the root and the offspring of David, the bright, the morning star'. Also, 'the Spirit and the bride say, Come. And he that heareth (and readeth) let him say, Come. And he that is athirst, let him come: he that will, let him take the water of life freely'.

331

APPENDICES

<u>Contents – Appendices</u>

1. 'SOLOMON' – THE KING AND SHEPHERD – 'MY BELOVED'

We are introduced to his love from the very beginning

There is no recorded breakdown in his love

His expressions of love are more excellent than hers

His love elevates the one he loves

His love leaps over all barriers

His loved one speaks of the love she had come to know
 'thy love is better than wine' – in experience inwardly – worship, 1.2
 'make mention of thy love more than wine' – in expression – witness,
  1.4
 'his banner over me was love' – in identification – warfare, 2.4

He had revealed the true character of love to her, 8.6f, for
 it was 'as strong as death' – strength of its irresistible call
 'jealousy is cruel as the grave' – unyielding in its claims of possession
 it is 'a very flame of the Lord' – revealing the heart of its originator, a
  veritable theophany (God is love)
 'Many waters cannot quench' nor 'floods drown' it – unquenchable
 she has been purchased at infinite cost – it expends itself in sacrifice

His love is positively and practically expressed
 He draws her, 1.4, brings her into his chambers, 1.4, directs her, 1.8
 He glowingly describes her, 1.15; 4.1–5,7,9–16; 6.4–9; 7.6–9a[7–10a]
 He surpasses her own assessment of herself, 2.2
 He provides food, shelter, fruit, security for her, 1.7; 2.3ff
 His love is overwhelming, 2.5; 5.5
 He embraces her, 2.6; 8.3
 His love is patient, 2.7; 3.5; 8.4
 He energetically takes the initiative, leaping, skipping, standing, look-
  ing, 2.8
 He appeals to her to 'come away', 2.10
 He tells her how he longs to see her, and to hear her voice, 2.14; 8.13
 He is sensitive to the cycles of love, 2.7,9,17; 3.5; 8.4
 His love brought her to glory, 3.6–11
 His love is self-sacrificing, 4.6
 His love is longsuffering, 5.2–5
 His love cannot rest until he regains his loved one, 6.11f
 His desire is toward her, 7.10[11]
 He is thrilled when she says appealingly 'Let us . . .', 7.11f[12f]
 His love is for those who lean upon him, 8.5

She describes him as 'thou whom my soul loveth', 1.7
'him whom my soul loveth', 3.1,2,3,4

He is specially 'my beloved', 1.13,14,16; 2.3/ 2.8,9,10,16,17/ 4.16/ 5.2,4,5,
6(2),8,10,16; 6.2,3(2)/ 7.9,10,12,13[10,11,13,14]/ 8.5,14
'thy beloved', 5.9(2); 6.1(2)

He is also 'my friend', 5.16

His love demands a plural of majesty [Heb.dodheka] to express its worth,
1.2,4

The virgins love him, 1.3, and make mention of his love, 1.4 [Heb.
ahabh], cf. daughters of Jerusalem that paved his palanquin with love
[ahabhah], 3.10

'What is thy beloved more than another beloved?' Only once does she
speak in considerable detail concerning him, 5.10–16. A few other descriptive phrases were added to this elsewhere, producing the following
picture:

his ointments have a goodly fragrance, 1.3
thou are fair, my beloved, yea pleasant, 1.16
the kisses of his mouth, 1.2
his left hand under her head, 2.6; 8.3
his right hand embraced her, 2.6; 8.3
his hand, 5.4

his hands, 5.14	(as) rings of gold set with beryl
his head, 5.2	is filled with dew
his head, 5.11	is (as) the most fine gold
his complexion, 5.10	is white and ruddy
his hair, 5.2	(is filled) with drops of the night
his hair, 5.11	bushy, and black as a raven
his eyes, 5.12	like doves beside water brooks, washed with milk, and fitly set
his cheeks, 5.13	as a bed of spices, (as) banks of sweet herbs
his lips, 5.13	(as) lilies, dropping liquid myrrh
his body, 5.14	(as) ivory work overlaid with sapphires
his legs, 5.15	(as) pillars of marble, set upon sockets of fine gold
his bearing, 5.16	is like Lebanon, excellent as the cedars
his mouth, 5.16	is most sweet

yea, he is altogether lovely, 5.16

Also other similes/metaphors used in describing him are:

thy name is as ointment poured forth, 1.3
he is (as) a bundle of myrrh, that lieth betwixt my breasts, 1.13
he is (as) a cluster of henna flowers in the vineyards of En-gedi, 1.14
he is as the apple tree among the trees of the wood, 2.3
he is like a roe or a young hart, 2.9,17; 8.14
Oh that thou wert as my brother, 8.1

2. THE LOVE THEME

The words used
  verb ʿahabh, 7x
  noun ʿahabhah, 11x, 5x with article, 6x without article
  noun dodh, in plural, 6x
  noun dodh, in singular with first person suffix = my beloved 33x,
    elsewhere only Isa.5.1
  noun with its possessive suffix raʿyathi = my love, 9x, elsewhere only
    Jud.11.37*

her describing His
  thy love is better than wine, 1.2
  his banner over me was love, 2.4
        generically
  as strong as death, 8.6
  jealousy cruel as grave
  flashes are flashes of fire
  a very flame of the Lord
  many waters cannot quench, 8.7
    neither can floods drown
  cannot fail, 8.7

effect on her
  thou whom my soul loveth, 1.7; 3.1,2,3,4
  we will make mention of thy love more than wine, 1.4
  sick of love, 2.5
              5.8
  there will I give thee my love, 7.12[13]

effect on others
  therefore do the virgins love thee, 1.3
  rightly do they love thee, 1.4
  paved with love, 3.10
  drink O loved ones, 5.1

His description of hers and His ways with her
  how fair is thy love, 4.10
  thy love is better than wine, 4.10
  how fair and how pleasant art thou, O love, for delights!, 7.6[7]
  stir not up . . ., 2.7; 3.5; 8.4

His comparisons of 'my love'
  1.9, mare
  2.2, lily among thorns
  6.4, thou are beautiful, O my love, as Tirzah

His descriptions, general
  1.15, thou art fair
  4.1, thou art fair
  4.7, thou art all fair

His calls
  2.10,13, rise up, my love, my fair one, and come away
  5.2, open to me, my sister, my love . . .

'my beloved' = her of him [Heb.dodhi]

general description
  thou art fair, yea pleasant, 1.16

descriptive metaphor
  a bundle of myrrh, 1.13
  a cluster of henna flowers, 1.14

descriptive comparative simile
  as the apple tree among the trees of the wood, 2.3
  like a roe or a young hart, 2.9,17; 8.14

physical and more literal description
  the voice (sound) of my beloved, 2.8; 5.2
        cf. spake and said, 2.10
  put in his hand, 5.4
  white and ruddy etc., 5.10

her possession of him
  my beloved is mine etc., 2.16; 6.3(2); 7.10[11]

appeals to him
  turn . . . be like a roe or a young hart, 2.17
  let my beloved come into his garden, 4.16
  come . . . let us go forth into the field, 7.11[12]
  make haste . . . and be thou like a roe, 8.14

her/his response
  I rose to open, 5.5
  I opened, 5.6
  precious fruits . . . which I have laid up for thee, 7.13[14]
  her mouth . . . like best wine that goes down smoothly for him, 7.9[10]
  (he) had withdrawn himself, 5.6

her appeal to others re him
  if ye find him . . . tell him, 5.8

others and her beloved
  what is thy beloved more than another beloved (4), 5.9
  whither is thy beloved gone . . . turned him (2), 6.1
  Who is this . . . leaning upon her beloved? 8.5

her knowledge of his whereabouts
  my beloved has gone down to his garden, 6.2

3. HE IS ALTOGETHER LOVELY

WE HAVE OBSERVED already that Poem 4 embraces that period of salvation history beginning at the descent of the Holy Spirit and continuing until the church is complete. At the present time God is still bringing into blessing a remnant of Israel which is within His elective purposes of grace. Paul, the converted scholar of New Testament period Judaism, is a fine representative of these. When divine light had dawned upon him, he said 'even though we have known Christ after the flesh, yet now we know him so no more'. That is, he had a well-defined picture of the kind of Messiah for whom he and his people waited, but since being confronted by the glorified Jesus the inadequacy, not to speak of the mistaken nature of this view, simply had to go. It was the crucified and now glorified One who had transported him from the vantage point of mere men to the mountain peak of divine revelation. Is not this a fruit of God's new creation work? All things have become new. Is He not now also producing out of saved Jews and Gentiles 'one new man, so making peace'?

Poem 4 presents the national neglect of Israel's Messiah with its consequent troubles, out of which a remnant comes to appreciate Him. This remnant is apprehended by the divine fulness and the exalted glory of her Messiah, the Son of the living God. With her eyes and heart ravished by her Beloved, she unfolds His loveliness in Song 5.11–16. All of us who have come to know Him, whether Jew or Gentile, feel a deep inner sympathy with this part of the Song. We are all lost in wonder as we gaze, with her, upon our Lord in glory.

One general observation is called for. Apart from the first and last features of her full-length portrait, His head and His mouth or palate, she senses the need for more than one simile to describe the indescribable. Consider this One, then, in whom dwells all the fulness of Godhead bodily.

1. **His Head** – as most fine [Heb.kethem] gold [Heb.paz], v.11. There could be no more emphatic way of contrasting His life on earth and His present glory than by recalling His earlier appealing word 'my head is filled with dew', v.2. The golden head is not to be understood as the Torah, or as the gold-covered Holy of holies

as proposed by the Talmud and Robert respectively. It is rather the head of her Beloved now glorified as His loved one now conceives it. This fine gold represents the fact of His deity, His divine wisdom, and His glorious Headship.[1] The two distinct words used for gold and combined only in verse 11 in the Old Testament, are used in a number of similes regarding wisdom.[2] Her glorious Head is the One 'in whom are all the treasures of wisdom and knowledge hidden', which again will provide a complete answer to any tendency to turn back to Judaism's shadows. She might say to this One 'How precious are thy thoughts unto me, O God! How great is the sum of them! If I could count them, they are more in number than the sand: when I awake I am still with thee'. How she rejoiced in having such an One as her Beloved whose thoughts were toward her.

2. His Locks – bushy, black as a raven.

He had referred to His head and locks which were 'filled with dew ... with the drops of the night', v.2, as strengthening the force of His loving appeal. The head and locks in combination are the two aspects of His beauty to which she gives first place in her adoring description. Praise God that His approach in appealing grace has brought her to appreciate His surpassing glory. The word 'bushy'

---

[1] She acknowledges Him as 'the head of the body, the church'. She has learned that she is above criticism regarding meat, drink, feast days, new moons, or sabbaths, now that she holds fast 'the Head, from whom all the body, being supplied and knit together through the joints and bands, increaseth with the increase of God'. She acknowledges that He is 'the head of every man', which resolves relationships in the local assembly. She rests in the fact that He is 'the head of all principality and power', and has been given to the church as 'head over all things', Col.1.18; Eph.5.23; 2.19; Eph.4.15; 1 Cor.11.3; Col.2.10; Eph.1.22.   [2] 'Gold' [Heb.kethem‡] in Song 5.11. Occurs 9 times, three of which refer to wisdom, Job 28.16,19; Prov.25.12//[Heb.zahabh = gold]: 'gold' [Heb.paz‡] in Song 5.11,15. Occurs 9 times, twice of wisdom, Job 28.17//[Heb.zahabh = gold]; Prov.8.17//'choice silver', and twice of the Word, Ps.19.10[11]; 119.127 both//[Heb.zahabh = gold]. Another word for 'gold' [Heb.zahabh‡] in Song 1.11; 3.10; 5.14. Occurs often, but the greatest concentrations of uses are in connection with the Tabernacle (ca 100 refs in Exod.25–40), then with Solomon's Temple and reign. The word combined with the participle of the verb [Heb.pazaz] is used of Solomon's throne which was overlaid 'with the finest gold [zahabh muphaz]', 1 Kings 10.18.

[Heb.taltallimt, plural] describes the mass of hair He had.[3] In this He is seen as the true Nazirite for whom 'there shall no razor come upon his head' ... 'his separation to God is upon his head'.[4] If He is detached from her, she knows that His separation to His God is for her. His hair is also black as the raven. He is quite different from Ephraim of whom Hosea wrote 'Strangers have devoured his strength, and he knoweth it not: yea, gray hairs are here and there upon him, and he knoweth it not', 7.9. With her Beloved there is no sign of decay or deterioration; she sees Him in all the vigour of manhood. As the Lord He purposes to roll up as a mantle the earth and heavens that He has made, and 'as a garment they shall be changed: but thou art the same, and thy years shall not fail'. The thrilling thought for her is that the glorified Man she has come to know is unchanging too. 'Jesus Christ is the same yesterday and today, yea and for ever'.[5]

3. His Eyes – like doves beside the water brooks;
washed with milk, and fitly set, v.12.

It is remarkable that the eyes which feature so often in His descriptions of her beauty, are only once singled out by her for the greatest descriptive detail of His beauty.[6] When the Messiah was in the world, we are told that on one occasion, having constrained His disciples to go by boat before Him across the Lake of Galilee, 'he departed into the mountain to pray'. Although separated from them by a considerable distance, and though it was about the fourth watch of the night, He was able to see them 'distressed in rowing', and 'cometh unto them walking on the sea'.[7] This anticipates the ministry of the Man in heaven, whose kindly eyes

---

[3] cf. word for a mound or even the artificial mound resulting from the building up of the several destruction levels of an ancient town known as a 'tel' [Heb.tel], Jer.30.18; 49.2. The simile in the plural 'mounds' or hillocks may refer to the banks of hair, or even its waviness.   [4] Read Num.6.1–21, esp. vv.5,7.
[5] Heb.1.12; 13.8. Contrast His hair being white as co-equal with the Ancient of days, where the emphasis is upon His mature discernment, His perfect judicial wisdom, Dan.7.9,22; Rev.1.14.   [6] For detail on 'doves' [Heb.yonaht] see pp.53f, n.2–9. As a term of endearment see 2.14; 5.2; 6.9, and in simile for her eyes see 1.15; 4.1, and for his eyes, 5.12. Other references to her eyes at 4.9; 6.5; 7.4[5] and to His, 8.10.   [7] Mark 6.45f,48.

341

are always upon His loved ones in the world. 'The Lord looketh from the heaven; he beholdeth all the sons of men . . . Behold, the eye of the Lord is upon them that fear him, upon them that hope in his mercy'. 'The eyes of the Lord are toward the righteous, and his ears are open unto their cry'.[8] The similes all bear upon the dark and lively pupils which are the more beautiful against the background of the whites of His eyes. He has described her affectionately as 'my dove', and has seen her 'eyes as doves', but all this is a reflection of Himself which He sees in her, so that she says 'I was in his eyes as one that found peace'.

4. His Cheeks – as a bed of spices,
(as) banks of sweet herbs, v.13.

In chapter 1 the Beloved was attracted by the beauty of the loved one's cheeks. Now it is her turn to describe His cheeks [Heb.lechi, 1.10; 5.13‡]. He was determined to enhance the nations cheeks at the Exodus with 'plaits of gold'. She now longs after her glorified Beloved's fragrant cheeks. It had been so different when He was in the world, before His exodus and return to the Father. Generally the nation had seen no beauty in Him that they should desire Him. He had been willing to give 'his cheek to them that smiteth', and they smote 'the judge of Israel . . . upon the cheek'. Submissively He gave His 'cheeks to them that plucked off the hair'.[9] Praise God, that is all behind Him. He is glorified now in heaven, and those who love Him long to see His lovely face. He is there as the one anointed 'with the oil of gladness above his fellows' as the reference to the garden terrace bed suggests. The word 'spices' [Heb.bosem] here is used of all four spice ingredients of the anointing oil and for the sweet incense.[10] Also the word translated 'sweet herbs' [Heb.merqacht] belongs to a family which is represented in the production of the spice mixtures of the anointing oil and the holy incense.[11] Here, then, are apt similes of the fragrant ministries found in the glorified Messiah, who is uniquely

---

[8] Ps.33.13,18; 34.15[16].   [9] Lam.3.30; Mic.5.1[4.14]; Isa.50.6; cf. Mark 14.65;
15.19; John 18.22; 19.3.   [10] Exod.25.6; 35.8, cf. v.28.
[11] cf. Exod.30.25,33,35; 37.29.

above all the kings in David's royal line as the world will soon know, and above Aaron as the appointed great high priest, even God's king-priest for ever after the order of Melchizedec. For all those saved ones today, the precious oil with which His head has been anointed runs down upon His beard, and from thence comes down upon the skirt of His garment to enhance our spiritual discrimination of all His personal moral perfections.[12]

5. His Lips – are (as) lilies, dropping liquid myrrh.

Her lips are like a thread of scarlet as to colour, His are like lilies [Heb.shoshannim], not as to their white colour but as to their attractive shape. They were petal-like, as was the ornamented brim of the great sea in Solomon's Temple.[13] In the days of His flesh His lips were not unclean as were those of the prophet and his people alike. They were lips of righteousness and truth.[14] When Messiah was among His people He was given 'the tongue of them that are taught, that I should know how to sustain with words him that is weary'. He stood out among men: 'Thou art fairer than the children of men; grace is poured into thy lips'.[15] Consequently many of His contemporaries 'wondered at the words of grace which proceeded out of his mouth'. His gracious lips befitted the one who was 'full of grace and truth'. His ministry now from heaven is even further enhanced. An ocean of cleansing and blessing flows through His lips and out of His inward parts as He speaks to the heart of His own today. 'My grace is sufficient for thee: for my power is made perfect in weakness'.[16]

If her lips are to Him sweetness itself, they 'drop (as) the honeycomb', then His lips are to her precious for the fragrance they exude, whilst 'dropping liquid myrrh'.[17] As He prepared His disciples for His exodus, He often spoke of the bitterness of those sufferings through which He was to pass. His lips dropped liquid myrrh long before His pierced hands dripped with myrrh. Now that He is exalted all His garments smell of myrrh, and His lips continue to drip with myrrh. He speaks as the one that was slain,

---

[12] Ps.133.2.   [13] 4.3; 5.13; 1 Kgs.7.20//2 Chron.4.5.   [14] Isa.6.5; Prov.10.21,32; 12.19.   [15] Isa.50.4; Ps.45.2[3] (note this is a shoshannim psalm, title [v.1]).   [16] Luke 4.22; John 1.17; 2 Cor.12.9.   [17] 4.11; 5.13.

who became dead but is now the Living one. He tells us that He is aware of our toil and patience, that there is tribulation for us, that faithful ones may be killed, that we shall be kept from the hour of trial, and that He is coming quickly. His continuing graciousness is expressed in terms of Golgotha's fragrant work on our behalf. He is kissing His own with the kisses of His lips, His love is better than wine!

6. His Hands – (are as) rings of gold set with the beryl, v.14.

Men pierced His hands at the cross. He showed Himself alive after His resurrection saying to His own 'Behold my hands'. 'The Father loveth the Son, and hath given all things into his hands'. Now He lives in heaven, and the golden hands of the glorified Lord mightily aid His own who are in the world. His hands as golden rings encircle and enfold those who belong to Him. The hand of the Lord is not shortened: He has redeemed and has power to deliver with a strong hand as in the past. He has said 'I give unto them eternal life; and they shall never perish, and no one shall snatch them out of my hand'. The believer today may depend upon His almighty help as Joseph had proved it, for 'the arms of his hands were made strong, by the hands of the Mighty One of Jacob'.[18] Those same hands, as of a master workman, are forming His own people for His own pleasure too, cf. 7.1[2].

Our Beloved's golden hands are also set [Heb.male´; 5.2,14‡] with the beryl. In 5.2 He spoke of His head being 'filled with dew', capturing something of what it meant to Him to be left out in the cold by His loved one. The hands of that same One, viewed from the standpoint of His glorified station in heaven, are filled with the beryl. These contrasting states indicate something of the tension between our Lord's present splendour and glory in heaven and His sensitivity to the lack of response to His loving overtures to men on earth. The word 'filled' is used often in connection with installing the priest into office. His consecration to the service of God was described literally as a filling of the hands. This may suggest yet another aspect of the glories of our Lord officiating on His people's behalf in heaven.[19]

---

[18] Luke 24.39f; John 20.25,27; 3.35; cf. 13.3; 10.28; Isa.50.2; 59.1; Exod.13.3,14,16; 6.1(2); 13.9; Deut.6.21; 7.8; Gen.49.24.   [19] Exod.28.41; 29.9,29.

7. His Body – is as ivory work overlaid with sapphires.
The word translated 'his body' [Heb.me ̄aw] only occurs in the
plural. It refers usually to the inward parts, or seat of the emotions,
and is translated 'heart' (AV bowels) in verse 4. There is no other
OT instance where the word refers to an external feature of the
body. The sole use of its Aramaic equivalent in Daniel 2.32
[Aram.me ̄a ̄] is translated 'belly', referring to that part of
Nebuchadnezzar's image between the chest and the thighs. This
may have influenced the selection of the word 'body' as an appropriate translation here, standing as it does in a list of external
physical features. However, the plural form and its usual associations may suggest here that the compassions and inner emotions
of the Beloved are as patent to His loved one as are His features.
In this sense it is used of the divine compassions toward Ephraim
in the very context leading up to the new covenant. The Lord says
'for as often as I speak against him, I do earnestly remember him
still: therefore my bowels are troubled for him; I will surely have
mercy upon him'. Again, Isaiah asks 'Where is thy zeal and thy
mighty acts? the yearning of thy bowels and thy compassions are
restrained toward me. For thou art our father, though Abraham
knoweth us not, and Israel doth not acknowledge us'. In both
cases 'mercy' or 'compassions' provide the parallel to our term.
Projected here therefore are the inward affections and divine compassions of Israel's glorified Messiah which are transparently
observable to those who yearn after Him.[20] While the Lord was in
the world He often was moved with compassion and it was evident
to those who looked on. So it is today, although He is beyond the
range of human sight. He continues to have compassion upon
whom He will. Moreover, He will arise soon and have mercy upon
Zion.[21] His loved one sees and she adores.

The simile 'as ivory work' which she adopts suggests the unchanging, imperishable character of His compassions which 'fail
not'. Ivory would also suggest that they have been proven through
and remain beyond His death, mysteriously wrought through
sufferings and now guaranteed incorruptibly in resurrection. All is
enhanced with the overlay of blue sapphires as the very heaven

[20] Jer.31.20; Isa.63.15.   [21] Matt.9.36; Luke 10.33; Rom.9.15; Ps.102.13[14]; cf.
Isa.54.7,8,10.

for clearness. Higher than the heavens, Ezekiel saw 'the likeness of a throne, as the appearance of a sapphire stone: and upon the likeness of the throne was a likeness as the appearance of a man'. There can be no doubt as to the identity of this theophanic figure. It is the Lord, the One who is now higher than the heavens in a glorified body. He is enthroned now in heaven, Himself resplendent with heaven's glory, where the place of His feet is 'as it were a paved work of sapphire stone'. If Israel's foundations are to be laid in sapphires, this is the only One capable of bringing it about. Soon He is to come out of those ivory palaces where He is the living guarantor of that incorruptible reign of glory which Solomon's ivory throne could only faintly represent.[22]

8. His Legs – (are as) pillars of marble,
set upon sockets of fine gold: v.15.

The Lord takes no pleasure in the legs of a man. Their strength is most transient and unsure, so that 'it is not of him that runneth'. Yet the bride finds great delight in the legs of her glorified Messiah. They are marble, indicating the strength and stability of His standing in the heavenly Temple. They tell a doubly assuring tale like the two massive pillars Jachin and Boaz astride the Temple's porch entrance, for in her Beloved all is established and in Him is strength. Though spoilers may come, she may be confident as Isaiah was that 'The Lord is exalted; for he dwelleth on high ... And (consequently) there shall be stability in thy times, abundance of salvation, wisdom and knowledge'.[23]

Man's imperial dream looking down the Times of the Gentiles must eventually lie shattered before being finally scattered. However grandiose or awe-inspiring that image might seem, the whole thing rests upon feet made of a mixture of iron and brittle pottery. Conversely, her Beloved's legs are firmly set upon sockets of fine gold which had been produced through the crucible of suffering. The five pillars at the door of the Tabernacle were set on bronze bases, and the four supporting the veil were upon silver bases. Here the fine gold bases would suggest that proven

---

[22] Lam.3.22; Exod.24.10; Isa.54.11; Ezek.1.26; Ps.45.8[9]; 1 Kgs.10.18//
2 Chron.9.17.   [23] Ps.147.10; Rom.9.16; 1 Kgs.7.15; Isa.33.6.

righteousness altogether suited for the Temple room of heaven of which the Spirit makes us aware because our Lord has gone to the Father and we behold Him no more.[24]

9. His Aspect – is like Lebanon, excellent as the cedars.

The word 'aspect' refers sometimes to the external appearance or visible form of a person. In 2.14 for instance the Beloved desired to see His loved one. Its most significant use in this sense for our purpose is concerning the Servant of the Lord. We are told that 'his visage was so marred' and that there was 'no beauty in him that we should desire him'. How all this has been changed for the ascended Christ is brought out by the use of the word here in 5.15, which takes on the nuance of a vision, a supernatural vision of the glorified One. At Sinai 'the appearance of the glory of the Lord was like devouring fire on the top of the mount in the eyes of the children of Israel'.[25] Here the Lord's elevation and his majestic bearing in the present, ravishes the vision of His bride free from any element of terror. For 'He that descended is the same also that ascended far above all the heavens, that he might fill all things'. Christ Jesus who came down and humbled Himself is now highly exalted. She sees Him as the one who is 'far above all rule, and authority, and power, and dominion, and every name that is named, not only in this world (age), but also in that which is to come'. He is indeed excellent [Heb.bachur], the greater than David chosen out of the people for exaltation in the future, and even now seen as 'with God elect, and precious'. Stateliness, straightness, splendour and strength combine in the simile of 'the cedars of God' which tell forth in measure the majesty and the mystery of the man now glorified in heaven.[26]

10. His Mouth – is most sweet: v.16.

Finally, she refers to His palate [Heb.chen], translated 'taste' in 2.3, where all that He was, as an 'apple tree', was sweet to her. Here, as in 7.9[10], the word is translated 'mouth'. She is not referring to the external shape of His lips, but to the sweetness, or

---

[24] Dan.2; Exod.26.37,32; John 16.8–11; [25] Isa.52.10; 53.2; Exod.24.17.
[26] Eph.1.21; 4.10; Phil.2.5–9; Ps.80.1; 89.19[20]; 1 Pet.2.3.

sweet things [Heb.mamtaqqim, plural] which she enjoys out of His mouth. She describes the surpassing sweetnesses which the breathings of His love bring to her. While He was here in the world, His mouth made known to her what He had heard from His Father, His mind and commandments. This was His divinely appointed role as the Mediator. How this had brought great joy to her.[27] Now, as her heavenly Bridegroom, He speaks to her heart of all that she is to Him. There is a closeness, an intimacy suggested in this that provides a fitting climax to her tenfold description of her Beloved. The Israel of God today may know Him thus, along with the power of His resurrection and the fellowship of His sufferings. Is not our glorified Lord altogether lovely to you?

---

[27] John 15.11,15; 17.7,8,13.

INDICES

INDICES

HEBREW WORDS AND PHRASES

Legend: 123 or 123,124 = page(s) number of entry
123 + 4,5 = page number and footnotes
123.56 = entry in footnote only
Word(s) indented belong to the same root as the normal margin
entry above

ALEPH

ʿebh 264.19
ʾabhibh 264.19
ʾabhobhoʿah ʿeleha 27.37: see ʿel
ʿeghoz 74 + 56, 57; 264.18; 265.20
ʾadhom 246
ʾadhoni 30 + 57
ʾahabh 34 + 10; 39 + 1; 40.5,6; 44.24;
    189.12; 322
ʾahabhah 41 + 8–14; 42 + 16; 44.24
  baʿahabhah 307
  beʿahabhathah 28
  weʿani ʿahabhteykha 306
  meʿahabhim 34 + 6
ʾahaloth 106–108 + 29–34
ʾahalim 106.29
ʿoth 126 + 4
ʿoz 311
ʿechadh 247.45
ʾachaz 76.62
  ʾachuzzah 76.62
ʾach li 231.35; 286 + 136
  kheʿach li 286.136
ʾachoth 231.35
  ʾachothi 231
  ʾachothi khallah 286.136: see kallah
ʾayyeh qinʿathekha 301; 303: see
  qinʿah
ʾayyal 60 + 36, 38
  ʾayyalah 60 + 37
  ʾayyeleth ʿahabhim 28
ʾayom 256.36
  ʿemah 254.36
ʾakhal 233; 234.43
ʾel 282.118
  ʾabhoʿah ʿeleha 27.37
  yabhoʿah ʿeleha 27.37
ʾalluph 29.50
ʿeleph 314
ʾim ... weʿim 288.149

ʿemah 254.36: see ʿayom
ʾamar 76
  ʾamarti 281.112
ʾani 309
ʾappekh 277
ʾerez 67 + 15–24
ʾaryeh 56
ʾesh 302.26
ʾish 22
  ʾish shelomi 312: see shalom
ʾishshah 22
  ʾesheth neʿurekha 29.50
  weʾesheth berithekha 29 + 50
  nathan ... leʿishshah 25.21: see nathan
  laqach ... leʿishshah 27.36
  baʿal haʾishshah 30 + 55, 56

****

BETH

be ... 307.41
bebhaʿal hamon 314
baghadh 31 + 71
bo 153
bachar 41 + 8–14
beten 88 + 19
  bitnekh 275
bayyom 310: see yom
bethʿabh 22; 24
  beth hayyayin 198
bekhirah 309.43
bakkepharim 102.8: see kaphar
beʿedhen 95.12: see ʿadhan
baʿal haʿishshah 30 + 55, 56
  baʿal neʿurekha 29.50
batsal 82.3
  chabhatstseleth 82 + 3, 4
baqash 215.30; 249.26; 268.39
barah 257.45
  barar 257.45
barosh 66 + 6–14

351

basam 116.2
  besem 116.2; 117.8
  bosem 116.2
  besammim 116–119 + 2–12
batteynu 195
bath nadhibh 266
batta'anughim 279
bath-rabbim 277

****

GIMEL

ge' gedholah 265.20
gan 94–98 + 1–23
  gan' edhen 95.13
  ginnah 95.8
gephen 76–79 + 63
geshem 132.38

****

DALETH

dabhaq 22; 29.52
daghal 200.47; 247
  deghel 199; 200.47
  dagalu (Akkadian) 200.47
dodh 45 + 27, 28; 46 + 32; 90.27
  dodhay 90.30; 284
  dodhi 45 + 27, 28; 80; 90.27, 30; 195;
    245 + 15; 281.115
  yedhidhoth 46 + 32
  yedhidhyah 47
dudha'im 89, 90 + 25, 30; 284
dalath ro'shekh 278

****

HE

hayyoshebheth 315
halakh 153; 282.119
har 178.22

****

ZAYIN

zebhach 112.60
zahabh 248 + 24; 340.2
zakkah 109.41, 43
zamir 55 + 10
  mizmor 55

****

CHETH

chabhatstseleth 88 + 3, 4: see batsal

chabher 316.66
  chabhertekha 29 + 50
choach 84 + 7
chul 271.51
  machol 271.51
  mecholah 271.51
  machalah 271.51
  Abel-mecholah 271.51
chazah 270 + 48
  chozeh 270
chazar bithshubhah 268.37
chittah 88, 89 + 17
chamadh 248
  machamaddim 248
chammah 130, 131 + notes
chammuqey yerekhayikh 274
chen 42
  matsa' chen be'eynay 311.49
chesedh 34; 42
charuzim 18
choreph 132.36
chashaq 41 + 8–14
chatham (Aramaic) 299.16
chotham 299
  chothemeth 299.17
  samtikha kachotham 300

****

TETH

tum'ah 31.67
  nitma'ah 31 + 67

****

YODH

yedhidhoth 46 + 32: see dodh
yedhidhiyah 47: see dodh
yadha' 27.36; 42 + 17
Yah 302.28
yom 131 + 31, 32
  bayyom 310
  leruach hayyom 154.3
  sheyyapuach hayyom 154.3
yonah 53; 54 + 2–4; 225
  yonathi 54 + 5–9; 226
yoreh 132.38
  moreh 132.38
yayin 76, 79 + 63
  beth hayyayin 198
ya'adh 127.10
  'edhah 127.10
  mo'edh 127–130 + notes

ya῾alath chen 28
yapheh 190.13; 195 + 30
 yaphah 190.13; 252 + 33; 279 + 130
yatsa῾ 283 + 120
yaradh 132.38; 250 + 27

****
KAPH

ki 300
kallah 230 + 32
kallu 17.30
kaphar 283 + 124; 306 + 38
 kepharim 283.124
 bakkepharim 102.8
 kopher 102, 103 + 8–11
 Kephar Nachum 102.8
karah 306 + 38
karkom 104, 105 + 21, 22
kerem 76, 77 + 63
 karmi shelli 315
kethem 248 + 24; 339; 340.2

****
LAMEDH

labhan 108.35
 labhen 108.35
 lebhanah 108.35; 130, 131 + notes
 lebhonah 108–110 + 35–49;   109.40;
  130.27
 Lebhanon 130.27
lehabhah 303.30
 shalhebheth Yah 302
lo 305
lun 283
laylah 131 + 33–35
lamadh 287.142
 lamedh 15.21
 telammedheni 287
laqach ... le῾ishshah 27.36
 wayyeqqech 27.37
laqat 251 + 30

****
MEM

meghedh 69.28; 285 + 130
mah ... wemah 288.149
 mah yaphith 279
 mah na amt 279

mohar 25 + 17
moreh 132.38
maweth 303
 khammaweth 301
mizmor 55.10
machol 271.51: see chul
 mecholah 271.51
 machalath 271.51
 Abel-mecholah 271.51
machamaddim 248: see chamadh
machaneh 272 + 56, 57
 machanayim 272 + 56, 57
mayim rabbim 303
 bha῾u mayim ῾adhnaphesh 304
 ba῾thi bhema amaqqey mayim 304
 ki ta῾abhor bammayim 304
 mimmayim rabbim 303
 mimma amaqqey mayim 304
 shibboleth mayim 304
malqosh 132.38
minchah 112.60
mo῾edh 127–130 + notes: see ya῾adh
me῾im 242 + 8; 345
ma῾al 31 + 69
me῾unnaghah 252.34
matsa῾ 215.31; 249.26; 311 + 48, 49
 matsa῾ chen be῾eynay 311.49
mitspeh 277.94: see tsaphah
mar 110–113 + 50–63
 mor 110.51
mar῾ah 68.22: see ra῾ah
 mareh 68.22
merkhabh 266.26: see rekhebh
 merkhabhah 266 + 26
merqachim 287.145: see reqach
marar 178 + 25
mishmar 173.10: see shamar
 mishmereth 173.10
mattan 25.17; 306 + 38: see nathan

****
NUN

na῾ah 190.13
 na῾wah 252 + 34
 na῾weh 190.13
na῾aph 34.7
nadhabh 267.32
 nadhabhah 267.32

353

qetsi`ah 106.26
qasheh 301

****
RESH

ra`ah 68.22; 270 + 49
  ro`eh 68.22
  mar`ah 68.22
  mar`eh 68.22
ro`shekh 278
  dalath ro`shekh 278
rebhabhah 247
rabhats 57 + 18
rahabh 255
ruach haqqadhim 133.41
  ruach zil`aphoth 133.41
reach 121–124 + notes
  reach nichoach 122.24, 29
  haricho 123 + 34
rachel 59 + 25, 26
racham 42
rekhebh 266.26
  merkhabh 266.26
  merkhabhah 266.26
rimmon 72, 73 + 44–55
ra`ah 57 + 17; 58.21; 147.11; 234.44;
    251.29
  rea 45 + 26
  re`ah 45.26; 245.15
  re`i 45 + 26; 245 + 15
ra`yah 245.15
  ra`yathi 45 + 25; 194 + 26
raphaq 296
ratsah 253.35
  ratson 253.35
  Tirtsah 253.35
raqqah 73.51
reqach 287.145
  roqeach 287.145
  merqachim 287.145

****
SIN

seh 59
samtikha kachotham 300: see chatham

****
SHIN

she`ol 302.24
She`ar Yashubh 269
shibboleth mayim 304
shaghach 270.49

shadhayikh 276
shubhi 268
  chazar bithshubhah 268.37
shu`alim 56
shazaph 190.14
shir 47 + 35
  shirah 47.35
  shir hashshirim 48
shakhabh 27.36
shakhar 233; 234.43
shalhebheth Yah 302: see lehabhah
shalom 270 + 47; 311–13
  Shalom `Achshav 312
  `ish shelomi 312
Shulammith 269; 312
Shelomoh 269.43; 312, 313
  lishlomoh 15.21
shemekha 18; 120
shemen 18; 119, 120
  shemenekha 120
  shemen turaq 120

****
SHIN

shamar 173.10: 174 + 13
  shomrim 173
  mishmar 173.10
  mishmereth 173.10
shemesh 130, 131 + notes
shor 275
  sharrekh 275
shesh 83.6
shoshan 83.6
  shoshanah 83–86 + 6–15
  shoshanim `edhuth 85
  shushan 83.6
shathah 233; 234.43

****
TAW

te`enah 70, 71 + 35–43
tor 55 + 11,12
telammedheni 287: see lamadh
tel 341.3
  taltallim 341 + 3
Tamar 74–76 + 58–60
  tomer 75.58
  timorah 75.58
tappuach 69, 70 + 29–34
Tirtsah 253.35: see ratsah
teshuqah 91.32; 282.118

INDEX OF GREEK WORDS AND PHRASES

SUBJECT INDEX

A

Aaron's anointing a figure, 117.9

Abraham, God's special friend, 189.12, Sarah owned him lord, 30, named his son, 30, sought wife for his son, 24, his love for Isaac, 40.6; 168, enjoyed God's love, 42.15, God's covenant with him and embryo nation, 171.7; 188f, a blessing to all families of earth, 316, and the God of glory, 188f; 322

Absalom and his sister Tamar, 75.59

Access to Father now for Jew and Gentile, 256.42

Achsah's wedding present, 25.17

Adam names all, his authority, 30, his union with Eve, a mystery, 33; 144.7; 168.2; 246, a type of Last Adam, 33

Adjuration refrains, 60.30; 61; 63.49

Adulteress, Israel as a spiritual, 34.7

Adultery, forbidden, 31.64f, swift and severe judgment of, 30.60, may be committed by betrothed, 25.22; 30f.61 and in marriage bond, 30.60, stalks unchecked today, 34, figuratively used of Israel, 34.7, spiritual leads to physical, 35.14, Israel's an offence to God, 34; 36; 37.22

Advents, first falls between Messiah's

eisodos and *exodos*, 219, foundation laying, in lowly grace, 282, submissive, sacrificial, 273, second, of Messiah in glory, 264–7; 282, when Israel is saved and shares in His glory, 273f

Age, this and the coming, 300

Agriculture, cycle matches festivals programme, 127; 129; 137

Aijalon, meaning, 60, name of a Levitical city, and of city in Zebulun, 60.38, also of river, 72.46

Allegory, Song viewed as by many Jews and Christians, 144f; 169f, objections to this approach, 144f.8. Differs from typology, 145f. Ezekiel uses, 308f.42, one use of word in NT, 145.8

Almighty, The, a fount of blessing, 276.83

Aloes, tree, word, all refs to in OT, 106f.29, associated with myrrh, 107, word a hapax in NT, 107.31

Amos, prophesies Lord's bounty, 80; 96

Analyses of Song, basic, 152, showing Poem 4 as parenthetic, 160, general, 159.61, in detail, 161–4, some notes on, and reason for differences, 164f

Angels, hosts surround God's throne, 247.21, Jacob made aware of them,

357

drawn upon to describe, 73. Used more of women in the Bible, 194.*28*, the law cannot produce, 274, destroyed by drudgery, 313, ashes to be exchanged for, 86, the Shulammite's superlative, 197, and tenfold, 272–9. Of the Lord put on Israel, 86; 194.*29*, Israel's under yoke of kingdom, 279, Israel's is an exceeding, 36. The king's is in the Song, 195.*30*. Nation saw none in God's Servant, 198.*42*. Jesus' superlative, 229

Beginning, in light of the end, 96; 131; 265.23; 296

Belly, word and uses, 88.*19*; 275

Beloved, 335f, word bound up with love theme, 45; 46.*30, 31*, is her frequent description of him, 45.27; 245.*15*, glowingly and uniquely described by her, 57; 244; 339ff. Messiah's glory excels Solomon's, 68. His initiatives, 156f; 205, he comes down to see, 261, and determines to apprehend her – 'I wills', 281. Dual role of in Song, 147. See Appendix 1, 335f

Beth-haggan, near modern Jenin, 94.*1*

Bethlehem, ruler to come forth from, 175; 298, place of Jesus' birth, 175, Golgotha's shadow cast as far as, 112

Betrothal, word, 25.*20*. Occasion of NE couples' first real encounter, 144, formal and binding, 24ff, committed father to give girl to wife, 25.*21*. Joseph/Mary instance, 26.*25*. Israel's to the Lord, 33

Bible, theocentric character of, 40.*5*, message of, man is not able, 42, various levels of understanding, 146

Biblical imagery, uses of things in simile, metaphor, typology/eschatology, 65; 80.*83*

Birds, in the Song, 53ff, singing heralds summer, 135; 210

Black, maiden confesses herself to be, 78; 190, advance in self-understanding, 83. Beloved's hair, as a raven, 55

Blessing, God's bestowed in harvest, 88. Jacob spoke of Joseph's from the Lord, 276.*83*. Israel to be made a, 85f.

God's present, on election of grace, 244; 257, world wide in character, 251, and eternal, 257

Blindness, affecting part of Israel now, 276.*92*, spiritual, of many of Israel's leaders, 226.*30*. Divine miracle alone can remove, 226, demands Messiah's ability, 226.21; 276. Seven instances of Jesus removing, 226.22; 277.*91*, one two-stage removal of, 226.*18*. Developing spiritual perception after removal of, 227.

Boaz, wealthy man, 169; 186, purchased Ruth as wife, 306.*38*, marriage typologically significant, 168f; 306.*38*. Name of pillar in porch of Temple, 73.*50*; 85

Body, God prepared for our Lord a, 123, He delighted to serve God in His, 123.*30*, now has a glorified, 249. Viewed spiritually, 345f

Breakdown, in marriage relations, 30ff, in relations between man and God, 32, in marriage relationship between the Lord and Israel, 32f

Breasts, particular emphasis in Song, all references, 276.*82*, simile for affections, 228, metaphorical of consolations of Israel in Isaiah, 276.*84*

Bridal tent, where marriage consummated, 27.*37*

Bride, word, uses in Song, 230.*32*, introduced in First Advent section, 230, Adorned for wedding, 26, veiled, 26.*29*, awaits bridegroom's coming, 26, comes out to meet him, 26, with her companions, 26.*31*, taken to bridegroom's house, 26. Typologically important ones, 167ff. Similes for, 98f, two sevenfold portraits of, 254f. Israel as, intimately associated with her Messiah/Bridegroom, 150, yet to be adorned with jewels as, 230f.*34*. Used metaphorically of church, 231.*36*, which is also a city, 257.*44*

Bride-price, not contemned, 305f. *See under* Compensation

Bridegroom, decked with garland, 26, goes out to meet bride, accompanied by his friend and companions,

26, brings bride to his home, 26. In Song represents King Messiah, 150. In simile of Lord's future joy over Israel, 274.67. Building a bride today, 231.36

Bring out/in, beginning guarantees the end with God, 265.23. *See under* Beginning

Brother(s), *see* Family. Responsible for sister where no father, 310. Her's over-demanding at first, 190; 212f, at last appreciate what grace has done, 308ff. She could wish her Beloved is her brother, 285. Resurrected Messiah called His own brethren, 285

Budded(ing), word, all uses in Song, and elsewhere, 265.21, land as bursting into life, 283

Burnt offering, daily, and accompanying offerings, 120, a basic divine requirement, 127.12

C

Calamus, word, main uses in OT, 105.23f, all references, 105.24, what it is, 105.25, used in perfumes, 105

Calendars, take count of days, 126, lunar months, 127; 128.17ff, solar years, 126; 128.16. Israel's is a lunar/solar, complications, 128.19, sacred extends over seven month cycle, the time-scale of divine purpose, 129; 137

Call of God, to Abraham, 189, to the nation as forsaken, 38, to return from the Exile, 206–10, from the Diaspora, 307f

Canaanite, and Mesopotamian love poetry corrupting, cultically based, 143. Pantheon, a corrupting influence, 43

Canon, Song's place in, rejected by some, 143, justified, 137, primarily because of sacred significance, 149.13. Song's place in should influence interpretation, 145

Captivity, Israel restored from, 80. *See under* Call of God

Carmel Range, references in Song, 15.17 terminates Sharon Plain on N, 15; 82,

beautiful and impressive, 15. Used in similes, 278

Cedar, the word in the Song, 67.16, identified, 67.15, described, 67f, stately, glorious and fragrant, 311, the wood of palaces and temples, 67.18f; 195. Lebanon famous for, and became a synonym for, 67.21. A simile of majesty, 196, and for Israel and the righteous, 67.20. Used metaphorically of the sister's displayed glory, 311

Ceremonial, of holy anointing, in OT, 105; 106.26, of holy incense, in OT, 109.40–46, of Christendom, 108.37. Apart from obedience it is unacceptable, 109.47

Change(d), Greek word in Psalm titles for 'lilies', 86.9, 11. In future, Israel to be, 86.9, dramatically, 273; 275, by her God, 264

Chariots, word, all uses in Song, 266.26, Pharaoh's, a matchless force, 56; 191f, Pharaoh's doomed at Reed Sea, 56.15

Chiefest, word, all OT uses of verb and noun, 199.47, as unique rallying centre, 247

Children, an heritage of the Lord, 28, to be trained up in fear of the Lord, 28

Choice, one, meaning of words, 257.45. Samson's, of a woman, 24. God's, of Israel to be His wife, 33, God's, and His love for Israel, 41

Christ, *see* Messiah

Christological approach to Scriptures essential, 285

Church, union of Christ and, mirrored by Adam and Eve union, 144. Fathers viewed Song as allegory concerning Christ and, 144f. Revealed by Jesus to Peter, 227.24. First established at Jerusalem, opposition resulted in expansion, 240. Titles of local churches, 251, as flock, 58.21. Christ's headship and, 340.1, Christ gathers at His coming, 252.31.

Cinnamon, word, Hebrew/Greek, all uses of, 106.26, description and uses, 106, one of ingredients of anointing oil, 106.28

City, supplies many similies in Song,

19. Of the great King, 46, Messiah entered, 75.*58*, the inviolable, to fall, 176.*17*, its sanctuary to be destroyed, 243. Two chosen as similes of loved one, 252f

Cleansing, Lord's, better than that of water, 246, purging sins and conscience, 230.*31*

Cleave, word, 22; technical term in covenant making, 29.*52*, God calls Israel to, 43

Clothe, God does, the field, and us, 87. With salvation, 230f

Clusters, word, all references in Song, 76.*61*; 280.*111*, used of dates, grapes and henna, 76.*61*, specifically of henna, 78.*72*

Come, word, frequently with another to heighten appeal, 282.*119*, in appeal to her, and him, 282, quickly, 317.*69*

Comely, word, all references to, 190.*14*, all uses considered, 252.*34*

Commandments of the Lord, Israel to keep. Of Christ, the church to keep, 43. Keeping, the means of enjoying the land, 69.*25*, and of abiding in God's love, 43

Companion, word, in Song etc, 316.*66*, of wife of one's youth, 29, used of his and hers, 316

Compassion, word for God's, 42

Compensation, word, 25.*17*, bride price paid to father, 25, what the Lord gives for His own, 306

Compilation, the Song as a, 141.*2*; 161.*7*

Consummation, of marriage, 22, is to take to wife, 27.*36*; 220, to go in to, 27.*37*. The sevenfold delight at, 233f

Cool of day, word, when shadows lengthen into night, 154.*3f*

Countryside, as a cradle of love, 46, quietness, beauty, privacy of, 261; 283f

Covenant, character of marriage, 30; 50, making, cleaving, technical terms, 29.*52*, relationship in marriage, projected in Song, 29; 46. Binds God to Israel, in steadfast love, 33f; 36; 41f, everlasting, 37; 308, unconditional/conditional, 214.*24*. God remembers His, 37.*23*; 308, confirming His faithfulness to, 295, called upon to have respect to, 209.*12*, His mercy and, 43. Rainbow a sign of Noah's, 126.*4*. God's, with Abraham, 171.*7*, irrevocable character of, 214.*24*; 256, passed on to Issac/Jacob, 189, to be established at the end, 316. God's with David, 17; 180, David and the ark of, 67; 122; 283, Temple as epitome of, 198f. The new, established by Messiah, 230, quaranteed and mediated by Messiah, 230.*31*, to be enjoyed by all Israel, 263; 271; 285.*132*; 308, in which all know the Lord, 287.*143*. The new, and Edenic hopes, 96, and the Lord's Supper now, 285.*132*. Of peace, realized at last, 312.*53*. Servant given as a, 294.*14*, Israel as people of, 124

Creation, purpose of God in, for man and woman, 21; 122; bound up with man and his fortunes, 129, sensitive association between man and, 69.*26*. Cameo, an embryo for future of the race, 22. Fourth day of, and function of the lights, 125.*1f*. God's purpose in, to glorify Himself, 33, His purpose for, to be achieved, 96.*17*, its groans to cease, Israel to be restored, 69.*27*; 98; 172, to be redeemed, 91, and nature and the nation to be in perfect harmony, 283f; 288

Cross, *see* Golgotha. Myrrh, frankincense and the, 178f. Lord went to, for His own, 229

Cruel, the word, 301

Curse, God's, thorns as evidence, 84; 197, executed on proven adulteress, 31, and on those who curse Abraham, 189

Cycle(s), of sun/moon, 126.*5*; 127.*15*; 128, of seasons, 125–38, evidence of God's faithfulness, 130. Of time, seasons apparent in Song, 130; 137. In the Song, are progressive, 151, and bring God's final purpose closer, 107, three of, are associated with Lord's first advent, 108. Love, of hart and hind, 62.*47*, key place of, 63. Of nature and salvation history are associated, 128

D

Damascus, in Syria, 15, implies expansiveness of Israel, 277.*95f*

Dance(ing), word, 271f.*51–55*, and singing at weddings, 26.*32*, in celebration of Israel's fulfilment, 271

Dangers incessant through Song, 211f; 311f

Daniel, and cutting off of Messiah, 243.*10*

Date(s), of Song, range of proposed, 14.*5*, tenth century BC, 13.*4*

Date, fruit of the date-palm, 75, honey produced from, 75, clusters in simile, 280.*111*

Daughter(s), of Pharaoh's dowry, 25.*17*. Prince's, Shulammite described as, 19; 47.*34*; 273. Of Jerusalem, 238; 244; 249. Of Zion, 219; 223f. Of multitudes, a title for Israel in future, 277. Of Zelophehad, 253.*35*

David, the son of Jesse, 17, taken from sheepfolds, to be shepherd of God's people, 147, super-warrior, 15; 247, enemies scattered by God, 265.*24*, vastness of kingdom, 277.*96*. Payed bride-price, 25.*19*, son Solomon, 47; 147, daughter Tamar, 75.*59*, his Shunammite companion, 269.*42*. God's covenant with, 180, made him a Messianic symbol, 268.*39*, his prayer realized only in Messiah, 17.*30*. Jesus the Messiah, son of, 224.*11f*

Day, word, 131.*31*, and night, 125. Of gladness, 24, of king's espousals, 131; 219f; 223. All waits dawn of new, 130, when God remembers covenant of days of her youth, 308, and the sister is spoken for, 131; 307–13. Of the Lord, wonders during, 126.*8*; 131.*29*, witness during, 131

Dead Sea, Engedi on, 15; 102.*5*, amazing changes of, in kingdom age, 79.*73*

Deal treacherously, word, uses, 31.*71*

Death, affects body, often in parallelism with Sheol, 302.*24*, paradise the abode after in Judaism, 97.*21*, a power we cannot withstand, 301. The phrase strong as, 301. Messiah's, its sacrificial character, 229f. 29–31; 178f. Jesus glorified has the keys of, 302.*24*

Deer, word, of male and female, 60.*36f*

Defiled, word, seven occurrences, 31.*67*, used to describe adulteress, 31

Delights, Messiah finds plurality of in His own, 224–8, in nation, 279

Deliver(er), Lord came down to, at Exodus, 265.*23*, He is yet to, out of deep waters, 304, to come out of Zion, 263; 278.*102*. He will bring blessing to nation at end, 296, and be peculiarly close to her, 296f.*11*

Design, evident in composition of Song, 151–4, reveals literary art of author, 151, not a compiler's skill, 161.*7*

Desire, word, meaning and use, 282.*118*, 3 Biblical uses of, 281f, words in Song, 248.*23*, in the OT, 91.*32*, an idiom for a strong, 285.*135*. A husband's toward wife, 29, the Beloved's for her, 90; 279–81. Israel's, 279. Shulammite's, for uninhibited pure love, 286–9

Development, in the Song, 154–59

Dews, a seasonal indicator, 52; 135, a great summer boon, 134, condense on Carmel and Galilean mountains, 134. Emblem of Spirit's ministry, 241f

Diaspora, since destruction of Herod's Temple the longest, 176, will cease when Messiah, Kingdom come, 284; 307

Disciples, taught to take up cross, 59, sent out to lost sheep of nation, 237f, blessed by opening up of OT, 285. Fearful of Jews after Jesus' death, 231, then thrilled by resurrection appearances, 231, when they tasted His love, 232. Uniquely set apart for Him, 231, enquire re. future of Israel, 237, sent to Jew first, 240, commission extended to world, 238

Divorce, OT legislation re., 23.*10*. Nauseous to God, 29, permitted by

Moses, not commanded, 29. Israel not divorced by the Lord, 38. Jesus and, 30.*54*

Doe, female gazelle, all references, 60.*32*, wrongly translated roe, 60, with hind, another female species, in adjuration refrains, 61

Door, metaphorical use of, 310

Dove, word, 53f, a rock pigeon, 54.*2*. Similes re., 54, eyes as, 54.*8*; 225f. My dove, endearing term for bride, 54.*5*; 241.*3*

Dowry, only Biblical instances, 25.*17*

Drama, Song as, with real people, 142f

Drink(ing), *see* Eating and

Drink offering, accompanied daily burnt offering, 122, revealed Lord's unbroken joy in God, 122

Duty, can interfere with love, 56; 212f; 313

E

Eating/Drinking, motif, words, uses, nuances, 234.*43f*. Spiced wine at wedding banquet, 119.*12*. At inauguration of covenant, 234.*44*. At the Lord's Supper, anticipation of an eschatological banquet, 234.*45*; 287f

Eden, word, Heb/Grk, 95.*12,13*. Original conditions there, 98, peaceful and secure, 57, garden par excellence, of delights in OT, 95.*11, 13*. Its blessedness to be restored, even multiplied at end, 57.*16*; 316

Egypt, wisdom of, 18, Solomon's links with, 16.*22*. As house of bondage, 42, Israel liberated from, 41.*9*; 42; 193

Egyptian, love poetry genre, 16.*22*, nearest parallel to Song, 143. Classified list of nature found, 65.*2*. Spoils taken when Israel left, 192

Eisodos, Messiah's first advent, 177.*20*. *See* Incarnation

Elders, a shepherd role in NT, 58.*21*

Election, closely associated with God's love, 41.*9*. Of those beloved for fathers' sakes, 278.*102*. Of grace, 244;

257; 262, before foundation of world, 256

Embalming, substances used in, 107f.*31*

Endearing expressions, 'my ...' multiplicity in Song, 166. His for her, 45.*25*; 54.*5*; 207f; 230.*32*; 231.*35*; 241.*3f*. Her's for Him, 124; 231.*35*

Ended, meaning of in Ps. 72, 17.*30*

Enemies, destroy city and sanctuary, 242.*10*. David's scattered by God, 265.*24*

Engedi, all references, 78.*73*; on W. shore of Dead Sea, 15; 102f, description, history, 78f

Ephraim, used of N. Kingdom, 302, urged to go up to Zion, 150.*14*

Espousals, crowning day of Solomon's, 148; 223. The Lord's love and Israel's, 33.*3*; 36

Eve, relationship to Adam mirrors a nobler one, 143.*7*, her sin brought sorrow, 91, her desire towards her husband, 91.*31*; 282.*118*

Evening/morning in Genesis 1, 130f

Everlasting, God's love as, 37; 40; 41.*2*; 150.*14*. Covenant, 37; 308. Joy, Israel's portion, 314

Ewes, word and all uses, 58f.*26*

Exile, Israel's return from, 206–10

Exodus, Israel's from Egypt, 42; 191f; 198; 302; 323, and Pharaoh's chariotry, 56.*15*; 191f; 263, and revelation of Yahweh, 302, guaranteed the inheritance, 129. Typology, and the prophets, 208. Return from Babylon as an, 209. Messiah's, after finishing His work, 177.*20*. His second advent as another, 265; 331

Eyes, range of literary use of, 227.*23*. Of the loved one, 225, overcome the Beloved, 255. For Church Fathers and Jewish writers, 145; 194. As balanced spiritual perception, 225–28; 227.*24*. Things as seen by the Lord, 312. Restoring sight of, a Messianic work for Rabbis, 277

Ezekiel, and marriage motif, 36f, and two-sister allegory, 308, and future of David's house, 68.*23*, and beauty of Israel, 194.*29*

F

Face, turned to God, 36. Loved one's in Beloved's description, 224. Glory of God in Jesus Christ's, 245

Fair(est), word and synonyms, 190.*13*; 194.*27*, as formula of commencement, 153; 155; 252. Emphasizing beauty of maiden, 153, all, as superlative phrase, 229

Faithfulness, wife's to husband, 31, of God to the covenants and to Israel, 33f; 130; 295.*6*

Faithlessness, word for, 32.*71*. Of Israel to God, 37

Family(ies), terms used in love relationships, 45f. 26–31; 230.*32*; 231.*35*; 241.*3*; 261; 286.*136*. Parents' roles in, 28. All earthly blessed through Abraham, 171.*7*

Father, God as, sent His Son, 40, well-pleased in His Son, 123.*31*, revealed His Son to babes, 227.*24*, knows our needs, 87. Throne of, shared by Messiah now, 262, believers have access to, 256. Kingdom of, Messiah's joy in, 288.*147*. Idolater confesses asherah as, 36

Father(s), house of, Hebrew phrase, 22, head of house, 24; 28.*46*, arranges marriage, 24, with mother trains up child, 28. Of nation, God's covenant with, 171.*7*; 256, Messiah confirmed God's promises to, 244

Fauna, in the Song, 53–63

Favour, word, 42, to find, theme, 311.*49*. Blessing of God's, 54.*6*, loss of God's, 54.*7*

Fawns, young gazelle males, 62, until mature under mother's care, 62; 297

Fear, of the Lord, Messiah's delight in, 123.*34*, child trained up in, 28. The disciples; of the Jews, 232. In future the land to know none, 284

Feast, of joy at wedding, 26f.*34,35*; 233f. 43–5. *See* Banquet

Feeding, word, 251.*29*. The flock, 57.*17*, as ministry of Messiah, 57.*21*, the role of a ruler, 147.*11*; 251.*29*

Feet, word and verb, 274.*68*

Festival(s), generally, 128f, the three great annual, 274. Of the Passover, 129.*20*; 197. Of Weeks, 275.*80*. Of Tabernacles, 287. Of the New Moon, 128.*17*

Field, flowers and grasses of, 81–91, home of beautiful hinds, 283, lilies of, 87, clothed by God, 87.*15*, to exult when Lord comes, 283.*122–3*

Fig, green, word for, 71; 135. The tree and its fruit, word for, 70.*35*, description, 70f. Used mostly figuratively, 71, and often in eschatological contexts, 71.*41*. It refused kingly office, 72.*42*. Lord's use in His teaching, 72.*43*

Figures of speech, in simile and metaphor, 65, used in different contexts, 65; 93. Drawn from human relations, 33–38; 44, fauna, 53–63, and flora, 65–80; 93

Finding, word, uses, 215.*31*; 249.*26*, place in drama of Poems 2, 4, 172f. Many found Messiah at His birth, 175.*15*; 214–16.*32f*, at opening of His public ministry, 175.*16*; 216. Theme climaxes in Poem 6, 311. *See* Sought

Fir Tree, word and species, 66.*6,7*, often used in parallel with cedar, 66.*8*; 195, description, 66. Significant uses of, 66.*9–14*

Fire, word, 302.*26*. Israel not burned in, 304. Attends divine appearances, 302. *See* Flame

Firstfruits, of barley, 127.*13*. Name of a festival, 129. Israel of God now as, 98

Flame, word and kindred, 303.*30*

Flesh, and bone, 29.*53*. To become one, 22.*6*; 29; 233

Flock, most common word, 58.*22*, another word for, 58.*23*, used metaphorically, 58.*23*, of Israel, 59.*27*, and churches, 58.*21*

Flood, waters of, bring judgment and salvation, not to cover earth again, 99, Israel to be brought through, 304

Flowers, general, 81–9, the word, 82.*2*. Spring varieties, description and distribution, 81f, shrivel and fade, a figure of the transitory, 81f.*1*

Form and Distribution, of stanzas, 165f

Formulae, of commencement, 152, of termination, 151f

Fountain, as metaphor for maiden, 95, and of those who believe now, 95.*10*. *See* Waters

Foxes, word, 56, and their counterpart, 213

Fragrance theme, 115–24

Frankincense, word family, 108.*35*, in the NT, 110.*48*; in the Song, 108f.*38f*, and OT, 109.*40–6, 49*. Not native to Israel, 108. Description, 108.*36*; 109.*39*. One of spices of holy incense, 179. Concerns Messiah's life and death for God, 112f; 179f

Friend, word, 189.*12*. Word Beloved uses most to address her, used only once of Him, 245.*15*. Used of Abraham as God's, 189.*12*, of a man's wife, 29.*50*. With pronominal suffix, 'my love', in the Song, 45.*25*; 189.*12*. For friend of bridegroom see 26.*30*

Fruit, word, 69.*28*; 285.*130*. First signs of, farmer first to partake, 134, ingathering at Tabernacles, 127.*15*. Of vine dried, 137. Beloved's is sweet to her, 137, hers is to be for Him, 136; 280.*111*; 281. To be prolific in kingdom age, 296, Israel to enjoy as one of God's boons, 150.*14*. Of vine, enjoyed by Messiah in kingdom, 288.*147*. Righteous bring forth in old age, 280.*108*. Of the womb is with the Lord, 90

G

Galilee, mountains of Lower and Upper, 134, Plain of Gennesaret in, 74.*56*. Enjoys boon of dews in summer, 134. Village of Shunam in, 146; 219. The place where love cycle opened, 298, and chief sphere of Jesus' ministry, 223.*5f*

Garden(s), word, 94.*1, 7*, distinguish use of singular and plural, 94; 250; 95.*9*; 99; 250; 316. See for detail 93–9. Planned, planted, protected, 94,

variety found in, 94; 101, kings often had beautiful, 94.*2*, Solomon's, 94.*6*. Bride both garden and a fountain of it, 94f, her own yet his, 79.*78*; 95.*8*. Of the Lord, is Eden, paradise, 96f.*18–22*. In similes re Israel, and forecasts re her future, 96.*14–18*. Typical Arab garden today, 101

Gates, fruits laid up at for Him, 90. Israel's called Praise in kingdom age, 310f.*47*

Gather, word, 251.*30*. Lord doing so today from nations, 251, and also the church at coming, 252.*31*. Elect from E and W at Lord's second advent in glory, 252.*31*

Gazelle, confusion of translation, 60, male = roe, female = doe, 60f, details and description, 60f.*30f*, 34f, 40f. In similes in Song, 61.*45f*; 228; 251, in adjuration refrains, 60.*30*; 201; 288f

Gehenna, distinct from Sheol, 302.*24*

Genre, of Egyptian love poetry, 16.*22*. Of Song, 18

Gentiles, Messiah given as light to, 298, God taking a people out of, 251, Lord's present ministry to, 256. Fulness yet to be brought in, 263. Did not seek righteousness, 241, yet found Him, 242

Gethsemane, garden of, 94.*4*, in Kidron Valley, 265.*20*

Gifts, word, 25.*17*, for bride and parents, 306. Hosea stripped wife of, 34. Father gives daughter to wife, 25.*21*; 27. Shulammite to give to beloved, 284f

Gilead, great mountain range E of Jordan, 15; 60; 178.*24*; 219, where Mahanaim located, 272.*56*, goats on its slopes, 60. Balm of, word for, 116.*6*

Glory, Messiah's, seen even now, 245, to be seen by all in future, 196.*36*, in Messianic kingdom, 17. God bringing many sons to, 124. Of Solomon's, reign, 14; 19

Goats, word and description, 57ff. God appointed as sin offering, 59.*28*; 255.*39*. Hair black, used for tents and Tabernacle, and as simile for

the king captive, 273; 278. His as black as raven, 55; 340f

Hand, His, embraces her, 200; 288, sight of His moved her, 242; 344, myrrh from His upon her's, 242. His mighty to keep, filled to serve, 344

Harlot(ry), *see* Adultery

Harmony, between man and nature, 69.*26f*, between Israel and creation at end, 129.*22*; 312f

Harts, word, male fallow deer, 60.*36*, with roes (male gazelle) in similes of Beloved, 61, description, 60f, maturing, mating habits, 62.*47*; 297, figurative use of, 61.*39, 43, 44*

Heart, word, 242.*8*. Beloved knows thoughts of her, 18, spoke to assure her, 224. Her's moved when she saw his hand, 242. Jesus spoke to, 224

Henna, word and homonyms, 102.*8*; 124; 283, description, 78f.*73*; 102.*3*, found in land, 102.*6, 9*, uses of, 102, in simile, 78.*72*; 136

Hill(s), of Moreh, 146. Frankincense, and Golgotha, 109f; 179f; 229. Day/night temperature variation on, 133.*40*. As places where idolatry practiced, 36. In eschatological contexts 73.*54*

Hinds, female of fallow deer, 60.*37*; 61; 283, mating habits, 62f, linked with does in refrains, 60.*32*; 61; 201; 216

History, and the divine will, 129.*21*, and God's saving programme, 180; 188; 206; 221; 240f; 262f; 295f. Of Israel, main phases, 289; 321–31

Hold, word, 76.*62*. *See* Possession

Holiness, God's unsullied, 37, God's outraged, 35

Holy, One of Israel, 304. Of Holies, 48f. Anointing oil, 105f

Horse(s), word, 56.*14, 15*. Egypt famed for, 56, cannot save, 56.*15*, overthrown by the Lord, 192

Hosea, and development of marriage motif, 34f, learned to love as the Lord, 35.*15*; 306

House, meaning of plural, 195f. God's and the king's inseparable, 196. The righteous planted in the Lord's,

280.*109*. Maiden brought to the king's, 195. Mother's, 119.*12*, as the land of Israel, 175; 286f

Husband, role in marriage, 28, appreciation of wife, 28.*41*, suspecting wife's unfaithfulness, 31.*66*. And wife relationship in divine purpose, 168.*3*.

Israel's Maker is her, 34; 38

I

Imagery, dominant use of, 65. Drawn from Fauna, 53–63, from Flora, 65–124

Immanuel, as result of Incarnation, 175, the child born, the Son given, 286

Incarnation, of Messiah, Son of God, 175; 214ff, a mystery and miracle, 177

Inheritance, and land promise to Abraham, 189, of land of Israel, 70, in to which God brought nation, 192f; 254, and which Israel will enjoy at last, 283; 314f. Messiah Israel's hope of, 70, to take possession of it by the saints, 315, given nations for an, 314.*58*. Father's perpetuated to family through sons, 24. And the daughters of Zelophehad, 253.*35*

Interpretation of Song, difficulty of, 167.*1*. Jewish, 144; 169f. Various proposals, 141–50. Different levels to be recognized, 19, as literary bridge, 19

Isaac, wife sought for, 24, typologically important, 168

Isaiah, and instruction of Hezekiah, 71.*38*, significance of sons' names, 268f. And God's governmental ways with Israel, 242.*9*; 313f, describing Israel from feet to head, 273.*59f*. His use of marriage motif, 37f, salvation oracle, 304, and ministry of comfort, 266.*29*. Describes nation's return to the land, 268f.*40*, her future walls etc, 311.*47*, and God's glory upon her, 274.*67*

Israel, name of patriarch, nation, ten tribes, N. Kingdom, 70. Built through Rachel and Leah, 59.*25*. Beloved for fathers' sakes, 262, chosen to shew forth God's excellencies, 264, has princely prerogatives, 273, described as chief of nations, 150, of whom is the Messiah, 252. Vine/vineyard motif used for nation, 80.*80*. Also marriage motif for the nation loved, and her heart spoken to, 33f; 150; 225.*15*, there was pure, first love, 35f. God described her as mine, 36; 304, my people, 266.*29*, His beauty seen upon her, 36; 86; 273ff. Liberated from Egypt to cleave to, obey, serve, 42f. Brought into land 199.*45*, enjoyed her promised inheritance, 192–201; 323f, but she failed to reciprocate God's love, 37, was unfaithful to her God, 34; 37, was warned, 35, and put out of it, 34. Considered herself divorced, 34.*9*, forsaken, 38. Not treated by God as my people, 266.*28*. Exiled, 206, then her return facilitated, 206–10; 324f. Post-exilic characteristics, 210–14. Visited by her Messiah, 214ff; 325, and He was found by some at first advent, 215f. Majority did not respond to Messiah's appeal, 240; 242, not knowing time of their visitation, though challenged and warned by Lord and in Acts, 176f; 243. Religious still seek after their own righteousness, 241, and their house is left desolate, 176. Has experienced tragic two millennia, 243, yet miraculously preserved through centuries, 176. Though back in land today, 263, still no king, sacrifice, 176; 268. Nation to pass through trouble to triumph, 264.*14*, causing terror among nations, 254; 263f. God yet to speak to her heart, 225.*15*, assure her of His love, 304, pardon her iniquities, 278.*98*, through Messiah's death, 171.7, as Balaam saw her, 59.*28*. He will redeem, restore, 35.*15*, save, 150.*14*; 172; 263; 314, heal, 127.*9*, cause all to be righteous, 311. Messiah to be the consolation of, 175.*15*. She is to return to the Lord, 268f.*40*, to be discipled to the kingdom, 285.*134*, enjoy the

Lord's delight in her, 282.*118*, to grow as a lily, 86, like trees planted of Lord, 107; 311, be blessed and made a blessing, 86; 107; 264; 315, to blissfully and peacefully enter millennium, 99; 312, a suited partner to share Messiah's glory, 274.*73*, fruit of intimate relationship with Him, 124, when the feast of Tabernacles will find fulfilment, 127ff; 199. Prophecies re nation to be fulfilled, 176. Her beauty will be recognized, and no joy be lacking, 275. Her reconciliation brings harmony to creation, 69.*27f*, and the nations, 313. Her priestly ministry in the Millennium, 315.*63*

Israel, the land, 70, fruitful, 71.*37*, both beautiful and varied, 81, specially so in future, and which nation is chosen to inherit, 284; 311; 314f

Israel, Modern State of, 68, extensive cultivation, 75, achievements, 176, David's Tower in Jerusalem, 15.*15*. Hated/loved by many, 176, developed military prowess, 263. Orthodox call to secularists to make return, 268.*37*. Peace Now movement, 312. A prophetic pointer, 263

Israel, Servant of the Lord as embodiment of, 70; 298.

Israel of God, proof that hardness of nation only in part, 263, and it is not totally set aside today, 240; 262. Name given to remnant of nation saved today, 68.*24*; 241, witness of His grace among it, 237, a kind of first-fruits of the nation, 98, described in bridal term, 230, and represented in Poem 5, 241. Has found Messiah through trouble, 241, the veil having been taken away, 244, her eyes turn to the Lord, 255, her appreciation of Him surpasses all previous understanding, 244f; 257, seeing beauties in Him, 245, which nation fails to see, 248. It is precious to Messiah now, 252-7, enjoying present blessings, 252; 254, God's love, 241, satisfaction in the Lord, 256, along with persecution because of its faith, 257

J

Jachin, pillar in Solomon's Temple, 73.50; 85

Jackals, details re, 56, spoilers of vines, 147, demanding attention to duty, 212f

Jacob, The patriarch, love for Rachel, 168, served to meet bride-price, 25.19, beyond claims of duty, 58f; 168. Return from Haran, 15.18, to Mahanaim, 272, and the land, 168. Long, unhappy disciplinings, 190f, and then to Egypt with family, blessed Pharaoh, 191. Typological importance, 168, name changed to Israel, 272f, play on names after change, 255; 298. The nation, house of, rejected their God, 36, to be a day of trouble for, 176; 275, national ungodliness to be removed, 263, tribes of to be raised up, 298, a seed to come out of, to inherit land, 284.127, future blessing subject of singing, 150.14

James, and God's present work among nations, 251

Jealousy, word, negative and positive, 301, law of, 31.66. Lord's name is, 34.8; 301, He brooks no rival, 301.22

Jenin, modern town at entrance of Jezreel Valley, 15, means garden, 94.1

Jeremiah, used marriage motif to expose/denounce Judah, 35f, and of joy of celebration, 146. And the new covenant, Edenic hopes, 96, and uniting of divided nation, 312.54

Jericho, city of palms, 74.58; 219, and famous for balsam, 116.7

Jerusalem, in Song, 15.14, topography of, 15.15, elevated, attractive, 252.34, climate of, 133.40, and the wilderness contrasted, 222. Defences of, 19. David brings ark up to, 67.14. Daring Moabite raid aimed at, 79.73. Place God chose to place His name, 253f, yet to be chosen by Him, 299, the city of the great king, 46; 75.58, psalmist prays for peace of, 176. Unpalatable ministry of prophets to, 175f.

Jesus ascended to, 222f.7, wept over, 176.17, as capital of the Beloved, 219; 223.8; 253. Guilty of killing its own prophets, 176.

First church, of Jewish believers, there, 240, universal witness launched from there, 238

Jesus, The Messiah, Lord, Son of God, which see, 252. Visited Jerusalem and Galilee in His ministry, 223.5ff, knew what was in man, 18. And disciple He loved, 228.27, spoke to His own in Upper Room, 224ff. Spoke of sufferings at men's hands, 59, warning the nation, 242. Died for the nation, 251. Scriptures are concerning Him, 285.131

Jewel(s), on priest's breastplate, 274.72, simile of beauty, preciousness, 274

Jewish, Interpretations of Song, 144; 169f, Feliks re Song, 149. Apocrypha, and paradise, 97.21.

Believers, the founder members of church, 237f; 244, and witnesses in Acts, 233; 238; 240; 243, and also today, 245, part of God's new creation, 252. See under Israel of God

Jezreel Valley, 15; 94.1, Shunem overlooks, 269

John, The Baptist, called nation to repentance, 222.2, a similar ministry to be raised again in Israel, 295.7

John, The Beloved Disciple, 228.27

Jordan Valley, Gilead towers over, 60, date-palm cultivation in, 74.58

Joseph, firstborn of Rachel, 285.130, experienced brothers' hatred, 190f.17. Jacob's blessing of, 276.83, Moses' blessing of tribe, 285.130. Typological associations of, 169.4; 171; 191.18

Joseph, ben Messiah, 170ff

Joseph, of Aramathaea, and burial of Jesus' body, 107; 113

Judah, Jeremiah/Ezekiel pillory for sin, 36f, more privileged of two parts of nation, 308.42, to be reunited with N. Kingdom, 312.54, and inherit land, 284.127, and become the Lord's portion, 299.

Messiah sprang from, 298

Judaism, features of post-exilic, 210–14,

Rabbinic approach to Song, 169f, Rabbi Aqibha, 169, and paradise, 97.21. Orthodox, pleads for people's return to God, 268.37

Juice, word, noun and verb, 73f.54, literal and metaphorical use, 73; 287f. *See under* Eating and Drinking

K

Keepers, word, 314.59, Solomon leased vineyards to, 78, maiden made keeper of vineyards, and describes her charms as a vineyard not kept, 77f

Keys, to interpretation of Song, 171–180, in arrangement and cycles of seasons, 137, and mark-time nature of Poem 4, 159ff, and the flame of Yah, 302

Kidron Valley, 264f.20

King, and Solomon, 13.2f, who is the beloved, 19, retinue of mighty men, 132; 224. And shepherd roles interwoven, 58.21; 147.10, not a problem, 147ff. An itinerary to N resulted in meeting maiden, 147, his carriage brings her to wedding, 219

Israel's Lord and King also her Shepherd, 150. Jesus born king of Jews, 110.48, He is king of grace and glory, 222, of righteousness and peace, 267, rode into His capital city, 223.8, and is yet to rule over Israel, 91, who are to rejoice in Him, 272, and to be seen in His beauty, 195.30, 32. He is held in her tresses, 273.65

Israel has been without king for millennia, 176; 268, ct. Reuben and Gad, 277.93

Kings, brought spices to Solomon, 116.3, and are to come to Israel's rising, bringing gold/frankincense, and praises, 110.49; 314f

King's, garden, S of City of David, 265.20. Week, a Syrian wedding celebration, 142

Kingdom, N, capital of, 15.16; 253, S and United, capital of, 253. Of God, on earth in future, 262; 314.56. Of

Heaven, likened to treasure/pearl, 306. Israel a disciple to at end, 285.134. Messiah to drink wine in, 80.82; 234.45; 287f. Righteousness reigns in, though sin exists, 98. Edenic conditions in, 57.16; 96; 98.23; 197, anticipated by feast of Tabernacles, 129, glory God's end-purpose, 96.17, multiplied light in, 126f.9, each man sits under vine/fig in, 71.41

Kinsman, Boaz, an example, 89.23; 230.32. And Shulammite's desire, 286. *See under* Family Terms

Kinship, terms, 231.35. *See* Kinsman

L

Lamb, Servant of Lord as a, 59, praised in heaven as, 247. In Kingdom to dwell with wolf, 57.16

Land, God gave to Israel, 80, guaranteeing it to her at Exodus, 129, and bringing her into it, 188. Flower-strewn in spring, 82, obedience the key to its fruitfulness, 68f, bounty not enjoyed by Reuben/Gad, 277. Note 'our land', 156. Post-exilic period in, 206ff. Messiah came to, 216. Sphere where Israel yet to arouse, find, Messiah, 298, He is to be given to people to raise up land, 298.14. To become hers at last, 315.63, according to proportions of Abrahamic promise, 277; 314f, as planted there by God, 80, as His goal for her, 265.23. It is to be married, 285.133, land and people then in concert, 284. To be surpassingly bountiful, 96; 283, the glory of Lebanon will be given to it, 196.36, God's blessing will make it flourish, 283

Leah, the firstborn daughter, 309.43, tender eyes, 225, her wedding gift, 25.17, hated by Jacob, 90, hoped to regain his love, 41.7, her womb opened by Lord, 89, with sister Rachel built house of Israel, 59.25, mother of 6 boys, 90, was called blessed, 257.46.

Beloved, 94–7; 229–32, and a blessing to others, 95; 232f. As the nation within the nation, 150

Man, God's purpose for seen at creation, 21f; 122, began in garden, 95.*11*, and association with word Woman, 22. For Man/Woman relations, see chap. 2. His love to God and fellows, 39, his fall and bondage to sin, 42

Man, of sorrows, 113, child, 294.*14*

Mandrake, word, 90.*27*; 284f, details, 89ff; 136; 284f

Mar(a), meaning and uses, 110.*51*

Mare, feminine singular use, 56.*14*, in contrast to stallions, 56; 191f; 263

Marriage, see chap. 2. To be kept pure, 31.*64f*; 144.*6*. A royal, 46.

Solomon's typological, 232ff. Unions with typological dimension, 167ff, and specific divine purpose, 168.*3*.

And the Lord's relationship with Israel, see chap. 3 for motif in prophets.

It involves a mystery, 144.*7*. A boon, 144, involving cares, 23.*10*, and responsibilities, 28.

Sevenfold metaphorical consummation of in Song, 233f

Martial metaphors in Song, chariots, 191f; 266.*26*, banner, 200.*47*; 254, mighty men, 222; 224, terrible as, 254.*36*; 263ff, willing people, 267.*32*

Mary, anointing the Lord, 107.*17ff*

Meal offering, 122f

Messiah, last Adam, second Man, 246.*18*, Son of man, 247, greater than Isaac, 168, than David, 304f, than Joseph, 171.*8*, than Solomon, 86; 245.

Out of Israel, 286, of tribe of Judah, 148, David's Son and Lord, 17.*30*, Root and offspring, 317.*69*, Lord, Son of God, God, 244f, the subject and key of all Scripture, 216; 285, called Israel typologically, 70; 298. His incarnation, 214ff, a body prepared for Him, 123.*30*, the child born, and Son given, 123. He grew in wisdom etc., 123. He was anointed for His work, 112, delighted in God's will, 123.*30f*,

came to Israel's lost sheep, 237, satisfied remnant, 175; 214ff, His glory revealed to few, 148, He fed them, 58.*21*. His fragrant moral graces, 105f. He had a shepherd role, 148, had public and private ministry, 221–9. He alone can give sight, 277.*91*. Visited Jerusalem, 223f.*7*, delighted in God's will, 123.*30f*.

Mary's anointing of, 104.*17*, glorified God on earth, 122f.*32*, love for God and His people tried, 304.

He is the kinsman redeemer, 286.*136*; 304, His is a reconciling, atoning, sweet savour sacrifice, 112; 123; 178ff; 229. He suffered, 126.*7*; 171.*7*, He gave Himself not only His substance, 307, was bound to the altar, 273.*66*, the Servant stricken, 266.*29*, whose resurrection was demanded, 171. Consequences of His being cut off, 243.*10*.

Post-resurrection ministry, 229–32, guarantor of Israel's redemption, 171; 246, promise of Spirit, 238, above all His fellows, 117.*9*, His ascent to heaven, 171; 232ff, present exaltation, 267.*33*, glorified, 86f, as First and Last, 113.*63*, as Son of God, pre-eminence of, 247, minister of circumcision 244f, on Father's throne, 262, yet engaged among His own, 249–52, as source of blessing, 95.*10*, the altogether lovely, 68.*24*; 248. He bequeathed peace to His own, 312.*52*, commissioned his disciples for universal ministry, 238; 250f. Appeals neglected, by many, 240–4, now known in new, glorious way by His own, 238; 244ff, by Israel of God, 68.

And Kingdom. Essential link between suffering and glory, 126f; 171, not two Messiah's, but two advents, 170f. Second advent, 264–7, He is coming back, 282, in dyed garments, 295, to redeem, save all Israel, 295f. His desire, patient waiting for this, 90f; 281f.*118*, preparing of nation for Him, 295f. At last sought out by Israel, 298f. His final joyous union with Israel, 63, Israel's blessing under, 68.*23*, intimate relationship with, 123f; 300, His graces seen in her, 123f, His joy as He drinks wine new, 74.*55*; 234.*45*; 287f, enjoys new and old, 285.

King and His reign in Pss., 17; 46, roles in nation and land, 298; 314; 267.*33*; 277f.*97*, to sum up all in heaven and earth, 315.*62*, universal King of kings, 314

Messianic age, see Poems 5, 6. Anticipated in Lord's love for Solomon, 17; 42.*16*. Great stages toward, 289, fulfilment of Israel's history, 169f, end-purpose of salvation history, 172.

Israel enjoys Messiah's love, 294, earth filled with glory, 17, a morning without clouds, 131; 264, one of peace, 312f.*53*, and its banquet when Messiah returns, 119; 234.*45*; 288, paradise, nature restored, 98

Messianic programme, its perspective two-dimensional, 171f

Millennial reign, God's goal for earth, 180, its rest suggested by Sabbath, 280, not simply paradise restored, 316.

Israel united with Messiah in, 78, a kingdom of priests, 315.

Decoration in its Temple, 280.*109*.

Administration in, 313ff.

Nations' wealth pours in to Israel in, 314. Satan in pit during, 314.*56*

Month, lunar, 128.*19*

Moon, word family, 130.*27*. And seasons, 127f, and festivals, 128, object of worship, 36, in similies, 130f

Moses', blessing of Joseph, 69.*28*; 285.*130*

Mother('s), in Song, 286f.*138f*, role in family, 28, house, 119; 282; 297, as Israel, 150; 175; 257; 261; 282, calls loved one her choice one, 257.*45*

Motifs, chief, in prophets, man/woman relations, 33–8. Love, in Song, 44. Zoological, 53–60, especially flock and shepherd, 57–60; 234.*44*, deer/gazelle, 60–3. Botanical, 65–124, especially grape vine, 76–80, and the garden, waters, 93–9; 231f, fragrance,

115–24. Seeking and finding, 172f; 215.*30f*; 249f.*26*; 311.*48f*. Eating and drinking, 119; 233f.*43ff*. Common in ANE love language, 143f

Mountain(s), word, 178.*22ff*, Gilead, 178, Myrrh = Golgotha the watershed of Song, 178f; 229. Of separation, 214; 316. Of spices, 316f. Of the Lord, Temple mount, 316. Of Olives, where Messiah returns, 265.*20*. In kingdom to drop sweet wine, 73f.*54f*; 80; 288.*146*, singing when Israel restored, 283.*123*, of God's inheritance, 254, when Judah an inheritor of my, 284.*127*

Mountain-valley, word, 83

My, God, Israel to own, 230; 263; 266.*29*, Messiah as, 244.

People, often in OT, 266.*29*, Israel was in past, 266.*28*, to become so in future, 263, nation's covenant confession, 266, Servant smitten for, 266.*29*.

My, in titles used of her: love, 45.*25*; 194, fair one, 194.*27*, dove, 53f; 210; 241.*3*, undefiled, 241.*4*; 257.*45*, sister, 231.*35*, bride, 230f.*32, 35*, garden, 98f; 233f, princely, willing people, 266f.

In titles used of Him: beloved, 45f.*30*, friend, 245.*15*; 249, brother, 286.*136*

Myrrh, word, and description, 110–13, all uses in OT, 111.*54ff*, in NT, 113.*61ff*. In holy anointing oil, 111.*55*; 112; 179.

Mentioned at birth in life and death of Messiah, 224; 232, points to His sufferings, 113; 224; 242, fitted Him for service as our priest, 112; 179.*26*. Obtained by Him for her, 220, hence associated with them both, 111.*57f*; 242

Myrrh Mountain, key to Song, 112, where and what it is, Golgotha, 178f; 229f, panoramic view of Song from, 179f

Mystery, of Christ and the church, 33.*1*, of man with maid, 44, divine mystery in the seasons, festivals, 129, in the Song, 144, regarding Israel's temporary hardening and salvation, 262f

373

N

Name, meaning of the term, 120, divine, unfolded to Abraham, his made great, 189

Names, significance of, Abel-mecholah, 271.*51*, Baal-hamon, 314, Bether, 210, Beulah, 38; 285, Hephzi-bah, 38; 282; 285, Isaiah's sons, 268f, Joseph, 130; 285, Mahanaim, 272.*56*, Manasseh, Ephraim, 191, Mara, Myrrh, Naomi, 110.*51*, Shulammite, Solomon, 269. *43*; 312

Narcissus, of Sharon, 82f.*5*, winter flowering, 83

Nard, identified, 103.*12*, all occurrences, 103.*16*, description and uses, 103f, Mary's use of, 104

Nation, depicted as woman, 295.*5*, as mother of Messiah, 150, of the remnant, 150, of responsible leaders, 150; 212, role as servant, 298.*14*.

And land associated, 38.*25*; 96; 312, in harmony with land, 137.

In post-exilic period, 210–14.

Jesus died for, 251, it neglected His great salvation, 240–4, saw no beauty in Him, 245, continued in obstinacy, 276.

In the land again, 263, tribution distress not in Song, 131; 295, to be allured by Lord, 295.*6*, apprehended by Him, 281, shall long for Him, 282–9, find Him as Immanuel, 286, to be regathered, reunited, 96; 308, to find peace, 311f, her final joyous union, 63, and rest in his love, 289

Nations, have gospel sent to them now, 250ff, righteousness to spring forth before in future, 96; 110, given to Messiah for His inheritance, 314.*58*, their wealth to come to Israel, 314.*60*, blessings to be mediated through Israel, 316, to go up to worship the king, 316.*65*, not deceived by Satan in millennium, 314

Nature, laws of, God's almighty control, 128. OT interest in, 65.*3*, supplies setting and imagery for Song, 19; 66, and many lessons, 65, in har-

mony with lovers' moods, 66. Sin disturbs nature, 69.*27*, its harmony yet to be restored with the nation, 69.*27*; 283f, to deliver its boons to nation, 137

Navel, word, kindred terms, uses, 275

Nazirite, purity of, 246.*18*, concluding of vow of, 119

Near East, climate of in Song, 137, heat, calls for skin care, 120.*14*, environment and the Bible, 39. Mores, 286, practices re bride-price, 305, customs re family, 308. Love terms, *see under* Family Terms

Neck, word, 276.*85*, descriptions of, 190; 276.*87*, in metaphor for obstinacy, 276.*86*

New, birth of nation, 275, covenant blessing to know the Lord, 287.*143*, covenant joy, 271, covenant love, 305, heart, heavens and earth, name, spirit, 285.*132*, songs, for saved Israel, 47.*36*; 272, and nature, 283. And old, 285.*134*. For other points re new covenant *see under* Covenant, Creation, counts with God now, 252, and the Lord's Supper, 285.*132*

Nicodemus, first approach to Jesus, 107, anointed His body at end, 107f; 112f

Night, word in Song, 131.*33*, use of plural in Bible, 215.*27*, beloved's appeals to her in, 131f.*34f*

Noah, his offering a sweet savour, 121.*22*, God's promise to, 132, found grace in God's eyes, 311.*49*

Nose, word, 277f.*97*

Nut, *see under* Walnut

O

Oases, at Elim, Jericho, 74.*58*, and Israel's final salvation, 67

Oath, of cursing, 31, God's to fathers, 41

Obedience, as reciprocation of love, 42, inseparable from love, 43, of Israel results in fruitfulness, 69.*25*

Offering, Noah's sweet savour, 121, phrase for sweet savour, 122.*24*,

Q

centre in the wilderness, 222, War Scroll, 200, hoped for a brighter day, 126f.*9*

R

Rachel, meaning of name, 59, Laban's daughter, 59, Jacob's love for, 41.*7*, her wedding gift, 25.*17*, requested Leah's mandrakes, 89; 284f.*129f*, in part built nation, 59.*25*, mother of Joseph/Benjamin, 253, as the little sister, 309.*43*

Rain(s), words related to, 132.*38*, God gives upon obedience, 69, the early and latter, 81; 132; 156, stop when winter past, 132.*37*; 264.*20*, influence on sowing/growing, 133.*39*, latter ensures final maturing of grain, 133

Raisins, word, all references, 76.*63*, maiden appeals for, 200

Ram skins, and the Tabernacle, 246

Ransom price, for Israel and divine love, 306, costliness ensures effectiveness, 307. *See under* Compensation

Raven, word, 55.*13*

Rebecca, Isaac's love for, 41.*7*; 168, and her wedding gift, 25.*17*

Rebellion of man and future astral changes, 126.*8*

Reconciliation, effected by Messiah's Golgotha work, 229

Redeemer, to be one near of kin, 286; 304, the Lord is Israel's, 38, He is to come to nation, out of Zion, 263–82, draws nation with bands of love, 278, Israel's appeal to when the threshing is past, 275.*80*

Redeemed, the Lord the rallying centre for, 247, year of the Lord's, to come, 295, Israel as the Lord's, 304, of the Lord to return, 268

Redemption, resurrected Messiah the guarantor of Israel's, 171, drama of Israel's, 98, day of Jacob's trouble precedes Israel's, 176. Of Jerusalem, 175. Of Israel in Ps. 45, 46. Final, of Israel, 208

Redemptive programme, God's, demands a double-advent Messiah, 171f

Refrains, and their place in the Song, 151, tabulation of, 155

Regeneration, the, kingdom age described as, 98

Relationship terms, *see under* Family

Remnant, godly, at present is Israel of God, 244, precious, history traced, 240f, saved, 243f; 262, their enhanced appreciation of Messiah, 244–9; Appendix 3. Of nation yet to return, 268f.*40*

Repent, significance of word, 268.*37*. *See under* Return

Rest, to make flock to, word, 57.*18*. Canaan a foretaste of resting in His love, 324, God's, when Israel restored, 38; 41.*14*; 279.*106*; 305.*35*; 329f. Israel to rest in the Lord's love at the end, 289, sabbath, remains for people of God, 279f, not achieved while thorns exist, 197

Restoration of all things, 172.*9*; 317.*69*

Resurrection, of righteous in Judaism, 97.*21*. Messiah's, physical and bodily, 231, post-resurrection ministry, 180; 229–32; 270.*45*; 326. Of the saints, 302.*24*

Return, word, nuances, 268. Orthodox call nation to, 268.*37*, essential for nation to, 270, nation's, to the Lord, 85; 268.*37*; 329. Israel's, to the land after Exile, 205–10

Righteous, and access to tree of life in Judaism, 97, and paradise in Judaism, 97.*21*. Israel all to be, 311.*47*, flourish like palm, 280

Righteousness, of the Law, 280, sought after by Israel, 241; 244. Obtained by the elect today, 244. Governs all God's ways with Israel, 295. Israel to confess Lord as our, 270, and is to be covered with robe of, 230f.*34*, her girdle also is to be, 275f, not her own, 280.*110*. Is to go before nation, 274, Israel's to spring forth, 96. Reigns in kingdom age, 98, the work of, to be peace, 312

Rivers, will not overflow the people of God, 304. In desert for those who return, 67. Flow out of believer's inward parts, 95

Roe, word for, translation, description of, 60f.*31–35*; 201.*49*, found among beauties of nature, 87; 211

Rose, word, identity and description, 82f, and the maiden's sense of lowliness, 196

Ruddy, word, associations, 246f.*18*

Ruler of Israel, from everlasting yet from Bethlehem, 294.*14*

Ruth, Naomi's daughter-in-law, 230.*32*, urged to stay in Boaz' field, 186, lay at Boaz' feet, 89.*23*, appealed to near kinsman, 275.*80*, hers a typologically significant marriage, 168f, desire for her fruitfulness, 59.*25*

S

Saadia Hagaon, and the difficulty of interpreting Song, 167, his proposed solution, 170, strength and weakness of, 171

Sacrifice, Hebrew and Greek term, and offering, technical terms, 112.*60*, sweet savour in Pentateuch and Ezekiel, 122.*24*. Christ alone has offered a sufficient, 110, 112f; 178f; 229; 305, a costly 306f, a sweet savour, 112.*60*. Typology of and the believer's giving, 112.*60*

Saffron, word, a hapax, 104.*21*, description of, 104f

Salvation, God of, 178, of the Lord, at Reed Sea, 192.*20*. None by means of Egypt/Asshur, 56.

God's personified in Messiah, 298, Simeon privileged to see God's, 216.*33*. Always a witness to, 237, extended universally today, 252, embracing remnant today, 242; 244.

Future, of Israel, taught by Paul, 262, Israel's demands Messiah's might, 295, to be published upon mountains, 207.*4*, Israel to be clothed in, 230f.*34*, beautified with God's,

272–8, Israel's to be as a lamp, 266. The reign enjoyed by saved nation, 98

Salvation History, initiated by and reveals God's love, 41. Song deals with course of, 46; 124, as older Rabbis saw it, 169f, Song sweeps the whole range of, 17, theme of in the poems, 185, thread of in Poem 1, 188f, in Poem 2, 206, in Poem 3, 221, summary of in Poems 1–3, 237, in Poem 4, 240–4, in Poem 5, 262f, in Poem 6, 295f, summary of through Song, 321–31.

The first advent and, 108.*34*, watershed in the first advent, 180, startling change in programme of, 238, Messianic goal of, 172.

Typologically presented, 93, imagery used in unfolding, 65, two different stages in presence or absence of thorns, 88. And the water theme, 99. And the nature cycle, 128. And the festivals, 127ff. Key place of seeking and finding in, 172–7; 214ff. The Shulammite's place in, 269. Ps. 45 and the grand climax of, 46

Samaria, Tirzah on mountains of, 15.*16*, Ostraca, and cities of Ephraim, 254.*35*. As one of two sisters, 308

Sandals, feet shod in, 274.*70*

Saviour, the Lord is Israel's, 304, the incarnation of the, 216

Say, a use of the word, 281.*112*

Scenes, a proposed sequence of 14 in Song, 16.*24*, contrasting, in Poem 1, 187, in Poem 2, 206, in Poem 3, 221, in Poem 4, 239f, in Poem 5, 262, in Poems 5 and 6, 293

Scenery, as affected by seasons in Israel, 125, springtime, 135.*44*, summertime, 135.*45*. Constantly changing in Song, 188, varying, in Poem 6, 294f, provides apt imagery for the poet, 93

Scorched, word, 190.*14*

Sea Daffodil, lily of the sea-shore, 83

Seal, word, uses, 299f.*16–19*

Seasons, word family, 127.*10*, in Israel, 132ff, cycle of in Song, 134–8, luminaries and the, 125, moon

disturbs whole of nature, 69.26, has brought curse and thorn, 88.17, of nation brought prophets' denouncing, 176, led to exile of nation, 209f.
Offering, and goats, 59f.
Purgation made for sins by Messiah, 230, He bore sin away, 305.
Sense of sin yet to cause nation to return, 268.37. It exists but will be suppressed in kingdom, 98
Sinuhe, and the Yarmuk region, 77.68
Sister, word, 231.35, for two sisters compare Leah/Rachel, 43, the little one, 307f, the two complement each other, 310, the two and Jer. 31, 312, the two and Ezek. 16, 308f.42. As an endearing love term, 231.35; 241.3
Smell, word, 121.19ff, first use definitive, 121.22, generally of appealing odours, 115; 121. Sweet, of sacrifices, to God, 121.22, used of Christ's offering, 110; 112f; 123; 178f; 229. *See* Aroma
Smyrna, place name in NT, 113.63
Solar year, exact duration of, 127f.16
Solomon, second child of Bathsheba, 47, son and successor of David, 17, his name in Song, 13.1f. His divine choice and call, 17, the king of glory, 14; 245, incalculably wealthy, 305, yet became shepherd for a season, 149, in his love for Shulammite, 46f, which he wrote of in Song, 16.23; 48. His role in Song denigrated by some, 142f; 305.36; 313, who hold shepherd-lover view, 57f.20. Early phase of life represented by Song, 14; 48. His early reign provides setting, 13–16, when all dwelt safely, 71, his kingdom divided after his death, 253. Built the Temple, 98f, in which lily-work has prominant part, 85, prayed at its dedication, 268.38.
He had penetrating wisdom, 18, taking in fauna, 53ff, and flora, 65.1, and opened up the beauties of nature, 81. Two psalms credited to him, 15f.21; 17, wrote three substantial works, 48, his Song provided prophets with the love motif, 19; 44.

He had a sense of messianic role, 17.26; 42.16, reign a messianic anticipation, 85.8; 149; 311, though excelled by King Messiah, 150
Son, of David, the Messiah, 68, yet He is also the Son of God, 177, has been given, 175, He is Immanuel, 175.15, the Son of God's love, 124, who glorified God upon the earth, 122f, was sent to be the propitiation, 40, came out from and has now returned to God, 177.20, the beginning of new creation, 124, and appointed Heir of all things, 256
Sons, the Shulammite's mother's, responsible in the family, and nation, 150, discouraged her relationship, 186, sought to safeguard and keep her busy, 147; 210; 212f, concern for little sister, 308–11
Song, word, 47.35, the Targum's ten outstanding songs, 49.42f, of the Sea, 271.52; 302f.23. The book, title of, 47ff, why the most excellent, 49f, setting and author, 13–16; 151, significance, 16ff, style, 18f, and Psalm 45, 46f, and Psalm 72, 17, its love-theme influence on prophets, 44, Rabbi Aqibha's assessment of, 49, its place in Jewish liturgy, 8; 149. Interpretation of, 141–50, its difficulty, 167.1, literal sense does not exhaust meaning, 17f; 143; 149, not record of a love triangle, 57.20; 147; 305f, enigmatic character of, 302, as a commentary on Isa. 62.5, 146.9. Structure of, 151–65
Soul, word, 215.29; 242.8, once of his overwhelming desire, 265.25
Speakers, identification of, 164ff; 264; 268.35; 281.115; 297
Spices, word, generic and specific, 116–19; 116.2,5; 117.8, 10, figurative of bride's appeal, 135, of his graces produced in her, 250, of the fragrant ministries of glorified Messiah, 342
Spiced, word, a hapax, and family, 287.145
Spirit, of God, touches heart to produce songs, 47, as the voice of redemption

T

Y

Z

BIBLICAL REFERENCES

Passage and verse references – Song of Songs

4^2–5^1 169
4^{7-14} 229–232
4^{7-9} 220
4^{7-8} 326
4^8–5^1 169
4^{9-11} 165; 326
4^{10-16} 220
4^{12-15} 165
4^{12-14} 326
4^{13}–5^1 240.2
[4^{15}–5^1]   232–234; 327
4^{16}–5^1 221

Ch 4

 1 45.25; 54.2,8,9; 58.23; 59.28; 153; 155; 162; 178.24; 190.13; 194.26; 225.17; 241.3; 255; 341.6
 2 15.19; 58.23,24; 59; 99.25; 162
 3 72.44; 73.51; 135.45; 162; 190.13; 252.34; 343.13
 4 15.15; 19; 153; 155; 162; 276.85
 5 28.42; 57.17; 60.32,35; 61 & n45; 83.6; 87.14,16; 153; 155; 162; 251.29; 276 & n82; 280.111
 6 109.39; 111.56; 112; 130.27; 131.31; 135.46; 154; 155; 162; 165; 177.21; 178.24; 229; 234; 326
 7 45.27; 153; 155; 162; 165; 190.13; 194.26; 241.7
 8 15.19,20; 56; 130.27; 153; 155; 162; 178.22; 230 & n32; 277.95
 9 19; 162; 230.32; 231 & n35; 241.3; 286.136; 341.6
10 46.29; 76.63; 79.77; 115 & n1; 116.2,4; 117.8; 121.17,21; 135.45,46; 153; 155; 162; 190.13; 220.1; 230.32; 231 & n35; 234.44; 241.3; 286.136
11 15.20; 121.19,20; 130.27; 162; 220.1; 230.32; 231; 234.44; 343.17
12 94.3,7; 95.8; 99.25; 144.6; 162; 230.32; 231 & n35; 241.3; 286.136; 299
13 69.29; 72.44; 102.8,9; 103.11,16; 118; 135.45,46; 162; 232; 283.124; 284.125; 285.130
14 103.11,16; 104.21; 105.24; 106.26; 107.29,30; 108.38; 111.56,57; 116.2; 118; 130.27; 135.46; 162; 232
15 15.20; 94.3,7; 95.9; 99.25; 130.27; 144.6; 162; 250; 316.64
16 46.30; 69.28; 94.7; 95.8; 116.2,4; 117.8; 135.45,46; 153; 154; 155; 162; 165; 166; 220.1; 233.42; 234.43,44; 250; 285.130

Chap(s)

5   175
5^2–6^9 158; 160; 162f; [235–257]; 262; 293; 327
5^2–6^3 170
5^{2-8} 153; 172; 238ff; 327
5^{2-7} 169
5^{6-8} 155
5^8–6^1 169
5^9–6^3 238
5^{9-16} 244; 327
5^{10-16} 166; 245
5^{11-16} 248; 339–348

Ch 5

1 46.29; 76.63; 79.78; 94.7; 95.8; 111.56,57; 116.2; 135.45,46; 152; 153; 154; 155; 162; 166; 220.1; 230 & n32; 231.35; 233; 234.43,44; 238; 241.3; 245.15; 286.136
2 45.25; 46.30; 54.2,5; 99.25; 131.33; 132.34; 134; 152; 155; 162; 165; 166; 194.26; 206.2; 220.1; 231.35; 241.3,4; 281.116; 339; 340; 341.6; 344
3 99.25; 162; 166
4 46.30; 162; 165; 242
5 46.30; 110.51; 111.52,56; 112.59; 162; 166; 242 & n8
6 46.30; 162; 165; 166; 215.30,31; 242; 249.26; 265.25; 283.120
7 155; 162; 166; 215.31; 243; 249.26; 277.94
8 15.14; 44.24; 46.30; 155; 162; 166; 200; 215.31; 249.26
9 46.30; 153; 155; 162; 164; 166; 190.13; 194.27
10 29.48; 46.30; 163; 200.47; 247
11 14.9; 19; 163; 248; 339f; 340.2
12 54.2,8,9; 163; 225.17; 341.6
13 83.6; 86 & n12; 110.51; 111.56,58; 116.2; 117.9; 163; 287.145; 342f; 343.13,17
14 14.9; 19; 163; 242.8; 248; 276.88; 340.2; 344
15 14.9; 15.20; 19; 67.16; 68.22; 130.27; 163; 248; 311; 346f
16 15.14; 46.30; 68.24; 163; 234.44; 245.15; 248; 249; 347

Chap(s)

6^{1-3}	249; 328
6^2-7^{10}	170
6^{4-9}	170; 239; 252–257
6^{4-7}	165; 252–256
6^{5-7}	153; 155; 158.6
6^{6-8}	256f
$6^{10}-8^4$	158; 160; 163; [259–289]; 293; 328
$6^{10}-7^{10}$	170; 261; 263–282
6^{11-12}	264–267; 329

Ch 6

1 46.30; 153; 155; 163; 164; 166; 190.13; 194.27; 215.30; 249 & n26; 251.30
2 46.30; 57 & n19,17; 58.21; 83.6; 87.14,16; 94.7; 95.8,9; 116.2; 118.10; 163; 166; 220.1; 250 & n27; 251.29,30; 316.64
3 46 & n30,31; 57 & n19,17; 58.21; 83.6; 87.14; 154; 163; 166; 214.24; 220.1; 228.26; 251.29; 252; 281.117
4 15.14,17; 45.25; 153; 155; 163; 190.13; 194.26; 200.47; 241.3; 252.34; 253; 254.36; 263.13
5 15.19; 58.23; 59.28; 163; 253; 341.6
6 58.23; 59 & n25; 99.25; 153; 163
7 72.44; 73.51; 163
8 14.6,10; 163; 165
9 28.42; 29.48; 54.2,5; 152; 163; 165; 241.3,4; 257.45; 270.49; 273.62; 286.138; 341.6
10 108.35; 130.28; 152; 153; 155; 157.5; 163; 165; 166; 190.13; 200.47; 254.36; 257.45; 261.1,4; 263; & n13; 293.1; 328
11 72.47; 73.52; 74.57; 76.63; 79.74; 82.2; 94.7; 95.8; 136.47; 155; 163; 165; 250.27; 261.2; 265.21; 270.49; 281.114; 283
12 163; 165; 200.47; 261.2,4; 265.25; 278.100; 299.15
13 27.35; 163; 165; 166; 200.47; 261.1,3,4; 267–272; 268.35; 270.48; 271.51; 329

For Hebrew verse numbering in Chap. 7 add 1 in each case.

12 13.1; 69.28; 76.63; 77; 78.71; 163; 164; 165; 294 & n3; 314.59
13 94.7; 95.9; 164; 166; 206.2; 250; 294; 315; 316.64,66
14 46.30; 60.31,36; 61 & n46; 116.2; 118.10; 124.37; 152; 164; 166; 178.22; 228.26; 294; 315; 316.68

Genesis

Ch 1

4	125.2
5	125.2
14–19	125.1
27	21.1
28	168.3

Ch 2

	21
1	17.30
4–25	96.17
7	21.2
8	94.4,5;
	95.11,12;
	97.19
9	94.4,5;
	95.11,12;
	97.19
10	94.3;
	95.11,12;
	97.19
15	94.5;
	95.11,13;
	97.19,20
16	95.11; 97.19
18	21.3
19	21.2
20	21.3; 30.58
21–24	168.2
21	22.4
22	22.4
23	22.5; 143
24	23.10; 143

Ch 3

1–7	23.9
1	95.11
2	95.11
3	95.11
6	198.42
7	70.36
8	95.11;
	134.43;
	154.3
10	95.11
16	91.32;
	282.118
17	69.26; 84.7;
	197.37
18	69.26; 84.7;
	197.37
19	69.26; 84.7;
	197.37
23	95.11,13;
	97.19,20
24	95.11;
	97.19,20

Ch 4

1	27.36; 42.17
2	42.17
5	42.17
7	91.32;
	282.118
16	95.12
17	27.36
19	22.7; 27.36
22	195.31

25	27.36

Chs 6–8 99.26

Ch 6

2	27.36
8	311.49

Ch 8

7	55.13
8–12	54.5
21	121.22;
	122.29
22	130.24;
	132.39

Ch 9

1	168.3
7	168.3
12	126.4
13	126.4
17	126.4
20	76.64
25	49.40

Ch 11

5	250.27
7	250.27
29	27.36

Chs 12–34 323

Ch 12

1–3	189.11
3	316.65
19	27.36

391

Biblical References

Ch 13

10	97.*19*

Ch 15

14	55.*12*
17	302.*26*

Ch 17

8	76.*62*

Ch 18

1	134.*42*
2	134.*42*
3	311.*49*
12	30.*57*
21	250.*27*

Ch 20

3	30.*56*
11	281.*112*

Ch 21

3	30.*58*
8	145.*8*
9	145.*8*
10	145.*8*

Ch 22

2	40.*6*

Ch 24

4	22.6
15–20	24.*11*
28	24.*16*
30	25.*17*
47	25.*17*
53	25.*17*
59	25.*17*
65	26.*29*; 226.*18*
66	26.*28*
67	26.*28*; 27.*37*; 41.7

Ch 25

23	88.*19*
24	88.*19*
28	40.*6*

Ch 26

9	281.*112*

Chs 28–35 191.*17*

Ch 28

3	168.3

Ch 29

6	59.25
9	24.*16*
11	24.*16*
12–14	29.53
16	309.*43*
17	194.*28*
18	41.7; 309.*43*
20	25.*19*
21	27.*37*
22	27.*34*
23	27.*37*
24	25.*17*
26	309.*43*
28	25.*19,21*
29	25.*17*
30	41.7
32	41.7

Ch 30

	285.*130*
13	257.*45*
14	89.*26*; 90
15	27.*36*; 90.*27*
16	27.*36*; 90.*27*; 307.*41*
22	90.*28*

Ch 31

38	59

Ch 32

1	272.*37*
2	15.*18*; 272.*37*
14	59.26
25	274.*71*
31	274.*71*

Ch 34

2	22.6; 25.*18*
3	22.6; 41.7
4	22.6
8	25.*21*
12	25.*17,18,21*

Ch 35

11	168.3

Chs 37–50 191.*17*; 323

Ch 37

3	40.*6*
4	40.*6*
9	264.*14*
10	264.*14*
11	264.*14*
25	116.*6*
27	29.53

Ch 38

6	75.*58*
11	75.*58*
13	75.*58*
18	299.*17*
24	75.*58*
25	299.*17*

Ch 39

7	27.*36*
10	27.*36*
12	27.*36*
14	27.*36*

Ch 41

5	105.*23*
6	133.*41*
22	105.*23*
23	133.*41*
27	133.*41*
39–46	169.4
42	299.*17*
50–52	169.4
51	191.*17*
52	191.*17*

Ch 43

11	116.*6*

Ch 22
16 25.*18*
17 25.*18*

Ch 23
15 127.*13*;
    264.*19*
16 127.15
23 199.45

Ch 24
10 346.22
11 234.*44*
17 347.25

Ch 25
5   246.*18*
6   116.3;
    117.*9*;
    342.*10*
31 105.23;
    265.21
32 105.23
33 265.21
34 265.21

Ch 26
14 246.*18*
32,37 347.*24*
33 49
34 49

Ch 27
21 127.*10*

Ch 28
11 299.17
17–21 274.72
21 299.17
33 73.49
34 73.49
36 299.17
41 344.*19*

Ch 29
9   344.*19*
18 122.24
25 122.24
29 344.*19*
37 48.39

38–42 127.*12*
41 122.24

Ch 30
10 48.39
23 105.24;
    106.26; 28;
    116.3,5;
    117.9
24 106.26
25 287.*145*;
    342.11
33 342.11
34 109.*41*
35 287.*145*;
    342.11
36 48.39

Ch 32
9   276.*86*

Ch 33
3   276.*86*
5   276.*86*
12 42.*17*;
    311.49
13 311.49
16 311.49
17 311.49

Ch 34
5   250.27
9   276.*86*;
    311.49
14 34.*8*; 301.22
18 127.*13*;
    264.*19*
20 307.*41*

Ch 35
5   267.32
7   246.*18*
8   116.3;
    342.*10*
22 267.32
28 116.3;
    117.*9*;
    342.*10*
29 267.32

Ch 36
3   267.32
19 246.*18*

Ch 37
11 265.21
19 265.21
20 265.21
29 342.11

Ch 39
6   299.17
14 299.17
24–26 73.49
30 299.17
34 246.*18*

Ch 40
10 48.39

Leviticus

Ch 1
9   122.24
13 122.24
14 54.4
17 122.24

Ch 2
1   109.42
2   109.42;
    122.24
3   48.39
9   122.24
12 122.24
14 264.*19*
15 109.42
16 109.42

Ch 3
    137
5   122.24
16 122.24

Ch 4
31 122.24

Ch 5

11	109.42

Ch 6

15	109.42;
	122.24
21	122.24
25	48.39

Ch 7

1	48.39

Ch 8

21	122.24
28	122.24

Ch 10

17	48.39

Ch 11

3	61.40
15	55.13

Ch 14

13	48.39

Ch 17

6	122.24

Ch 18

6–18	23.10

Ch 19

18	45, 310.45

Ch 20

11	23.10
12	23.10
14	23.10
17	23.10
19	23.10
20	23.10
21	23.10

Ch 21

7	27.36

Ch 23

5–7	127.13
10	127.15

11	127.15
13	122.24
15–21	275.80
18	122.24
34–43	127.14
40	75.58

Ch 24

7	109.43
9	48.39

Ch 26

3	69.25
4	132.37
10	285.134
14	69.26
15	69.26
19	69.26
20	69.26
31	122.24

Numbers

Ch 1

52	200.47

Ch 2

2	200.47
3	200.47
10	200.47
17	200.47
18	200.47
25	200.47
31	200.47
34	200.47

Ch 3

32	49.40

Ch 5

11–31	31.66–70
15	109.42
21	274.71
22	274.71
27	274.71

Ch 6

	341.4

10	54.2,4

Ch 8

4	265.21

Ch 9

15	302.26
16	302.26

Ch 10

10	128.17
14	200.47
18	200.47
22	200.47
25	200.47

Ch 11

5	82.3
11	311.49
15	311.49
17	250.27
25	250.27

Ch 12

5	250.27

Ch 13

23	71.37;
	72.44,45;
	280.111
27	71.37

Ch 14

3	268.36

Ch 15

3	122.24
7	122.24
10	122.24
13	122.24
14	122.24
24	122.24

Ch 17

8	265.21

Ch 18

7	48.39
17	122.24

Ch 19	
2	246.*19*

Ch 20	
5	71.*37*

Ch 21	
8	266.*30*
17	47.*35*; 49.*42,43*
25	277.*92*

Ch 23	
12	255.*39*
21	59.*28*

Ch 24	
6	95.*15*; 106.*29*; 107.*30*
11	281.*112*

Ch 25	
1–9	35.*14*

Ch 26	
33	253.*35*

Ch 27	
1	253.*35*

Ch 28	
1	193.*23*
2	121.*23*
3–8	127.*12*
6	122.*24*
8	122.*24*
11–15	128.*17*
13	122.*24*
16–25	127.*13*
24	122.*24*
26–31	275.*80*
27	122.*24*

Ch 29	
1–6	128.*17*
2	122.*24*
6	122.*24*
8	122.*24*
12–38	127.*14*

13	122.*24*
36	122.*24*

Ch 32	
37	277.*92*

Ch 36	
11	253.*35*

Deut

Ch 4	
19	129.*23*
37	41.*8*; 283.*120*
38	41.*8*; 199.*45*

Ch 5	
9	301.*22*
10	43.*20*

Ch 6	
4	42.*18*
5	123.*33*; 310.*45*
21	344.*18*
23	199.*45*

Ch 7	
7	33.*2,3*; 41.*9*
8	33.*2,3*; 41.*9*; 304.*31*; 344.*18*
9	43.*20*

Ch 8	
8	72.*44*; 77.*68*; 88.*17*

Ch 9	
6	276.*86*
13	276.*86*

Ch 10	
12	43.*20*
15	41.*8*
16	276.*86*

17	49.*40*
19	43.*21*
20	29.*52*

Ch 11	
1	43.*20*
13	43.*20*
14	132.*37*
22	29.*52*; 43.*20*

Ch 12	
8	193.*22*
9	193.*22*
15	61.*40*
22	61.*40*

Ch 13	
3	43.*20*
4	29.*52*; 43.*20*
6	45

Ch 14	
5	61.*40*
14	55.*13*

Ch 15	
22	61.*40*

Ch 16	
1	264.*19*
10	267.*32*
13–15	76.*64*; 287.*144*

Ch 17	
3	129.*23*
14–20	19.*36*

Ch 19	
19	43.*20*

Ch 20	
7	25.*24*; 27.*36*

Ch 21	
13	27.*37*

Ch 22

13	27.36; *38*; 62.48
16	62.48
22	30.*60*
23	25.22; 31.*61*
24	25.22; 31.*61*
25–27	25.*23*; 31.*62*
28–29	25.*18*; 26.25
30	23.*10*

Ch 23

5	41.*10*

Ch 24

1–4	23.*10*
1	27.36; 311.*49*
3	62.48

Ch 26

7–8	192.20
16–19	214.24

Ch 22

20	23.*10*
22	23.*10*
23	23.*10*

Ch 28

7	192.20

Ch 29

12	214.24
13	214.24

Ch 30

6	43.20
16	43.20
20	29.52; 43.20

Ch 31

10–13	127.*14*
19	47.35
21	47.35
22	47.35
27	278.86
30	47.35

Ch 32

10	222.3
13–16	285.*130*
14	88.17
44	47.35

Ch 33

2	247.21
12	46.32
13–14	69.28
15–16	69.28

Ch 34

3	74.58

Joshua

Ch 5

14–15	272.56

Ch 10

12	49.42; 60.38; 126.6

Ch 11

3	277.94

Ch 12

24	253.35

Ch 13

17	277.92
26	272.56; 277.92
30	272.56

Ch 15

16–18	25.*19,21*
19	25.*17*
32	72.46
62	79.73

Ch 17

3	253.35

Ch 19

13	72.46
42	60.38
45	72.46

Ch 21

24	60.38; 72.46
38	272.56
39	277.92

Ch 27

5	29.52; 43.20
19	277.93

Ch 23

8	29.52
11	43.20

Judges

Ch 1

12.13	25.21
16	74.58

Ch 3

13	74.58
21–22	88.*18*

Ch 4

5	75.58
10	27.34
21–22	73.51

Ch 5

1	49.42,43
2	267.32
9	267.32
12	4.7
26	73.51

Ch 6

17	311.49

Ch 7

22	271.51

Ch 9

2	29.53
8	119.13
9	119.13
10	72.42
13	275.77

Ch 14

2	120.14
27	75.58

Ch 15

25	264.20;
	311.49

Ch 17

24	272.56
27	272.56

Ch 18

24–27	173.10

Ch 19

13	29.53
32	272.56

Ch 21

1	250.26

Ch 22

	49.42,43
1	47.35
2–4	212.21
10	250.27;
	265.24
34	61.43

Ch 23

1	279.105
4	264.16
6	197.38
7	197.38
17	307.41

Ch 24

24	307.41

I Kings

Ch 1

	17.26
1–11	13.4; 14
3	269.42

Ch 2

8	272.56

Ch 2 (continued)

17	269.42
21	269.42
22	269.42
23	307.41
37	264.20

Ch 3

1	14.11;
	16.22; 169.4
4–13	17.26
12	53.1
15	19

Ch 4

12	271.51
14	272.56
21	14.13
23	61.41
24	14.13
25	14.13;
	71.41; 77.67
26	14.11;
	266.26
29	19.35; 53.1
30	16.23;
	18.34; 19.35
31	18.34; 19.35
33	53; 65.1

Ch 5

2–5	17.26

Ch 6

6	67.19
10	67.19
15	66.10; 67.19
16	67.19
18	67.19
20	67.19
26	67.19
29	75.58;
	280.109
32	75.58;
	280.109
35	75.58;
	280.109

Ch 7

2	67.18
15	346.23

Ch 7 (continued)

18	73.50
19	83.6; 85.8
20	73.50;
	343.13
22	83.6; 85.8
26	83.6; 85.8;
	265.21
33	266.26
36	75.58;
	280.109
42	73.50
49	265.21

Ch 8

10	198.44
11	198.44
15–21	17.26
27	49.40
33	268.38
35	268.38
47–48	268.38
56–58	198.44

Chs 9–10

	16.22

Ch 9

6	25.17;
	268.36
16	14.11
19	14.11
22	14.11

Ch 10

1–3	18.33
2	116.3
8	14.12
9	41.10; 42.16
10	116.3
17	67.18
18	276.89;
	340.2;
	346.22
20	14.12
21	14.12; 67.18
25	116.3
26	14.11;
	266.26
27	14.12
28	14.11

Ch 11
1–8	14.7

Ch 14
6	206.2
17	253.35
20	267.32
21	195.31
31	195.31

Ch 15
13	264.20
21	253.35
33	253.35

Ch 16
6	253.35
8	253.35
9	253.35
15	253.35
17	253.35
23	253.35
24	15.16
25	15.16

Ch 17
4	55.13
6	55.13

Ch 18
40	264.20

Ch 19
18	244.12

Ch 21
2	94.4
8	299.17

Ch 23
6	264.20

II Kings

Ch 4
8–37	269.42

Ch 5
18	72.44

Ch 6
20	277.91

Ch 9
17	173.10
18	173.10
20	173.10
27	94.1

Ch 11
6	173.10
7	173.10

Ch 15
14	253.35
16	253.35

Ch 17
14	276.86

Ch 18
21	105.23
31	71.41

Ch 19
23	66.8; 67.15
34	94.1

Ch 20
6	94.1
7	71.38
8–11	126.6
13	116.3

Ch 21
3	129.23
5	129.23
18	94.2

Ch 25
4	94.2
17	73.50

I Chron

Ch 2
4	75.58

Ch 3
9	75.58

Ch 6
31	48
32	48
80	272.56

Ch 8
13	60.38

Ch 9
29	109.44
30	116.3

Ch 11
2	147.11
20	48
21	48

Ch 12
8	61.42
9	60.31

Ch 13
8	48

Ch 16
3	76.63
8–10	49.43
10	249.26
11	249.26
31	283.122

Ch 17
1	67.18
6	147.11
21	257.45

Ch 18
6	277.96

Ch 23
22	173.10

Ch 25
6	48
7	48

	13	47.34
	14	45.26
	15	189.10

Ch 47
| | 4 | 41.10 |

Ch 48
| | 1 | 47 |

Ch 49
| | | 85 |
| | 14 | 302.24 |

Ch 50
| | 13 | 109.47 |
| | 14 | 109.47 |

Ch 51
	9	108.35
	12	200.48;
		267.32

Ch 53
| | title | 271.51 |

Ch 54
| | 4 | 200.48 |

Ch 55
| | 6 | 54.3,6 |

Ch 56
| | 1 | 54.6 |

Ch 57
| | 1 | 198.41 |

Ch 59
| | | 86.9 |

Ch 60
		85
	1	83.6
	5	46.32

Ch 63
| | 7 | 198.41 |

Ch 68
		86.9
	13	54.3,7
	18	303.28
	34	301.20

Ch 69
		85
	1	83.6
	2	304.32
	6	249.26
	9	301.23
	14	304.32
	15	304.32
	30	47
	36	43.20

Ch 70
| | 4 | 43.20; |
| | | 250.26 |

Ch 72
	1	15.21; 17
	3	312.53
	5	126.5
	7	265.21

Ch 73
| | 25 | 248.23 |

Ch 74
	1	58.22
	19	55; 130.25;
		209.12

Ch 75
| | 5 | 276.86 |

Ch 78
	14	302.26
	63	26.32
	70–72	147.11

Ch 79
| | | 86.9 |
| | 13 | 58.22 |

Ch 80
		85
	1	83.6; 347.26
	2	147.11
	8–11	80.83
	10	67.20
	12–16	80.83

Ch 81
| | 3 | 128.17 |
| | 16 | 88.17 |

Ch 83
| | 16 | 249.26 |

Ch 85
| | 5–10 | 312.53 |
| | 13 | 276.69 |

Ch 88
| | title | 271.51 |

Ch 89
	19	347.26
	36	126.5
	48	302.24

Ch 90
	16	273.64
	17	86.90;
		273.64;
		279.105

Ch 91
| | 1 | 198.41 |
| | 7 | 247.21 |

Ch 92
		49.42; 280
	title	279.107
	12–15	279.107
	12	67.20;
		75.58;
		265.21
	13	265.21

Ch 93
| | 5 | 190.13 |

Ch 94
| | 7 | 303.28 |

Ch 95
	6	274.73
	7–11	242.6;
		243.10

Ch 96
	1	47.36;
		283.122
	6	301.20
	10–13	283.122

Ch 98
1   47.36

Ch 100
3   58.22

Ch 102
11   154.4;
        211.17
14   345.21

Ch 104
16   67.20
19   127.11
20   125.2
28   251.30

Ch 105
3   249.26
4   249.26

Ch 106
1   303.28

Ch 108
6   46.32

Ch 109
23   154.4;
        211.17

Ch 110
1–3   267.33
1   172.9
4   267.34

Ch 111
1   303.28

Ch 112
1   303.28

Ch 113
1   303.28

8   273.61
9   273.61

Ch 118

14   303.28
25   224.10
26   224.10
27   273.66

Ch 119
47   43.20
97   43.20
113   43.20
116   200.48
119   43.20
127   43.20; 340.2
133   274.69
140   43.20
159   43.20
165   43.21
167   43.20

Ch 121
5   198.41

Ch 122
6   312.51
7   312.51

Ch 127
1   15.21; 17;
        173.11
2   46.32
3   28.40; 88.19

Ch 130
3   303.28
6   174.14

Ch 132
11   88.19

Ch 133
2   117.9;
        343.12

Ch 134
3   18.32

Ch 135
1   303.28

Ch 136
11   283.120

Ch 139
13   88.19

Ch 144
4   154.4;
        211.17
9   47.36

Ch 145
14   200.48
20   43.20

Ch 146
1   303.28
8   277.91

Ch 147
1   252.34;
        303.28
2   55.13
7   55.13
10   56.15;
        346.23
14   275.81
17   133.40

Ch 148
1   303.28
9   66.4

Ch 149
1–3   272.55
1   47.36;
        303.28
4   253.35;
        272.58

Proverbs

Ch 2
17   31.63

Ch 3
4   311.49
6–8   275.76

Ch 4
7   306.40

Ch 5

5	302.24
15–19	144.6
18f	28.41; 29.50

Ch 6

3	255.37

Ch 7

1–27	106.27
4	231.35
17	106; 26; 107.29
18	45.28
27	302.24

Ch 8

11	306.40
17	340.2

Ch 10

21, 32	343.14

Ch 12

4	28.44
19	343.14

Ch 13

25	88.19

Ch 17

7	252.34

Ch 18

3	88.19

Ch 19

10	252.34

Ch 21

31	56.15

Ch 22

6	227.23
11	43.21

Ch 25

11	69.29
12	340.2

Ch 26

1	252.34
22	88.19

Ch 27

18	71.39

Ch 30

15–20	65.3
17	55.13
24f	65.3

Ch 31

1–31	28.45
23	28.47
28f	257.45

Ecclesiastes

Ch 1

2	49.40

Ch 2

4–6	94.6

Ch 3

1	62.48
8	62.48

Ch 7

1	120.15

Ch 9

8	108.35
9	27.39

Ch 12

5	82.2

Isaiah

Ch 1

6	273.10
9	244.11
11	109.47
18	108.35; 246.18

29–31 96.14

Ch 2

3	316.65

Ch 3

24	116.4

Ch 4

5	302.26; 303.30
6	132.37; 198.41

Ch 5

1–7	315.61
1–6	76.65; 94.1
1–3	314.57
1	45.28; 47.35

Ch 6

1–3	246.17
5	343.14

Ch 7

6f	57.16
14	286.138
23	314.56

Ch 9

1	223.6
2	216.34; 223.6
6f	177.19

Ch 10

21	269.40
22	244.11; 269.40
23	244.11

Ch 11

1	198.43
3	123.34; 278.97
6–9	129.22

Ch 12

2	303.28

Ch 13
  10   126.8

Ch 14
  8   66.8

Ch 17
  7   274.73

Ch 18
  5   82.2

Ch 19
  6   105.23

Ch 21
  5   173.10
  6   173.10;
      174.12;
      296.9
  8   277.94
  11f 174.13

Ch 23
  15   47.35

Ch 24
  23   126.8

Ch 25
  4   198.41
  6   199.46;
      234.45
  9   199.46

Ch 26
  3   200.48
  4   303.28
  18   271.51

Ch 27
  6   265.21
  8   133.41

Ch 28
  15   302.24

Ch 30
  17   192.20

  29   47; 49.42;
       127.9

Ch 31
  1   56.15
  3   56.15
  5   94.1

Ch 32
  2   198.41
  17f 312.53

Ch 33
  6   346.23
  9   196.36
  17   195.32
  20–22 270.50

Ch 34
  11   55.13

Ch 35
  1   82; 196.36;
      265.21
  2   196.36;
      265.21;
      278.98
  5   226.21;
      277.91
  6   61.43;
      274.71
  9   277.95
  10   269.40

Ch 36
  9   56.15
  16   71.41

Ch 37
  24   66.8; 67.15
  35   94.1

Ch 38
  6   94.1
  11   303.28
  21   71.38

Ch 39
  2   116.3

Ch 40
  1   266.29
  2   225.15
  3   295.7
  4   207.7
  6–8   82.1
  9–11 297.11
  11   59.27;
       147.11

Ch 41
  8   189.12
  19   66.8,12

Ch 42
  1   253.35
  7   226.21;
      277.91
  10   47.36

Ch 43
  1–4   304.31
  3   306.38
  4   41.11;
      306.38
  23   109.45
  24   105.24
  44.7–
  45.7 207.7

Ch 48
  14   41.11
  17   287.142
  22   270.44;
       311.50

Ch 49
  1   298.14
  3   298.14
  5   298.14
  6   298.14
  8   253.35;
      298.14
  16   310.46
  18   231.34
  26   74.54

Ch 50
  1   38.24;
      287.139

2	344.*18*
4	225.*16;*
	343.*15*
6	342.*9*

Ch 51

2	257.*45;*
	287.*139*
3	96.*15,18;*
	287.*139*
9	301.*20*
10	269.*40*
13	274.*73*
16	266.*29*

Ch 52

6	266.*29*
10	347.*25*
7	190.*13;*
	274.*70*
8	174.*14*
14	68.*22*

Ch 53

2	68.*22;*
	198.*42;*
	248.*23;*
	347.*25*
7	59
8	266.*29*
9	107.*32*

Ch 54

1	38.*25;*
	271.*51*
2	270.*50*
4	287.*142*
5	38.*25;*
	99.*26;*
	287.*142*
6	38.*25;*
	253.*35*
7f	345.*21*
9	99.*26*
10	312.*53;*
	345.*21*
11	346.*22*
13	287.*142;*
	312.*53*

Ch 55

1	234.*45*
5	270.*45*
10–13	283.*123*
12	312.*53*
13	66.*11*

Ch 56

6	43.*20*

Ch 57

3	34.*7*
21	270.*44;*
	311.*50*

Ch 58

	264.*14*
11	96.*15;* 99.*27*

Ch 59

1	344.*18*
20	263.*11;*
	297.*11*
21	263.*11*

Ch 60

	311
1	208.*10*
2	274.*67*
5	314.*60*
6	110.*49*
13	66.*10*
18	311.*47*
21	311.*47*
22	309.*43;*
	311.*47*

Ch 61

10	26.*29;*
	231.*34*

Ch 62

1	266.*27*
2	270.*47;*
	285.*133*
3	274.*67*
4	38.*25;*
	278.*101;*
	282.*118;*
	285.*133*
5	146.*9;*
	231.*34;*

	274.*67;*
	278.*101;*
	285.*133*
6	174.*14*

Ch 63

1	295.*8*
4	295.*8*
7	295.*8*
8	193.*25;*
	266.*29*
9	41.*9;* 193.*25*
11	99.*26*
12	99.*26*
15	301.*23;*
	345.*20*

Ch 65

3	96.*14*
8–10	280.*111*
9	284.*127*
10	196.*36*
17	285.*132*
19	279.*106*
22	266.*29*

Ch 66

3	109.*46*
10–12	276.*84*
10	287.*140*
11	287.*140*
12	312.*53*
13	287.*140*
17	96.*14*
22	285.*132*

Jeremiah

Ch 2

2	33.*3;* 36.*16;*
	222.*3*
10	80.*80*
20	36.*17*
24	36.*18;* 62.*48*
25	36.*18*
27	36.*18*
33	36.*18*

Biblical References

8	29.50			**Ch 3**	
12	69.29;			16	88.19
	72.44; 75.58		**Jonah**	19	61.43; 86.9

Ch 2

Ch 2
3   96.13,14;
    97.20
10 126.8
16 230.33
21–27 284.126
22 71.41
23–24 275.80
30 126.8
31 126.8;
    131.29

Ch 3
15 126.8
18 73.54;
    288.146

Amos

Ch 2
9   67.15

Ch 3
2   42.17

Ch 5
4–6 250.26
15 43.21
20 126.8
21–23 109.47

Ch 8
3   47.35
9   126.8
10 47

Ch 9
4   227.23
13–15 80
13 73.54;
    288.146
14 96.16

Jonah

Ch 2
3   304.32
5   304.32
6   304.32

Ch 4
8   133.41

Micah

Ch 4
4   71.41
11 270.50

Ch 5
1   342.9
2   298.14
4   147.11

Ch 6
6   109.47
7   88.19
8   43.21

Ch 7
14 147.11

Nahum

Ch 2
3   66.9

Habakkuk

Ch 1
7   254.36

Ch 2
1   174.12
14 17.31

Zephaniah

Ch 1
15 126.8

Ch 2
3   250.26

Ch 3
    279.196
17 41.14;
    305.35

Haggai

Ch 2
7   198.42
9   312.53
19 71.41;
    72.44;
    284.126
23 299.17;
    300.18

Zechariah

Ch 3
10 71.41

Ch 4
3,11 80.83

Ch 6
12,13 85.8

Ch 8
19 43.21

Ch 9
9   223.8

411

Ch 10

2	251.*29*
3	59.*27*

Ch 11

2	66.*8*
4	147.*11*
7	147.*11*
9	147.*11*
16	147.*11*;
	251.*29*

Ch 12

10	270.*44*

Ch 13

7–9	264.*14*
7	147.*11*;
	251.*29*
9	214.*24*;
	266.*29*

Ch 14

4	265.*20*
10	72.*46*
16	316.*65*

Malachi

Ch 1

2	41.*13*
7,8	193.*23*

Ch 2

10–12	31.*71*
14	29.*50*
16	29.*51*; 34.*9*;
	38.*24*

Ch 3

1	295.*7*

Ch 4

2	131.*30*
3	74.*54*

Matthew

Ch 1–2   325

Ch 1

3	75.*58*
18	25.*20*;
	26.*25*;
	216.*32*
22	175.*15*

Ch 2

2	175.*15*
6	58.*21*;
	147.*11*;
	175.*15*
8	216.*32*
11	110.*48*;
	113.*61*;
	224.*13*

Ch 3

1	222.2
3	222.2
12	89.*22*
17	123.*31*

Ch 4

1	223.*4*
6	224.*14*
15–17	223.*6*
16	216.*34*

Ch 5

5	272.*58*
20	213.*23*

Ch 6

28f	87.*15*

Ch 8

22–26	277.*91*

Ch 9

15	26.*30*
20–22	256.*41*
27–31	277.*91*
27f	226.*22*
36	345.*21*

Ch 10

6	238.*1*
16	54

Ch 11

5	226.*21*
7–10	222.2
25–27	227.*24*
28	213.*23*

Ch 12

22	226.*22*
42	86.*13*
50	231.*35*

Ch 13

7	84.*7*
22	84.*7*
24–30	197.*39*
28–30	252.*31*
44f	306.*39*
48	252.*31*
52	285.*134*
56	231.*35*

Ch 14

13	223.*5*
15	223.*5*

Ch 15

14	226.*20*
24	238.*1*
30f	226.*22*

Ch 16

1–3	126.*3*
3	132.*37*
16–18	227.*24*
21	227.*24*

Ch 17

2	246.*16*
5	123.*31*

Ch 19

5	22.*6*
12	23.*10*
28	98.*23*

414

Acts

Ch 13

1	225.*16*
3–11	241.*5*
3	344.*18*
23,25	228.*27*
34	229.*28*

Ch 14

1	225.*16*
14	43.*19*
27	312.*52*

Ch 15

10	43.*19*
11,15	348.*27*
12,17	229.*28*

Ch 16

8–11	347.*24*
28	177.*20*
33	312.*52*

Ch 17

4	123.*32*
7,8,13	348.*27*

Ch 18

1–3	94.*4*
1	265.*20*
18	133.*40*
22	342.*9*

Ch 19

3	342.*9*
26	228.*27*
28–30	126.*7*
38–42	107.*31*
39f	113.*61*

Ch 20

25, 27	344.*18*

Ch 21

7	228.*27*
16	58.*21*
20	228.*27*

Acts

Ch 1

4f	233.*40*
6	238.*1*
8	233.*40*

Chs 2–7 240.*2*

Ch 2 233

1	208.*9*
20	126.*8*;
	131.*29*
27f	108.*33*

Ch 3

8	274.*71*
19f	98.*23*
21	172.*9*;
	317.*69*
25	171.*7*

Ch 7 276.*87*

2f	189.*11*

Ch 8

1	251.*28*

Ch 9

36	60.*34*

Ch 15

12–14	252.*32*

Ch 20

28	58.*21*

Ch 27

20	132.*37*

Ch 28

2	133.*40*

Romans

Ch 1

21–23	43.*23*

24–27	43.*23*
26f	23.*8*

Ch 5

10	229.*29*
22	241.*4*

Ch 8

18–25	69.*27*
20–22	129.*22*
38f	304.*31*

Chs 9–11 243

Ch 9 298

5	252.*32*
15	345.*21*
16	346.*23*
27,29	244.*11*

Ch 10

20	242.*9*

Ch 11 262

1–10	262.*9*
4f	244.*12*
7,10	277.*91*
11–27	263.*11*
17–20	80.*83*
21–25	80.*83*
25–28	278.*102*
25	277.*91*
26f	297.*11*
28	262.*10*

Ch 15

8	245.*13*

Ch 16

1	231.*35*
4	251.*28*;
	276.*87*
16	251.*28*

I Corinthians

Ch 1

2	251.*28*

415

Ch 2
10 340.*1*
19 274.*73*

Ch 3
18 30.*59*

I Thessalonians

Ch 2
7 28.*46*
11 28.*46*

II Thessalonians

Ch 2
1 252.*31*

Ch 3
5 265.*22*

I Timothy

Ch 2
12–14 30.*59*
13 21.2

Ch 3
5 147.*10*

Ch 4
1–3 23.*10*

Titus

Ch 2
3–5 30.*59*

Philemon

Ch 2 231.*35*

Hebrews

Ch 1
3 230.*30*
8 179.*26*
9 117.9;
179.*26*
12 341.5

Ch 2
14f 241.3
17 230.*30*

Ch 3
7–11 242.6
8–11 243.*10*

Ch 7
298.*14*
14 241.3
22 230.*31*
26 246.*17*

Ch 8
6 230.*31*
8,13 230.*31*;
285.*132*

Ch 9
13f 246.*19*
15 230.*31*;
285.*132*
26 179.*29*;
229.29
28 230.*30*

Ch 10
5 112.*60*
7,9 123.*30*
10 230.*30*

Ch 12
24 230.*31*

Ch 13
4 23.*10*; 144.*6*
8 341.5

James

Ch 2
15 231.*35*
23 189.*12*

I Peter

Ch 1
24f 82.*1*

Ch 2
3 347.*26*
7 245.*14*
9 245.*14*;
264.*15*
10 245.*14*

Ch 3
1–6 30.*59*
6 30.57

Ch 5
2 58.*21*

II Peter

Ch 1
16–18 246.*16*
17 123.*31*

I John

Ch 4
7–21 229.*28*
7–10 303.29
7 40.3
8 40.2

417

10f	40.4
16	40.2
19	40.4

Revelation

Ch 1

11	113.63
14	341.5
18	302.24

Ch 2

	97
7	97.22
8–11	113.63
8	113.63

Ch 5

11f	247.21

Ch 6

12f	126.8

Ch 7

17	58.21

Ch 8

12	126.8

Ch 10

8–10	88.19

Ch 11

3–12	80.83

Ch 12

	298
1f	264.14;
	286.138
3–6	295.5
5	58.21;
	147.11
14–17	295.5
14	48.38

Ch 14

15f	89

Ch 15

3	129.21

Ch 17

14	49.40

Ch 18

13	106.26;
	110.48

Ch 19

9	234.45
15	58.21;
	147.11
16	49.40;
	314.60

Ch 20

2–4	314.56
21.1–	
22.5	257.44
21.9–	
22.5	96.17

Ch 21

	253.35
1.5	129.22
2,9	231.36
12	310.45

Ch 22

12,16	317.69
17	231.36
20	317.69

SOURCES AND AUTHORITIES REFERRED TO IN THE TEXT

LEXICAL WORKS

BDB = A Hebrew and English Lexicon of the OT, by Brown, Driver and Briggs, Oxford, '77
22.6; 200.47; 286.135; 288.149; 307.41

Holladay = A Concise Hebrew and Aramaic Lexicon of the OT, by W L Holladay, Brill, '71
60.36

TDOT = Theological Dictionary of the OT, eds. Botterweck and Ringgren, Eerdmans '77
31.71; 231.35; 257.45; 300.18

TWOT = Theological Wordbook of the OT, eds. Harris, Archer and Waltke, Moody, '80
231.35; 234.44

DICTIONARIES, ENCYCLOPEDIA, GENERAL REFERENCE WORKS

ANET = Ancient Near Eastern Texts Relating to the OT, ed. J B Pritchard, Princeton, '50
77.68

AOT = Anthropology of the OT, H W Wolff, SCM, '74
32.72

AOTS = Archaeology and OT Study, ed. D Winton Thomas, '78
102.5

CDP = Church Doctrine and Practice, eds. Heading and Hocking, Precious Seed, '70
90.3; 95.10

CIBPI = Current Issues in Biblical and Patristic Interpretation, ed. G F Hawthorne, Eerdmans, '75
40.5

DNTT = Dictionary of NT Theology, ed C Brown, Zondervan, '78
108.36

EAE = Encyclopedia of Archaeological Excavations in the Holy Land, M Avi-Yonah and E Stern, Oxford, '75
253f.35

EBT = Encyclopedia of Biblical Theology, ed. J B Baur, Sheed and Ward, '70
34.10; 40.5

Hist. Geog. = The Historical Geography of the Holy Land, G A Smith, '31
133.39

IDB = The Interpreter's Dictionary of the Bible, Abingdon, '62
60.36; 69.29; 110.50; 116.6; 143.5; 149.13; 299.17

ILOT = An Introduction to the Literature of the OT, by S R Driver, T & T Clark, 1892
57.20

IOT = An Introduction to the OT, by R K Harrison, Tyndale, '70
57.20

KYB = Know Your Bible, Vol. 1, OT, by W Graham Scroggie, Pickering and Inglis, '50
57.20

NBH = Nature in our Biblical Heritage, N Hareuveni, Neot Kedummim, Israel, '80
83.5

NMB = Nature and Man in the Bible, Yehuda Feliks, Soncino, '81
60.36; 62.47; 66; 67.21; 84.7

PB = Plants of the Bible, by M Zohary, CUP, '82
66; 67.17; 69.29; 82.4; 89; 102.3; 103; 105.22, 25; 108.36; 110.50; 116.6

PWB = The Plant World of the Bible, Yehuda Feliks,
116.6

SCHURER = The History of the Jewish People in the Age of Jesus Christ, by Emil Schurer, revised and edited by Vermes and Millar, T & T Clark, '73–87
116.7

TBD = Treasury of Bible Doctrine, eds. Heading and Hocking, Precious Seed, '77
120; 257.43

TSBH = Tree and Shrub in our Biblical Heritage, by N Hareuveni, Neot Kedummim, Israel, '84
67.15; 70.35; 84.7

TWB = A Theological Word Book of the Bible, ed. Richardson, SCM, '82
98

JOURNALS

AJSL = American Journal of Semitic Languages and Literatures
269.41; 302.27

CBQ = Catholic Biblical Quarterly
141.2; 146.9; 149.13

JBL = Journal of Biblical Literature
141.2; 199f.47

JETS = Journal of the Evangelical Theological Society
16.21

VT = Vetus Testamentum
301.21

ZAW = Zeitschrift fur die alt-testamentliche Wissenschaft
161.7

COMMENTARIES AND SPECIAL STUDIES

Bruce TiT = This is That, by F F Bruce, Paternoster, '68: 147.11

Carr SoS = The Song of Solomon, G L Carr, Tyndale, '84: 143.5; 313.55

Clarke Pss = Analytical Studies in the Psalms, by A G Clarke, Ritchie, '76
17

Clarke SoS, The Song of Solomon, Ritchie
57.20

Cohen Pss = The Psalms, by A. Cohen, Soncino
17; 46.33

Delitzsch SoS = Canticles and Ecclesiastes, by F Delitzsch, T & T Clark, 1899
27.35; 54.8; 83.6

Falk LL = Love Lyrics from the Bible, by M Falk, Almond Press, '82
57.20; 145.8; 161.7; 305.36

GAS = The Book of the Twelve, by G A Smith, Hodder and Stoughton, '08
133.39

Gordis SoS = The Song of Songs and Lamentations, Jewish Theological Seminary, '74
99; 302.27

Goulder Song = The Song of Fourteen Songs, M D Goulder, Sheffield, JSOT Sup. 36 '86
16.21, 24; 54.8; 141.2; 151.1; 305.36

Heaton = Solomon's New Men, by E W Heaton, Thames and Hudson, '74
16.21

Loewe BM = Biblical Motifs: Origins and Transformations, ed. A Altmann, '66
170.5

OTL Kings = 1 and 2 Kings (Old Testament Library), by J Gray, SCM, '77
65.2

Perowne Pss = The Book of Psalms, by
  J J S Perowne, Bell, 1898
  17
Pope SoS = The Song of Songs, by M
  H Pope, Doubleday, '80
  170.6; 265.20
Reuss
  143.5
Rowley SotL = The Servant of the Lord
  and other essays on the OT, by H H
  Rowley, Blackwell, '65
  141.1
Thirtle = The Titles of the Psalms, by J
  W Thirtle, Froude, '04
  86.9

**JEWISH AND MOSTLY ANCIENT
SOURCES**

Ibn Ezra: 56.14
JOS. Ant = Josephus' The Antiquities
  of the Jews
  116.7
JOS. Wars = Josephus' The Wars of the
  Jews
  74.56; 94.2; 102.6; 110.50; 116.7
J Kapah ed. Hamesh Megilloth: 170.6
Kimchi the Elder: 17

Midrash Rabbah on the Song
  48.37; 194; 306
Mishnah – Eduy: 143.5
  Kerith. 6a: 103.13
  Yad. 49.41
Qumran – War scroll: 200.47
  IQH 127.9
Rabbi Aqibha on the Song
  49.41; 97.21; 169
Rabbi Hoshaya: 84.7
Rambam: 56.14
Rashi: 56.14
Saadia Hagaon: 167.1; 170
Talmuds, Jerusalem (jT), Erubim 1.19b:
  60.33
  Babylonian (bT), Ber. 3a: 55.12
    Hag. 14.b: 97.21
    Hullin 59b: 60.33
    Yom. 21.b: 214.25
    Sanh. 91b: 127.9
Targum on the Song, 49.42; 55.12; 169f;
  178; 279; 283.121; 301; 306; 312
Tosef. Sot. 15.9: 103.15

CHURCH FATHERS

Origen: 49.43
Theodore of Mopsuestia: 143.5